# The Miracles of the Kasuga Deity

Number XCVIII of the Records of Civilization:
Sources and Studies

# The Miracles of the Kasuga Deity

ROYALL TYLER

COLUMBIA UNIVERSITY PRESS

NEW YORK

The author and publisher gratefully acknowledge the support toward publication given them by the Norwegian Research Council and the Institute for Medieval Japanese Studies, Columbia University.

COLUMBIA UNIVERSITY PRESS
NEW YORK   OXFORD

Library of Congress Cataloging-in-Publication Data

Tyler, Royall.
The miracles of the Kasuga deity / Royall Tyler.
p.   cm.—(Records of civilization, sources and studies : no. 98)
Includes translation of the Kasuga Gongen genki.
Includes bibliographical references.
ISBN 0-231-06958-8
1. Kasuga Gongen genki.   2. Kasuga Jinja (Nara-shi, Japan) in
literature.   3. Legends, Shinto—History and criticism.   4. Legends,
Buddhist—Japan—History and criticism.   5. Japanese
literature—1185–1600—History and criticism.   I. Kasuga Gongen
genki. English. 1990. II. Title. III. Series.
PL790.K35T95 1990
895.6′32209—dc20        89-22237
                                      CIP

Printed in the United States of America

Book design by Charles Hames

*For my father*
*and in memory of my mother*

# Contents

CONTENTS

# Acknowledgments

I thought of this project while in Kyoto on a Japan Foundation grant in 1978–79, but began it only in 1980. Most of the work was done outside Japan, but the necessary research would have been impossible without another year in Kyoto, 1982–83, thanks to a Fulbright grant. Hiroyoshi Hisahiko, the director of the Nara Prefectural Library, deserves special thanks for his help. Early on, John Keenan explained little passages from Hossō writings that to me were impenetrable. Toward the end, Robert Sharf, who has trained as a priest of Kōfu-kuji, supplied useful materials and information on present Kōfukuji as well.

The late Kageyama Haruki kindly introduced my wife and me to Kasanoin Chikatada, the present head priest of the Kasuga Shrine, and to Ōhigashi Nobukazu, the Shrine's adviser on cultural affairs. Mr. Ōhigashi generously allowed me to copy his transcriptions of the shrine documents, which have since been published in vol. 13 of *Shintō taikei,* and discussed Kasuga history with us on several occasions. One spring morning he led us up Mikasa-yama, and as we neared the top a brilliant sun burst through the clouds. Shimizu Yoshiko of Kansai Daigaku took us to the Yōmei Bunko where the director, Nawa Osamu, spent days showing us the Yōmei Bunko copy of *Kasuga Gongen genki.* Once when rain was threatening, Mr. Nawa teased us that the weather might keep him from bringing that day's portion of precious scrolls in from the storehouse; but then he appeared anyway, carrying them under a big, black umbrella.

Finally, this book would have been poorer without the insight and knowledge of my wife, Dr. Susan C. Tyler, who also made the maps and traced the pictures. Her own work on Kasuga devotional art makes her an expert on the shrine. We chose to study Kasuga entirely independently of one another, but being together has allowed us to hold a Kasuga seminar whenever we wish. All mistakes and shortcomings, however, are my own. They are certainly there. I hope the work's overall value will outweigh them.

# Conventions and Official Titles

In all translated passages in this book, and of course particularly in *Kasuga Gongen genki* itself (hereafter simply "the *Genki*"), I have liberally capitalized names, titles, and other words; whereas in the introductory chapters and glosses I have followed current practice and kept to lowercase initials. Capitalization is a useful device in English to mark respect. If it gives these translations a slightly old-fashioned air, no harm will have been done. The book distinguishes between "shrine" and "sanctuary," since the Kasuga Shrine consists of several subshrines ("sanctuaries") for which a separate word was needed. As for divine beings, Myōjin ("resplendent deity"), Daimyō-jin ("great resplendent deity"), Gongen ("avatar"), and Kami are retained wherever they occur in the original. Otherwise, I resorted to "Deity" or, occasionally, "God."

The major translations *(Sakakiba no nikki* and the *Genki)* are intended to be easy to pick out from the glosses and other accompanying material, so that anyone wishing to skip the glosses should be able readily to do so. The comments and notes follow each section of translated text.

Dates in the translations are spelled out, but elsewhere are noted schematically: Kenkyū 7.9.27 (1196). Intercalary months are indicated thus: Ten'ei 1.int7.12. Premodern Japanese years do not correspond exactly to modern ones, so that a date like Jishō 4.12.28 (when the Taira forces burned Nara) technically belongs in 1181. However, since Jishō 4 corresponds in the tables to 1180, this date would be given here as Jishō 4.12.28 (1180).

In the notes to the *Genki,* the date when the incident related would have occurred (if it really happened) is given first. Dates given in the original are repeated here, with their year equivalent in the modern calendar. After the dates come sections entitled "Possible Source," "Related Materials," "Background," and so on. Historical background material for the stories fills out the often rather sketchy *Genki* accounts. These sections are followed by the notes proper. For items that recur, I have not each time referred the reader back to the original note, which can always be located in the index. In a few cases, the notes to a *Genki* story are followed by a section entitled "Significant Variants." Further comments on this item will be found in chapter 2, under "The state of the *Genki* text."

## OFFICIAL TITLES

Official titles are a great problem. For the translations (though not necessarily for the glosses or introductory chapters) I felt obliged to translate them all, with three exceptions explained below. One wonders how valuable it is to do so. On the one hand, many titles could be eliminated or somehow diluted for a general audience, while for a scholarly audience they could simply be left in the original. On the other hand, the existing English equivalents for the civil titles, admirably worked out by other scholars, were too familiar and too convincing to ignore. William and Helen McCullough (1980:2:789–831) have explained them so well that there was no need to do so here.

The religious titles were another matter. The main ones have been explained by the McCulloughs (1980:1:396–97), but previously worked out equivalents are less consistent, less satisfactory, and less complete. The most difficult were *hōin, hōgen,* and *hokkyō.* I finally gave up on them and left them in the original. For instance, the translation of *Genki* 11.1 speaks of "Hōin Egyō."

The main group of ecclesiastical titles is that of the *sōgō* ranks. Kōfukuji monks were normally appointed to the lowest of these after serving as lecturer *(kōji)* for the Yuima-e. The *sōgō* ranks appear in these translations as follows (from lowest to highest); "provisional" preceding any of them translates the Japanese *gon.*

| master of discipline | *risshi* |
| minor prelate | *shōsōzu* |
| prelate | *sōzu* |
| major prelate | *daisōzu* |

grand prelate        *sōjō*
major grand prelate   *daisōjō*

The names of the various roles played by monks at the Yuima-e, as explained in chapter 4 under "The Yuima-e," appear as follows:

| | |
|---|---|
| selector | *tandai* |
| lecturer | *kōji* |
| questioner | *monja* or *ichimon* |
| witness | *shōgi* |
| definer | *ryūgi* |
| auditor | *chōshu* |

Another set of titles, prominent particularly in *Genki* 11.4, alludes to certain important ceremonies including the Yuima-e.

| | |
|---|---|
| graduate | *tokugō* |
| lecturer designate | *gikō* |
| past lecturer | *ikō* |

Otherwise, there is a scattering of other titles:

| | |
|---|---|
| the venerable | *shōnin* |
| most worthy | *daitoku* |
| superior | *jishu* |
| entrant | *nyūji* |
| personal attendant | *jijū* |

Titles of offices at the Kasuga Shrine are translated as follows:

| | |
|---|---|
| overseer | *shō-no-azukari* |
| head priest | *kannushi* |
| clansman | *ujibito* |
| shrine guard | *shinden-mori* |
| shrine servant | *jinnin* |
| shrine maiden | *miko* |

# Introduction

One easily gathers from well-known commonplaces about Japanese history that the Heian world ended in the late twelfth century, and that the old court, if not extinguished thereafter, at least faded into insignificance. But this is not quite true. Minamoto no Yoritomo (1147-99), who established the Kamakura Bakufu, seems not to have wished to offend the Kyoto nobles, who took him on the whole for a loyal supporter. The system of rule by retired emperors *(insei)* survived, according to some scholars, at least until the Jōkyū Rebellion of 1221; while others hold that although weakened, it lasted until Go-Daigo put a stop to Go-Uda's *insei* in 1321 (Uwayokote 1975:36, 57). Certainly the Kyoto court remained politically alive, and throughout the thirteenth century, even as its authority slipped away, could nourish dreams of the Bakufu's end from its own faith in the eternal collaboration of the emperor and his Fujiwara regent.

Some of the old and wealthy religious establishments associated with the court did even better. Kōfukuji and the Kasuga Shrine in Nara continued to control vast estates and powerful populations of armed monks and shrine servants *(jinnin);* and Yamato province remained, as it had been before, under the temple's sway.

Kōfukuji was the senior clan temple of the Fujiwara aristocracy. Although it was peopled by the sons of the highest nobles, its interests and those of the great houses in Kyoto did not always coincide. There was one thing, however, upon which Kōfukuji and the Fujiwara of the court could certainly agree, and that was devotion to the Kasuga Shrine. The Kasuga deity was the tutelary deity *(ujigami)* of the Fujiwara, while for Kōfukuji he was not only a protector but also the source of legitimacy for the temple's power. In the first years of the fourteenth century, this convergence of enthusiasm produced one of the major artistic achievements of the Kamakura period: the superb *emakimono* ("set of painted handscrolls") entitled *Kasuga Gongen genki* ("The Miracles of the Kasuga Deity").

This book is a study of the text of *Kasuga Gongen genki*. It comprises eight chapters on the *Genki* and its world, and a fully annotated translation of the *Genki's* stories. The work has not been approached this way before. Most of the secondary writing about it concerns one of two issues: what the paintings tell us about the architecture, costume, and manners of the time, and how the *Genki* was conceived and executed. Some historians have cited specific passages of the text to support one point or another. However, no one has written more than a few paragraphs on the content of the *Genki,* and no one has glossed its text.

This is not really surprising. The *Genki* belongs to a large, and still ill-defined, class of medieval works that include temple or shrine origin legends *(engi)* and collections of miracle stories *(reigenki)*. These have not received the same attention as medieval tale literature *(setsuwa bungaku),* the best-known examples of which have been carefully studied and figure in standard collections of classical Japanese literature.

The relative obscurity of works like the *Genki* seems not entirely to be explained either by their subject matter (though nowadays secular works often seem to be more attractive than religiously inspired ones) or by their literary quality. The *Genki* itself may not have the exceptional appeal of *Uji shūi monogatari,* perhaps the best of the *setsuwa* collections, but as long as one understands a little of its world, it makes better reading than *Kojidan,* for example, which since 1981 has been available in an annotated edition with modern Japanese translation. In fact, the *Genki* is very interesting. It is true that *Kojidan* and the other *setsuwa* collections cover a wider range of material and so are more generally useful, if not always more appealing. However, something else seems to have kept scholars away from such works as the *Genki.*

Perhaps the first problem is that the *Genki* and many other works like it mingle text and painting. The paintings being immediately attractive and impressive, the work as a whole tends to end up being left to art historians, and abandoned by those who represent literature —that is, the study of written compositions. And since art historians understandably do not consider it their business to study texts, the texts associated with their artifacts continue to be neglected. Historians of religion too may value such works, but they feel no greater urge to study texts. Meanwhile beautiful books filled with reproductions of *engi* or *reigenki* paintings continue to be published with, in the back, the same raw transcriptions of the *kotobagaki*—a term suggesting that the text *accompanies* the paintings as prose passages accompany the poems in an imperial anthology.

Another reason for relative neglect in the case of the *Genki,* especially, may be the work's aristocratic character. Gorai Shigeru (1978b) left no doubt that to one whose sympathies lie with the common people, the *Genki* is simply offensive. Even to one less passionately committed, the *Genki* may seem anomalous in an "age of warrior rule"; and the religion it represents was actively opposed to the "new Buddhism" that arose in Kamakura times. The *Genki* paintings have been mined for images of folk life, but the deeper interests of the gentlemen and monks who worked on the *Genki* may appear obsolete. So may the religion of the *Genki.* By the standards of those who study Buddhist doctrine it is not Buddhism, and it falls into precisely the twilight zone proscribed by Shinto since the Meiji Restoration.

These considerations help explain why the *Genki,* as text, has been rather neglected. Yet taking it up was like opening a window onto a world whose periphery one has glimpsed here and there, but whose center one has never seen before. Surely there is no more vivid expression of Fujiwara pride—a nostalgic one, of course, since by the time the *Genki* was made, Fujiwara glory was less lived than remembered. The work's very insistence that the Kasuga deity lives on, like his children, with undiminished vigor, evokes the lengthening shadows of decline. But above all, one looks through the *Genki* onto the living pattern of *honji-suijaku* religion: a mode of faith that held the deities of Japan were "traces manifested below" *(suijaku)* by the eternally enlightened, "original ground" *(honji)* buddhas.

I have tentatively suggested elsewhere (R. Tyler 1987:46–47) that the mode of faith this pattern belongs to deserves better acknowledgment as a distinct phase of Japanese religion. The phase involved a particular understanding not only of Buddhism and the native deities, but also of geography. Its intense interest in *place* and landscape, as demonstrations of the deepest truth, is as obvious in the Kasuga cult as in *honji-suijaku* religion as a whole. Jacqueline Pigeot's meticulous analysis of the treatment of place names in classical poetry led her to the interesting conclusion (1982:162, n. 193) that the classic notion of *uta-makura* (like the classic notion of *honji* and *suijaku* deities) did not become clear until the twelfth century. Kasuga, one of the geat *uta-makura,* supported a complex body of religious and poetic lore that tells a great deal about the conservative side of Kamakura religion.

The *Genki* leaves no doubt that this faith was upheld and nurtured not only by the greatest nobles at court but by their sons and brothers at Kōfukuji as well. In this sense, the Kasuga cult as seen through the *Genki* casts doubt on the "popular" in "popular religion," at least as the expression applies to the Kamakura period. Bernard Faure (1987:48), to take a recent example, wrote of Keizan (1268–1325), the third-generation successor to Dōgen, that he "had since his youth been influenced by popular religion and the *shugendō* of the Hakusan branch of Tendai." "Popular religion" and *shugendō* are here placed in the same class. Yet considering those who upheld the Kasuga cult and the *kenmitsu bukkyō* ("esoteric-exoteric Buddhism") of Kōfukuji —which included *shugendō*—one may ask whether "popular" is a useful word. The conventional distinction between "aristocratic" (or possibly "orthodox") and "popular" may not necesarily apply to the religion represented by the *Genki,* however lofty its patrons. Kuroda Toshio suggested that *honji-suijaku* religion is inseparable from *kenmitsu bukkyō,* the form Buddhism took in Heian times, and he specifically included provincial shrines in his appraisal. Kuroda wrote (1980:152):

> In the medieval period, the "divine virtue" of almost all [local deities] was represented, directly or indirectly, as the salvation of sentient beings by the buddhas and bodhisattvas. In terms of faith, therefore, this is *shintō* less as a distinct faith in the kami *(jingi shinkō),* than as one aspect of *kenmitsu bukkyō.*

In his study of *Daijōin jisha zōjiki,* the vast diary of the Kōfukuji superintendent Jinson (1430–1508), Suzuki Ryōichi concluded (1983:61) that the only focus of Jinson's complex religious devotion was the Kasuga deity. Jinson, a son of the regent and man of letters

Ichijō Kanera (1402–81), inherited a tradition to which the *Genki* gives elegant and at times moving expression.

One should not call Jinson foolish, Buddhist prelate that he was, if he looked ultimately to Kasuga rather than, for example, Amida. Chapters 5 and 6 below, and the *Genki* text itself, help explain why. Instead, one should admire in the Kasuga cult a mode of religious faith that was more important and distinct in its time than many now recognize, and that was worthy to sustain such great monks as Gedatsu Shōnin (1155–1212) and Myōe Shonin (1173–1232). This study will have done well if it contributes to a better understanding not only of the *Genki* as a work but of all that the *Genki* represents.

# Part One

# 1

# *The Work*

*Kasuga Gongen genki* is one of the rare Kamakura-period *emakimono* to be written and painted on silk. Consisting of twenty scrolls, with a twenty-first for the table of contents and preface, it opens with an introduction (1.1); presents ninety-three sections of text illustrated by the same number of paintings (1.2–20.1); and closes with a final summation (20.2). The table of contents lists fifty-six story titles, apart from the introduction and conclusion. This translation, on the other hand, divides the text into seventy-two numbered tales that celebrate the enduring potency of the Kasuga deity, his readiness to chastise those who displease him, and above all the zeal with which he protects those who trust in him. The criterion for this division into seventy-two has generally been to consider each discrete dream, oracle, or other act of communication by the deity as a separate item, except where narrative continuity in the original made it unreasonable to establish a break.

The preface to the *Genki* provides the basic information about the work. Takashina Takakane (fl. 1309–30), the head of the imperial office of painting *(edokoro),* did the paintings. The stories were compiled by the Kōfukuji monk Kakuen (1277–1340), in consultation with two senior monks of the same temple: Jishin (1257–1325) and Hanken (1247–1339). The text was written out by "the Former Regent Mototada and his three sons." These personages were Takatsukasa Mototada (1247–1313); Fuyuhira (1275–1327); the Kōfukuji monk Ryōshin (1277–1329); and Fuyumoto (1285–1309). The *Genki* was dedicated in Engyō 2.3 (1309) by "The Minister of the Left."

# SAIONJI KINHIRA

This last gentleman was Saionji Kinhira (1264–1315). The point is not quite self-evident because two men were minister of the left during Engyō 2.3. Takatsukasa Fuyuhira resigned the post on Engyō 2.3.14, while Kinhira replaced him on 3.19. However, according to *Kugyō bunin* for Tokuji 3 (Engyō 1), Fuyuhira had already been appointed regent *(sesshō)*, and also head of the Fujiwara clan, on Engyō 1.11.11. His relinquishing the post of minister of the left on Engyō 2.3.14 was simply the "second announcment" *(dainido hyōji)* of this step. Wada Eishō (1917) proved the case by citing *Kanmon gyoki* for Eikyō 10.2.27 (1438), which mentions that the *Genki* was commissioned by "Chikunai no Sadaijin," together with the Tenshō-era (1573–92) *Eishun o-kikigaki* (by Eishun, d. 1596, the author of *Tamon'in nikki)*, which names the man who commissioned it as "Chikurin'in no Sadaijin Kinhira." *Chikunai* and *Chikurin'in* are both known as names for Kinhira. As Miya Tsugio suggested (1983:19), the "Chikurin-den" of *Genki* 1.3 may intentionally allude to him.

How did Kinhira come to conceive so ambitious an offering to the Kasuga deity? He wrote in his preface: "Unable to restrain my zeal to honor the Deity, I have gathered this collection together to the best of my ability, so as to increase the faith of all men." One need not disbelieve his sentiments to look for something more precise. Koresawa (1963:16) suggested that Kinhira was directly inspired by the prodigy of the spirit fires on Kagen 2.9.28 (1304), as related in *Genki* 20.1. The alarming oracle of 1306, mentioned in *Sakakiba no nikki* (ch. 8) but apparently not recorded anywhere, might also have played a part. Most writers have speculated that the conception of the project had to do with Kinhira's political fortunes. The following account of these fortunes relies principally on Kondō Kihaku (1952, 1958), Nagashima Fukutarō (1963), and Miya Tsugio (1983).

The Saionji house had prospered ever since the time of its founder Kintsune (1171-1234), the second son of Fujiwara no Sanemune. Having married the niece of Minamoto no Yoritomo, Kintsune had close ties to Kamakura. After a brief eclipse at the time of the Jōkyū Rebellion he rose to be chancellor, and he also functioned as *kantō mōshitsugi,* the court official in charge of liaison with Kamakura. Kintsune's son Saneuji (1194–1269) became still more powerful, serving like his father as chancellor and *kantō mōshitsugi.* After 1246 the latter office belonged permanently to the Saionji house.

Since the Saionji were a cadet Fujiwara line, a Saionji could not become regent or head the Fujiwara clan. That remained the privilege of the "five regent houses" *(go-sekke),* which arose during the thirteenth century from splits in the Fujiwara "northern house" *(hokke):* the Konoe, Kujō, Ichijō, Nijō, and Takatsukasa. Mototada and his sons who wrote out the *Genki* text were of course Takatsukasa, and by the time the *Genki* was dedicated it was Mototada's eldest son, Fuyuhira, who bore both the above titles. However, the Saionji achieved something just as impressive. Thanks to Saneuji, they captured from the regents the right to supply imperial consorts. Saneuji's daughter became Go-Saga's empress, and the mother of Go-Fukakusa and Kameyama.

Kinhira therefore had every reason to be proud of his line, and to value his own position as the senior Saionji. His younger sister by the same mother became the consort of Emperor Fushimi, and another was loved by Retired Emperor Kameyama. Kinhira himself rose quickly, as might be expected, and was named minister of the right in Einin 7 (1299). Then trouble came. In Kagen 3.int12 (1305) Kinhira was punished by Retired Emperor Go-Uda, who confiscated his two proprietary provinces, dismissed him as head of the left imperial stables, and had him confined to his home. Go-Uda's reasons are unclear, but they may have had to do with his displeasure over attempts to make Tsuneakira, Kinhira's grandson, crown prince.

Kinhira must have felt this affront deeply. He was apparently moved to address himself to Kasuga, because on Kagen 4.2.8 (1306) he completed a copy of the *Fukūkenjaku shinju shingyō* (*Taishō* 20/ 402, no. 1094), which is now in the Tokyo National Museum (Kondō 1952). The copy is in gold on dark blue paper. Fukūkenjaku (Skt. Amoghapāśa) is a major *honji* for the Kasuga deity, and the sutra in question often appears in the diaries of Fujiwara courtiers.

Twelve days later Kinhira was pardoned, thanks to the intervention of Kamakura. Perhaps he took it that his devotion to the Kasuga deity had "worked." At any rate, on Tokuji 2.1.16 (1307), he began a seven-day retreat at the shrine. He probably prayed that his daughter Neishi, who had been Go-Fushimi's consort since the first month of the previous year, should bear a son, and that in this and other ways the fortunes of the Saionji house should be fully restored. And perhaps this is when he conceived the *Genki,* which was dedicated only two years later. One can understand in this way his statement in the *Genki* preface, "After I conceived this gesture of devotion, great good fortune blessed my house."

For good fortune did come his way. First, in Engyō 2.1 (1309), Neishi was awarded the title *(ingō)* Kōgimon'in and named "titular mother" *(junbo)* of Hanazono, who had just become emperor on Engyō 1.11.16 (1308). Then in Engyō 2.2 his son Sanehira (1290–1326) was appointed provisional middle counselor. The following month Kinhira himself was named minister of the left, as already noted. He resigned on Engyō 2.6.15, apparently feeling no need to press the point further. Yoshida Kenkō wrote in *Tsurezuregusa* 83 (Keene 1967:70):

> Nothing stood in the way of the lay priest of Chikurin'in and minister of the left rising to be prime minister [i.e., chancellor, *dajōdaijin*], but he said, "I doubt that being prime minister will make much difference. I'll stop at minister of the left."

However, these things did not happen before another round of difficulties, one discussed particularly by Nagashima (1963). Kinhira, like his forebears, was *kantō mōshitsugi.* Late in Tokuji 2 (1307) there erupted one of Kōfukuji's many quarrels with Kamakura. Caught between Kōfukuji and Kamakura, Kinhira aroused the temple's hostility. The affair was not settled until Engyō 1.7 (1308). Nagashima (1963:22) suggested that Kinhira may have commissioned the *Genki* as a gesture of thanks, and consequently that work on the *Genki* may not have begun until after that date. Whether this is plausible or not depends on one's understanding of how long it would have taken to complete the *Genki.* Kondō Kihaku maintained in several articles that two years would have been only barely enough.

One can imagine too that the idea of honoring the Kasuga deity in this manner might have been in the air at the time. Kinhira could have sought the deity's favor in other ways, some of them even more expensive, as many Fujiwara had done before him. It was not yet wholly clear that the days of Fujiwara glory were over. The clan had reason to feel like affirming the vitality of their ancient role. Moreover, the Mongol threat had heightened court interest in Kasuga as in other important shrines; and the teachings of great monks like Gedatsu and Myōe Shōnin had given a new intensity to Kasuga faith. The overall message of the *Genki*—that the full Teaching is present at Kasuga—is a stirring one, of much broader significance than the political fortunes of a man, a family, or even the Fujiwara nobility as a whole. There is no need to deny Kinhira and his collaborators the imagination to be inspired by such thoughts.

Certainly, Kinhira may have known about other recent, ambitious picture-scroll projects. *Ippen Shōnin eden* had been completed in 1299, and *Sannō reigenki,* a set of nine scrolls celebrating the miracles of the deity of Mt. Hiei, had been completed ca. 1288 (Nakano 1975:42). Given the vigorous rivalry (quite visible in the *Genki*) between Kasuga-Kōfukuji and Mt. Hiei, Kinhira may have felt it was high time to go Hiei one better in honor of Kasuga. Moreover, the *Genki* may not have been his only gift to Nara. Nagashima Fukutarō (1977) argued that the twelve-scroll *Genjō Sanzō e,* a beautifully illustrated life of the great Chinese pilgrim and translator Hsüan-tsang (600–64), was painted by Takakane on Kinhira's order, and presented by Kinhira to Kōfukuji when he offered the *Genki* to Kasuga.

## MOTOTADA AND HIS SONS, AND KAKUEN

According to the *Genki* preface, Mototada and his sons, "zealous to honor the Deity, vowed that in order to ensure the efficacy of their work, no outside brush should be involved." As the tutelary deity of the Fujiwara, the Kasuga deity preferred not to be served by persons outside the Nakatomi or Fujiwara clans. Moreover, it was the head of the Fujiwara clan who had overall responsibility for the Kasuga cult, so that the approval and participation of the head of the clan (Fuyuhira when the *Genki* was dedicated, but formerly Mototada) was no doubt essential. Fuyumoto's participation followed.

The role of Ryōshin is a little less obvious. Older than Fuyumoto, Ryōshin was nonetheless a monk and therefore not in quite the same class as his brothers. In fact, his part may reflect his unusual position. Ryōshin wrote out scrolls 17 and 18, which concern Myōe Shōnin, and this is precisely the section of the text missing from *Kasuga goruki* (discussed below). At any rate, Nagashima (1963:18) pointed out that Ryōshin was competing for power at Kōfukuji with Jishin,

Hanken, and Jishin's newphew Jinkaku, who was superintendent at the time. No doubt he was glad of his chance to distinguish himself.

Kakuen, the monk formally charged with compiling the *Genki* text, was Kinhira's younger brother. At Kōfukuji he was the head of Tōbokuin, a subtemple allied with the powerful Ichijōin headed by Ryōshin. Though far from junior, Kakuen was perhaps not yet senior enough to take sole responsibility for the work. As Nagashima observed (1963:18), it was important that all major factions at Kōfukuji should be represented in he project, to make the effort truly unanimous. Kakuen therefore consulted with Jishin of Daijōin, the great rival of Ichijōin, as well as with Hanken of Sanzōin.

## POSSIBLE PRECURSORS TO THE *GENKI*

All writers on the *Genki* agree that considering how quickly the work was put together, some sort of collection of Kasuga miracle stories must already have existed. Kondō (1958) insisted particularly on this point. Tale collections of all sorts were known then, and the example of *Sannō reigenki* has already been mentioned. Moreover, judging from an entry in *Daijōin jisha zōjiki* (for Kōshō 3.3.12 [1457], discussed by Nagashima [1977:50–51]), a full-scale precursor to the currently known *Genjō Sanzō e* existed already in the time of Shin'en (1153–1224). The Kasuga Shrine still has accounts of shrine history older than the *Genki,* and these contain material that appears in the *Genki.* Some concrete evidence on the subject is available.

The earliest reference to a collection of Kasuga tales is in *kan* 7 of *Kyōkunshō* (1233) by Koma no Chikazane (1177–1242) (ZGR: 179–80). Relating the story told in *Genki* 6.1, Chikazane attributed it to a *miyashiro no genki* ("record of miracles of the shrine") compiled by Gedatsu Shōnin. *Eishun o-kikigaki* also mentioned this work, saying: "Some items in the *{Genki}* . . . are from Gedatsu Shōnin's old record *(kyūki),* while some were gleaned from the records of a wide range of families." The content of the *Genki* suggests that Gedatsu Shōnin's record did indeed come to form the nucleus of the work. This subject is discussed in chapter 5, under "Gedatsu Shōnin, the *Genki,* and Shaka."

The diary of the Kasuga Wakamiya priest Nakatomi no Sukekata contains three relevant entries. Nagashima (1963:19) set them forth in convenient form. (1) On Bun'ei 6.4.20 (1269, erroneously cited by Nagashima as Bun'ei 4.4.20), Sukekata noted that Shinshō (1247–86) of Ichijōin had summoned him and asked about the history of the shrine. Shinshō was on retreat at Kasuga at the time. When Sukekata answered as best he could, Shinshō pressed him with detailed questions. Then he ordered Sukekata to submit a written document or documents to him. (2) On Bun'ei 12.1.4 (1275), Sukekata paid a new year visit to Shinshō, then superintendent, at Ichijōin. Shinshō said: "A record of the Daimyōjin's miracles *(daimyōjin no genki)* must exist. You will have to send it to me." Sukekata said he would do so. (3) On 8.17 of the same year (now designated Kenji 1), Sukekata wrote that he had sent "the old record[s] of this shrine" to Shinshō, as requested.

Noting the persistence of Shinshō's interest, Nagashima attributed it partly to his family background. Shinshō's grandfather, Konoe Iezane, had been deeply devoted to Myōe Shōnin and to the Kasuga shrine that Myōe built at his temple, Kōzanji. Shinshō's father, Kanetsune, had also been assiduous toward the Kōzanji Kasuga shrine. Moreover, court interest in both Kasuga shrines had been heightened at about the time of Sukekata's diary entries by the Mongol threat.

Nagashima (1963:20) concluded that Shinshō stimulated the compiling of some sort of *genki* collection, probably put together by Sukekata in consultation with certain monks of Kōfukuji. One might add that Sukekata and colleagues would surely have consulted the collection made by Gedatsu Shōnin. This resulting work would then have been available to Kakuen, who would have had to add the material of *Genki* 19.1 and 20.1. If this is correct, then the material of 17.1–18.4 must have been specially edited for the *Genki,* instead of having been included in the older collection. Since a long, detailed account of these extraordinary events already existed (see the discussion following 18.4), there would have been no need to incorporate it into anything less than a full-scale, finished work.

Of course all of the above is speculation. No one can be sure about any sort of "proto-*genki,*" unless he accepts that *Kasuga go-ruki,* or the version of it described by Takahashi Teiichi (1982), is that document.

*Kasuga go-ruki* (the manuscript of which is still owned by Kōfukuji) is very close indeed to the text of the *Genki* except that it lacks the material corresponding to scrolls 17 and 18. After positing the existence of one or more still earlier compilations, Kondō (1953, 1958) suggested that *Kasuga go-ruki* must be the work on which the *Genki* is most immediately based.

Takahashi, for his part, assigned just the same role to a manuscript he himself discovered, and which he dated no later than late Muromachi. It bears the interesting title *Zennyū butsudōshū* ("Collection on Gradual Entry into the Buddha's Way"). Takahashi's discussion of the manuscript and its significance is weakened by his silence regarding *Kasuga go-ruki,* which he seems not to have known about. At any rate, all his information about *Zennyū butsudōshū,* including a list of discrepancies between it and the *Genki* text, suggests that it is none other than a copy of *Kasuga go-ruki* under another title. Unfortunately Takahashi's published text of the manuscript (in *Bukkyō bungaku kenkyū,* vol. 2, March 1964) is almost impossible to find; Miya, too (1983:21), noted that he had never seen it. For the time being, one can only assume that it is *Kasuge go-ruki* and say no more about it.

A detailed comparison of *Kasuga go-ruki* and the *Genki* text reveals many small discrepanies, the signifiance of which is obscured by the fact that *Kasuga go-ruki* has been published only in a transcription that may not be entirely reliable. The single most obvious difference (apart from the matter of scrolls 17 and 18) is that *Kasuga go-ruki,* in the passage corresponding to *Genki* 3.3, speaks of Sukefusa and Gyōson; whereas the *Genki* has been visibly emended to name Sanetsune and Zōyo. For Kondō (1958:83–84), this proves that *Kasuga go-ruki* is indeed a previous state of the *Genki* text.

Even if true, however, the idea does not seem very interesting. In its present form, which includes the material corresponding to *Genki* 20.1, *Kasuga go-ruki* cannot be earlier than the end of 1304. Need it have been written before a full-scale *Genki* projected was conceived? Moreover, if Kakuen, the main *Genki* compiler, had nothing more to do than pick up a copy of the text we now know as *Kasuga go-ruki,* he would hardly have deserved to be mentioned in the preface; and in any case *Eishun-o-kikigaki,* though relatively late, suggests otherwise. Kondō (1958:82) even proposed that *Kasuga go-ruki* was the *kotobagaki* of a fully illustrated *genki* that was *different* from the one discussed in this book. He suggested, in other words (partly on the analogy of *Sannō reigenki* and its successors), that two complete *Ka-*

*suga genki* were made between 1304 and 1309. This seems wholly implausible. It is much more likely that if *Kasuga go-ruki* really is earlier than the *Genki,* it is simply an advanced draft of the *Genki* text itself—after all, there must have been one. However, Nagashima (1963:20), for his part, considered *Kasuga go-ruki* to be later than the *Genki.* The issue is difficult to decide.

In the meantime, Kondō (1957) proposed another piece of evidence regarding precursor collections. This was a single sheet he found in the Kanazawa Bunko, entitled *Kasuga Gongen genki shō.* The sheet contains rather disjointed notes corresponding mainly to *Genki* 1.5 and 4.5. Kondō surmised that it is in the writing of Ken'a (1263–1338), the second abbot of Shōmyōji in Kanazawa, or at least of a contemporary of Ken'a. He concluded (1957:12, 1958:86) that these notes were taken from the document or documents that formed the basis for *Kasuga go-ruki.*

However, *Kasuga Gongen genki shō* seems at least as likely to be notes scribbled down, not always accurately, from hearing a reading of the *Genki* text. Moreover, if this is the kind of material the *Genki* or the *Kasuga go-ruki* compilers had to work with, one can only say that they were talented writers. It is perhaps well to remember that in proposing his ideas, Kondō never touched on—and seems to have ignored—the *Kyōkunshō* mention of a *miyashiro no genki* and the material from Sukekata's diary. These omissions do not strengthen his case.

## A "MOCKUP" OF THE *GENKI*

As one might expect, Takakane, who did the *Genki* paintings, prepared a full set of sketches *(nakagaki)* before executing the final version. These are mentioned in *Kanmon gyoki,* the diary of Prince Sadafusa (a son of Emperor Go-Hanazono) under the date Eikyō 10.2.27 (1438) (ZGR:521, cited in Nagashima 1944:245):

> Narutaki-dono lent me the set of the *nakagaki* of the illustrated *Kasuga engi* (20 scrolls). It belongs to Hagiwara-dono. How extraordinary to see it again! The final set was offered to the Kasuga Shrine . . . [The *nakagaki*] I borrowed is by Takakane too. I suppose it is an heirloom in Hagiwara-dono's family, which must be why Narutaki-dono has it now.

It is not clear whether this *nakagaki* included the text. Perhaps it still exists, though it is unknown in modern times.

## THE *GENKI* THROUGH THE CENTURIES

Once presented to the shrine, the *Genki* was carefully kept there. The shrine still owns the special, lacquered stand on which it was to be displayed, but the work was seldom seen. If required at Kōfukuji it could normally be taken only to Tōbokuin (*Daijōin jisha zōjiki* for Entoku 2.8.1 [1490]). Moreover, according to the diaries of Konoe Motohiro for Genroku 14.4.27 (1701, cited in Wada 1917) and of the Kasuga priest Mitsutomo for Hōreki 10 (1760, cited in Ōhigashi 1983b:4), no shrine priest or Kōfukuji monk less than forty years old was allowed to see it. Mitsutomo, a high-ranking priest, did not even ask to see it until he was in his forty-first year.

There were exceptions, however. In the *Daijōin jisha zōjiki* entry just cited, Jinson noted that the *Genki* was back from being shown to Emperor Go-Tsuchimikado in Kyoto, and was now at Tōbokuin. He went on:

> The superintendent [Shōkaku, a son of Nijō Mochimichi] has sent word to Tōbokuin that he wants to view it in private. Tomorrow, apparently, the monks who are sons of senior nobles *(ryōke-shu)* will see it, and it will be shown to the superintendent in the evening. The day after tomorrow it will be returned to the Shrine. I have never heard of its being shown anywhere except at Tōbokuin, but since the superintendent wants a look at it. . .

The *Genki* is known to have gone to Kyoto four times, as listed by Nagashima (1944:245); and Ōhigashi (1983a:86–87) recently added to its travels a visit to Edo Castle in Kyōhō 10 (1725).

Early in the Ōei era (1394–1428), Ashikaga Yoshimitsu managed to get the *Genki* for an *e-awase* ("picture competition") party. Later on, it went three times to the imperial palace: Entoku 2.7 (1490); Kyōroku 2.3 (1529); and Genroku 14.4 (1701). Nagashima (1944:246) described as follows the imperial viewing of 1490, on the basis of the Entoku 2.7.22 entry in the diary of Sanjōnishi Sanetaka:

That day the Emperor [Go-Tsuchimikado] proceeded to his Kuroto-no-gosho. Sanjōnishi Sanetaka and Nakamikado Nobutane read the *kotobagaki*—Nobutane scrolls 11, 12, and 13, and Sanetaka the rest. All present were deeply moved. In order to perform his duty, Sanetaka had fasted and bathed on the previous day.

On its trip to Kyoto in 1529, to be viewed by Emperor Go-Nara, the *Genki* was carefully looked after and securely guarded. It left on Kyōroku 2.2.29. When it returned to Nara on 4.12, a delegation from Ichijōin came as far as Uji to greet it (Nagashima 1944:247, quoting without attribution *Oyudono no Ue no nikki*, ZGR *hoi*, vol. 3).

Thus the *Genki* was treated by the court not just as a treasure but as a sacred object imbued with the presence of the Kasuga deity himself. However, the excursion to Edo Castle seems to have been less solemn. The *Genki* was taken to Edo and back by two priests from the shrine, and stayed under the shogun's care for five months. No doubt it was well looked-after, and eagerly viewed by a good many people, but its associations can hardly have been as impressive in Edo as they were in Kyoto.

Later in the eighteenth century an unfortunate laxness seems to have set in. Miya (1983:23) has discussed how, sometime during the An'ei era (1772–80), the *Genki* was apparently removed from its place at the shrine. The circumstances remain a mystery. According to a note appended to the Tokyo National Museum copy of the *Genki* (the copy is dated Kōka 2 [1848]), Kajūji Tsunetoshi (1748–1804), a major counselor in Kyoto, was amazed one day to learn that a private person in the city was in possession of the *Genki,* having allegedly obtained it from a certain merchant family. Tsunetoshi informed the shrine, and it turned out that the *Genki* really was gone. When he recovered the work, happily intact, he entrusted it to the regent, Takatsukasa Masanori. Masanori returned it to the shrine with the order that it should never again be allowed to stray. Ōhigashi Nobukazu (1983:88), on the other hand, has found evidence that this account may not be correct. Whatever really happened, the *Genki* in the late eighteenth century was treated a bit casually. The decline in its dignity parallels the decline suffered by Kasuga and especially by Kōfukuji at about the same time.

In due course the *Genki* found its way back to the Takatsukasa house, which in Meiji 8 (1875) offered it to the imperial household (Miya 1983:23). It remains imperial property to this day, and is now no easier to see than it was in the fourteenth century.

## WIDER KNOWLEDGE OF THE *GENKI*

Although the *Genki* was inaccessible, its existence was known. Those interested in it—that is, in the Kasuga deity—had therefore to be content with the text, of which copies appear to have been available. For example, according to *Daijōin jisha zōjiki* (end of the entry for Entoku 3.7 [1491]), Daijōin owned a *Kasuga genki* in one scroll, which can only have been the text alone (Kondō 1953:279). Kondō (1953:280) also cited a similar manuscript among the Yasuike documents listed as belonging to the Tenri University Library.

Among those who continued to read such copies, or to teach others from them, no doubt fewer and fewer recognized the people, places, and circumstances mentioned in the work. As in the case of other *engi* as well (Kondō 1953:280), there developed a need for more information that was met by *kikigaki:* in effect, compilations of notes on the text. Several from the late Muromachi period survive, including the *Eishun o-kikigaki* already mentioned. Kondō (1953) published another that appears to be, like Eishun's, from the sixteenth century. The existence of these *kikigaki* shows that interest in the subject was still alive nearly three hundreds years after the *Genki* was completed, and that at least some knowledge of the work must have reached many people who could not possibly have hoped ever to see the original.

## COPIES OF THE *GENKI*

The only way—a very expensive one—to make the whole *Genki* accessible to a wider audience was to copy it. Such copies began to be made in the Edo period, although even then no copy could be made without the permission of the head of the Fujiwara clan (Ōhigashi 1983b:6).

Ōhigashi Nobukazu (1983b:6) listed the presently known complete copies of the *Genki*. They are as follows.

(1) One owned by the Kajūji family. Ōhigashi dated it a little earlier than the Yōmei Bunko copy. Its fate is unknown, though it existed as late as 1807 when the last part of the present Kasuga copy was made from it.

(2) The Yōmei Bunko copy *(Yōmei Bunko-bon)* was made between 1716 and 1735 by the Rinpa artist Watanabe Shikō (1683–1755), a retainer of the Konoe house. The text was written out by "Konoe Yorakuin," no doubt a senior member of the Konoe family at that time (Kyoto Kokuritsu Hakubutsukan 1981:221). This copy is owned by the Yōmei Bunko in Kyoto, where in 1983 I had the privilege of seeing it. The paintings are beautifully executed (on paper), and the condition of the scrolls is excellent. At the rate of four scrolls per visit, it took five weekly visits to see the whole *Genki* properly. Simply looking at each picture of so large a work takes a good deal of time.

(3) The Kasuga copy *(Kasuga-bon,* formerly *Kuwana-bon)* was copied partly from the original and partly from no. 1 above. It was begun at the order of Tayasu Munetake (1715–71), the second son of the shogun Yoshimune, and finished by Munetake's son, Matsudaira Sadanobu (1758–1829), in 1807. Ōhigashi (1983a:87) suggested that Munetake may have first been shown the *Genki* by his father as a boy, in 1725, when the *Genki* was in Edo. Munetake obtained access to the original, for the purpose of making the copy, with help from the Konoe family, probably in the 1760s. The first, completed copy was lost in a fire. Munetake had the work begun again, but only half the copy (through scroll 10) was finished by the time he died. The the *Genki* disappeared, as related above, and after its recovery all access to it was cut off. Sadanobu had to have his father's copy completed from the copy then owned by the Kajūji family (Ōhigashi 1983a:87–89).

Since 1983, the Kasuga copy has been the property of the Kasuga Shrine. It is remarkable for having twenty-two scrolls, rather than the usual twenty-one. The extra scroll consists of the text of *Genki* 1.1, together with Munetake's critique of it. The learned Munetake, well versed in *kokugaku* thought, could not stomach 1.1, and felt obliged to set it apart so as not to mar the rest of the work.

(4) The Tokyo National Museum copy *(Tōkyō Kokuritsu Hakubutsukan-bon)* no. 1 was copied from the original in 1845.

(5) The National Diet Library copy (*Kokuritsu Kokkai Toshokan-bon*) was made from the Kasuga copy in 1870.

(6) The Tokyo National Museum copy no. 2 was made from the original in 1935.

Thanks to modern printing, the *Genki* has become widely accessible in the twentieth century, although it cannot be said that photographs are as satisfactory as a proper copy. Perhaps the first photographed reproduction was published in 1929 by Yūzankaku, and others (listed in the bibliography) have followed more recently.

# 2

# *The Text*

This chapter, inevitably a little disjointed, will discuss several important aspects of the *Genki* text. The first issue will be the text itself, and the extent to which the various published transcriptions of it are reliable. Then will come a discussion of how the work is organized. In this connection a synopsis of the text will be provided. Comments on the text's literary character will follow. A final section will touch on the relationship of the *Genki* to *setsuwa* and to *engi* literature.

## THE STATE OF THE *GENKI* TEXT

The state of the *Genki* text should need no special comment. After all, the original still exists and has been published more than once in transcription. Yet a genuinely thorough study should no doubt establish a correct reading for each line and word. This book does not do so because I cannot possibly read the original more authoritatively than those who have already transcribed it.

The different transcriptions of the text (listed in the bibliography) do not always agree with each other. Moreover, the published text of *Kasuga go-ruki* does not agree precisely with any version of the *Genki* text. Sometimes it is helpful, but sometimes one cannot help suspecting faulty transcription. Proper names are particularly troublesome, but there are other discrepancies as well. No version of the *Genki* text is entirely free of apparent errors. Especially in the case of proper names, research can detect a mistake or validate a reading, but other instances are more elusive. In a few cases, the last element in the notes that follow each story in this translation discusses significant variants. Much more often, the translation simply incorporates the reading that investigation showed to be correct, or at least best.

Even the original copyists (Mototada and his sons) seem to have made mistakes. Evidence to this effect occurs in 5.1, for example, where most transcriptions have the deity say, "The path of enlightenment too is the path of my heart" *(waga kokoro no michi)*. However, one *Genki* transcription and *Kasuga go-ruki* have instead, "The path of enlightenment too is the path of my mountain" *(waga yama no michi)*. The latter version makes much better sense for the *Genki*, and as it happens, the conclusion (20.2) alludes to this statement in a way that leaves no doubt on the subject. Yet the *kokoro* does seem to be in the text at that place. Apparently Mototada, who copied this passage, misread, or for some reason emended, the *yama* that must have been there before him.

## THE CONTENT AND ORGANIZATION OF THE *GENKI*

*Kasuga Gongen genki* demonstrates the Kasuga deity's direct involvement in human affairs as protector, judge, source of validating authority, guide to paradise, and deliverer from hell. The stories are presented in two major chronological sequences. The first and smaller sequence concerns the civil nobility, and covers the years 937 (1.2) to ca. 1220 (8.2). The second has to do with monks, particularly those of Kōfukuji, and lasts from ca. 880 (8.3) to 1304 (20.1). The two sequences are framed by an introduction and a conclusion that evoke respectively the origins of the shrine and the deity's undiminished efficacy in the present.

One can make finer distinctions as well. The opening story of the first sequence (1.2) is still introductory in character, since it establishes for the deity a Buddhist authority that will be important throughout the work. Similarly, the first story (8.3) of the second sequence governs everything that follows, for in it the deity sanctions the Buddhism of Kōfukuji. Again, the last two stories of the second sequence (19.1,20.1) not only evoke the *Genki*'s recent past (1301 and 1304) but also constitute a sort of "grande finale" to the whole work. Otherwise, the stories presented in the *Genki* can be divided into subsets of which some, like the one featuring Fujiwara no Tadazane (3.1–4.2), are clear-cut. Others are hazy. Consequently the subsets indicated below are not the only ones that could be proposed.

A more ingenious analysis can be imagined. Too much subtlety would be misleading, however. Those who put the *Genki* together had limited material to work with, and their chronological method still further restricted their freedom to make artful arrangements. Some subsets indicated below may be due partly to chance. On the other hand, it is clear that the stories in the *Genki* do not always appear in strictly chronological order. This suggests that the compilers did indeed arrange their material, within certain limits, so as to group it according to theme.

## A Synopsis of the *Genki*

| No. in this book | *Dan* no. in original | Date of event | Synopsis |
| --- | --- | --- | --- |
| **INTRODUCTION** | | | |
| 1.1 | 1.1 | | Identifies the four main Kasuga deities and accounts for their presence at the shrine; evokes the founding of the shrine; stresses the deity's protection of Kōfukuji; and affirms the deity's continuing potency. |
| **SEQUENCE 1** | | | |
| The deity's Buddhist standing | | | |
| 1.2 | 1.2 | 937 | In an oracle the deity assumes the title Jihi Mangyō Bosatsu. |
| The flourishing of the Fujiwara line | | | |
| 1.3 | 1.3 | 948 | The deity appears as a lady to a minor Fujiwara and shows him where to build his home. |
| 1.4 | 1.4 | 992 | The deity appears, again as a lady, to another minor Fujiwara, and promises him a strong and prosperous line. |
| Protection of the Fujiwara (1) | | | |
| 1.5 | 1.5 | 1092 | The deity possesses Retired Emperor Shirakawa, on the way to Kinpusen, and charges him |

A Synopsis of the *Genki* (*continued*)

| No. in this book | *Dan* no. in original | Date of event | Synopsis |
|---|---|---|---|
| | | | with neglect of Kasuga and the Fujiwara. Shirakawa makes a propitiatory vow. |
| 2.1 | 2.1 | 1093–1100 | Shirakawa donates a copy of the Buddhist canon to the shrine; the plaque (*gaku*) for the Sutra Repository, already written by Korefusa, is discovered thanks to an oracle from the deity. |
| 2.2 | 2.2 | 1113 | Shirakawa wants to stop a Kōfukuji expedition against Mt. Hiei; Akisue counters by reminding him of how the deity protects him. |
| 2.3 | 2.3 | Between 1094 and 1099? | Having forgotten his sword in the palace, Moromichi sends a lady back to fetch it, but the deity protects it from her touch. |

Protection of the Fujiwara (2): Tadazane

| | | | |
|---|---|---|---|
| 3.1 | 3.1 | 1098 | When the newborn son of the future regent Tadazane dies, the women of the household substitute someone else's baby for him. The deity possesses Minamoto no Toshifusa, Tadazane's father-in-law, to reveal the truth. |
| 3.2 | 3.2 | 1114 | A chain of poems in praise of Mikasa-yama. |
| 3.3 | 3.3,3.4,3.5 | 1110 | Tadazane imprisons the Kasuga priest Sanetsune, then falls ill. Zōyo, summoned to heal him, discerns a divine curse. When Sanetsune prays to Ka- |

|       |       |                            | suga for Tadazane, Tadazane recovers. |
| ----- | ----- | -------------------------- | ------------------------------------- |
| 4.1   | 4.1   | Between 1131 and 1156?     | Tadazane dreams of *tengu* monks, and calls for his home's protector deity. A Kasuga priest comes in and the *tengu* flee. |
| 4.2   | 4.2   | 1116                       | Tadazane goes to Kasuga to announce his retirement from the world. The deity gives him an oracle and some advice. |

Rewards and punishments

| 4.3   | 4.3   | 1183                       | The Regent Motomichi, fleeing Kyoto with the Taira, is stopped by a supernatural messenger from Kasuga. |
| ----- | ----- | -------------------------- | ------------------------------------- |
| 4.4   | 4.4   | 1160                       | Angered by Saionji Kinnori's neglect, the deity lets Kinnori die. |

Rewards and punishments: Sanesada

| 4.5   | 4.5   | 1177                       | As a reward for loyalty, the deity has Gotokudaiji Sanesada reappointed major counselor. |
| ----- | ----- | -------------------------- | ------------------------------------- |
| 4.6   | 4.5   | 1184                       | Forced from his post as palace minister by Minamoto no Yoshinaka, Sanesada is reapppointed following a portentous dream. |

Rewards and punishments:
the deity grants paradise or hell

| 5.1   | 5.1, 5.2, 5.3 | Ca. 1180–90          | Fujiwara no Toshimori prospers as a result of his monthly pilgrimages to Kasuga, and is helped by the deity to paradise. |
| ----- | ------------- | -------------------- | ------------------------------------- |
| 5.2   | 5.4           | Between 1190 and 1211? | Sueyoshi, Toshimori's son, continues his father's monthly pilgrimages. The deity protects him from a *tengu*. |

## A Synopsis of the *Genki* (*continued*)

| No. in this book | *Dan* no. in original | Date of event | Synopsis |
| --- | --- | --- | --- |
| 6.1 | 6.1 | Ca. 1130–52 | Touched by the loyalty of Koma no Yukimitsu, a dancer, the deity saves Yukimitsu from hell. |
| 6.2 | 6.2 | 1198–99 | Taira no Chikamune abused some Kasuga shrine servants. The deity takes his life and has him escorted to hell. |
| 6.3 | 6.3 | ? | Some boys make a snake drop a copy of the Heart Sutra. The deity is angry, since the snake is a former devotee whom the deity was trying to help. |
| 7.1 | 7.1 | 1212 | Obliged to give up his post at court because of a death in the family, Tsunemichi finally gets it back when he prays to Kasuga. |
| 7.2 | 7.2 | Ca. 1225–29 | A nun dreams she should say "Namu Daimyōjin" because this invocation combines the power of all five Kasuga sanctuaries. |

The deity demands commensurate offerings

| | | | |
| --- | --- | --- | --- |
| 7.3 | 7.3,7.4 | 1217 | The deity tells a Kōfukuji monk in a dream to have the dancer Chikazane do Ryōō for him. The performance goes beautifully. |

The deity is the Great Teacher
and the *Yuishiki ron* is his text

| | | | |
| --- | --- | --- | --- |
| 7.4 | 7.5 | Ca. 1180 | A lady learns in a dream that the deity is "the Great Guide who assures Rebirth." |
| 8.1 | 8.1 | Ca. 1213–19 | The deity assures a nun that he is present in the famous Shaka of the Shakadō in Saga. |

| | | | |
|---|---|---|---|
| 8.2 | 8.2 | After 1183 | A single house is spared an epidemic because a Kōfukuji monk forgot a scroll of the *Yuishiki ron* there. |

SEQUENCE 2
The deity validates
the Buddhism of Kōfukuji

| | | | |
|---|---|---|---|
| 8.3 | 8.3 | Ca. 875–85 | The deity validates simultaneous study of Hossō and Esoteric Buddhism by Zōri, a Kōfukuji scholar. |

The deity's patronage
of true piety and learning (1)

| | | | |
|---|---|---|---|
| 8.4 | 8.4,8.5 | 949 | Disappointed at not being named lecturer for the Yuima-e, Ichiwa leaves Kōfukuji. At Atsuta, the deity tells him to go home and promises that he will be lecturer next year. |
| 8.5 | 8.6 | Ca. 955 | The deity resolves the confusion of Hōzō, a Kōfukuji monk, concerning the correct text for his part of the Yuima-e. |
| 8.6 | 8.7 | Ca. 1150–57 | A Kōfukuji monk wanders away to the East, where the deity appears to him and reassures him. |
| 9.1 | 9.1,9.2, 9.3 | 969–1047 | A poor woman puts her son under Kūsei of Kōfukuji. When she dies, the deity returns her to life. When she really dies, the boy, now a monk, devotes himself to praying for her. |
| 10.1 | 10.1, 10.2 | 998 (pt. 1) | Rin'e, praying at the shrine, is disturbed by bells and drums. |
| | | 1017–25 (pt. 2) | He vows that one day he will silence the music. When he |

## A Synopsis of the *Genki* (*continued*)

| No. in this book | *Dan* no. in original | Date of event | Synopsis |
| --- | --- | --- | --- |
| | | | does so, the deity lets Rin'e know that he is displeased. |

**Piety and learning (2): Eichō**

| No. in this book | *Dan* no. in original | Date of event | Synopsis |
| --- | --- | --- | --- |
| 10.2 | 10.3 | 1058 | The imperial envoy to the Yuima-e dreams he sees the regent bow before Eichō's room. |
| 10.3 | 10.4 | Ca. 1082–96 | A weird, supernatural monk comes to Eichō, who calls on the deity. A shrine servant comes and frightens the monk away. |
| 10.4 | 10.5 | Between 1060 and 1096 | Eichō sees the deity from behind and asks to see his face. The deity refuses because Eichō is not yet truly seeking liberation. |

**The deity's loyalty to the monks who serve him (1)**

| No. in this book | *Dan* no. in original | Date of event | Synopsis |
| --- | --- | --- | --- |
| 10.5 | 10.6 | Between 1039 and 1047 | The Tendai abbot Kyōen, reading the *Yuishiki ron* on Mt. Hiei, sees the deity dancing on a pine in his garden. |
| 10.6 | 10.7 | Ca. 1050–93 | The Kōfukuji monk Kyōe moves away but the deity continues to protect him. |

**The deity's loyalty to the monks who serve him (2): Egyō**

| No. in this book | *Dan* no. in original | Date of event | Synopsis |
| --- | --- | --- | --- |
| 11.1 | 11.1 | 1135–64 (pt. 1) 1110–25 (pt. 2) | Egyō of Kōfukuji was once called to read the Lotus Sutra for Enma in hell. In his youth, when he thought of leaving the temple, the deity scolded him and promised him high rank. |
| 11.2 | 11.2 | 1129–33/4 | Retired Emperor Toba exiles Egyō, who eventually calls |

down the deity to find out
when he will be allowed back.

The threat of the deity's wrath

| 11.3 | 11.3 | 1166 | Someone posts on the First Torii of the shrine a dream that suggests the deity is angry with Kōfukuji and is leaving. |
| 11.4 | 11.4 | 1166 | To placate the deity, Kōfukuji holds a solemn doctrinal debate. A monk dreams the deity is returning. |

The deity's attention
to his monks' welfare and conduct

| 12.1 | 12.1 | 1140 | Zōshun, an important Kōfukuji scholar, sees the four main Kasuga deities, converses with the first, and goes over in his mind the Kasuga *honji*. |
| 12.2 | 12.2 | 1156–59 | During a forty-day rite at Kōfukuji, deer come daily to listen. |
| 12.3 | | 1165 | Keichin, from Tōdaiji, meets Jizō at Kasuga. |
| 12.4 | 12.4 | Ca. 1125–50 | Onkaku gets nowhere at Kōfukuji, but prospers at Iwashimizu Hachiman. Then he dreams the deity visits Hachiman, and tells how he had kept Onkaku poor so that he should reach rebirth faster. Onkaku hurries back to Kasuga and achieves rebirth. |
| 13.1 | 13.1, 13.2, 13.3 | 1165–1230 | Seiga, born at Kasuga, is entrusted to Shōren'in, a Tendai temple. Displeased, the deity makes him ill, but finally allows him to become a monk at Kanjuji. |
| 13.2 | 13.4 | 1174 | The Fourth Sanctuary visits the studious Jōon. |

## A Synopsis of the *Genki* (*continued*)

| No. in this book | *Dan* no. in original | Date of event | Synopsis |
|---|---|---|---|
| 13.3 | 13.5 | 1189 | Zōkei leaves Kōfukuji temporarily, but is brought back by a mischievous stratagem of the deity. |
| 14.1 | 14.1 | ? | A Kōfukuji monk wanders off to study Tendai *shikan*. The deity lets him know in a dream how deeply he disapproves. |

The deity's displeasure: Ryūkaku

| | | | |
|---|---|---|---|
| 14.2 | 14.2 | 1139 | Superintendent Ryūkaku, rejected by the monks, prays for the deity's help. The deity complains about him too. |
| 14.3 | 14.3 | 1139 | The deity complains about Ryūkaku to Ryūkaku's colleague. |
| 14.4 | 14.4 | 1139 | The deity reproves Ryūkaku. |

The virtue of the Yuishiki ron

| | | | |
|---|---|---|---|
| 14.5 | 14.5 | ? | A monk chanting the Lotus Sutra at Kasuga is reproved for not chanting the *Yuishiki ron*. |
| 14.6 | 14.6 | Late 12th c.? | A house escapes a great fire in Kyoto because there is a scroll of the *Yuishiki ron* in it. |
| 15.1 | 15.1, 15.2 | ? | A monk kicks a student monk for sleeping in the gallery of the shrine. The deity, angered, makes him ill because the student had been studying the *Yuishiki ron*. |

Further instances of the deity's protection

| | | | |
|---|---|---|---|
| 15.2 | 15.3 | ? | Kyōei of Kōfukuji, who must officiate at a ceremony, needs "host gifts." The vestal of Ise, alerted by the deity in a dream, sends him what he requires. |
| 15.3 | 15.4 | 1224 | Jisson, who must conduct a |

| | | | |
|---|---|---|---|
| | | | ceremony, is incapacitated by asthma. A deer appears to him in a dream, and he recovers. |
| 15.4 | 15.5 | Between 1226 and 1230 | In time of famine, a Kōfukuji official hoards rice for the superintendent and withholds it from a group of starving monks. The deity intervenes in a dream. |
| 15.5 | 15.6 | Between 1180 and 1230 | The deity heals and protects a monk in whom he has no special interest, but who has always been loyal. |

The deity and Gedatsu Shōnin

| | | | |
|---|---|---|---|
| 16.1 | 16.1 | 1195 | Gedatsu Shōnin having retired to Kasagi, the deity possesses him in order to scold him. |
| 16.2 | 16.2 | 1196 | Gedatsu Shōnin installs the deity as the protector of the Hannyadai on Kasagi; the deity rides there on Gedatsu's head. Later, the deity reveals to Gedatsu that his *honji* is Shaka. |
| 16.3 | 16.3 | 1199 | Through Gedatsu Shōnin, the deity delivers a long discourse on the Hossō tradition. Then he begs Gedatsu to settle at Kōfukuji and to write down what he knows. Last, he chides Gedatsu for urging the Shaka *nenbutsu* on Amaterasu at Ise. |
| 16.4 | 16.4 | Ca. 1240 | Shōen, a disciple of Gedatsu, describes the deity's hell and a sort of purgatory reserved for former monks of Kōfukuji. |

The deity and Myōe Shōnin

| | | | |
|---|---|---|---|
| 17.1 | 17.1 | 1203 | When Myōe Shōnin decides to go to India, the deity possesses his aunt and begs him not to go. |

A Synopsis of the *Genki* (*continued*)

| No. in this book | *Dan* no. in original | Date of event | Synopsis |
|---|---|---|---|
| 17.2 | 17.2, 17.3 | 1203 | The deity possesses the woman again, assures Myōe of his boundless admiration and love, and urges him to study and teach. Finally the deity promises to bless a new Kasuga cult. |
| 18.1 | 18.1 | 1203 | When Myōe Shōnin goes to Kasuga, the deer there bow to him. Later, at the shrine, he dreams he goes to Vulture Peak. |
| 18.2 | 18.2 | 1203 | The deity talks to Myōe again about how he is to be represented in painting, and gives Myōe a parting verse. |
| 18.3 | 18.3 | 1203 | Back at Kasuga, Myōe dreams again of Vulture Peak. He also dreams of holding in either hand a steel hammer. |
| 18.4 | 18.4, 18.5 | 1203 | The next day, Myōe visits Gedatsu Shōnin at Kasagi. Gedatsu gives him two relic particles. At the shrine, Myōe finds that these particles are the two hammers he dreamed of before. He sees the deity come to inhabit the relic particles. |
| Final scenes 19.1 | 19.1–19.5 | 1301 | Bandits raid the shrine and steal all the sacred mirrors. Kōfukuji troops destroy them and their stronghold. One by one, amid wondrous signs, the mirrors are found and returned. |
| 20.1 | 20.1 | 1304 | Kōfukuji has acted against the bakufu, and a bakufu show of force is imminent. Then the |

trees on Mikasa-yama die.
Dismayed, the bakufu gives in
to the temple's demands.

CONCLUSION
20.2        20.2

The lesson of all this is that in
the gap between Shaka and
Miroku, enlightenment is fully
present and accessible at the
shrine, and Mikasa-yama is
every buddha's paradise.

## THE *GENKI* AS LITERATURE

Works like *Kasuga Gongen genki* are included only sporadically in
medieval tale *(setsuwa)* literature. Still, the *Genki* is as much of a tale
collection as most *setsuwa* compilations, and a more satisfying one
than some. Both as text and as painting it justifies the devoted efforts
of those who executed it, and it is certainly a well-done piece of
writing. Gorai Shigeru (1978a:2) insisted that it is far more important
to understand the purpose of an *emakimono* than simply to "appreciate" *(kanshō)* it. From a certain perspective this is no doubt true, but
still, an *emakimono* like the *Genki* gives one much to enjoy, and part
of the pleasure surely comes from the text.

The language is Japanese, without admixture of kambun, in keeping with the work's purpose, which is to honor the Kasuga deity.
Although the style is occasionally, as the context demands, formal or
rich with Buddhist vocabulary, it is more often pleasantly light for so
solemn a work. Formality is understandably most obvious in the
introduction (1.1), where a terse decorum sometimes makes the text
a little hard to follow and perhaps encourages the sort of criticism
leveled at this passage by Tayasu Munetake. As for Buddhist vocabulary, 16.3, for example, is thick with it, but only because it transcribes
the words of the deity himself, speaking through the scholarly as well
as saintly Gedatsu Shōnin. One might expect the conclusion of the
*Genki* (20.2) to be as formal as the introduction, and perhaps it is; but
it is not as stiff. Unlike the introduction, it conveys deep feeling: the
exaltation of one who composes a declaration of faith. In fact, one
can hardly imagine a finer evocation of *honji-suijaku* religion.

Between introduction and conclusion, the *Genki* has moments of beauty, humor, and liveliness that give the text considerable charm. However, relatively fewer good passages occur in the first sequence, where many items are brief or little developed. One reason is that the ambitions and pretensions of courtiers, whether rewarded or chastised, are not necessarily attractive. No doubt the low point occurs in 4.5 and 4.6, where Gotokudaiji Sanesada's fussing about getting reappointed, however natural, seems particularly unedifying. Moreover, the humor in 2.3 is no doubt visible only to us, for surely the compilers did not mean to make Moromichi look silly. Perhaps the liveliest stories in this section of the *Genki* are those of Sanetsune's imprisonment (3.3) and of Tsunemichi (7.1), who gets the deity to intercede so effectively on his behalf. Hanken's dream (7.3) is impressive too. It is noteworthy, though, that Sanetsune was a Kasuga priest and Hanken a Kōfukuji monk: these two stories are centered on people who belonged not to the court but to the Kasuga-Kōfukuji community.

The reason why the second sequence of stories is generally more interesting than the first, apart simply from its greater length, is that it features the monks of Nara: Kōfukuji above all, but also Tōdaiji where Myōe Shōnin must have formed his connection with the Kasuga deity. The senior Fujiwara at court may have been the titular head of the Kasuga cult, but the cult really lived in Nara among the monks: the *Nanto daishu* ("assembled monks of the Southern Capital") as contemporary documents generally call them, meaning particularly Kōfukuji. The Kasuga deity was their local patron. Unlike the nobles in Kyoto, who honored other shrines as well, their loyalties were largely undivided. As a result, the second sequence is the richer of the two, and conveys greater intimacy with the deity.

The fullness of Kasuga lore at Kōfukuji is clear already in the second story (8.4) of this sequence, a well-developed tale about a locally famous, relatively early monk. This version was not even the only one known at Kōfukuji ca. 1300, since a rather different one was recorded in *Sanne jōikki,* the annual record of the Yuima-e. The exemplary career of another famous monk is told expansively in 9.1. As to humor, the delightful incident recounted in 10.1 may not be meant principally to raise a smile. After all, Lady Nijō (the author of *Towazugatari*), who heard it when she visited Kasuga in 1290, wrote,

"This tale strengthened my faith and filled me with awe" (Brazell 1973:203–4). Still, a smile will do it no harm. And surely the end of 14.5 is at least partly a joke, carefully planned not so much by the deity (who despite his impish form is represented as being quite seriously malicious) as by the teller. As to the misfortunes of poor Zōkei in 13.3, perhaps "humorous" is not quite the right word; but the side of the deity revealed here is not at all like his mature solemnity elsewhere. Items 11.1, 11.2, and 20.1 show plainly just how deeply the deity's withdrawal, or the threat of it, could affect Kōfukuji. The court's devotion to Kasuga was distant in comparison.

If the last two stories in the *Genki*'s second sequence, and especially the final one (20.1), resemble a sort of gala closing scene, the climax of the work is undoubtedly to be found in scrolls 16 through 18, and above all in scroll 17. In scroll 16, the text begins to move beyond the limits of the preceding material by presenting three fascinating scenes from the life of Gedatsu Shōnin. This is not the first time three or even more successive stories have treated the same person, but the items about Gedatsu give a new feeling of depth and completeness. Moreover, the deity's running argument with Gedatsu, over Gedatsu's move away from Kōfukuji, gives this monk's relationship with the deity a remarkable vividness. One is therefore almost disappointed by 16.4, fascinating though it is, because it is merely another story and not a moment or two more with an extraordinary man. Yet the item that follows (17.1) begins an even more remarkable series. Two whole scrolls are filled with the astonishing visitations granted by the Kasuga deity to Myōe Shōnin.

The material for this long passage was ready to hand in documents written by Myōe's disciples, but the work of the *Genki* compilers is all the more obvious for that. There is no need to stress the value of the original documents, especially *Kasuga Daimyōjin go-takusen ki*. From the literary standpoint, however, the *Genki* version is more satisfying. Skillfully edited, it smooths the rather fragmented text of *Kasuga Daimyōjin go-takusen ki* into a continuous account. No doubt some detail is lost in the process, and perhaps even some accuracy— though surely no reader can fail to wonder what in the world *he* or *she* would have seen, heard, smelled, felt, and thought in Myōe's place. One is grateful that the older document has been preserved. But the result (especially in 17.2) is perhaps one of the finest and most unusual passages in medieval Japanese literature. The emotion of the scene described in 17.2 comes through convincingly, and the deity conveys at once a humanity and a divine nobility far beyond anything to be found in the rest of the *Genki*. Scroll 17 alone lifts the *Genki* beyond the commonplace, giving it a distinction that honors the faith it represents, and commending it to the attention of readers in another place and time.

## THE *GENKI* AND *SETSUWA* LITERATURE

The *Genki* shares some of its material with other medieval writings, especially *setsuwa* collections. For one thing, many of the people, places, etc. mentioned in the *Genki* appear elsewhere in *setsuwa* literature. The notes to the tales, below, acknowledge these instances, especially those that concern supernatural visitations, rebirth in paradise, or other issues favored by the *Genki*. In other cases, the *Genki* may share whole stories with other works. The table below lists all the occurrences of *Genki* stories (or partial stories) elsewhere, whether in variant form or in a form close to that of the *Genki* text. Or rather, the table lists all those occurrences that I have been able to find. There are surely more.

The difficulty of identifying source materials for the *Genki* has been noted in chapter 1. In the case of five stories, however, plausible sources can be named. The two Kasuga Shrine documents *Koshaki* and *Kasuga go-sha go-honji narabini go-takusen ki* seem to have supplied 1.2, 2.1, and 3.2; while *Kyōkunshō* (by the Kasuga *bugaku* dancer Koma no Chikazane) may have contributed 6.1 and 7.3. (However, 10.5 is not the same as the *Kyōkunshō* version.) Besides these, two stories from *Senjūshō* (4.2,8.4) recur in extremely similar tellings in the *Genki,* and a third (8.6) appears in the *Genki* in a variant form. The relationship between *Senjūshō* and the *Genki* was discussed by Takagi Yutaka (1985), who pointed out also certain similarities of vocabulary and of course the continuity between the ideas in the *Genki* introduction and those in *Senjūshō* 9 *(Nihon wa shinkoku no koto)*. No one can say, however, whether the *Genki* stories were taken directly from *Senjūshō* or whether the two works share a common influence.

Aside from these few apparently direct links between the *Genki* and other writings, twenty-five *Genki* stories can be found elsewhere in one or more variant versions older than the *Genki* itself; while later variants exist for fourteen stories. The earlier *setsuwa* collections that include such variants are *Gōdanshō, Shūi ōjō den, Ima monogatari, Hosshinshū, Kyōkunshō, Jikkinshō, Kokonchomonjū, Senjūshō,* and *Shasekishū;* while the two later ones are *Shingonden* and *Sangoku denki.* There is a wide range of difference between these variants and the *Genki* versions. For example, the *Chūyūki* entry corresponding to 2.1 is fuller than the *Genki,* but otherwise there are no discrepancies between the two; the *Shasekishū* version of 17.1 and 17.2 is very brief; and the *Shingonden* variant for 3.3 is wholly unlike the *Genki* account. A proper study of the relationship of the *Genki* to other documents and writings remains to be done.

Occurrences of *Genki* Stories Elsewhere
(Titles of *setsuwa* collections are shown in boldface)

| | Nearly the same as *Genki* | Variant | Date |
|---|---|---|---|
| *Chūyūki* | | 2.1 | Relevant entry 1093 |
| **Gōdanshō** | | 10.5 | Early 12th c. |
| **Shūi ōjō den** | | 10.6 (partial) | 1132 |
| *Kasuga go-sha go-honji narabini go-takusen ki* | 1.2,3.2 | | 1175 |
| *Kasuga Daimyōjin hotsuganmon* | | 10.6 | Ca. 1200 |
| **Hosshinshū** | | 10.4 | Ca. 1214 |
| *Kasuga Daimyōjin go-takusen ki* | | 17.1–18.4 | 1233 |
| **Kyōkunshō** | 6.1,7.3 | 10.5 | 1233 |
| **Ima monogatari** | | 4.5,5.1 | Ca. 1240 |
| *Koshaki* | 2.1 (partial) | 3.3 | Date contested |
| *Nihon kōsōden yōmonshō* | | 8.3 | 1251 |
| **Jikkinshō** | | 12.1 | 1252 |
| **Kokonchomonjū** | | 2.1,4.5,12.4, 17.1,17.2 | 1254 |
| *Kōzanji Myōe Shōnin gyōjō* | | 17.1–18.4 | 1255 |

Occurrences of *Genki* Stories Elsewhere (*continued*)
(Titles of *setsuwa* collections are shown in boldface)

| | Nearly the same as *Genki* | Variant | Date |
|---|---|---|---|
| **Senjūshō** | 4.2,8.4 | 8.6 | Mid-13th c. |
| *Heike monogatari* | | 4.2 | 13th c. |
| *Zoku kyōkunshō* | | 10.5 | Ca. 1270 |
| **Shasekishū** | | 10.4,16.2 (partial), 16.4,17.1,17.2,18.1 | 1283 |
| *Kōshō Bosatsu no go-kyōkai chōmon shū* | | 10.6 | Ca. 1285 |
| *Jizō engi* (Freer Gallery) | | 7.3 | Unclear |
| *Towazugatari* | | 10.1 | Relevant entry 1290 |
| *Kōfukuji ruki* | | 11.2 | (Composite) |
| *Sanne jōikki* | | 8.4 | (Date of entry unclear) |
| *KASUGA GONGEN GENKI* | | | |
| **Shingonden** | | 3.3 | 1325 |
| *Kasuga Gongen genki shō* | | 1.5,4.5 | 2d quarter 14th c.? |
| *Kōfukuji ryaku nendaiki* | | 1.5,2.2,20.1 | Mid-14th c.? |
| **Sangoku denki** | | 16.4 | 1431? |
| *Kasuga ryūjin* | | 17.1–18.2 | 15th c. |
| *Tamon'in nikki* | | 4.1 | Relevant entry 1543 |
| *Honchō kōsōden* | | 8.3,8.4,8.6, 10.5,12.4 | 1702 |

## THE *GENKI* AND *ENGI* LITERATURE

Though in some respects a *setsuwa* collection, the *Genki* may be classified as an *engi:* that is, as an example of the large body of medieval Japanese writings whose most obvious common characteristic is to tell the legendary origins of temples and shrines. Already in *Kanmon gyoki* (see ch. 1), Prince Sadafusa referred to the *Genki* as *Kasuga engi*. In the only annotated collection of *engi* texts published so far, Sakurai Tokutarō (1975:469) cited the *Genki* as a model *jinja engi* ("shrine *engi*"), a type he described as stressing the bond between a deity and the members of his community *(ujiko)*.

So many *engi* are illustrated, or provide important information about temples and religious objects, that they have generally been understood to belong to the domain of art historians. However, lately they have begun to draw the attention of scholars not primarily concerned with art. Sakurai's volume is an example. Another is a group project, recently announced by Tashima Kazuo of the Kokubungaku Kenkyū Shiryōkan, to study the *content* of *Hie Sannō rishōki,* the text to the nine-scroll version of the *emaki* entitled *Sannō reigenki.* Tashima noted (1986:1) that although the text has been in print for a long time, almost all the attention the work has received so far has gone to the paintings. Moreover, he promised that the project would, among other things, establish the work's relationship with "the rest of *setsuwa* literature." The approach to the *Genki* in this book is similar.

Despite Sakurai's judgment, one can wonder whether the *Genki* really is an *engi*. Most authorities, like Sakurai, take it that the term *engi* is ultimately the same word as the Sino-Japanese translation of the Sanskrit *pratitya-samutpāda* ("co-dependent origination"). Gorai Shigeru (1982:8) disagreed, but his definition too refers to the idea of origins. Is *Kasuga Gongen genki* about the origins of the Kasuga Shrine?

Not really. It devotes even less space to origins than *Hie Sannō rishōki,* which does not much stress the subject either. The truth is that there is still no consensus on where the boundaries of the *engi* genre lie. In fact, according to Yoshihara Hiroto (1986:122), *jisha engi* ("shrine and temple *engi*") have not yet been recognized as a genre at all by historians of literature. In the meantime, various scholars in religion or art have proposed conflicting classification schemes. (Nakano Genzō [1975] gave a particularly useful treatment of the subject.) No doubt the problem will be sorted out in the future, especially as work on the literary aspect of *engi* progresses. In the meantime, the status of the *Genki* as an *engi* remains unclear.

# 3

# *The Shrine*

The intimate relationship between Kōfukuji and the Kasuga Shrine was like that between a king and a queen in some old tale. To speak of one, in the time of the *Genki,* was to speak of the other, though neither ever lost its identity. Kōfukuji—to pursue the metaphor—was like the king; high-principled, mettlesome, prone to grasp what he could reach, and at times a nuisance to the world at large. The shrine resembled the queen: modest, beautiful, wholly loyal, and in fact the living spirit of the kingdom. To understand this, one must know something about the temple and the shrine, and something of the Kasuga cult. The most practical way to begin is to describe what the shrine looks like, how it is situated, and what deities it honors.

## THE SHRINE AND ITS DEITIES

The Kasuga Shrine stands at the foot of Mikasa-yama (283 m.), a hill in the range along the eastern edge of the Yamato plain. Mikasa-yama is clearly an ancient *kamunabi:* a sacred hill linked with the cult of ancestral spirits and powers such as mountain and water deities. Behind it rise the Kasuga hills (Kasuga-yama), where there are still many traces of ideas and practices associated with the spirits of the dead. Regular in form, and somewhat detached from its neighbors, Mikasa-yama seen from the west against the higher peaks beyond it looks rather like a deity in a medieval painting, seated before a folding screen. *Genki* 3.2, and many poems, show that the hill could be addressed as the Kasuga deity; and in 8.4 the deity speaks as the hill. Mikasa-yama presides over all the *Kasuga mandara* that became popular toward the end of the Kamakura period. Its presence is fundamental to the cult. Even today it is closed to all except shrine priests and certain local religious devotees.

The shrine below Mikasa-yama consists of a main sanctuary complex; a much smaller complex for the Wakamiya; and many secondary shrines (sessha and massha). Kōfukuji lies about a kilometer away, to the west. Tame deer roam the whole area, as they have for many centuries, because the deer is the Kasuga deity's mount. The row of main sanctuaries, which one would expect to face west, directly away from Mikasa-yama, faces south instead. Around the sanctuaries cluster various buildings including the heiden and several massha. A broad, walled gallery (kairō), pierced by four entrances, surrounds the whole, except in the northeast corner, which is protected by a simple wall. A stream runs through the compound. The southern entrance is the elaborate Nanmon ("South Gate"). The southwest entrance, around the corner from the Nanmon, is the Keigamon: in the past, the "private" entrance used ceremonially by ranking members of the Fujiwara clan. Most of the complex, with its brown, cedar-bark roofs, is painted a felicitous orange-red, and trimmed in white and green. Though the shrine has been rebuilt at intervals over the centuries (according to Nagashima, 1955:472, it was supposed to be rebuilt every twenty-one years), it has looked this way since the late twelfth century. Most of the present buildings date physically from the nineteenth century, although they reproduce the older ones.

There are four main sanctuaries in the compound, lined up next to each other. In the Genki, as in other documents of the time, the four deities are most commonly referred to not by name but by number: First Sanctuary, Second Sanctuary, etc. In other words, no distinction is made between the deity and the structure the deity inhabits. The First Sanctuary, on the east end of the row, closest to Mikasa-yama, is Takemikazuchi, who came to Kasuga from Kashima. This is the seat of honor, so to speak; Takemikazuchi has always been the ranking presence at Kasuga. The Second Sanctuary is Futsunushi from Katori, and the Third is Amenokoyane from Hiraoka. These three are male. Himegami, the Fourth Sanctuary, occupies the western end of the row and hence the lowest place. She is female. Although recent authorities connect her exclusively with Hiraoka, she was understood in the time of the Genki to be an emanation of the Ise Shrine. By the

Map 1. The Kasuga-Kōfukuji Area

Key:

1. Kintetsu Railway Station
2. Nan'endō (Kōfukuji)
3. Central Kondō (Kōfukuji)
4. Kōfukuji Museum
5. Kōfukuji temple headquarters
6. Sarusawa Pond
7. Nara Hotel; approximate location of Daijōin
8. Gangōji Gokurakubō
9. Araike
10. First Torii of Kasuga
11. Yōgō no matsu
12. Nara National Museum
13. Himuro-sha
14. Sagi no ike
15. Man'yō Garden
16. Mizuya jinja
17. Kasuga Shrine
18. Wakamiya
19. Sanjūhassho-sha
20. Shin'yakushiji
21. Mikasa-yama
22. Nandaimon (Tōdaiji)
23. Daibutsuden (Tōdaiji)
24. Kaidan'in (Tōdaiji)
25. Nigatsudō (Tōdaiji)
26. Sangatsudō (Tōdaiji)
27. Tamukeyama Hachiman

N

1 cm = 70 m

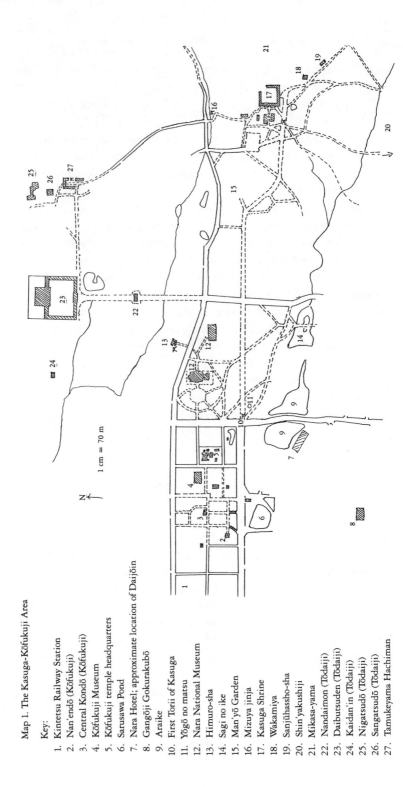

Map 2. The Kasuga Shrine

Key:

1. Hitokotonushi-sha
2. Naishimon
3. Shōjōmon
4. Keigamon
5. Kairō (Gallery)
6. Enomoto-sha
7. Nanmon
8. Naoraiden
9. Heiden
10. Chūmon
11. Main sanctuaries. Right to left (east to west):
    Takemikazuchi, Futsunushi, Amenokoyane, Himegami
12. Wall
13. Chakutōden
14. Fuji no torii
15. Haraido jinja
16. Second Torii
17. Shamusho (modern shrine office)
18. Wakamiya
19. Tajikarao-sha
20. Hosodono
21. Path up Mikasa-yama

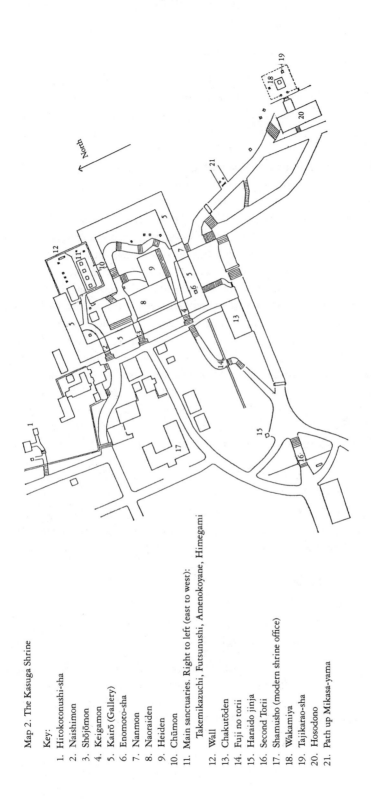

end of the Heian period all these *suijaku* deities had one or more *honji* who figured too in the Kasuga cult.

About 100 meters south-southwest of the main complex is the Wakamiya, technically a *sessha* of the Kasuga Shrine. This deity, named Amenooshikumone, is supposed to be the child of Ameno-koyane and Himegami. His sanctuary faces west.

Pilgrims approach the shrine from the west, along a broad, graveled avenue. In the time of the *Genki* this avenue led quite obviously from Kōfukuji to the shrine, though nowadays the link is less clear. One passes first through the First Torii, which figures in several *Genki* stories. On the right is the famous *yōgō no matsu* ("pine where the god appeared") discussed in the notes to *Genki* 10.5. In the late twelfth or thirteenth centuries one would have admired, on the left, the Kasuga Shrine's two five-story pagodas; Saigyō did so in *Senjūshō* 5/14. Now one sees instead the old and new buildings of the Nara National Museum. Continuing on, the Saigyō evoked in *Senjūshō* wrote: "I gradually made my way into the shrine grounds where stood a grove of tall, luxuriant cryptomeria, traversed by six paths like the six-forked crossroads of the afterworld" (tr. Moore 1982:188). The spot is still a grove of tall trees, but the modern visitor finds there, on the left, the entrance to the "Man'yō Garden" where plants mentioned in the *Man'yōshū* are cultivated. Saigyō next "crossed the bridge of accumulated merit and drew near the shrine at last. There were the four [sanctuaries] and the towering two-storied [Nanmon] gate." He omitted various other structures that lay (or lie) along the way. Still, he could have noted the Second Torii, which he passed through just before reaching the shrine. He might not have recognized, though, to his left after having done so, the Fuji-no-torii ("Wisteria Torii"), which gave Fujiwara clan members private access to the Keigamon.

# THE LEGENDARY ORIGINS OF THE KASUGA SHRINE

There are two versions of the origins of the Kasuga Shrine. One is told in the legends that constitute the canonical history of the shrine. The other is set forth, more tentatively, in the writings of modern scholars. The two are not quite the same. Though the second is no doubt more accurate, in the *Genki* the first is assumed to be true.

No concerted study of the Kasuga origin legends seems yet to have been done, but the legends themselves are now published (ST). Of these, *Koshaki* ("An Ancient Record of the Shrine") bears the earliest date: Tengyō 3 (940). Unfortunately the only extant copy of *Koshaki* was written on used paper, with on the reverse side a part of a calendar containing a date corresponding to 1234. Some scholars (for example, Tsuji 1944:470) therefore maintain that, in reality, *Koshaki* cannot be earlier than the mid-Kamakura period; others, however (for example, Nishida 1978:70), accept the date of 940 as plausible enough. In any case, *Koshaki* (ST:6–9) contains a good account of the origins of the shrine, and attributes it to none other than Nakatomi no Tokifū (731–818) who, together with Hidetsura (713-807), accompanied the deity Takemikazuchi to Kasuga. One may choose not to believe that Tokifū really wrote this passage, or that the date given for it (780) is entirely trustworthy. However, skepticism does not affect the account's usefulness as background for the *Genki*.

Takemikazuchi, Iwainushi (that is, Futsunushi), and Amenokoyane figure in the opening part of Tokifū's narrative. The text first reviews their mythological role, stressing (as does *Genki* 1.1) their service to Amaterasu and their essential role in the pacification of the land. It evokes particularly their glorious success in restoring light to the world in the episode of the Heavenly Rock Cave. (Though not mentioned here, Iwainushi appears to be inseparable from Takemikazuchi.) When Amaterasu has come forth from the cave, she praises the deities, assuring them that it is "thanks entirely to the power of their own vows" that they have brought forth "the light of my sun and moon." And she continues, "Therefore I shall call you Kasuga [Spring Sun] no Daimyōjin." Next, after confirming the definitive suppression of the evil forces led by her brother Susanoo, she charges the deities to continue to aid her. At last they all descend to Japan, each to a different place: Amaterasu to Watarai country in Ise; Amenokoyane to Suku-no-yama in Shimanoshimo county, Settsu province; and Takemikazuchi and Iwainushi to Shiga village in Kashima county of Hitachi. The text explains that "the deities descended from the heavens, each riding a cloud; and the Nakatomi clan rode down upon the wings of cranes."

Generations later, the deities announced to the Emperor and especially to the Head of the [Fujiwara] Clan, to their shrine servants, and to the clansmen: "Our seats are too far from the Capital. We will move closer." Then each came to seek his dwelling-place, and the Nakatomi clan accompanied them.

Here the text names the three Kasuga deities again, this time adding Himegami to their number. The location of the "home" shrine for each is given too:

Iwainushi-no-mikoto: Katori county, Shimōsa province
Amenokoyane-no-mikoto: Hiraoka village in Kawachi county, Kawachi province
Takemikazuchi-no-mikoto: Shiga village in Kashima county, Hitachi province
Hime-no-mikami-no-mikoto: Ise Daijingū

Regarding Himegami, the text appends this note: "[Himegami] dwells in the shrine-hall of the [other] three deities. Therefore she is called the Aidono ["Who Shares the Hall"] Deity."

Now comes the journey that culminated in the establishment of the Kasuga Shrine: that of Takemikazuchi from Kashima to Kasuga. Takemikazuchi is represented as having undertaken it at his own pleasure. No version of the story gives more than a few words to the arrival at Kasuga of any other deity, and from version to version these few words may disagree with one another. It is as though Takemikazuchi had been escorted all the way in a limousine, while the other deities were left to follow as best they could, and nobody really cared just how they got there as long as they turned up. It is interesting that this picture changed completely soon after the *Genki* was made, though it is not entirely clear why. *Sakakiba no nikki* (1364; see ch. 8) emphasizes Amenokoyane instead, and the two fifteenth-century Noh plays *Uneme* and *Saho-yama* have Amenokoyane, not Takemikazuchi, settling on Mikasa-yama as the beginning of the shrine. The following legend seems to have been ignored.

During his move to Mikasa-yama from His dwelling-place in Hitachi province, His mount was a deer, and He used a persimmon branch for a whip.

First, on Jingo-keiun 1.6.21 [768] He reached the village of Natsumi in Nabari county, Iga province. While bathing in the river called Ichi-no-se, He performed a wonder with this whip: when He planted it in the riverbank, it became a tree, took root, and grew.

From there He crossed the river and dwelled for several months upon Komō-no-yama in the same province. At that time Tokifū and Hidetsura roasted chestnuts. He gave a chestnut to each, saying, "If you and your descendants are to serve Me generation after generation, without interruption, then if you plant these chestnuts they will take root and grow." So they planted the chestnuts, as He had suggested, and the chestnuts did take root. That is when Tokifū and Hidetsura acquired the clan {muraji} name Nakatomi Ueguri ["Nakatomi Plant-Chestnut"].

On Jingo-keiun 1.12.7, He settled upon Abe-no-yama in Shikinokami county of Yamato province.

Takemikazuchi's momentous progress is the subject of the *Kashima-dachi mandara* ("departure from Kashima" *mandara*), which constitute a subgenre of Kasuga devotional art. The deer is usually white. The painting may well include (at the bottom, and smaller) the loyal Tokifū and Hidetsura. It is not surprising that this pair, who were to found two of three main priestly houses of Kasuga (respectively, Tatsuichi and Ōhigashi), should have acquired during the journey a distinctive clan name.

On Jingo-keiun 2.19 He manifested himself upon Mikasa-yama in Soenokami county, in the same province. Once He had done so, Amenokoyane and Iwainushi-no-mikoto each began offering him *nusa* there. The reason why Mikasa-yama is the most renowned sacred spot in all of Japan, is that each [of these Deities] has chosen to dwell there. The Emperor together with the Head of the Clan, and particularly the shrine servants and the clansmen, entrust themselves to the protection [of these Deities], as they have vowed to do. Moreover, the Deities protect and uphold the Hossō Daijō ["Mahāyāna"] School. It is for this purpose that they all gathered in this place.

This passage corresponds fairly well to its counterpart in *Genki* 1.1. Here, the deities join Takemikazuchi in order to serve him, although in the *Genki* Takemikazuchi, ever the magnificent host, invites the deities to come.

In an oracle to Empress Shōtoku [r. 764–70] the Deity said: "I shall make my august residence at the foot of this mountain, facing south," etc. Astonished, the Empress issued an edict that the land there should be inspected [so as to determine precisely the right spot]. At last, in Jingo-keiun 2.11.9, at the hour of the tiger [ca. 4 A.M.], they erected the shrine pillar[s] and completed the hall[s].

One gathers from the statement concerning the residence of Himegami that this original shrine consisted of a single hall, in which all three male Kasuga deities (Takemikazuchi, Iwainushi, and Amenokoyane) were present. However, since the authenticity of *Koshaki* as a whole, and certainly of this account, is in doubt, one can draw no firm conclusion.

Now when Tokifū and Hidetsura respectfully moved the Deity, the Deity announced to them: "When you move Me, you must have me ride on a *sakaki* [tree]. Why? Because in the future you are to revere the *sakaki* as my true body *(shōtai)*." In compliance they mounted Him upon a *sakaki*. Tokifū and Hidetsura, of the Nakatomi Ueguri clan, carried this *sakaki* on their shoulders when they reverently moved the Deity and established his residence.

The Kasuga deity's vehicle is indeed the sacred *sakaki* tree, as *Genki* 11.3 and 16.2 vividly confirm. *Shika mandara* ("deer *mandara*"), a genre closely related to *Kashima-dachi mandara,* show not a god in human form upon the deer's back but a *sakaki*. Moreover, when the combined forces of Kasuga and Kōfukuji marched on Kyoto to press a grievance, Kasuga shrine servants ( *jinnin,* or "god-people") carried

before them the *sakaki* of their deity, the *shinboku* or "god-tree."
*Hyakurenshō* for Kyūan 6.8 (1150) states, "In this *shinboku* hang
several mirrors called the true bodies *(mishōtai)* of Kasuga no Daimyōjin" (cited in Miyai 1978:110).

> Now Tokifū said, "Where should we live? Please show us." The
> Deity answered, "I shall throw a *sakaki* toward the southwest.
> Understand that the place where it falls belongs to me," etc. . . .
> So they sought in that direction, in accordance with the divine
> utterance, and found the *sakaki* at the northeast corner of
> Hachijō-nibō-gotsubo in Sakyō [the "left" district of the Capi-
> tal], in Soenokami county. Prostrating themselves, they made
> this place their home and served the Deity there.
>
> As they did so, the Deity said further: "I will accept offerings
> set before Me by the Nakatomi Ueguri clan; but offerings set
> before Me by another clan, I will not accept. If you allow such
> offerings to be made, I will strike [the offender] with terror. At
> the same time, the trees on My mountain will die. When this
> news reaches the clansmen they will be overcome with fear, for
> they will know that I have ascended to the empyrean, and am
> gone. If they wish Me to return to my seat, let the Nakatomi-
> Ueguri place offerings before Me for seven days, and pray with
> all their hearts. Then I shall return to My original seat."
> [Colophon:]
> The above is set down as a record for future generations.
> Hōki 11.8.3 [780]
> By Nakatomi Ueguri-no-muraji Tokifū

It is only natural that the Nakatomi-Ueguri (whether Tokifū or his
descendants) should have insisted on the inalienable prerogative of
their clan to serve the Kasuga deity; and it is just as natural that the
deity, whose complex identity includes that of ancestor of the entire
Nakatomi lineage; should have been understood to legitimate their
claim. The matter was of no small significance, as the background of
*Genki* 3.3 makes plain. Moreover, the Deity's standing threat to
abandon Kasuga if roused for any reason to just anger—thus leaving
the trees on Mikasa-yama to die—is important in *Genki* 11.3–11.4
and 20.1.

# THE MODERN UNDERSTANDING

Modern writers have discussed why these deities should have been brought to Kasuga from their several, scattered shrines; and especially *when* the Kasuga Shrine was really founded. None believed the date 768, on which the legendary accounts are unanimous.

Some sort of divine presence was clearly honored in association with Mikasa-yama before Takemikazuchi and the others came. Mori Ikuo (1987) discussed archaeological traces, some only recently discovered, that leave no doubt on the subject. He and Ueda Masaaki (1987) both concluded that probably the Wani clan, once powerful in the Kasuga area, supported this pre-Fujiwara cult. Indeed, Kasuga shrine legends mention an earlier deity whom the new arrivals talked into yielding them his land. They first got him to trade Kasuga for Abe-no-yama. When the deity, distressed at receiving no offerings there, came back to complain, they suggested a spot before their own hall where, they assured him, he would have plenty of visitors. The deity accepted (*Koshaki,* ST:5). He is still at Kasuga under the name of Enomoto no Myōjin, and figures in *Genki* 11.3 and 13.1. Enomoto is enshrined in the gallery of the main shrine, just west of the Nanmon.

As *Koshaki* suggests, originally the Kasuga deities were indeed "too far from the Capital." Since the Fujiwara claimed them as *ujigami* ("clan divinities"), they naturally wished to have them properly enshrined in the brilliant, new capital of Nara, founded in 710.

The Fujiwara clan itself came into being thanks to the crucial role played by Fujiwara no Kamatari (614–69) in the Taika Reform of 645. Kamatari was a Nakatomi, and the divine ancestor of the main line of the Nakatomi is Amenokoyane, enshrined at Hiraoka.

Some authorities hold that Kamatari was born in Yamato, and that he therefore belonged to this main Nakatomi line; while others affirm that he was born at Kashima (Grapard 1984:249). If so, he would indeed have regarded Takemikazuchi as his tutelary deity. In any case, Kamatari clearly possessed important property at Kashima, and so would have been likely to regard Takemikazuchi as his tutelary deity even if he was born elsewhere (Miyai 1978:41). As for Futsunushi (or Iwainushi), he is closely linked to Takemikazuchi in the mythology, to the point of being sometimes hard to distinguish from

Takemikazuchi, and his shrine at Katori has an ancient and geographically convincing tie to Kashima. Therefore, without going into the complexities of the subject (Miyai 1987:9–43, 61–68), Takemikazuchi and Futsunushi at Kasuga can be considered inseparable.

Kamatari was granted the Fujiwara surname in 669, and after 698 the use of the name was limited to his direct descendants. Fuhito (659–720), his most important son, firmly consolidated the Fujiwara position at court by marrying one daughter to Emperor Monmu and another to Emperor Shōmu. He also established Kōfukuji. Why should it not also be Fuhito who established the Kasuga Shrine?

The earliest recorded doubt about the official founding date of 768 is to be found in *Kasuga-sha shiki* ("A Private Record of the Kasuga Shrine"[1295], ST:68–69). The author, the Kasuga priest Nakatomi no Sukenaga (1266–1338), noted the existence of a puzzling council of state decree *(kanpu)* dated 755: it speaks of the four Kasuga deities being honored in the empress's residence. The decree that Sukenaga saw has since been lost, but modern investigators have found other clues. The case is reviewed, for example, by Nishida (1978). A famous exhibit is the Tōdaiji map of 756 *(Tōdaiji sangai shishi no zu)* in the Shōsōin. It shows a "god-place" *(shinchi)* at precisely the location of the Kasuga Shrine. Ueda Masaaki (1987:9–10) has suggested that this "god-place" may have been the *yashiro* ("shrine") mentioned in *Man'yōshū* nos. 404 and 405, which date from the mid-Tenpyō period (729–49). Perhaps this *yashiro*—probably a sacred grove rather than a building—was dedicated to the original deity of the area, the Enomoto no Myōjin mentioned above. However, the evidence as a whole suggests that at least three male Kasuga deities were indeed celebrated in Nara before 768. In fact, a Tenpyō 11 (739) entry in *Shoku nihongi* (cited in Nishida 1978:21) shows that the Nakatomi-Ueguri clan too existed earlier.

Of course, "earlier than 768" still does not mean the time of Fuhito, and in fact most of the evidence has to do with the 750s or 760s. Nonetheless, Nagashima (1944:8) took it as evident that Fuhito did indeed establish the Kasuga Shrine. Miyaji Naokazu in "Kasuga-jinja no seiritsu" *(Shintō ronkō* 1, cited in Nishida 1978:41–44) thought the idea compelling. Nishida himself (1978:41) suggested that although the shrine must have been founded by Fuhito, the first permanent sanctuary building must have been erected in 768. Until then, the shrine was probably a *yōhaisho,* or "place for distant worship": a sacred spot from which the deities of Kashima, Katori and Hiraoka could be worshiped at a distance. Temporary sanctuaries might have been put up for each festival and dismantled afterwards—in which case the deities would have been summoned to Kasuga, and into these sanctuaries, only at festival time. At any rate, Nishida (1978:71) cited the oracle given by the Kasuga deity to Empress Shōtoku—the one mentioned in *Koshaki* as having inspired the building of the permanent shrine—and expressed confidence that it was genuine. Shōtoku was Fuhito's granddaughter.

## A HISTORY OF THE KASUGA SHRINE

Ultimate responsibility for the Kasuga Shrine lay with the head of the Fujiwara clan, whose duties included oversight of the clan's ancestral shrines and temples. No doubt the continuing consolidation of Fujiwara fortunes was connected with a dramatic rise in the official ranks of the Kasuga deities between 777 and 859. In 777 Takemikazuchi was awarded the upper third rank and Futsunushi the upper fourth, but Amenokoyane and Himegami were not mentioned at all. By 850 the four held respectively the upper first, upper first, junior first, and upper fourth. Amenokoyane too reached the upper first rank in 859, while Himegami acquired the upper third (Miyai 1978:36–38). Thus in 859 the three male Kasuga deities reached the highest standing the court could offer them. (According to *Kasuga shiki* [ST:69], the Fourth Sanctuary attained the upper first rank ca. 1200.) Moreover, the mid-ninth century appears to be the time when the *Kasuga matsuri* became a completely regular observance. In Jōgan 8 (866) a high priestess *(itsukime)* was appointed to Kasuga, on the model of the Kamo Shrine. It is true, however, that by the end of the century her office had lapsed.

Nothing in the *Genki* alludes to these developments. The deity did not claim the standing of a bodhisattva until 937 (*Genki* 1.2), though Hachiman, prominently enshrined at neighboring Tōdaiji, had done so in 783. As for the Fujiwara, up to the end of the eleventh century the *Genki* has only two items (dated 948 and 992) about minor Fujiwara in Yamato province.

It is not clear why. Imperial pilgrimages to Kasuga began in 989 (or possibly 985), and by 1100 there had been at least seven more; while Kaneie began the tradition of formal pilgrimages by the Fujiwara clan head in 986 (Saeki 1929; Miyai 1978:94–95). *Shunki* for Chōryaku 4.8 (1040, cited in Miyai 1978:107) has this entry: "I place my whole trust in Kasuga no Myōjin's desire to avert all disasters." In one text of *Ōkagami,* the ailing Michinaga (who in the past had been to Kasuga on pilgrimage) is said to have gone to the west corridor of his mansion and "bowed to the south, asking leave of the Kasuga god to renounce the world" (McCullough 1980:302). One does not gather that the deity was neglected, though Michinaga's bow toward Kasuga was certainly simpler than the grand pilgrimage of his successor Tadazane in 1116 (*Genki* 4.2). In the *Genki,* at least, the court nobility did not really become engaged with Kasuga until the Kasuga deity found himself obliged, in 1092, to rebuke Retired Emperor Shirakawa (1.5). Shirakawa's response was to offer Kasuga a copy of the Buddhist Canon. In the next year, 1093, the *sakaki* of Kasuga led several thousand Kōfukuji monks on their first reliably recorded march to the Capital. (Nagashima 1959:8).

If the *Genki's* evidence is to be believed, Buddhism was essential to the rise of a devotional Kasuga cult. The worldly power of Kōfukuji and the Buddhist teaching both played their part. As to power, it was during the eleventh century that Kōfukuji rose to be sovereign in Yamato. In the realm of faith, Kasuga seems not to have touched the deepest feelings of the court aristocracy (however meticulously the Fujiwara may have acted as members of their clan) until the kami were fully accepted as manifesting enlightenment, and until the continuity between the buddhas and the divine presence at Kasuga was clearly established. In his classic survey of *honji-suijaku* thought, Tsuji Zennosuke dated this sort of transition to the early twelfth century (Tsuji 1944:460–61). The dates supplied by the *Genki* support his finding. Shirakawa's offering was the first in a long series of gifts that loudly affirmed the Buddhist dimension of the Kasuga cult. By the late twelfth century, it was understood that Kasuga no Daimyōjin could escort a devotee's soul to paradise (5.1), save it from hell (6.1), or consign it to the same ghastly destination (6.2). By the late Kamakura period, private devotion to Kasuga (as distinguished from the ritual forms required of the highest nobles by ancient precedent) amounted to a complex paradise cult of which *Kasuga mandara* paintings were the icons.

These developments had long been prepared by the Kasuga cult that flourished at Kōfukuji, as well as by the temple's acquisitive designs. The Kasuga deity was after all the temple's patron. Nagashima (1944:31) went so far as to write, "It is no exaggeration to say that the development of Kōfukuji had as its background the divine power of the Kasuga Shrine." Perhaps for this reason, the *Genki's* stories about Kōfukuji monks begin earlier, and more convincingly, than those about civil nobles. In the first one (8.3), from the late ninth century, the deity did nothing less than sanction the combination of esoteric and exoteric Buddhism that thereafter became normal at Kōfukuji. And in 949 (*Genki* 8.4), one year after blessing a country gentleman (1.4), the Kasuga deity spoke to a promising Kōfukuji monk like the true guardian of the temple's interests. By about 1100 Kōfukuji was the supreme power in Yamato province, and had come definitively to dominate its protector. Nonetheless, the Kasuga deity remained not only the temple's battle-standard, as it were, but also the very source of its temporal authority.

Shirakawa's magnificent offering of the Canon, together with a building to house it, was followed in 1116 by Tadazane's gift of the Kasuga Shrine's first five-story pagoda; the second was donated by Retired Emperor Toba in 1140. Both were erected on shrine land taken over by Kōfukuji in the tenth century, so that they symbolized perfectly the bond between the temple and the shrine. In 1178 the monks gave the shrine, despite the court's hesitation, the gallery already described (*Gyokuyō* for Jishō 2.2.16), and, at about the same time, other touches such as the Nanmon and the Keigamon, "which [intentionally] make the Shrine look a little like the Byōdōin, one of the few surviving Heian period Pure Land temples, or like a Pure Land palace in a painting" (S. Tyler 1987:126). The last major Buddhist addition was Shion'in, 1215. This complex, within the Kasuga Shrine grounds, included a thirteen-story pagoda that enshrined the *honji* of the four main Kasuga deities. (Both pagodas burned down in 1411, while Shion'in, after burning down in 1480, was rebuilt and lasted into the late Edo period.) In the meantime, Kasuga had acquired a new deity and a new sanctuary.

The Wakamiya is a puzzle. Many features of this deity and his sanctuary invite speculation that the Wakamiya must be the original divine presence at Kasuga, and the true spirit of Mikasa-yama; yet the sanctuary was not built until 1135. Moreover, the way this new sanctuary suddenly emerged fully armed, as it were, with all the honors accorded a major deity, suggests a complex background of which surviving records give no hint.

*Kasuga shaki* (GR 2b:60) claims without corroboration that the Wakamiya deity first appeared in 933. However, it goes on to make a much better supported statement: the Wakamiya was seen on Chōhō 5.3.3 (1003) by Nakatomi no Koretada (d. 1004). After 1135 the Wakamiya was served by a new priestly line, the Chidori, founded by the Sukefusa discussed under *Genki* 3.3. A document belonging to this Chidori house (Nara-ken Kyōikukai 1914:1:138) describes the event. In the third month of 1003 a translucent, gelatinous mass formed on the underside of the floor of the Fourth Sanctuary. The mass soon grew so large and heavy that it fell, and from it emerged a little snake. The snake crawled up the northwest pillar of the structure and disappeared into the sanctuary. Koretada, who saw all this, realized the snake was the Fourth Sanctuary's child.

At first the newborn deity was left with his mother. Later, however, the Fourth Sanctuary possessed a child medium and demanded to know why only she, and not her son as well, was receiving offerings. So a small sanctuary for the young deity was established between the Second (Futsunushi) and Third (Amenokoyane) Sanctuaries— that is to say, precisely in the middle of the line of four sanctuaries, in a space then as now called the Shishi-no-ma, or "Lion Room" because a lion is painted on its back wall. Finally, in 1135, the Wakamiya was installed in his separate sanctuary building. The very next year, the famous Kasuga Wakamiya Festival *(Onmatsuri)* was held for the first time. Thereafter the Wakamiya played an active part in the life of the Kasuga Shrine.

Despite the mystery surrounding the Wakamiya, it is at least clear that the Kōfukuji monks must have welcomed his appearance. Though devoted to Kasuga, and to all that Kasuga meant for their own temple, they had no access to the regular Kasuga Festival that honored the four main deities twice annually in spring and fall (Nagashima 1959:9). For this occasion monks were classed with persons in mourning and pregnant women, and obliged to keep their distance (Miyai 1978:90–91). The Wakamiya gave them a major Kasuga festival of their own, and their temple's power turned it into the great annual festival of Yamato province. No doubt their enthusiasm had something to do with the instant importance, and even with the existence, of the Wakamiya's new sanctuary. Nagashima (1959:9) went so far as to state flatly that Kōfukuji established the Wakamiya in order to strengthen its hold on the Kasuga Shrine.

In the late Heian period the Kasuga deity became, as already noted, a spiritual judge and guide, capable at least of interceding for the individual soul and bringing it to salvation. This trend coincides with the gradual diffusion of the Kasuga cult throughout Yamato and to many other areas of Japan as well—wherever the Kasuga Shrine or Kōfukuji had estates. An early example (cited in Miyai 1978:111) is a document dated Kōwa 2.6.2 (1100) that mentions a Kasuga shrine in the province of Echigo. By the late twelfth century, when misbehavior of monks and shrine servants in the deity's name had long since become a major problem, the spread of such Kasuga *massha* on the estates aroused the court's concern (Miyai 1978:112). Moreover, the Kasuga deity was being installed as the local protector of other temples, at least by Gedatsu Shōnin and Myōe Shōnin.

Courtiers were also beginning to put shrines to the Kasuga deity in their homes. Kujō Kanezane (1149–1207) evoked his own home shrine in a passage (*Gyokuyō* for Juei 3.5.16) that has been translated and discussed by Susan Tyler (1987:24–25). A later passage from *Hanazono Tennō shinki* (Shōchū 2.12.25 [1325]), quoted in full by Nagashima (1944:226–27), concerns a certain Kiyotsune who, being too poor to visit the shrine in person, had installed a painting in his home—no doubt a form of *Kasuga mandara*—and honored it precisely as though it actually was the shrine. Meanwhile, in the early thirteenth century, Myōe Shōnin became the first spiritual leader to urge Kasuga devotion upon people outside the Fujiwara clan. In his activity, and in the spread of Kasuga shrines to distant estates, one may see the trend toward popularization that is so often cited in connection with other developments in Kamakura religion. This trend is apparently responsible for the development of Kasuga *kō*, or devotional "confraternities," which were common in Yamato and nearby areas (Nagashima 1944:230–34).

Perhaps one could also apply the idea of "popularization," at least in the sense of increased *personal* participation, even to the heightened religious awareness of the aristocracy from the late twelfth century on. As far as Kasuga is concerned, Kujō Kanezane shows in *Gyokuyō* a more intimate involvement than, for example, his predecessor Fujiwara no Tadazane (1078–1162) in *his* diary *(Denreki)*. Moreover, pilgrimages from the court to Kasuga increased dramatically during the thirteenth century. Saeki Ryōken (Saeki 1929) collected all available references to pilgrimages by members of the imperial family. His list shows that while from 1200 to 1250 such pilgrimages occurred on the average about once every five years (a marked increase over the preceding half-century), between 1250 and 1300 the average was only two years. In fact, there were two pilgrimages in 1284, 1285, 1288, and 1298, and three in 1292. Such heightened court contact with Kasuga, and with other shrines as well, has been attributed to anxiety over the threat of the Mongol invasion (Ōhigashi 1983b:4). At any rate, this peak is part of the context in which the *Genki* was conceived. Court pilgrimages continued (according to Saeki's list) through 1307, and then dropped off. In this as in other ways to be discussed below, the *Genki* is a little like a magnificent sunset. The devotees of Kasuga did not rise to such heights again.

Devotion to the Kasuga deity continued, however, for centuries thereafter. One aspect of his popularity is the *Sansha takusen* ("Oracles of the Three Shrines") movement, the inspiration for which can be traced back to the end of the Heian period. In *Gyokuyō* for Jishō 4.5.16 (1180), Kanezane wondered whether the troubles then current might be due to the "designs" *(o-hakarai)* of Ise, Hachiman, and Kasuga; and it is precisely this trio of deities who are the "Three Shrines." Nagashima (1944:250–52) has discussed the phenomenon. The simple, unexceptional moral teachings associated with the movement became influential in about the sixteenth century and lived on through the Edo period. Unlike the earlier Kasuga cult, they had no visibly Buddhist character. In fact, Helen Hardacre has written (1986:37) of the *sansha takusen* confraternities that they "constituted one of the few pre-Meiji transdomainial assemblies for the propagation of Shintō ideas apart from Buddhism."

In 1868, when the separation of Shinto and Buddhism was officially begun, the monks of Kōfukuji (far fewer by then, and poorer, than they were in Kamakura times) were faced with the new government's demand that they should return to lay life. In reply, they pleaded in a body that since their temple had always served the Kasuga deity, they should be registered as priests of the Kasuga Shrine (Tamamuro 1977:168–75). Their petition was granted. The partnership between Kasuga and Kōfukuji was broken, and little of Kōfukuji remained.

## RITES, FESTIVALS, AND OFFERINGS

The *Genki,* which stresses personal devotion and personally bestowed boons, has nothing to say about festivals and other routinely scheduled rites. Still, one should mention the principal observances at the shrine as they were in the Kamakura period. The major festivals (the *Kasuga matsuri* and the *Onmatsuri*) continue to be celebrated today, though in rather different style and, under the solar calendar, at somewhat different times. The more Buddhist observances, however, have been abandoned at least since the beginning of the Meiji period.

The diaries of Kasuga priests regularly mention daily offerings *(hinami no go-ku)* made to the sanctuaries. There were also thrice-monthly offerings *(jun no go-ku)* and seasonal offerings *(sekku no go-ku)*. Such offerings were supported by designated estate holdings (Nagashima 1955:472).

The great festival to honor the four principal sanctuaries was the *Kasuga matsuri,* celebrated each year in spring and fall, on the first monkey *(saru)* day of the 2d and 11th months. Various ranking nobles attended, but the key participant was an imperial envoy (normally a middle captain) who brought offerings as well as dancers, musicians, and a distinguished company of gentlemen from the court. The offerings included horses, which were a normal gift to important shrines, and horse races were often held for the occasion. While in Nara the imperial envoy and his entourage, like most high-ranking pilgrims, stayed at the Saho-dono, originally the residence of Fujiwara no Fuhito.

The *Onmatsuri,* the festival of the Wakamiya, was actually a celebration for the whole shrine. It began on the 17th day of the 9th month. Kōfukuji levied funds for it from the entire province of Yamato, so that it had the character of a province festival as well. It involved (as it still does) bringing the Wakamiya deity down from his permanent sanctuary to a "travel place" *(tabisho)* along the avenue from Kōfukuji to the main sanctuary complex, and presenting various offerings and entertainments there for the pleasure of the deity and the assembled crowd. The central event was *dengaku* arranged by two Kōfukuji monks chosen annually for the purpose (Nagashima 1944:129).

Kōfukuji monks were also responsible for Buddhist rites at the shrine. The more important of these were the *Niki no go-hakkō* ("Biannual discourses on the Lotus Sutra"), which started on the 9th day of the 4th month and the 4th day of the 9th month; a *Daihannya-e* held annually on the 15th day of the 4th month; and a *Kasuga dokyō* held on the 24th day of the 9th month.

Many of the offerings presented on such occasions appear in the *Genki* stories. Rebuked by the Kasuga deity (1.5), Shirakawa first quickly sent the shrine a horse; and his formal pilgrimage of 1092 (2.1), like the pilgrimages of other great lords, shared some features of the regular *matsuri*. The dance he had presented (shown in the *Genki* painting) was an important offering. The Kasuga deity loved music and dance, as *Genki* 7.3 or 13.1 shows particularly vividly, for in these stories the deity requests them himself.

Despite the amusing collision between music and Buddhist learning in *Genki* 10.1, the deity appreciated the Buddhist texts that were offered him. Shirakawa certainly knew this when he gave the deity the Buddhist Canon, together with one hundred monks to read (for the deity) the sutras it contained (*Genki* 2.1). The *Genki* stresses the deity's protection of the *Yuishiki ron* (Skt. *Vijñapti-matratā-siddhi*)— the fundamental text of the Hossō school—to the point where one might imagine that he had little taste for anything else, but this is clearly an exaggeration. It was routine for a monk to offer the deity sutras, as indeed a monk was doing when the deity claimed his bodhisatttva name (*Genki* 1.2). Such offerings were called *hosse,* and at the Kasuga sanctuaries, as at most shrines, there was a *kyōsho* ("sutra place") provided for the purpose. Saigyō in *Senjūshō* found the shrine ringing with the Buddha's word (tr. Moore 1982:189):

At times I stood by the shrine altar, thrilled by the voices chanting the *Essence of Wisdom* {*Hannya rishubun,* Skt. *Prajñā-pāramitā-naya-śatapañcā-śatikā*]. Now and again I wandered before the Treasure Hall where voices ceaselessly recited Consciousness Only [Yuishiki] texts.

## THE ORGANIZATION AND ADMINISTRATION OF THE SHRINE

The organization of the Kasuga Shrine in medieval times has been described by Nagashima Fukutarō (1944:13–20, 1955:470–72), and some additional information can be found in an article by Ōhigashi Nobuatsu (1929:127–32). The descendants of Tokifū and Hidetsura, as already noted, came to be known respectively as the Tatsuichi and Ōhigashi houses. These provided the *shō-no-azukari,* until Kōho 2 (965) the single senior officer of the shrine. In that year the entire Nakatomi clan was in mourning, so that the Nakatomi priests could not serve at the shrine. Ōnakatomi no Tsunetaki was therefore brought in from Ise to act as *kannushi,* or chief priest. He stayed, and his descendants, known as the Nakahigashi house, continued in that office. Then in 1135 Nakatomi (Tatsuichi) no Sukefusa, the *shō-no-azukari* at the time, became concurrently the first *kannushi* of the Wakamiya. The office of Wakamiya *kannushi* continued in his line, the Chidori. Thereafter these three officers were known as the "three senior officers" *(sansōkan)* of Kasuga.

Each of the three had a ladder of subordinate officers under him, drawn likewise from the eligible houses. The senior and second-ranking officers (called *gon-no-azukari* or *gon-kannushi*) were referred to together as *shake* or *shashi* ("shrine officials"); and *shake* sons or younger brothers who did not yet hold office were called "clansmen" *(ujibito).* Entry onto the ladder of promotion toward the first two posts was by merit, for there was a relatively large pool of candidates to draw on. The Tatsuichi and Ōhigashi lines, which provided the *shō-no-azukari,* were actually split into between four and seven branch houses; and Chidori sons could serve under the *shō-no-azukari.* The Nakahigashi line, which supplied the *kannushi,* was divided into five branches. The Wakamiya *kannushi* succession, however, was hereditary in the single Chidori line.

The two main groups (Tatsuichi/Ōhigashi and Nakahigashi) also resided separately. The so-called *Shō-no-azukari gata* ("group") was sometimes referred to as *Nankyō* ("Southern Settlement") because they lived south of Sanjō-dōri. (Sanjō-dōri is the westward extension of the main avenue to the shrine.) The *Kannushi gata*, on the other hand, could be called *Hokkyō* ("Northern Settlement") because they lived north of Sanjō-dōri. Each group, and the Wakamiya group as well, had its own contingent of shrine servants *(jinnin)* who were therefore called *sanbō jinnin* ("*jinnin* of the three groups"): *Nankyō jinnin, Hokkyō jinnin,* and *Wakamiya jinnin.*

Shrine servants of this kind wore yellow robes *(ōe jinnin)* and resided near the shrine, unlike the white-robed shrine servants described below. They assisted the officers of the shrine and the clansmen in all matters, and appear in several *Genki* stories as the direct emissaries of the Kasuga deity. Yellow-robed shrine servants in fact normally mediated between pilgrims and the sanctuaries (or the deities) themselves, since the Nakatomi officers were inaccessible to most people. They too had their hierarchy. The highest-ranking among them were known as "permanent sanctuary guards" *(jōjū shinden-mori)*—one each for the Nankyō and Hokkyō groups. Under them came "sanctuary guards" *(shinden-mori),* and below these a variety of other offices. Like the *sansōkan* houses, these shrine servants lived in certain fixed areas of Nara.

The white-robed shrine servants *(byakue jinnin),* much less grand than the yellow-robed ones, lived on shrine estates all over Yamato and even in other provinces. Therefore they could also be called "scattered shrine servants" *(sanzai jinnin).* Many were minor officials or titular landowners *(myōshu)* on the estates, and they could also be the priests of local Kasuga or other shrines. Some were merchants. Those who were armed and who lived in Yamato could be referred to as "people of the province" *(kokumin).* The *kokumin* were included in the organization of Kōfukuji, and formed the backbone of Nara's military power.

The Wakamiya also had an organization of female shrine attendants *(miko)* known as *Yaotome;* and one of male *kagura* dancers and musicians called *Kagura-otoko.* A Wakamiya *miko* appears as a medium in *Genki* 4.4 and 4.5. The senior *miko,* at least, seem to have been the wives or daughters of *shashi* priests.

The *shashi* were appointed by the chief of the Fujiwara clan, but not without some comment from the superindendent *(bettō)* of Kōfukuji or even from the monks at large, collectively known as "the assembly" *(daishu)*. It was not unknown for the *daishu* to demand successfully that the chief of the clan dismiss a *shashi*. This action was called *shukan* ("the daishu's condemnation"). The published diaries of Kasuga priests show clearly enough that the shrine had next to no autonomy. One should remember too how badly the top officers of the shrine were outranked by the senior monks of Kōfukuji. Judging from the number of times his name appears in documents, Ōnakatomi (Nakahigashi) no Tokimori (1097–1180) was an influential *shashi;* yet he did well to rise as high as the senior fourth rank, upper grade. Sukefusa, another obviously powerful *shashi,* reached the same rank. Yet the senior monks of Kōfukuji were the brothers and sons of regents, and in any case the material power of Kōfukuji was incomparably greater. There could have been no contest between the two.

## PROBLEMS THAT CROPPED UP IN THE LIFE OF THE SHRINE

Most stories and pictures of the *Genki,* and other records of pomp and circumstance, make it easy to imagine the shrine as forever peaceful, holy, and inviolate. It is a bit of a shock to read *Genki* 19.1 and discover that the shrine could actually be invaded, and robbed of some of its most sacred treasures, by unprincipled ruffians. But even a cursory reading of Kasuga priests' diaries shows that, as one might expect upon more mature reflection, things did not always go smoothly. In fact, the shrine may well be more peaceful now, and safer too, than it was then.

There were, first, all the pressures and demands from Kōfukuji. Campaigns to press grievances in the Capital or elsewhere *(shinboku dōza,* or "movements of the *shinboku")* must have caused an uproar at the shrine. Pilgrimages by great personages from the court must have done so too, in other ways. There were repairs to look after, and lawsuits over estates and revenues to be pursued. Quarrels between shrine servants, or groups of shrine servants, could be violent, and were certainly troublesome.

There were other security problems also. Robbers occasionally stole even from the sanctuaries—presumably for individual gain rather than to score a point, like the bandits of *Genki* 19.1; and this entailed not only material loss but pollution. Persons unknown were sometimes thoughtless enough to relieve themselves against a sanctuary fence, so that the affected sanctuary had to be purified and the soiled boards replaced. A dog might die under a sanctuary, or even choose that spot to have puppies. Someone might bring a mare to the shrine, only to have her drop a foal much too close to the sanctuaries. (The gentleman responsible had to pay for the cleanup and the purification.) Then there were the deer, discussed by Ōya (1929), Tamura (1929), and various later writers. The Kasuga deer, then as now, were sacred, and it was forbidden to kill them. In fact, killing a "sacred deer" *(shinroku)* was punishable by death. Nonetheless, wounded deer sometimes died near the sanctuaries, or were seen to stagger past them. The culprits had to be pursued and dealt with. As likely as not, they were associated with Kōfukuji.

Finally, certain anomalous events could draw the attention of someone at the shrine and require interpretation by means of divination. The cry of a deer from near the sanctuaries could be treated this way. So could the collapse of a venerable tree, the falling of some ornament from a sanctuary or torii, or a migration of flying ants from near a sanctuary. The diary of Nakatomi no Sukekata for Kōan 3.8.3 (1280) contains a puzzling entry about "silver flowers" *(ginka)* that had "opened" on all five sanctuaries. Sukekata wanted to find out whether they were really silver or not, and sent shrine servants to gather some in a "small earthen container." When the objects were shown to two gentlemen who were probably diviners (one was an Abe), one declared that they were flowers, and the other declared that they were not. The issue remained alive for several days, the principal worry being whether the event boded well or ill. Apparently no one could say just what the "silver flowers" were, but it was officially decided, and reported, that they were a good sign.

# 4

# *The Temple*

Modern Kōfukuji consists of one three- and one five-story pagoda; two kondō ("golden halls"); two "round halls" (the Nan'endō and the Hokuendō); a headquarters compound *(honbō);* and a museum. These are situated in Nara Park, roughly between the Kintetsu railroad station and the First Torii of Kasuga. They do not at first seem to have much to do with each other. The *honbō* is largely concealed behind shrubbery. Usually, only two show signs of life: the Nan'endō and the museum. Being one of the "Thirty-Three Kannon [Temples] of the Kansai," the Nan'endō is often busy with pilgrims, while the museum, which houses a superb collection of Buddhist sculpture, is crowded with tourists. Surely few among the pilgrims or the tourists give a thought to Kōfukuji, or to what it once was.

The present contrast between Kōfukuji and nearby Tōdaiji is striking. With its Great Buddha a must for all visitors to Nara, Tōdaiji not only looks busy and prosperous but has a distinct personality. The Tōdaiji research library is a valuable scholarly resource, and the temple has a robust historical identity as well. Kōfukuji, on the other hand, is a wraith. This is understandable in the light of the past, but one would still prefer a less obvious lesson on evanescence.

That Kōfukuji was once a very great power is clear from chapter 3, and still more so from this one. Even Tōdaiji paled beside it. In late Heian or Kamakura times, Nanto (the "Southern Capital," i.e., Nara) often meant Kōfukuji alone. But one should remember too the temple's former religious importance. The scholarly genius of Eichō (1002–83) was widely acknowledged even beyond Nara, and Zōshun (1104–80) was a pillar of the Hossō tradition. Startling stories about Kūsei (878–957, *Genki* 9.1), Shinki (930–1000, *Genki* 10.1), Rin'e (950–1025), *Genki* 10.1), and Chūsan (935–76; *Senjūshō* 6/3, 7/4,

7/5) suggest that they were esoteric adepts and practiced *shugendō*, though the first three were all superintendents of Kōfukuji as well. Moreover, so great a Buddhist establishment was bound, like Mt. Hiei, to send talented monks out into the greater world, however anxious the Kasuga deity may have been to keep them at home.

Monks left Kōfukuji, for various reasons, to lead a life of single-minded devotion and practice. The Kakuei (1117?–1157) of *Genki* 8.5 is a striking example. *Senjūshō* 5/1 tells of Eigen who rose to high office but one day simply went away into the mountains of Shinano. *Senjūshō* 5/9 concerns Shinpan (986–1054, a Taira appointed superintendent in 1044), who withdrew at last from the world and died below Mt. Miwa, calling on the Kasuga deity.

Some of these monks achieved a place in history. The great ascetic Tokuitsu (749?–824?), who engaged in a celebrated debate with Saichō (767–822), founded mountain temples in Dewa and Hitachi. Jōyo (957–1047, *Genki* 9.1), a disciple of Kūsei, became famous for reviving Mt. Kōya. Kyōe (1001–93, *Genki* 10.6), originally a disciple of Rin'e, distinguished himself at the Odawara *bessho* in southern Yamashiro, and was sought out on Mt. Kōya by Retired Emperor Shirakawa. Jippan (1086–1144) began the revival of interest in monastic discipline *(ritsu)* that became so important in the late twelfth century. The Kasuga deity is said to have guided him to an orthodox *ritsu* master (*Tōshōdaiji ge:* 53, *Shōdai senzai denki:* 363).

A successor in Jippan's line was Gedatsu Shōnin, together with Myōe Shōnin the outstanding spokesman for the "old Buddhism" against the exclusive Amida *nenbutsu* practice advocated by Hōnen (1133–1212). Gedatsu Shōnin, for his part, strove to popularize the Shaka *nenbutsu*. Myōe, although originally from Tōdaiji rather than Kōfukuji, had so unusual a relationship with the Kasuga deity that the *Genki* compilers devoted far more space to him than to any other individual. He is credited with having attempted a revival of Kegon Buddhism. In sum, Kōfukuji played an important religious role in the late Heian and Kamakura periods, themselves a time of exceptional religious ferment. This role is an essential element in the spiritual background of the *Genki*.

# THE ORIGINS OF KŌFUKUJI
# AND OF ITS BUDDHISM

Perhaps the best survey history of Kōfukuji is an article by Nagashima Fukutarō (1959). What follows will often rely on that work. Miyai too (1978:157–362) has published much information on the topic, and Nagashima's earlier book (1944) is essential reading on this and other aspects of medieval Nara.

Kōfukuji, like the Fujiwara clan, began with Kamatari. *Fusō ryakki* (cited in Ueda 1985:250) states that Kamatari built a chapel in his residence in 657, though *Kōfukuji ruki* has a somewhat later date, associated with Kamatari's death in 669. This was the seed from which Kōfukuji grew. Fuhito moved the chapel to Asuka, where it was called Umayazaka-dera. Then, with the founding of Nara, he undertook the construction of a proper temple that he called Kōfukuji. The name appears to come from a passage in the *Yuima-gyō* (Skt. *Vimalakīrti-nirdeśa-sūtra*), a text that meant a great deal to Kamatari (Ueda 1985:272–73). However, since Kamatari had lived in Yamashina, southeast of what later became Kyoto, the temple continued often to be referred to as Yamashina-dera.

*Kōfukuji ruki* claims that Fuhito founded Kōfukuji in 710, the year the court moved to Nara, but modern research suggests that the real date may be closer to 720 (Nagashima 1959:2). By about 740 the temple was largely complete. The Hokuendō (721) is a memorial to Fuhito. The East Kondō (726) was built by Emperor Shōmu to pray for the recovery from illness of former Empress Genshō; and the five-story pagoda (730) was commissioned by Shōmu's consort Kōmyō (Fuhito's daughter), with the participation of Fusasaki (Fuhito's son and the founder of the dominant "northern branch" of the Fujiwara). The Nan'endō, dedicated in 813, was a late addition. Being important in connection with the Kasuga cult, it will be discussed separately below.

None of the Nara temples were confined to a single "sect." It was in principle possible to study any Buddhist school then current at any of them. However, they naturally tended to specialize. Just as Tōdaiji (founded in 745) was particularly strong in Sanron and Kegon studies, Kōfukuji prided itself upon its Hossō (Yogācāra) tradition.

Hossō Buddhism first reached Japan in the mid-seventh century

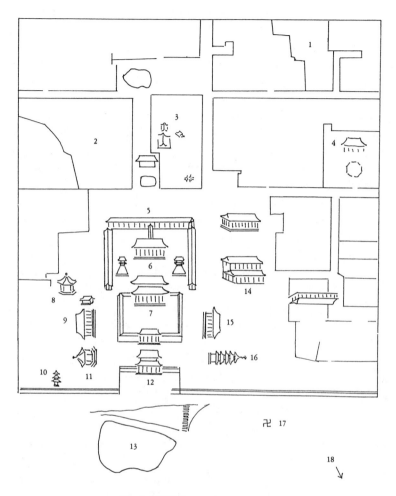

Map 3. Kōfukuji

Key:

1. Tōhokuin
2. Ichijōin
3. Kangakuin
4. Kanzen'in
5. Triple Dormitory
6. Kōdō
7. Central Kondō
8. Hokuendō
9. West Kondō
10. Three-story pagoda
11. Nan'endō
12. South Gate
13. Sarusawa Pond
14. Jikidō
15. East Kondō
16. Five-story pagoda
17. Bodaiin
18. Daijōin

through Dōshō (629–700), who had studied in China with Hsüan-tsang (Jap. Genjō, 600–64), the great pilgrim and translator. On returning to Japan, Dōshō settled at Gangōji (founded in 588, moved to Nara in 718). Then other Gangōji monks went to study with Hsüan-tsang. Later Gien (d. 728), also of Gangōji, learned Hossō from a Korean master who had studied in China under Chih-chou, a grand-disciple of Hsüan-tsang's great student K'uei-chi (Jap. Kiki, 632–82). Finally, Gien's disciple Genbō (d. 746) likewise went to study with Chih-chou, returning in 735 with a large collection of texts (including many esoteric ones) that was stored at Kōfukuji. In this way Kōfukuji acquired its own Hossō transmission. K'uei-chi, known by his formal title as Jion Daishi, has been honored there ever since.

Hossō was a vital school of Buddhism in China and Japan when Kōfukuji was new. The temple's pride in it can be seen in the tradition that the Kasuga deity came from Kashima expressly to protect the Hossō teaching there. It is also visible in the intensity of Kōfu-kuji's early rivalry with Gangōji over which temple should have pride of place as the center of Hossō studies—a contest won by Kōfukuji. One might note that Genbō's most distinguished student was Zenshu (723–97), mentioned by the Kasuga deity in *Genki* 16.3. Jikun (d. 777), the first superintendent of Kōfukuji, was a grand-disciple of Gien.

Despite this emphasis on Hossō, however, Kōfukuji in the Heian period was at least equally a Shingon temple. The teaching brought back to Japan by Kūkai (774–835) quickly took root in Nara, and Kūkai even spent some time as superintendent of Tōdaiji. The story (told in *Kōfukuji ruki*) that Kūkai consecrated the Nan'endō may or may not be true, but it suggests the standing of Shingon at Kōfukuji. The relationship between Kōfukuji and Mt. Hiei, the center of Ten-dai Buddhism, was one of intense, often destrictive rivalry, as *Genki* 2.2 or 14.1 makes plain. In contrast, Kōfukuji was normally friendly with Tōji or Mt. Kōya.

*Genki* 8.3 shows the Kasuga deity, in the late ninth century, ap-proving a Kōfukuji monk's combined practice of Hossō and Shingon. Thereafter, esoteric practioners like Kūsei and his successors could rise to be superintendent. Jōshō (912–83), who was superintendent of Kōfukuji in the 940s, served also as the head monk of Tōji (*Kōfukuji bettō shidai*). Moreover, about 950 Fujiwara no Morosuke

(908–60) gave Kōfukuji a Godaiin, dedicated to the group of five *myōō* (Skt. *mantrarāja*) centered upon Fudō (Skt. Acala) *(Kōfukuji ruki)*. Somewhat later, when Kōfukuji came to control Yamato, it claimed most of the temples in the province as dependencies *(matsuji)*. The majority of these were Shingon—an identification Kōfukuji never sought to change.

This combination of exoteric *(ken)* and esoteric *(mitsu)* Buddhism, known as *kenmitsu bukkyō,* is explicitly acknowledged in *Genki* 8.3. The biography of Jōshō in *Kōfukuji bettō shidai* particularly cites his contribution to it at Kōfukuji. In one form or another, it was the normal Buddhism of Heian times. *Kenmitsu bukkyō* has been nicely described by Kuroda Toshio (1980:21–22). The Buddhism of Mt. Hiei was an outstanding example, although in its case the main exoteric term of the pair was Lotus Sutra faith. Apart from historical reasons to uphold the two simultaneously, the intellectual and religious tension between *ken* and *mitsu* no doubt made it particularly interesting to affirm their unity *(dōitsu)*. As Kuroda pointed out, this unity was grasped not in logical terms (which was impossible) but, thanks to an understanding of "psychological mysteries" that joined diverse elements in mutual harmony. In this sense, the *kenmitsu bukkyō* of Kōfukuji and other great Heian religious centers was a close relative of *honji-suijaku* faith.

## THE RISE OF KŌFUKUJI

The court's departure from Nara did not trouble Kōfukuji for long, if at all. As the formal *(ritsuryō)* government lost control of crown lands, the clans, and especially the Fujiwara, extended their holdings. Profiting from this trend, Kōfukuji acquired more and more estates *(shōen)* in Yamato. The more it gained, the more it needed armed troops to protect its property, and the better able it became to support such troops. Like any thriving organism, the temple tended naturally to take over its territory.

In time this expansion touched the Kasuga Shrine. Nagashima (1987:52–53) stated, without identifying his source, that Fujiwara no Yoshifusa (804–72), as head of the Fujiwara clan, prohibited Kōfukuji from performing any act of worship at the shrine; but that in 947, the then head of the clan at last permitted a biannual Hokke hakkō *(niki no go-hakkō)* observance. By 1018, this observance had become a fully accepted part of the life of the shrine. Elsewhere, Nagashima (1959:8) noted evidence from the diary of Emperor Murakami that in Ōwa 2 (962), Kōfukuji managed to wrest from the shrine a tract of land on the shrine's own grounds, within the First Torii. It is on this tract that the Kasuga pagodas were eventually built. One document (cited in Nagashima 1959:8) claims that the very first Kasuga-Kōfukuji march on the Capital *(shinboku dōza)* occurred in 968, although, as already stated, the first confirmed one dates from 1093.

Kōfukuji continued to make gains during the eleventh century. In Jian 3 (1023), it unsuccessfully protested Fujiwara no Yorimichi's (990–1074) efforts to bring certain estates back under court control (Nagashima 1959:8, citing *Shōyūki*). In Eishō 5 (1050), on the other hand, it opposed Minamoto no Yorichika, a lieutenant whom Yorimichi appointed governor of Yamato, and obtained his exile to Tosa. As late as 1070, however, it was unable to prevent Fujiwara no Norimichi (997–1076, the current regent) from getting himself appointed concurrently governor of the province so as to oversee a necessary rebuilding of the Nan'endō. Moreover, when Emperor Go-Sanjō at first refused Norimichi's request, Norimichi declared the authority of the Kasuga deity impugned, and threatened the resignation of all the Fujiwara officers of the court. Go-Sanjō yielded. The story is told in *Zoku kojidan* 1.

Norimichi's appeal to the Kasuga deity's authority is one that Kōfukuji itself insisted on making to its own advantage. The Fujiwara clan and its senior clan temple were rivals not only over a province but also over the clan shrine. Nagashima (1959:9) put the matter as bluntly as possible: "Kōfukuji believed that by controlling the Kasuga Shrine, it could exclude the Fujiwara clan and make Yamato its own." The *shinboku dōza* of 1093 began a long series of such attempts to use the Kasuga deity against the Fujiwara. On that occasion Kōfukuji insisted that "Kasuga no Myōjin protects Kōfukuji, and Kōfukuji assists Kasuga no Myōjin. Temple and Shrine are one and the same. The Shrine's afflictions are the Temple's afflictions" (Nagashima 1959:9, citing *Fusō ryakki*). During a *shinboku dōza* expedition the sacred *sakaki* would be taken to Kyoto, accompanied by thousands of well-armed monks, and installed at the Kangakuin, the Fujiwara "academy" just south of the imperial palace compound. (Later on, however, its normal station became the Chōkōdō of chapter 8.) Sometimes the court sent troops to stop the monks, generally at Uji; but on the whole the divine reproach was difficult to oppose. One who did so risked expulsion from the clan *(bōshi)*, as decided upon ultimately by the Kōfukuji monks (Miyai 1978:114).

In this context, Shirakawa's Canon and the two pagodas speak eloquently. No doubt the court helped further Kōfukuji's designs in part because of the growing domination of Kōfukuji by the sons of Fujiwara nobles. When a Minamoto (a Koga Genji) was appointed superintendent of Kōfukuji in 1138, the monks rejected him *(Genki* 14.2–4). The court must also have cooperated, whether or not under pressure, in the establishment of the Wakamiya. And shortly after that event, Kōfukuji enjoyed another success.

Having fought one war with Kinpusen in 1093 *(Chūyūki* for Kanji 7.11.3, 7.11.17, 8.3.6), over its claim that Kinpusenji was a Kōfukuji dependency, Kōfukuji won another in 1145 *(Daiki* for Ten'yō 2.6.8, 2.7.12, 2.7.26, 2.9.13; *Kōfukuji ruki).* Thereafter Kōfukuji monks of the highest rank held the office of head monk *(kengyō)* of Kinpusen *(Kinpusen kengyō shidai).* It cannot be simple coincidence that the next year, on Kyūan 2.10.23 (1146), an important Kasuga *massha* was first erected near the Wakamiya: the Sanjūhassho-sha, which was built to enshrine the deities of Kinpusen (diary of Nakatomi no Sukefusa). Thus Kōfukuji took in not only Yamato proper but the potent, far-off Ōmine mountains.

Nagashima (1959:10) wrote that once Kōfukuji managed, through the Wakamiya and its festival, to seize definitive control of the Kasuga Shrine, it was able (through the shrine) to gain the final allegiance of the local landowners *(myōshu)* on estates throughout Yamato. In Hō-gen 3 (1158), the court sent a party of officials to carry out a survey of the province. They were turned back by Kōfukuji troops. Kōfukuji now continued gathering land and income-yielding dependencies to itself, even at the expense of so great a power as Tōdaiji. For example, Hasedera, claimed in Tōdaiji documents as a dependency of that temple, was nonetheless "seized" *(ōryō)* by Kōfukuji ca. 990 *(Tōdaiji yōroku:* 126a) and appears in all Kōfukuji documents as a dependency of Kōfukuji. Kōfukuji was uncontested in its domain. It could often even impose a superintendent on another of the other major Nara temples (Nagashima 1944:162).

Kōfukuji and Tōdaiji had little difficulty foiling an attempt by Taira no Kiyomori (1118–81), about 1159, to take control of the little remaining imperial land in Yamato. However, the resulting anti-Taira feeling helped make Kōfukuji sympathetic to the coup attempt led by Minamoto no Yorimasa (1104–80) in 1180, and so did a traditional sympathy with Miidera against Mt. Hiei. After Yorimasa's defeat and death, Kiyomori sent troops against Nara, under his son Shigehira. Tōdaiji and Kōfukuji both burned down. (This was not the first fire in Kōfukuji history but it must have been the worst, except possibly for the fire of 1717.) Still, both temples recovered relatively quickly from this disaster, favored especially by the active cooperation of Minamoto no Yoritomo (1147–99). The extraordinary efforts made to restore their buildings and art produced works of superb quality, and contributed to the development of thriving artist and craftsman guilds (za) in Nara. Meanwhile Yoritomo, the founder of the Kamakura shogunate, was sensible enough to recognize Kōfuku-ji's power. Although he placed a constable (shugo) in each province, he left Kōfukuji and Yamato alone. In its own province, Kōfukuji was the de facto constable.

During the thirteenth century Kōfukuji continued as prosperously as before, vexed only by three sorts of problems. First, there were the inevitable conflicts with other institutions that encroached (as Kōfukuji saw it) on Kōfukuji interests. Perhaps the outstanding example is the quarrel with Iwashimizu, which broke out in 1235 over the issue of water rights in neighboring estates. The affair has been treated at length by Kuroda Toshio (1975:79–140), and is discussed below under Genki 20.1. It continued to flare up into the fourteenth century.

Second, there were conflicts with Kamakura—often the consequences of the quarrels just mentioned. Uwayokote Masataka (1975:36–60) has examined the process by which the court, in theory responsible for settling such disputes, felt obliged to turn more and more to Kamakura, so that Kamakura tended as the decades passed to act more and more forcefully. A very early example occurred in 1198, in connection with the dispute that cost Taira no Chikamune so dearly (*Genki* 6.2). When an aroused Kōfukuji threatened to intimidate the court with an armed expedition, Yoritomo informed it that he would send troops against it if it did so, and that if necessary he would lead the troops in person (Uwayokote 1975:51). The quarrel with Iwashimizu brought repeated intervention from Kamakura. *Genki* 20.1 shows that Kōfukuji took the bakufu's armed might seriously. Nonetheless, Kamakura never sought to subjugate the temple. It sought only to keep the peace, acting as much as possible, in this respect, as a loyal servant of the court.

Third, there were the *akutō* ("bandits") who became a serious problem for Kōfukuji in the second half of the thirteenth century, threatening the temple both as an estate owner and as the holder of police power in Yamato province. Watanabe Sumio (1960) has discussed them. There were important incidents in 1278 and 1285, the year when Kōfukuji began a province-wide campaign to solicit anonymous denunciations *(rakusho)* against the *akutō*. The worst offenders, based in Takaichi-no-kōri of southern Yamato, were accused of armed robbery, arson, murder, gambling, and stealing rice crops by harvesting the fields at night. However, there were *akutō* even in Nara, as *Genki* 14.5 suggests. *Genki* 19.1 has to do with a sensational *akutō* outrage.

## FUJIWARA MONKS
## AND THE RISE OF THE *INKE*

The gradual, thorough takeover of Kōfukuji by sons of the Fujiwara, and especially by the sons of senior nobles *(kugyō)*, has been discussed most concertedly by Nagashima (1944:153–59), but no one who uses *Sōgō bunin* or *Sanne jōikki* to investigate the careers of Kōfukuji monks can possibly fail to notice the trend. Originally, the Fujiwara were only patrons of Kōfukuji. In Nara and early Heian times, the Kōfukuji monks were not usually of Fujiwara birth. Later, however, the enormous prestige of Buddhism, combined with the pressing need to dispose of excess sons, made the great temples more and more attractive to powerful families. Moreover, in the light of Kōfukuji's history it is easy to see how advantageous it might have been for a noble house to have a son in a high position there. (The temple would have benefited in equal measure.)

An easy test to apply in the matter is to examine the parentage of monks who served as lecturer *(kōji)* for the annual Yuima-e. In the 140 years between 859 and 999, fifty-five Kōfukuji monks acted as lecturer, and only seven of these were Fujiwaras. Between 1000 and 1180, however, 138 lecturers were from Kōfukuji, and eighty-four of them (well over half) were of Fujiwara extraction (Miyai 1978:197). After 1180, *Sanne jōikki* (the register of lecturers) reveals a still higher percentage of Fujiwaras, who moreover served at a younger and younger age. In fact, after the mid-Heian period, a non-Fujiwara monk was unlikely to be appointed lecturer at all. A fine example is the great, but unfortunately non-Fujiwara scholar Zōshun who appears in several *Genki* stories. Zōshun was not lecturer until 1168, in his sixty-fifth year. In contrast, Shin'en (1153–1224), a younger brother of Kujō Kanezane, was in his twentieth year when he served as lecturer in 1172.

The trend is equally obvious with respect to ecclesiastical *(sōgō)* rank. Over the centuries, a sort of inflation steadily reduced the value of a given rank, and one cause of this inflation was undoubtedly the need to promote Fujiwara sons more and more reliably, higher and higher. In the Nara period, the rank of minor prelate *(shōsōzu)* was ample for the superintendent of Kōfukuji. By Zōshun and Shin'en's time, a superintendent was normally a grand prelate *(sōjō)* or senior grand prelate *(daisōjō)*. As lecturer for the Yuima-e, the young Shin'en (in defiance of the principle that one was appointed to the lowest *sōgō* rank *after* having served as lecturer) was already a minor prelate. Zōshun, on the other hand, held no *sōgō* rank in 1168 and was not appointed provisional minor prelate *(gon-shōsōzu)* until 1178. Such things went on elsewhere as well, but surely not more than at Kōfukuji. In the Kamakura period and after, the trend became almost comical.

This Fujiwara invasion of Kōfukuji fostered the development of private subtemples that sheltered noble sons from temple life and upheld the dignity of their houses. Such subtemples were known as *inke*. Not that Kōfukuji had no *inke* before the Fujiwara began to move in. The earliest may have been the Tōin mentioned in *Genki* 15.1, where the texts brought back to Japan by Genbō were deposited in 738 *(Kōfukuji ruki:* 305b). Kitain, founded in 949 by Kūsei

(*Genki* 9.1), originally housed a line of monks whose interests were entirely worthy. However, even Kitain succumbed, for after about 1280 the heads of Kitain were from the Tokudaiji house (Nagashima 1944:169). In the Edo period, they came normally to serve also as deputy superintendent *(gon-bettō)* of Kōfukuji (Nagashima 1959:20).

The two key *inke* at Kōfukuji, Ichijōin and Daijōin, came to be known as *monzeki*. By the end of the Heian period they dominated Kōfukuji and usually supplied the superintendent. Still later, superintendents from elsewhere at Kōfukuji became rare, and after the Muromachi period the office simply alternated between the two. If Ichijōin controlled the West Kondō of Kōfukuji, Daijōin controlled the East Kondō. If (from the end of the twelfth century on) Ichijōin held that the *honji* of the First Sanctuary of Kasuga was Fukūkenjaku (Skt. Amoghapāśa), Daijōin maintained that the *honji* was Shaka (Skt. Śākyamuni).

Both *monzeki* were beyond the reach of the superintendent and of the other administrative organs of Kōfukuji (Nagashima 1959:15). Luxuriously appointed, their main buildings came to be built in *shin-den-zukuri* style, with four-legged gates and lovely gardens, like the mansions of the nobles in the Capital (Nagashima 1944:157). Each had its private personnel, administration, and property. An estate could belong not to Kōfukuji but, for example, to Ichijōin; likewise a temple could be a dependency particularly of one of the *monzeki*. Wealthy though both were, however, they were not quite equal. As the Kōfukuji superintendent Jinson (of Daijōin) remarked in the mid-fifteenth century, "Two-thirds of this province belongs to Ichijōin" (*Daijōin jisha zōjiki,* quoted in Nagashima 1944:56).

Ichijōin is not mentioned in the *Genki*—an omission that must be deliberate, although the reasons for it are uncertain. Nagashima (1944:163–66) has discussed its history. It was originally founded by Jōshō, mentioned above as having headed both Kōfukuji and Tōji, in the tenth century. Jōshō was a Fujiwara, but his aims must have been rather different from those of his eventual successors. Ichijōin became the property of the senior nobles after Kakushin (1065–1121), a son of the regent Fujiwara no Morozane (1042–1101). Kakushin's successors (including Shin'en) were all the sons of regents. Sons of both Kujō Kanezane and Konoe Motomichi (1160–1233) took over

Ichijōin, and for several generations the headship moved between the Konoe and Kujō. After Ryōshin (who wrote out *Genki* scrolls 17 and 18), however, the headship passed definitively to the Konoe.

Daijōin (Nagashima 1944:166–69) was founded in 1096 by Ryū-zen (1038–1100) at the wish of his father, a Fujiwara minor captain *(shōshō)*. Ryūzen's undistinguished successor was followed by Jinpan (1101–74, *Genki* 11.4), who appears in the records as being, like Kakushin, a son of Fujiwara no Morozane. Jinpan was succeeded by Shin'en, who thus headed both Ichijōin and Daijōin. Thereafter Dai-jōin remained in the Kujō house, though after the Go-sekke split in the Kamakura period, it came to be shared by the Kujō and the Ichijō.

## THE YUIMA-E

For the Fujiwara monks whose destiny it was to aspire to the highest ranks at Kōfukuji, the key step in their careers—a sort of graduation, or coming-of-age ceremony—was to serve as lecturer for the Yuima-e. The Yuima-e is prominent in the *Genki*. This seven-day rite was the most prestigious in the annual round of ceremonies associated with the Nara temples. Two other, analogous rites were associated with it as the "three imperial rites of Nara": the Yuima-e, the Saishō-e of Yakushiji, and the Gosai-e held in the Daigokuden of the Imperial Palace. The Yuima-e lecturer was appointed by the emperor on the recommendation of the head of the Fujiwara clan; and as in the case of the Kasuga Festival, the ceremony was attended by an imperial envoy *(chokushi)*, usually a middle captain. Having passed through the Yuima-e, the lecturer normally went on to serve likewise at the Gosai-e and finally at the Saishō-e. That is why the title of the register of lecturers for the Yuima-e, *Sanne jōikki,* means something like "the three rites in one." Once finished, he was nor-mally appointed to the first of the *(sōgō)* ranks, that of *risshi* ("master of discipline").

The most thorough study of the Yuima-e has been done by Ueda Kōen (1980 and 1985:249–89). Ueda stressed (1985:265) that the origins of the Yuima-e are inseparable from those of Kōfukuji itself. In 656, when Kamatari was ill at his Yamashina residence, he had a Paekche nun expound for him the fifth chapter of *Yuima-gyō.* This is the chapter in which the layman Yuima Koji (or Jōmyō; Skt. Vimala-kīrti), on his sickbed, receives countless enlightened beings, particularly Monju (Skt. Mañjuśrī). Kamatari's condition immediately improved. The later ancestral cult rendered to Kamatari at Tōnomine (ironically a dependency of Mt. Hiei) made the parallel between him and Vimalakīrti as plain as possible: it identified Kamatari with Vimalakīrti (Nara Kokuritsu Hakubutsukan 1964:pl. 78–81).

According to *Fusō ryakki* for 657 (cited in Ueda 1985:250), Kamatari not only built a chapel in his home that year but also instituted there a "vegetarian assembly" *(saie)*, which *Fusō ryakki* identifies as the origin of the Yuima-e. The date 658 is supported elsewhere (Ueda 1985:259–62), and there is some disagreement in the sources about the point at which any such rite became genuinely identifiable as the Yuima-e. Still, there is no doubt that the inspiration for the observance came from Kamatari himself. Whether or not the rite was performed regularly during the second half of the seventh century, Fuhito reinstituted it, in his father's honor, once the court had moved to Nara. At last in Shōwa 6 (839), the Yuima-e of Kōfukuji was established forever by imperial decree. In this early period the rite, although held at Kōfukuji, was not monopolized by it. Monks from other Nara temples had equal access to nomination as lecturer, and in time lecturers came even from Enryakuji. However, as Kōfukuji grew more and more markedly into a private Fujiwara institution (albeit one in frequent conflict with the Fujiwara of the court), access to the Yuima-e became restricted. Yet even in the Kamakura period distinguished outsiders might serve as lecturer. The famous Sōshō of Tōdaiji, studied by Hiraoka Jōkai, was lecturer for the Yuima-e in 1239, and for the Gosai-e and Saishō-e in 1240 (Ueda 1985:252).

The Yuima-e, a complex doctrinal debate, began annually on the 10th day of the 10th month and ended on the 16th. It took place in the Kōdō, except in years when fire had made the Kōdō unavailable. (For several years after the great fire of 1180, the Yuima-e was held in Zenjōin, then a part of Daijōin. Being somewhat isolated, on the site of the present Nara Hotel, Zenjōin had come through the disaster unscathed.) A detailed picture of the scene it presented is associated with *Genki* 11.2. Before the Kōdō altar, presided over by an Amida triad, stood two roofed daises for the debating pair. On the viewer's left of the altar was a statue of Yuima Koji, facing, on the right, a statue of Monju. These two images evoked the *real* debate, of which the annual one was only a reminder: that between Yuima Koji and Monju in the *Yuima-gyō*.

Each day of the rite had a morning and an evening session, as one gathers from *Genki* 10.2. When it was all over, there was a banquet described by Nagashima (1959:7) as a *naorai*. The banquet was accompanied by entertainments such as *ennen* dances. Also associated with the Yuima-e was the "imperial envoy's debate" *(chokushi bōban rongi)* mentioned in *Genki* 13.2, although it is not clear just when this event took place.

The key figures in the Yuima-e were the imperial envoy, the selector *(tandai)*, and the lecturer. The imperial envoy attested the supreme dignity of the rite. The selector (the first was the Zōri of *Genki* 8.3) chose the questions to be put to the lecturer, and no doubt generally supervised the observance. According to Nagashima (1959:7) he was supposed not to think up the questions himself but to receive them by divine inspiration from the Kasuga deity, in a dream. Each question was then asked the lecturer by a questioner *(monja* or *ichimon)*, and the lecturer's answering disquisition was rated by a witness *(shōgi)*.

Besides these figures there were also several definers *(ryūgi)*, most of whom came from other temples. Normally a monk could not be named lecturer until he had served as definer. (The Ichiwa of *Genki* 8.4 was the first lecturer to evade this rule.) Part of the Yuima-e procedure involved debates between the definers, which amounted to debates between scholars of different schools, particularly Sanron and Hossō. The entire rite was formally attended by a fixed number of auditors *(chōshu)*, some of whom can be seen, in the picture accompanying *Genki* 11.2, coughing or blowing their noses. The imperial envoy sat just outside the open doors to the hall, not quite in front of the main image on the altar. Members of the general temple population could also come and watch through the open doors, wearing their characteristic loose robes and the hoods *(katō)* that in gatherings were supposed to preserve their anonymity. One in the *Genki* illustration shows a flash of armor under his robe, and three are clearly women.

# THE ORGANIZATION OF KŌFUKUJI

There remain many uncertainties regarding Kōfukuji organization (Nagashima 1944:40), and in any case the functioning of the temple must have changed in many ways, despite all the weight of precedent, between the Nara period and the late Kamakura. The rise of Ichijōin and Daijōin, with their marked tendency to dominate Kōfukuji as a whole, is one obvious example. The best single source for information on how the temple actually worked at any time is no doubt *Daijōin jisha zōjiki.* This diary was surely the foundation for Nagashima Fukutarō's discussions of the subject (1944:40–49, 1959:14–17), though of course Nagashima used other materials as well. Hiraoka Jōkai (1981:322–417) discussed the organization of Tōdaiji in detail, but his findings, while helpful for Kōfukuji, are not necessarily directly relevant to it.

The head of Kōfukuji was the superintendent *(bettō),* the first of whom (Jikun) was appointed in 757. *Kōfukuji bettō shidai* is the register of these superintendents. They were named by the emperor on the recommendation of the head of the Fujiwara clan, although a document of appointment issued by the head of the clan was sometimes considered enough. In theory, the only criterion for the appointment was merit, but one need say no more about that. After 869 the superintendent was assisted by a deputy *(gon-bettō).* He also had a private secretary known as *shusse bugyō.*

Between the superintendent and the temple council *(sangō)* came the "five masters" *(goshi),* described in connection with Tōdaiji by Joan R. Piggott (1982:61). The senior among them was the *bechie goshi,* appointed for a one-year term. This group bore the real responsibility for running the temple. For instance, the dispatch to Kamakura described in the notes to *Genki* 6.2 was signed by the *bechie goshi.*

The temple council, in charge of daily affairs at the temple (as distinguished from the *inke,* especially the *monzeki*), was headed by a *jōza,* and composed besides of two *jishu* (translated in the *Genki* text as "superior"), four *gon-jishu,* three *tsuina,* and sometimes a *gon-tsuina.* It originated in 971, under Jōshō of Ichijōin. Appointments to it were generally made from among the monks of the *monzeki.* A register entitled *Kōfukuji sangō bunin* survives.

Three monks from the temple council, and one from outside it, were selected as directors *(mokudai)*. A director of repairs *(shuri no mokudai)*, the odd man in the group, figures prominently in *Genki* 15.4. He took care of temple buildings, grounds, and supplies. The others were the director of assemblies *(esho no mokudai)*, who made all arrangements for the Yuima-e and other rites, and oversaw the estates that provided the income to support them; the archivist *(kumon no mokudai)*; and the director of offerings *(tsū no mokudai)*, who oversaw offerings for the seven halls of Kōfukuji, including the huge endowment given the temple by Empress Kōken (r. 749–58, later Empress Shōtoku).

The lower officials under the superintendent were most commonly called *geshoshi*. One figures in *Genki* 4.6. These included the monks in charge of the forest in the Kasuga hills and the sacred deer; the master of liturgical chanting *(shōmyō)*; and musicians, dancers, painters, sculptors, and other craftsmen.

There was also a monk, called *daigyōji-sō* or *daidōshi*, in charge of each one of the seven halls of the temple: the Main Kondō, the East Kondō, the West Kondō, the Kōdō, the Five-Story Pagoda, the Hokuendō, and the Nan'endō. The temple even employed a yin-yang diviner *(onmyōji)*.

These single officers or small governing bodies did not have decisive power in all matters. General assemblies of the monks could make decisions, initiate temple actions, or resolutely oppose the superintendent and his colleagues. Early in the temple's history, the assembly of the monks at large was called *kōshu*. However, as the temple grew and evolved, differences in status and function made it difficult to sustain the idea of a single group. Class distinctions appeared. By the late twelfth century, the upper stratum *(jōrō)* had separated out as the "scholars" *(gakuryo)*, and the middle stratum *(chūrō)* as the "six directions" *(roppōshu)*. The general service class *(zōnin)* was simply called *gerō*.

The *roppōshu* got their name from the way the territory under the temple's sway (including the temple grounds proper and the various dependencies) was divided into six "directions." They included both younger scholars (who could rise into the *gakuryo*) and nonscholars. The two subgroups (scholars and others) were distinguished from one another, but both could bear arms. Some even served as guards *(hokumen)* for the *monzeki*. The *roppōshu* had investigative and other powers, and played the key role in mobilizing all the forces available to the temple in time of emergency. They could be compared to officers in the military sense, while the *gerō* were the temple's regular troops.

It is not entirely clear whether all three classes, or only the upper two, constituted the *daishu,* a term used in *Genki* 11.3 and certainly common in the documents of the time. No doubt the word was elastic. *Daishu* decisions (such as one to undertake a full-scale military expedition, or *hakkō*) were surely reached by the *gakuryo* and *roppōshu.* However, when the whole *daishu* set forth (as suggested by the title of *Nanto daishu nyūraku ki* [1139]), they obviously included the *shuto* as well.

*Shuto* too seems to be a variable term. On the face of it, it seems very like *daishu.* The word occurs, for example, in *Genki* 14.2, where the *shuto* violently expel a superintendent from the temple. Are the *shuto* so engaged different from the *daishu* on their way to torment the Kyoto nobles? Kuroda (1980:29, referring particularly to Mt. Hiei) wrote that the two terms mean the same thing. On the other hand, Hiraoka (1981:398) declared that their meanings are different; and Nagashima too (1944:44–45), writing about Kōfukuji, distinguished sharply between them.

The *shuto* as distinguished from the *daishu* were men who normally lived not at the temple but scattered throughout Yamato. Some 2,000 at a time, called *kanpu* ("immperially commissioned") *shuto,* were appointed to reside at Kōfukuji for a "four-year," that is, three full years, term. They guarded the temple and the shrine, and exercised the police power of Kōfukuji throughout Nara and Yamato province. The executive body of the *shuto* was called the *satashu;* and the first *shuto* council meeting of the year (on the 16th day of the 1st month) was known as *hōki-hajime. Hōki* ("the swarming of the bees") also designated the *ad hoc* councils at which the *shuto* decided they wished to swarm forth and chastise a miscreant—for instance, Mt. Hiei, either directly as in *Genki* 2.2, or through the unfortunate Tōnomine. Hiraoka (1981:398–99) has pointed out for Tōdaiji that the *daishu* (in the narrower sense) could start such an action, take charge of one threatening or already under way, or try to stop the hot-tempered *shuto.* It is likely that the same was true for Kōfukuji. At any rate, on military campaigns the *shuto* also led the *kokumin* of Kasuga, already discussed in the previous chapter.

There remain to be discussed the *dōshu* ("those of the halls"), who were attached particularly to the East and West Kondō. These practitioner monks were sometimes known also as *zenshu*, or "meditators." Although theoretically of a standing equal to that of the *gakuryo*, they were in fact looked at askance. The *dōshu* could bear arms, and early in the temple's history constituted its military strength, although later they were overshadowed in this respect by the groups just described. The *dōshu* of the East Kondō practiced the *shugendō* of Kinpusen (Suzuki Shōei 1975; *Ōmine tōzan honji Kōfukuji tōkondō sendatsu kiroku);* and also did certain practices in the Kasuga hills (*Saisai yōki nukigaki* for Jōji 5.1.1 [1366]). They, and not the Kasuga Shrine, took care of the Kasuga *massha* in the Kasuga hills (Ōhigashi Nobukazu 1980).

## THE NAN'ENDŌ

Most buildings of Kōfukuji need no special comment, but the Nan'endō (an eight-sided hall of moderate size) is different. No discussion of Kōfukuji and the Kasuga deity could leave it out. If the *Genki* does not mention or allude to the Nan'endō, that can only be because of a conscious choice on the part of the compilers. Information on it appears in various secondary writings, as well as in sources like *Kōfukuji engi, Kōfukuji ruki,* or *Shun'ya shinki.* Susan Tyler (1987:150–56) has treated it in the context of the Kasuga paradise cult.

The Nan'endō was finished in 813, long after the other major halls of Kōfukuji, as the family sanctuary of the "northern house" *(hokke)* of the Fujiwara. According to *Kōfukuji ruki* (DNBZa:296a, 306c), six or eight Minamoto died on the day of the dedication. And however unlovely, not to mention implausible, this legend may be (the Minamoto surname did not yet exist in 813), it conveys a truth. The Nan'endō was a sort of Fujiwara *sanctum sanctorum* where Minamoto gentlemen were *not* welcome. *Genki* 1.5 conveys something of this Fujiwara partisan feeling. Nagashima (1959:4) cited a document to the effect that no prayers could be offered at the Nan'endō even for a member of the imperial family.

The earliest section of *Kōfukuji engi* (dated Shōtai 3[900]) does not mention Kūkai, but *Kōfukuji ruki* (DNBZa:296a) describes how Kūkai took part in the founding of the hall "for the prosperity of the Fujiwara clan." He consecrated the base upon which the central image of the Nan'endō was to rest, and placed beneath it a golden tortoise. Whether or not Kūkai did this in historical fact, his gesture accurately sums up the Nan'endō as a model of Fudaraku (Skt. Potalaka), the paradise of Kannon (Skt. Avalokiteśvara). *Kōfukuji ruki* (DNBZa:306c) states: "Mt. Fudaraku is an eight-sided mountain upon which wisteria blossoms flourish. This hall [the Nan'endō] is modeled upon that mountain *(kano yama no arisama o utsushitaru nari)*." *Shun'ya shinki* (ST:193–94) concurs, adding: "This hall was built in the southwest corner of the Kōfukuji grounds, facing [Sarusawa] pond to the south. The pond, with waves upon it, is like the southern ocean [where Fudaraku is canonically located]."

Like the Sangatsudō of Tōdaiji, the Nan'endō enshrines Fukūkenjaku Kannon. The present image, together with the images of the Shitennō and the Hossō patriarchs also honored in the hall, was made by Kōkei (fl. late twelfth century) to replace the one burned in 1180.

The Sangatsudō image is certainly older than Kūkai, and the original Nan'endō image must have been too, for *Kōfukuji engi* states that it was made in Tenpyō 17 (745) for the Kōdō and moved to the Nan'endō in 813. Miyai (1978:242) cited evidence that Fukūkenjaku was enshrined in the Kōdō already in 736, and in another hall in 772. Clearly, this esoteric deity was important in the eighth century, perhaps in connection with texts and rites brought back to Japan by Genbō in 735. Gonsō (755–827) of Tōdaiji is even recorded as having left a sutra text on a peak of Kinpusen named "Fukūkenjaku Bosatsu no mine" *(Shozan engi:* 93). However, the Fukūkenjaku cult seems not to have flourished (except where it was already established) much past the eighth century. By 813 the choice of Fukūkenjaku for the Nan'endō was conservative, and no doubt reflected the wish of Fuyutsugu (775–826) to honor the first three generations of the "northern house"; his father Uchimaro (756–812), grandfather Matate (716–67), and great-grandfather Fusasaki (682–737). Or perhaps the choice was that of Uchimaro who, according to another tradition reported by *Kōfukuji engi* and adopted by *Shun'ya shinki,* conceived the image himself but died before it could be finished.

According to *Kōfukuji ruki* (DNBZa:296a), the Isagawa deity appeared among the workmen building the Nan'endō in the guise of an old man and spoke two verses that, when paraphrased, mean about the same thing: "Now that the Lord of Fudaraku dwells upon the Southern Hill [or Shore, the Nan'endō], how vigorously the wisteria billows of the North [the Fujiwara of the *hokke*] shall flourish!" One of this pair appears as no. 1854 in the *Shinkokinshū*, where it is attributed to "Kasuga no Enomoto no Myōjin"; and *Shun'ya shinki* divides the pair between *two* old men, Isagawa and Enomoto. Speaking of the *Shinkokinshū* poem, *Nanto shichidaiji junreiki* (ZZGR:565) specifies that Isagawa appeared "as a messenger of Kasuga no Myōjin," while *Kōfukuji ruki* (DNBZa:306c) and *Gaun nikken roku* (Hōtoku 1.3.9 [1449]) say that he *was* the Kasuga deity, whose involvement is clear anyway.

Fujiwara no Tametaka noted in his diary *(Eishōki)* for Ten'ei 1.6.15 (1110):

> Tonight I went to the Central Kondō [of Kōfukuji], offered lamps, and read scriptures. Then I went on to the Nan'endō and offered lamps as before. The ceremony was conducted by Ryūgon. At the southern altar I worshiped Kasuga no Daimyōjin. Then I faced the southeast and worshiped Kinpusen and Hachiman Daibosatsu.

This passage confirms a link between the hall and the Kasuga deity. It is tempting to think that the Nan'endō may often have been a *yōhaisho* ("place from which to worship at a distance") for Kasuga. In any case, the iconographically unique Fukūkenjaku of the Nan'endō was sometimes painted as equivalent to the Kasuga deity. S. Tyler (1987:151–53) discussed three such works. One, from the Kamakura period, shows the scenery of the shrine in conjunction with the Nan'endō image. A prayer to the Kasuga deity is written on the painting.

The Kasuga-Nan'endō continuity is most clearly expressed in words by many authoritative statements that Fukūkenjaku is the *honji* of the Kasuga First Sanctuary, which in the *Genki* and elsewhere often represents the whole shrine. It is interesting that no Kasuga or Kōfukuji document explains the content of this link, though the matter is hardly obscure. The most one finds is a tradition mentioned in *Kasuga*

*Daimyōjin go-honji narabini go-takusenki* (ST:37) that Fukūkenjaku is the Kasuga *honji* because he wears a deerskin (actually, an antelope skin) *kesa;* and because he loves the Fujiwara as a doe loves her fawn. *Shun'ya shinki* (ST:194) develops a related thought:

> Fukūkenjaku wears a deerskin over his left shoulder; and when the First Sanctuary, Takemikazuchi no Mikoto, moved from Kashima to the Mikasa Grove, it was a deer he used as his messenger. This suggests a deep and ancient tie between the two.

However, the Fukūkenjaku of the Nan'endō—a secret image, never seen and almost never photographed—does *not* appear to wear any such *kesa* over his left shoulder. The *kesa* exists in sutra descriptions and in other Japanese images of Fukūkenjaku, but apparently not at Kōfukuji. Perhaps the statue once wore a real deerskin that is now gone. But apart from the matter of the deerskin, Susan Tyler has suggested the far better explanation that Fukūkenjaku became identified with the Kasuga deity because the Kōfukuji image existed already (though not necessarily yet in the Nan'endō); and because the Kōfukuji monks, who could not then pray directly at the Kasuga Shrine, needed nonetheless to be able to address the deity.

## KŌFUKUJI AFTER THE *GENKI*

The history of Kōfukuji after the early fourteenth century is one of progressive disarray and decline. This account will rely, except where noted, on Nagashima (1959:16–22).

The events and emotions surrounding the Kenmu Restoration must have touched Kōfukuji in many ways. Go-Daigo made a secret pilgrimage to Kasuga, at night, on Genkō 1.8.29 (1331) (Saeki 1929: 125). Then in 1335 came Go-Daigo's flight and the split between the courts. Ichijōin aligned itself with Go-Daigo's Southern Court *(miya-gata),* and Daijōin with the Northern Court in Kyoto *(buke-gata).* Both mobilized all the warriors they could muster *(shuto* and *koku-min),* and the ensuing conflict engulfed Yamato in prolonged warfare. In the summer of 1351 (in the midst of a seesaw military conflict between the two courts, involving Kyoto itself), all-out war erupted between the two *monzeki,* and the Yuima-e had to be canceled *(Saisai yōki nukigaki* for Kan'ō 2, *Sanne jōikki).* Calm was restored the following year, but the Yuima-e nonetheless lapsed repeatedly, for up to a decade at a time, between 1353 and 1391, and often too in the following century.

Despite perils and disorders, however, Kōfukuji managed to keep its hold over Yamato until the mid-sixteenth century. It was the entry of the daimyo Matsunaga Hisahide (1510–77) into Yamato, in Eiroku 2 (1559), that really spelled the end. Thereafter the townspeople of Nara wrested control of their community from Kōfukuji, and in Tenshō 8 (1580) the temple was forced to permit a survey of Yamato that revealed these interesting figures. Ichijōin's holdings yielded an income of 1300 *koku* of rice, only 200 *koku* less than the income registered for Tōdaiji at that time; while Daijōin's yielded 950 *koku*. However, the income of Kōfukuji and the Kasuga Shrine as a whole totaled over 18,000 *koku,* from estates and from taxes (6,500 *koku* worth) that the temple collected as proprietor *(kokushi)* of Yamato. The Kasuga priestly houses *(shake)* all together enjoyed a private income of 500 *koku,* and their much more numerous subordinates *(negi)* a combined total of 900 *koku.*

In Tenshō 13 (1585) Hideyoshi put a stop to the taxing of Yamato by Kōfukuji, and cut 10,000 *koku* from its revenue. The remainder being too little even to support the regular rites of Kōfukuji and Kasuga, the temple was granted in Bunroku 4 (1595), after a new survey, enough to ensure that the rites could continue. However, there was no surplus to cover exceptional expenses. Kōfukuji had to apply to Edo for special grants to pay for major repairs, for *takigi nō,* or for the *sarugaku* for the *Onmatsuri.* The population of Kōfukuji dwindled and its dependencies drifted away, most of them becoming officially Shingon temples. Finally, in Kyōhō 2 (1717) a fire destroyed most of the temple. To raise money, Kōfukuji had to exhibit its treasures in Kyoto, Osaka, and Edo. Of all the buildings lost, only the Central Kondō and the Nan'endō were rebuilt.

At the Meiji Restoration, Kōfukuji did its very best to show the new government goodwill, managing even to present it with 3,000 *ryō.* Nonetheless, the *haibutsu kishaku* ("disestablishment of Buddhism and smashing of buddhas") movement hit Kōfukuji full force. Documents and objects were burned. The upper-class monks of the temple, in a body, became Kasuga Shrine priests. The highest of them were appointed to the peerage. In 1871 the last of the temple's property was confiscated. Kōfukuji was abandoned. Some of its structures became public buildings (a school, a courthouse), and both pagodas were offered for sale. The Kasuga meadows (Kasuga-no) became a public park.

At last in 1881 a head priest came once more to live at Kōfukuji, and an association (the Kōfukuji Kai) was formed to revive the temple. The Central Kondō was rededicated in 1889. The opening of the Kōfukuji Museum in 1959, on the former site of the Jikidō ("Refectory"), assured the temple an income. At present there are three ordained monks at Kōfukuji, running an establishment (mostly connected with the museum) of about three dozen employees.

# 5

# *The Cult*

A summary history of the Kasuga cult might go as follows. The Kasuga Shrine, intended from the first as the tutelary shrine of the Fujiwara, soon became the protector of Kōfukuji as well. The identities of the four original Kasuga deities, and of the Wakamiya who joined them in the twelfth century, were never forgotten, but the five tended to merge into an undifferentiated power or presence: Kasuga no Daimyōjin.

By the Kamakura period, the worship of this deity comprised (1) the official Fujiwara cult, exemplified by the Kasuga Festival; (2) the Kōfukuji cult, exemplified by the *Onmatsuri,* which celebrated the Kasuga deity as the patron not of the temple only but, by extension, of Yamato province also; and (3) personal devotion, that is, the quest for worldly boons and the quest for the pure land. The idea of Kasuga as a pure land seems to have been associated with a gradual, though certainly incomplete universalization of the cult: an increasing appeal to religious values not associated with status or birth. More and more people saw the Kasuga deity as a guide to paradise or a savior from hell. A name now often associated with this trend, among the civil nobles, is that of Kujō Kanezane, whose Kasuga faith is documented by his diary. Gedatsu Shōnin, among the monks, is discussed below.

The worldly power of Kōfukuji spread local Kasuga shrines far and wide, and brought countless people into the shrine's domain. Myōe Shōnin actively promoted Kasuga faith. By about the fourteenth century, the Kasuga cult was personally significant to many outside Kōfukuji and the Fujiwara clan; and thanks particularly to the *Sansha takusen* teachings, the name of Kasuga no Daimyōjin was honored by the common people of Edo times and even beyond. Thus the shrine retained a prestige that the temple, and the clan too, gradually lost. The *shinbutsu bunri* movement of early Meiji finished Kōfukuji, but began to draw Kasuga into a national, self-conscious Shinto religion.

Today, with little more than memories left from the past, the Kasuga Shrine still flourishes thanks to tourism and popular interest. The religious content of this interest, though hard to evaluate, should not necessarily be underestimated. Along the path from the main sanctuaries to the Wakamiya, on the side toward Mikasa-yama, there is a gap in the fence. Beyond the gap, a path disappears into the trees. From here, certain local people climb regularly to the top of Mikasa-yama—to the site known as Hongū Jinja, or "Shrine of the Original Sanctuary"—and perform religious rites. One does not know who they are, but they exist. Their impulse is continuous with the one that brought Takemikazuchi to Mikasa-yama, and made the shrine site a "god place" on the Tōdaiji map of 756.

This chapter will survey the Kasuga cult as it appears in the *Genki*, in both its worldly and its more spiritual guises. The Kasuga faith of Gedatsu Shōnin, who strongly influenced the *Genki*, will be specially emphasized. The discussion will then pass to the *Genki*'s striking bias toward Shaka rather than Fukūkenjaku Kannon as a principal *honji* for the deity; and to the idea, clear in the *Genki* as in many other medieval writings, that Japan is a divine land. A final passage will consider the Fourth Sanctuary's role as *gohō*.

## THE HEAD OF THE CLAN

Hori Ichirō (1974:30) wrote of tutelary deities *(ujigami)* in Japan:

Each family had its own shrine as a central symbol of its solidarity, dedicated to the ancestral spirit who had been enshrined and worshipped by its ancestors. This type of belief system is characterized by particularism and exclusiveness from other families, so that its main function is to integrate all the members of the family into a patriarchal hierarchy.

This nicely describes the *ujigami* function of the Kasuga deity. As to "particularism and exclusiveness," the deity's feelings about other clans have been described in chapter 4, in connection with the Nan'endō of Kōfukuji. Retired Emperor Shirakawa, possessed by the deity (*Genki* 1.5), said it quite jealously enough: "Ah yes, you Genji are doing very well, aren't you!" As to "a patriarchal hierarchy," the most plainly fitting of the deity's forms is no doubt that of the head of the Fujiwara clan.

Once the regent and head of the clan Fujiwara no Moromichi (1062–99) forgot his sword on leaving the palace, and sent a lady back in to fetch it (2.3). She found Moromichi (so she thought) seated within as before, with the sword safely pinned beneath his knee. Actually, however, the gentleman was the Kasuga deity. In *Genki* 10.2 the deity appeared explicitly as "the regent and head of the clan" (then Yorimichi, 990–1074) to salute a young monk's studiousness. At other times, though not recognizable as a known grandee, the deity certainly looked like *a* head of the clan. *Genki* 10.1 tells how a monk "had just dozed off when he saw emerge from the Second Sanctuary a noble gentleman in formal dress, bearing a *shaku*." This description, which fits many *Genki* pictures, evokes the presence of an ultimate Fujiwara lord who does indeed have at heart the "solidarity" of the Fujiwara clan.

This lord desired service and respect. He chastised, or at least declined to favor, persons who withheld these from him, while he protected and rewarded those who trusted in him. What could be more natural? Angered by the indifference of Saionji Kinnori (1103–60) in 4.4, the deity ended the gentleman's life; but in 4.5 he acknowledged Gotokudaiji Sanesada's (1139–90) loyalty by having him reappointed a major counselor. He was always ready to keep *tengu* away from an innocent victim (4.1, 5.2).

In this or in other guises, the Kasuga deity was as solicitous about Kōfukuji as the power responsible for the Fujiwara fortunes—hence the power responsible for founding Kōfukuji in the first place—was bound to be. The temple too was his community. Moreover, a monk could leave the community, unlike a civil Fujiwara noble who could not cease being a Fujiwara no matter what he did. The deity might go to great lengths (8.4, 13.3) to discourage a monk from leaving; yet he might appear (8.6, 10.6) to monk who *had* wandered away, but whom he had particular cause to like, to remind him that Kasuga was still with him. He could also (14.1) turn a monk from studying the doctrine of Kōfukuji's great rival, Mt. Hiei. Meanwhile, in the lay world, he promoted the *Yuishiki ron* (the fundamental text of the Hossō school) by having its mere presence in a house save the house from fire (14.6) or epidemic (8.2).

The deity could reward or punish monks just as he could civil nobles. In 15.5 he recognized a monk's loyalty by healing him. Some monks in the *Genki* provoked his reproof or outright wrath (10.1 or 14.2–4). In fact, the whole temple could be threatened by the deity's displeasure, since he was prepared to leave in order to bring the monks to their senses. When someone posted a public notice about a dream in which the deity did just this (11.3), Kōfukuji organized ten days of debates and doctrinal discourses at the shrine to draw him back. On the other hand, the deity could also leave in order to protect Kōfukuji and influence the secular power (20.1).

## THE SPIRITUAL GUIDE

As "head of the clan" the deity had lively interest in spiritual things —an interest even older than his patronage of Hossō studies, since Kamatari, the Fujiwara founder, was identified with Yuima Koji. When Fujiwara no Tadazane (1078–1162) went to Kasuga to take leave of the deity before quitting the world (4.2), the deity greeted him with some lines from the Hossō patriarch K'uei-chi (Jion Daishi, 632–82) about phenomena and noumena not being separate from consciousness. "You see," the deity went on, "you have no common purpose in mind, but intend to cast off your finery, and this makes me so happy that I am weeping for sheer joy." He then commented, like a Fujiwara ancestor, on the qualities of Tadazane's two sons and noted that both would be head of the clan, though neither seemed overly pious. In this passage the deity sounds a little the way Michinaga (Tadazane's great-great-grandfather), the pillar of every significant virtue including success and sheer luck, might have wished to sound under similar circumstances.

However, the Kasuga deity's spiritual role at times transcended anything appropriate for an acting "head of the clan." Like other *suijaku* deities (as the first chapter of *Shasekishū* makes plain), he became the voice of the Buddhist Teaching itself, urging faith, enlightenment, and compassion. Eichō understood this quite clearly (10.4) when, privileged to see the deity only from behind, he complained about not seeing the deity's face. " 'I appreciate your feelings,' answered the deity, 'and they please me very much. Here in my domain, however, you are not yet seeking the path of true liberation. That is why I will not face you.' " Eichō was inspired to mend his ways—or, more accurately, his will. Onkaku too (12.4) came at last to grasp that the deity's deepest concern was for the enlightenment of those under his care. Fujiwara no Toshimori (1120–ca. 1180) reached the same understanding (5.1) when, after a lifetime of well-rewarded devotion to Kasuga, he realized the vanity of worldly gain and heard the deity say, "The path of enlightenment too is the path of my mountain." *Genki* 7.4 puts the matter plainly when it describes how a lady saw, in a dream, a *sotoba* with this inscription:

> Those with heavy karmic impediments
> will have, thanks to Mikasa Daibosatsu,
> the Compassionate Lord, the Great Guide,
> Rebirth in the Land of Bliss.

## THE MASTER OF PARADISE AND HELL

Monks and laymen in late Heian or Kamakura times pondered their "next life" *(gose* or *goshō),* and aspired above all to be born into a paradise or "pure land" *(jōdo).* Several such paradises were acknowledged. Those accessible at Kasuga have been discussed in detail by S. Tyler (1987) and more briefly by R. Tyler (1987). The principal ones are Tosotsu; Fudaraku (Skt. Potalaka), the paradise of Kannon; and Ryōjusen (Skt. Gṛdhrakūṭa), the paradise of Shaka as the preacher of the Lotus Sutra. The *Genki,* which outside 20.2 alludes specifically only to Ryōjusen, mentions in its conclusion Ryōjusen; Fudaraku; Jōruri, the paradise of Yakushi (Skt. Bhaiṣajyaguru); and Shōryōzan (Wu-t'ai-shan), the paradise of Monju.

The *Genki* shows that the Kasuga deity gave access to paradise (5.1); that he could be in paradise whenever he wished (16.3); and that paradise, by whatever name, was in fact "present within the shrine fence" (20.2). The deity could also bring his devotees back from hell (6.1, 9.1), which itself was present at Kasuga (16.4):

> Our Daimyōjin's ways are certainly wonderful. He will not have anyone who has done Him the least honor, however great a

sinner that person may be, go to any other hell than the one He himself holds ready beneath the Kasuga Meadows. Each morning He fills the ablution vessel of Jizō Bosatsu, and from the Third Sanctuary asperses this hell with a wand. . . . Then He intones for the sinners essential passages and *darani* from the Mahayāna Canon. . . . Thanks to His ministrations, the sinners gradually rise and pass out of hell.

The devotees who merit such kindness are not necessarily Fujiwara nobles or Kōfukuji monks, for this oracle dates from ca. 1240 when the ideal of a broader appeal was well established. Yet the possibility that anyone with a sufficient link *(en)* to Kasuga, however acquired, could have so personal, not to say physical, a relationship to paradise and hell is unsettling. One should take seriously the deity's words just quoted: "The path of enlightenment too is the path of my mountain." But what do they mean?

Any answer must address the meaning of "this world." Japanese religion is generally reputed to be "this-worldly" and absorbed in the quest for "this-worldly benefits" *(genze riyaku),* a tendency that many authorities, Nakamura Hajime among them, have deplored (R. Tyler 1982). Kasuga is undoubtedly of "this world," since among other things the shrine and mountain can be photographed, visited, and managed as real estate. Yet the medieval concern with paradise, hell, and the afterlife—all three apparently imaginary or remote—could find comfort there. Did people really believe that the Kasuga deity's shrine and mountain (or many other Japanese mountains) were paradise?

The "this-wordly" view, claiming as it does that the Japanese respond to little beyond their senses, requires the answer yes. So does an article by Kawamura Tomoyuki (1980), who proposed that this aspect of the Kasuga cult demonstrates a decisive shift away from an old understanding of the pure land as the "other shore" *(higan),* and toward a belief that the pure land is "this shore" *(shigan).* Bruce Darling (1983:215–36) wrote in similar terms. Such an approach inevitably appeals to unambiguous commonplaces often associated with the cult of Amida. Miyai Yoshio's work on Kasuga and Kōfukuji, published in one of a four-volume set entitled *Jingi shinkō no tenkai to Nihon jōdokyō no kiso* ("The development of faith in the native deities, and the foundations of Japanese Pure Land Buddhism"), seems also to refer ultimately to the Amida cult.

One might instead grasp the Kasuga paradise cult in the context of late Heian and Kamakura *kenmitsu bukkyō,* which was absorbed in reflections upon the nonduality of enlightenment and the passions. Certainly the cult cannot be discussed satisfactorily by anyone unwilling to acknowledge, indeed to take pleasure in, paradox. This makes Susan Tyler's treatment of the subject especially valuable. Is the landscape before one's eyes necessarily "this world"? What happens to that landscape when one closes one's eyes, goes away, or dozes off and dreams? These questions are essential. *Did* people believe that Kasuga was paradise? Yes, especially Gedatsu Shōnin. But Gedatsu Shōnin knew quite well that it was not.

## THE KASUGA FAITH OF GEDATSU SHŌNIN

The Kasuga deity is said once to have called Gedatsu Shōnin, a Fujiwara and a Kōfukuji monk, his "Jirō" (*Shasekishū* 1/5, NKBT:70). His "Tarō" was Myōe Shōnin. Reading the *Genki,* one readily understands why. Myōe's spiritual house seems to have been wide open to the deity. Gedatsu Shōnin, on the other hand, argued, resisted, and worried the deity a good deal. He resembled a wayward younger son. But for all the trouble a younger son may cause, the bond between him and his father may be just as strong as the bond between the father and his firstborn, though perhaps different in character. As the deity cried, referring to this "Jirō" (17.2), "It is extraordinary how deeply one feels for him!"

Compared to the teachings of Hōnen or Shinran, the religious faith of Gedatsu, Myōe, or others of their background appears confusing, even chaotic. Lost in a forest of ideas, practices, oracles, and dreams, one gladly concludes that these men must all have been searching for what Hōnen found: an intelligible principle at last. That is the way Kamei Katsuichirō (1975:36), for example, seems to have felt about the monk and poet Saigyō (1118–90). With respect only to paradise, which is far from being the whole issue, "logic" surely requires that it at least be either *here* (preferably "within us") or *there.*

Gedatsu Shōnin, trained like all the scholar-monks of his temple in Buddhist logic *(inmyō,* Skt. *hetu-vidyā),* might have found this position not merely wrong but unfeeling. For him, the deities deserved deeper understanding. First, they were not to be rejected. His *Kōfukuji sōjō* (1205), a formal complaint against Hōnen's doctrine, lists nine separate charges. The fifth of these, "the error of rejecting the sacred deities," begins:

> The *nenbutsu* devotees divorce themselves forever from the deities *(shinmei).* They do not distinguish between [deities who are] Provisional Transformations (*gonge,* like the Kasuga deity) and [those who are] material (*jitsurui,* like potent stones, plants, etc.); and they have no respect for our ancestral mausolea and major shrines. . . . I leave aside here the lesser, material powers (*jitsurui no kishin).* But as to the manifest traces *(suijaku)* of the Provisional Transformations, these are the Holy Ones *(daishō)* revered by all the great monks of ancient times.

The distinction in this passage between *jitsurui* and *gonge* further confuses the issue of whether paradise is "real" or not, since on the face of it a stone or tree imbued with minor *mana* is not different in kind, only in size, from Mikasa-yama and the landscape of the Kasuga Shrine. The point, however, is that for Gedatsu Shōnin the *gonge,* present though they may be in particular places and forms, are wholly at one with the buddhas and bodhisattvas. To abandon them is to abandon one's forebears (both biological and spiritual), one's present, and one's normal access to enlightenment.

Gedatsu Shōnin left two explicit statements of his Kasuga faith: *Kasuga kōshiki* and *Kasuga Daimyōjin hotsuganmon.* Both express deep longing for rebirth into the Tosotsu Heaven of Miroku, who was not only Shaka's successor but also the source of the Hossō tradition. Both speak of devotion also to Shaka, whom Gedatsu Shōnin showed to be one with Miroku; and *Hotsuganmon* prays to Kannon for the gift of perfect compassion. Gedatsu Shōnin addressed *Kōshiki* to the Three Treasures, Shaka, Miroku, Amaterasu, Kasuga, and the Hachibu protectors. In the end, however, both pieces are prayers to the Kasuga deity.

Rebirth into the Tosotsu Heaven was understood to be especially difficult. In both *Kōshiki* and *Hotsuganmon,* Gedatsu Shōnin evoked the famous visit of the ascetic Nichizō (905?–985?) to the pure land

and hell of Kinpusen (*Fusō ryakki* 25); and stressed the way the Kinpusen deity Zaō Gongen, described by Nichizō as an emanation of Shaka, led Nichizō to the Inner Sanctum (Naiin) of the Tosotsu Heaven. The analogy between Kinpusen and Kasuga is obvious, and in *Hotsuganmon* is explicit. Gedatsu Shōnin desired the privilege vouchsafed to Nichizō.

However, Gedatsu Shōnin suspected that his faith and works might still be "insufficiently mature." If so, he wrote, then

> I pray to go first to a place close to humankind, and there serve the *gonge,* the Holy One. His body is not far to seek. My devotion (*kokorozashi*) is all for the Great Deity (*ōkami*) of Kasuga.

Shortly he went on:

> The sacred deities of our realm, our ancestral mausolea, and our major shrines are all *gonge* of the buddhas and bodhisattvas. This has been so since antiquity. Among them the Great Deity of Kasuga, during the Jōhei years [931–38, *Genki* 1.2], gave an oracle in which He dubbed himself Jihi Mangyō Bosatsu ["Bosatsu Complete in Mercy's Works"], [a title that] applied to his outer manifestation in action; and He rose to the junior rank of Bodhisattva. Shall I then—low, evil, and ignorant as I am—declare Him an unworthy guide? Yet how much more worthy are His inwardly realized sources (*naishō honji*): Shaka, Yakushi, Jizō, Kannon, and Monju [the five Kasuga *honji*].

Gedatsu Shōnin's sentiments resemble those vividly expressed in *Tōdaiji Hachiman genki* (ZGR:241a), a text far more inclined than the *Genki* to speak theoretically:

> The deities (*shinmei*) have the Buddha's Teaching as their inner realization (*naishō*), while the Buddhas have the deities for their external manifestation (*gaiyō*). Although source (*hon*) and trace (*jaku*) differ, they are mystically one. *Shari* ["relics"] are the body-karma of the Nyorai. . . . The Holy Teaching is the speech-karma of the World-Honored One. . . . The deities (*shinmei*) of the various shrines are the message-karma [or "intention-karma, *igō*] of the Great Holy One.

This attitude underlies the opening passage of *Genki* 1.1 and is nicely stated in *Genki* 7.2, which dates from ca. 1225–30, roughly ten to fifteen years after Gedatsu Shōnin's death. A nun dreamed she was told:

> Chant the invocation "Namu Daimyōjin." Other invocations manifest the virtue of only one Buddha or Bodhisattva. One saying of "Namu Daimyōjin," however, makes manifest the power of all Five Sanctuaries, and so its benefits are vast.

In other words, Mikasa-yama was the presence not just of the Kasuga deity in a narrow sense but of his *honji* who were compassion and enlightenment.

Further on in *Kasuga kōshiki,* Gedatsu Shōnin confirmed the Kasuga deity's acknowledgment of him as a younger son by evoking the deity as a father and master:

> I desire humbly to approach the August Deity as a beloved child follows his father; respectfully to obey His guidance as a loyal minister serves his sovereign. . . . He leads me without fail to arouse the mind of enlightenment; He himself bestows upon me the Bodhisattva Precepts.

The passage is a definitive expression of the process already suggested in this chapter: the elevation of the deity, in a devoutly Buddhist context, from clan protector to voice of the universal truth.

At last, *Kasuga kōshiki* passes on to the pressing question, What will happen to me when I die? Gedatsu Shōnin asked rhetorically, "If the Myōjin does not protect me then, when will He protect me?" He prayed to know beforehand the moment of his death, to be of firm mind when it came, and to be delivered then from all demon assaults from within or without. And he continued:

> When the moment comes the August Deity will appear *(yōgō)* in my room, filling me, body and mind, with His deep peace, and producing for me much beneficial karma *(shukuzen)*. Then He will make manifest those among the Three Treasures to whom I have a tie *(uen sanbō)*, and these will all grant me their aid. The *shari* I have will then, anew, reveal their wonders, and the True Teaching in which I take refuge will confer on me its power.

Already Shakamuni Nyorai of the Pure Land of Ryōzen, and Miroku, the Compassionate Lord of the Tushita Heaven, with all the blessed host of His Inner Sanctum, appear in welcome (*raigō*) before my eyes. Monju, Jizō, Jōmyō [Vimalakīrti], Kannon—peerless Three Treasures of this world and the regions beyond—give thought to Your Original Vows, do not cast aside Your disciple's devotion! If [Your vows] are not in vain, then I surely will be born into the Inner Sanctum of Chisoku [the Tosotsu Heaven]; if my works and prayers are valid, then I at last shall serve the Buddas [as countless as] grains of dust.

Against this background one understands perfectly Jinson's feelings when, on Meiō 2.10.27 (1493; cited in Kawamura 1980:47), he noted in his diary:

Last night I dreamed I saw the Pure Land of Mikasa-yama. On top of the mountain there were a Tahō-tō [enshrining Shaka and Tahō, Skt. Prabhūtaratna], palaces and towers, bodhisattvas and heavenly beings. The mountain's majesty was wholly beyond thought or words. How absolutely wonderful!

This paradise was Ryōzen, the same one Myōe Shōnin saw at the Kasuga Shrine in *Genki* 18.1. Which "shore" was it on? The question is meaningless. Gṛdhrakūṭa is just as real a place in India as Mikasa-yama is in Japan. What does mean something is to say that for Myōe, for Jinson, and especially for the endlessly difficult, devoted Gedatsu Shōnin, such a paradise was home.

## GEDATSU SHŌNIN, THE *GENKI,* AND SHAKA

One key to the religious faith of such monks as Gedatsu and Myōe Shōnin seems to be an intense longing for the Buddha. George Tanabe (1983:18–34) has made this clear. He wrote (1983:18):

During the five billion six hundred seventy million years that were thought to separate the time of Śākyamuni from the coming of Maitreya, the world is without an incarnate buddha. The experience of the absent deity and the remoteness of enlightenment . . . form an essential part of the context for understanding a monk like Myōe. The difficulty if not the outright failure in achieving the highest Buddhist ideals was recognized as a past and present fact that was due to the misfortune of living in a less than ideal time and place.

The text and notes to *Genki* 17.1–18.4 make plain enough Myōe Shōnin's longing for India, where Shaka lived and taught. Myōe's friend Gedatsu Shōnin wrote in *Kasuga kōshiki:*

> However, persons like myself, in a small land and in the latter age [of the Law], are not born so as to meet the living [Shaka]; nor do we go and see His holy places. For us, the Teaching of Lord Shaka is as though delivered in vain.

These words add new depth to the passages just quoted. The Buddha's absence nourished the radiance of Kasuga, rich as Kasuga already was with associations. Gedatsu Shōnin, seeing in his mind's eye the deity's final *yōgō,* was not unlike the monk in the far north, once of Kōfukuji, to whom the deity appeared one moonlit night and said (8.6), "You have left me, but I have not left you." The monk that night had been "weeping to recall the Kasuga sanctuaries." Gedatsu Shōnin too must have wept sometimes, thinking of the Buddha and his country. The Kasuga paradise meant that despite Gedatsu Shōnin's misfortune, enlightenment was accessible also, to *him,* in his own "small land" and desolate time.

The oneness of Shaka and Miroku only made this the more true. Shaka had taught in time and space. As the preacher of the Lotus Sutra, however, he was eternal and omnipresent, and he merged with Miroku whose enlightenment waits to take form in future history. Gedatsu Shōnin quoted the *Butchiron* (Skt. *Buddhadhūmi-sūtra-śāstra*) as follows: "Sometimes he [the eternal buddha] manifests *tōgaku* ["equal enlightenment"], sometimes *nehan* [nirvāna]." And he continued in his own words:

> This is certain: of old in India, on [the continent of] Enbudai (Skt. Jambudvīpa), He was called Shaka and manifested *nehan,* while now, above the clouds of Chisoku, He has become Miroku and dwells in equal enlightenment.

With respect to Kasuga, this affirmation is comparable to the idea (discussed in chapter 6) that the Kasuga deity is Roshana (Skt. Vairocana), whose enlightenment is equally unbounded by space or time. As those who held such a view were well aware, the *Kan Fugen kyō* (Skt. *Samantabhadra-bodhisattva-dhyāna-caryādharma-sūtra*), generally considered in Japan a part of the Lotus Sutra, states: "Thereupon the voice in the sky will speak thus, saying: 'Śākyamuni Buddha is called Vairocana Who Pervades All Places' " (Katō 1975:576).

Gedatsu Shōnin was probably not the first to understand the Kasuga deity as Shaka. The Kasuga deer themselves make a better reason to identify the deity with Shaka (who first preached in the Deer Park at Benares) rather than with Fukūkenjaku. Moreover, the original image enshrined at Kōfukuji was a Shaka; and when the Taira burned Nara, Kujō Kanezane worried that the loss of a small, silver Shaka, located between the eyebrows of the bronze Shaka in the Central Kondō, would mean the end of the Fujiwara clan. (*Gyokuyō* for Jishō 5.1.6; S. Tyler 1987:191). Perhaps this silver Shaka was one associated with Kamatari (*Kōfukuji ranshōki*, DNBZa:315).

The cult of *shari,* which had been offered to shrines since at least the mid-tenth century (Tsuji 1944:459–60), suggests the same link with Shaka. The cult flourished at Kasuga and Kōfukuji, and was associated with the Ritsu revival begun by Jippan and continued by, among others, Jippan's successors: Zōshun, Kakuken, and Gedatsu Shōnin. The Ritsu tradition began with Shaka himself, and the *shari* that Gedatsu Shōnin gave to Myōe Shōnin (*Genki* 18.4) came originally from Ganjin (688–963), who brought Ritsu to Japan. According to *Genki* 12.1 Zōshun identified the First Sanctuary as Shaka already in 1140.

After Gedatsu Shōnin time, however, the idea that the deity was Shaka seems overwhelmingly to have been associated with him. Kujō Michiie (1193–1252), Kanezane's grandson, composed late in life a prayer to the Kasuga deity *(Mine-dono go-ganmon)* in which he wrote (ST:206), clearly following Gedatsu Shōnin:

The Daimyōjin is a *suijaku* of the Buddhas and Bodhisattvas. If the Jōhei oracle is correct, He is already named Jihi Mangyō no Bosatsu. And they say He is a *suijaku* of our Great Teacher Shaka Nyorai.

By the late thirteenth century the idea seemed to have originated with Gedatsu Shōnin. *Kasuga shiki* (1295), quoting a verse that appears in *Genki* 16.2, says (ST:71):

> According to Gedatsubō no Shōnin's *Honjikō no shiki,* the First Sanctuary is Shaka. The Shōnin heard this verse in a dream:
>> Know me as I am!
>> The Buddha Shakamuni
>> came into this life,
>> and lo! the bright moon
>> now illumines the world.

Perhaps it was this dream oracle that prompted the Shōnin to write "Shaka" in his text.

The *Genki* shuns any allusion to Fukūkenjaku or the Nan'endō. This is particularly obvious in connection with 4.3, where Kanezane's brother Konoe Motomichi (1160–1233) is said only to have dreamed "the *suijaku mandara* that has become so popular." This statement is extremely discreet. Motomichi was associated explicitly with a list of Kasuga *honji* that specifies Fukūkenjaku for the First Sanctuary, and Fukūkenjaku is shown in much important Kasuga art.

Instead, the *Genki* insists on the identity between the Kasuga deity and Shaka. The opening words of the text (1.1) express a now familiar sentiment: "In Kasuga no Daimyōjin the Nyorai of the full moon's bright orb has tempered the effulgence of His eternal enlightenment." In fact, the link between the famous Seiryōji Shaka and Kasuga (8.1) apparently entered the *Genki* text ultimately through Gedatsu Shōnin. One should recall the *Miyashiro no genki* reported by Koma no Chikazane in *Kyōkunshō* (see ch. 1) as having been compiled by Gedatsu Shōnin. Perhaps the *Genki*'s determined bias toward Shaka constitutes evidence that this work, now lost, was the foundation for the *Genki* itself. At any rate, despite the dramatic events associated with Myōe Shōnin in scrolls 17 and 18, the spirit of Gedatsu Shōnin seems particularly to pervade the *Genki*.

This spirit, so dedicated to the propagation of living Buddhism, is probably sufficient to explain the *Genki*'s emphasis on Shaka. Fukūkenjaku, after all, was an arcane deity, not only long out of fashion but closely associated with the exclusive interests of the Fujiwara. It is possible too that more parochial considerations were involved. At Kōfukuji, Gedatsu Shōnin was a resident of Ryūgejuin, which was aligned with Daijōin. Perhaps this is why after his time (it is not clear just when, but certainly before the fifteenth century) the identification of the First Sanctuary with Shaka came to be known as the "Daijōin tradition," while the identification with Fukūkenjaku was called the "Ichijōin tradition." On the other hand, judging from the people involved in putting the *Genki* together, the work should show, if anything, a greater influence from Ichijōin. More subtle, or less official, factional pressures may also have played a role, but they are now difficult to trace. Despite the inaccessibility of the *Genki,* hidden as it was from all but a few, one is probably right to understand the work simply as expressing the best ideals of the *kenmitsu bukkyō* of Nara in Kamakura times.

## THE "DIVINE LAND"

These ideals involved the tension between "a small land in the latter age of the Law" and the distant (in time and space) but infinitely august land where the Buddha taught. The careers of Gedatsu and Myōe Shōnin show how unstable the balance between these two terms could be in one man's mind; for both despaired of Japan's impoverished remoteness *and* affirmed (through the *gonge*) Japan's spiritual centrality and richness. In fact, by moving from Kōfukuji to Kasagi (1193), Gedatsu Shōnin actually acted out this dilemma. As far as the Kasagi deity was concerned (*Genki* 16.3), he might as well have moved from India in the Buddha's time to Japan in his own. At Kasagu, Gedatsu Shōnin faced on a smaller scale the same challenge as Japanese Buddhism itself: to make enlightenment, which once lived far away, live again here and now.

The resulting tendency to affirm that enlightenment *is* alive in Japan is obviously continuous with affirmations that Japan is blessed by special divine favor. For example, *Ishiyamadera engi,* a text of the Kannon cult, states (p. 96): "It is with our land, among the sentient beings of the three thousand dust-mote worlds, that [Kannon] has the deepest affinity *(innen)."* Another example is the well-known contention that Japan was a *shinkoku,* that is, a "divine land" or a "land of the gods." Kuroda Toshio made the point when he wrote (1975:261):

> Therefore all medieval *shinkoku* thinking was more or less adorned with Buddhist logic. In fact, Buddhist doctrine occupied the commanding position, and *shinkoku* thought was systematized by the *honji-suijaku* teaching, which is an application of *hon* and *jaku* [Buddhist] logic.

The tension between India as, in effect, *hon* ("source") and Japan as *jaku* ("[manifest] trace") certainly produced statements compatible with older affirmations of Japan's divine virtue. The earliest reference to Japan as a *shinkoku* appears in the *Nihongi,* but perhaps the classic instance occurs in *Sandai jitsuroku* for Jōgan 11.5 (869), in a prayer inspired by a Silla raid on Japanese territory (Tamura 1959:309–11). Ross Bender (1980:72–74) has translated the entire passage. The key section runs:

> Our court has for a long time had no war, and we have neglected to be vigilant. A war is surely cause for apprehension and fear. However, Japan is called the Divine Land *(shimmei no kuni).* If the gods protect us, and in particular if the awesome Imperial Great Kami, who is the great ancestor of our court, protects and aids the empire, what invasion can succeed?

Tamura (1959:314) showed that Japan was most likely to be called a divine land in time of trouble. Here the issue is invasion, which in 1309 was not a remote thought. Only a few decades earlier, Japan had been distressed by prolonged anxiety about the Mongol threat, and alarmed by two Mongol invasion attempts. Prayers that the Mongols should be repelled had been offered in shrines and temples throughout the land, and moreover, these prayers had apparently worked. The triumph of the "divine wind" that twice destroyed the Mongol fleet only confirmed the proposition that "our major shrines are all *gonge* of the buddhas and bodhisattvas." Kuroda (1975:274) wrote that *shinkoku* thinking became markedly stronger after the Mongol invasions. Perhaps both elements—the spiritual and the proudly national—can be seen in this enthusiastic passage from *Genki* 20.2:

Since purity in accordance with the mind is itself the Pure Land, our own Kami are the Buddhas. How could the Shrine not be the Pure Land? Jōruri and Vulture Peak are present within the shrine fence. Why seek Fudaraku and Shōryōzan beyond the clouds?

Besides all this, however, the conception of Japan as a divine land has in the *Genki* a third aspect linked directly to the Fujiwara. No one seems to have questioned that "the awesome Imperial Great Kami [of Ise] ... is the great ancestor of our court," or that this deity, Amaterasu, was the single most important one in the realm. On the other hand, the standing of Kasuga, and especially of the Fujiwara themselves, rested entirely on the mythological help given Amaterasu by Takemikazuchi and Amenokoyane (*Genki* 1.1). Without this authority, the place of the Fujiwara regents beside the emperor could have been questioned. Kuroda (1975:266) noted that according to both *Yōtenki* and *Keiran shūyōshū* (texts associated with Mt. Hiei), the Hie deity was the "local protector of Japan" *(Nihonkoku no jinushi)* and no less than the father of Amaterasu. No spokesman for the Kasuga cult could possibly have asserted such a thing. It was no light matter that, as *Genki* 1.1 puts it, "the winds of Mikasa-yama [should] proclaim the Eternal Name, investing with great dignity the bond between [the Emperor and] the Regent."

On this score, the Kasuga Fourth Sanctuary played a vital role. Then as now this sanctuary was understood to be the consort of the Third Sanctuary, Amenokoyane. In the time of the *Genki,* however, the deity's connection with Hiraoka was at best uninteresting. Instead every Kasuga source identifies the Fourth Sanctuary as Ise, or as *dōtai* ("one in substance") with Ise. *Genki* 1.1 explains:

When [Amaterasu no Ōmikami] pushed open the door of the Celestial Rock Cave, She illumined the darkness that had engulfed the world, and so relieved the people's distress. This means that She and [Ameno]koyane no Mikoto are conjoined in profound union, and likewise that the Grand Shrine of Ise is manifest in the Fourth Sanctuary.

It was held that after the episode of the Heavenly Rock Cave, Amaterasu had given Amenokoyane a specific charge that sealed their relationship forever. According to *Kasuga-sha shiki* (ST:66):

Thereafter, when the Heavenly Grandchild descended to the Land of the Reed Plains, Amateru On-kami declared to Amanokoyane: "My descendants shall be sovereign in the Central Land of the Reed Plains. Your descendants shall govern the land generation after generation *(yoyo kunigara o tore)* on behalf of mine."

Precisely the same statement (worded a little differently) appears in the *Nihon wa shinkoku no koto* chapter of *Senjūshō* (9/1). This is the sort of compact to which Jien (a brother of Kujō Kanezane and a Tendai Abbot) alluded in *Gukanshō* as well (Brown 1979:211, 213) as the basis for the standing of the Fujiwara.

The opening paragraph of *Senjūshō* 9/1 puts the matter even more explicitly than the *Genki:*

Our realm is divine land. It is the power of our own deities that we have to thank for the Buddha's Way *(buppō) being* the Buddha's Way; it is their divine protective power that makes the Royal Way *(ōbō) be* the Royal Way. The Sovereign over the realm, the Son of Heaven who is revered as supreme above all, descends (awesome to tell!) from the Great Deity of Ise. The Head of the Fujiwara clan, venerated as the Regent responsible for all matters of government, is the scion of the Kasuga Deity. Who among [those who hold] the Hundred Offices [of government] is not thus of divine stock?

This passage proposes nothing less than the idealized pattern of the Heian state—a pattern quite out of date by the time *Senjūshō* must have been finished, and still more so by 1309. In *Gukanshō* (Brown 1979:228), Jien put the situation more realistically:

The Sun Goddess enshrined at Ise and the Great Illuminating Kami enshrined at Kasuga certainly consulted together and decided [how Imperial rule was to be supported] in the distant past. And the Great Hachiman Bodhisattva and the Great Illuminating Kami of Kasuga consulted together and decided [how Imperial rule is to be supported] in the present. . . . It is clear that the decision for the present, made after the state had been buffeted this way and that, has been made for these final reigns and requires that the sovereign have a guardian who has the power of both learning and military might.

But those who sponsored the *Genki* understandably found no place in the work for Hachiman or for any acknowledgement of the Minamoto power with which Hachiman was identified. They proposed instead a glorious but entirely nostalgic vision that made of the Kamakura bakufu no more than a ripple on the face of eternity.

## THE FOURTH SANCTUARY AS *GOHŌ*

In the *Genki,* the Fourth Sanctuary comes up in another connection that deserves a word or two. Apparently this sanctuary particularly was regarded as the *gohō* presence at Kasuga and Kōfukuji. The word is a bit confusing because Gohō as a proper noun is also the Japanese name of Dharmapāla (530–61), a figure immensely important in the Hossō tradition and therefore honored at Kōfukuji. As a common noun, however, *gohō* refers to a large class of relatively minor deities (or minor aspects of more important deities) who "protect the Teaching."

Perhaps "minor deity" is a misleading expression. *"Active* deity" might be better. A *gohō* typically served an ascetic practitioner, either to guide him to higher realms or to act as his agent in the procedure of healing or prognostication. An example of the first kind may be found in *Uji shūi monogatari* 15/8, where Fudō, a fundamental *gohō* figure in *shugendō,* takes Sōō (831–918) of Mt. Hiei to the gate of the Tosotsu Heaven. A celebrated example of a healing *gohō* occurs in *Uji shūi monogatari* 8/3, where the ascetic of Mt. Shigi sends his divine minion the Sword Guardian *(tsurugi no gohō)* to heal Emperor Daigo. In the *Genki,* the Fourth Sanctuary as *gohō* seems to be associated with oracles delivered, according to the classic pattern, by a woman medium in response to specific questions, and under the direct control of a male monk-adept. The Fourth Sanctuary's oracles therefore differed from those delivered spontaneously by the *miko* of the Wakamiya (*Genki* 4.4, 4.5).

It may be significant in this regard that the Fourth Sanctuary is female. In other words, although the Fourth Sanctuary's connection with Ise and her function (at times) as *gohō* are probably unrelated, they may be linked by her gender. It is not that *gohō* are necessarily female. However, this role might easily have been considered beneath the dignity of the three other (male) Kasuga sanctuaries. Moreover, a possible model for the Fourth Sanctuary as *gohō* is the female Nifu deity of Mt. Kōya. Enshrined from the start by Kūkai as the temple protector *(gohō garan shin)* of Kongōbuji, this deity clearly gave oracles since Kūkai himself received one (Miyai 1979:52, citing Kūkai's *Go-yuigō,* or "testament"). The matter deserves further study.

The Fourth Sanctuary's outstanding appearance as the *gohō* occurs in *Genki* 13.3 where a monk, made desperately ill on purpose by the Kasuga deity, receives a supernatural visitation during which a feminine voice first sings a song to the accompaniment of a *koto,* then chants a passage from the *Yuishiki ron.* Puzzled, one of the monk's colleagues decides to summon *(kanjō)* the *gohō.* Thereupon "the Fourth Kasuga Sanctuary came down and cried, "I've won, I've won!" The *Genki* illustration shows a female medium dancing in frenzy. Other probable instances are *Genki* 6.3, 11.2, 15.1, and 15.5. In the first, third, and fourth of these, *"gohō* divination" *(gohō-ura)* produces an oracle that reveals why the main figure of the story is ill. In the second, an ascetic *(ugen no sō),* apparently assisted by a young male medium, summons the Kasuga deity on behalf of Egyō (1085–1164), who had been unable to bring the deity down himself. The text only says, "Shortly the Daimyōjin did appear . . . ," but one may assume that "the Daimyōjin" was particularly the Fourth Sanctuary. *Genki* 13.1 provides the curious case of a girl spontaneously possessed by a *messenger* from the Kasuga deity, precisely while a healer was trying to call the deity in person into the healer's regular medium. Here, too, the object of the healer's summons was no doubt the *gohō.*

This interpretation is plausible because of what the great Kōfukuji scholar Zōshun dreamed in the sixth month of Hōen 6 (1140, *Genki* 12.1). Zōshun saw "the Daimyōjin's [four] palanquins" entering the Kōfukuji grounds from the First Torii of Kasuga. All except the First Sanctuary, who spoke to Zōshun, were invisible behind their curtains. (The *Genki* illustration shows the First Sanctuary as a gentleman in court dress.) The account concludes: "He could tell that the First Sanctuary was Shaka, the Second Miroku, and the Fourth the *gohō,* but he woke up without learning anything about the Third." It is of course possible to understand this *gohō* as being Dharmapāla. That is the way Kameda took it (1970a:374). However, Dharmapāla is mentioned nowhere else as a *honji* for the Fourth Sanctuary, and in truth the idea makes little sense. Certainly *Koshaki* (ST:10) identifies the *honji* of the Himuro-sha (a Kasuga *massha*) as Jinna (Skt. Dignāga), a sixth-century disciple of Seshin (Skt. Vasubandhu). The Himuro-sha, however, cannot compare in standing to the Fourth Sanctuary, which surely required a more elevated *honji* than any human patriarch. No doubt Zōshun's dream was idiosyncratic, as witnessed by his ignorance regarding the Third Sanctuary, but Dharmapāla would have made an odd companion to Shaka and Miroku. It is more likely that Zōshun acknowledged here the Fourth Sanctuary's oracular function.

# 6

# *Forms and Dreams*

So far, conciseness and the standards of English grammar have made it necessary to write of "the Kasuga deity" as though the deity were singular, and for that matter male. By now, of course, it is obvious that the truth is a little more varied. This chapter will review the full cast of characters covered by so plain a term. Not that the cast is as large as it could be. The Hie Shrine, for example, is more complex. Moreover, there is no room here for the galaxy of Kasuga *massha,* many of which could be included under "Kasuga no Daimyōjin" in the broadest sense of the name.

The many guises of "Kasuga no Daimyōjin" show vividly that a deity in Japan has no single form. They also demonstrate a key principle of medieval religion: that enlightenment reveals itself in accordance with the capacity and attunement of sentient beings. As a dream-monk explains in *Jizō Bosatsu reigenki* (ZGR:45b):

> When all the Buddhas travel the same road, I rejoice and the Buddhas do too. The inner realization *(naishō)* of the *honji* [Buddhas] is all the single, Dharmakāya *(hosshin)* Buddha. Since sentient beings vary in motivation *(ki),* [the Dharmakāya's] manifestations too are different from one another.

For us, finally, all these forms display the rich weave of convention, history, inspiration, and accident that clothes such a cult—one whose main concerns are not after all so very difficult or even unusual—in colors that belong to it alone.

# THE SEX AND NUMBER
# OF THE KASUGA DEITY

Despite the presence of the female Fourth Sanctuary, Kasuga no Daimyōjin as a whole is undoubedtly male. The Third and Fourth Sanctuaries by themselves are in principle a male-female pair like the Tatsuta deity *(Tatsuta no Daimyōjin no on-koto)* or the deity of Fuji *("Fuji Asama Daibosatsu no koto"* in *Shintōshū* 8); but this pair is overwhelmed by the First and Second Sanctuaries and the Wakamiya, who are entirely male. This is not to say that Kasuga no Daimyōjin cannot appear as a woman without being specifically the Fourth Sanctuary, for such a visitation does take place in *Genki* 1.3 and 10.6. However, the positions of the First Sanctuary, and to a lesser extent the Third Sanctuary, are in general so commanding that "Kasuga no Daimyōjin" must be referred to in English as "he." The sex of the medium, if any, makes no difference. The medium in *Genki* 17.1 and 17.2 is intensely feminine, but she nonetheless speaks (according to *Kasuga Daimyōjin go-takusenki)* as "this old man."

The question of number is a little more elusive. Although "Kasuga no Daimyōjin" is not exactly singular, it would be wrong to conclude that the term is therefore simply plural. The matter might have been clearer (if any speaker of an Indo-European language had been present to wonder about it) early in the history of the cult, when the identities of the deities were presumably more routinely distinct. However, it can probably be said that the forms appearing in the *Genki,* including Mikasa-yama itself, are not wholly singular *or* plural. The lady of *Genki* 1.3 and the gentleman of *Genki* 6.1 may be singular in form, but each alludes, explicitly or not, to a more complex presence. Perhaps the psychological phenomenon of multiple personality provides a rough analogy: in such cases the personality present at any given time says "I" with complete confidence, never having heard of the other "I's" who inhabit the same body (Mikasa-yama). Or perhaps the idea of a team, a family, or a state is helpful. If so, the lady and the gentleman just cited are "representatives" or "ambassadors plenipotentiary" and could say indifferently "I" or "we." Yet Kasuga no Daimyōjin is not organized this way. The First Sanctuary may be senior, but he does not run anything. The *Genki* contains no hint that the various aspects of Kasuga no Daimyōjin have a collective life apart from the divinity's acts of communication with humans. In order to resolve this conceptually puzzling matter, one should no doubt take into consideration the *human* community that supported the cult, but this would lead the discussion too far afield. It is easier to remember that superficially, at least, the problem is largely an artifact of language. Having no masculine or feminine gender and no singular or plural inflections to manipulate, the Japanese speaker does not need to worry about it.

## THE DEITY'S MANIFESTATIONS IN THE *GENKI*

The manifestations of Kasuga no Daimyōjin in the *Genki* are quite diverse. They may convey not only personal experience but also interpretation of this experience. No doubt most oracles and many dreams made the general identity of the divine power clear enough. One understands that the dreamer in 7.3 should have had no doubt about the two gentlemen he saw, even though they did not positively identify themselves. In other cases, however, dreamers (or those who passed on their stories) must have realized or decided only afterwards where a dream had come from. This is obviously the case in 15.2, where the dreamer has no idea who the gentleman of her dream may be. It may also be true of a dream like the one in 15.4, where the old monk's connection with Kasuga no Daimyōjin seems to be a matter of opinion.

One obvious conclusion to draw from the incidents told in the *Genki* is that Kasuga no Daimyōjin often did not deliver communications or assistance in person, but instead worked through messengers. In this he behaved precisely like any nobleman. This is particularly clear in a passage of 13.1:

> While the healer was at work, an oracle came through a young girl of the household. "I am Enomoto no Myōjin," the divinity said. "Kasuga no Daimyōjin sent me."

In other cases the deity sent shrine servants (4.3, 5.1, etc.); a Kasuga priest named Tokimori (4.1); a junior official of Kōfukuji (4.6); or Mizuya, a *massha* deity like Enomoto (13.3).

The simplest way to convey all this is in the form of a table. The one below, based on both the text and the paintings, takes into account all *Genki* stories in which the deity is given a form, however vague. It also includes the different sorts of mediums.

### Mediums

| | |
|---|---|
| A woman medium at the main sanctuaries | 1.2 |
| A woman medium at the Wakamiya | 4.4, 4.5 |
| A woman medium at the Atsuta Shrine | 8.4 |
| A woman medium under the control of a healer | 6.3, 11.2, 13.3, 15.1, 15.5 |
| A woman medium spontaneously possessed at home | 13.1 (Enomoto), 17.1, 17.2, 18.2 |
| A boy at the main sanctuaries | 4.2 |
| Retired Emperor Shirakawa | 1.5 |
| Minamoto no Toshifusa | 3.1 |
| Gedatsu Shōnin | 16.1, 16.3 |

### Forms of the deity in dreams and visions

| | |
|---|---|
| A lady | 1.3, 1.4, 10.6, 14.2 |
| A young boy | 13.2, 14.5 |
| A boy in his late teens | 7.3 |
| A mature gentleman | 6.1, 8.3, 8.6, 9.1, 10.1 10.4, 12.4, 15.2, 18.4 |
| Four persons in palanquins, with one gentleman visible | 12.1 |
| An old man | 10.5 |
| The head of the Fujiwara clan (Yorimichi) | 10.2 |
| A double of Fujiwara no Moromichi | 2.3 |
| Jizō | 11.4, 12.3 |
| A voice | 2.2, 5.1, 7.2, 11.3 |
| A *sakaki* tree | 11.3 |
| A *sotoba* | 7.4 |
| Countless fires in the air | 20.1 |
| A felt but unseen presence | 16.2, 18.1 |

### Messengers of the deity in dreams and visions

| | |
|---|---|
| One or more shrine servants | 4.3, 5.1, 5.2 6.2, 10.3, 14.6 |
| The Kasuga priest Tokimori | 4.1 |
| A mature gentleman | 7.3 |
| A junior monk-official of Kōfukuji | 4.6 |
| An old monk | 15.4 |
| "Someone unknown" | 7.1 |
| A white hand | 14.1 |

| | |
|---|---|
| Deer | 12.2, 15.3 |
| The Enomoto deity | 13.1 |
| The Mizuya deity | 13.3 |

All the anonymous mediums are of a kind attested elsewhere, and stories about mediums possessed spontaneously by various sorts of powers are not at all uncommon. As to Gedatsu Shōnin, Japan has had many visionary monks, or monks who have had sacred dreams *(reimu)*, but relatively few seem to have been such outright mediums as he. However, the most unusual mediums in the *Genki* are Shira-kawa and Toshifusa. Embarrassing incidents connected with them (if one believes them at all) could only have been recorded for the higher purpose of celebrating the Kasuga deity.

As to the dream and vision forms, the lady (a beautiful lady of the most noble bearing) and the various males from young boy to old man are all familiar in Heian or medieval writings. Divine voices alone are found elsewhere too. *Sakaki* is to be expected, since it is the Kasuga deity's canonical vehicle; and the deer is the deity's canonical mount, or messenger. The other forms of the deity or of his messengers are more idiosyncratic, but except for the remarkable fires of 20.1 are not particularly surprising in context. Perhaps the most striking of them is Jizō, since he is the only *honji* actually seen in the *Genki*.

## RECOGNIZED *HONJI* AND *SUIJAKU* FORMS

Discussing the religious importance of the *honji* forms, Susan Tyler wrote (1987:6): "In *honji suijaku* thought the chief creative effort is the identification of the Buddhist versions of the kami." It is therefore not surprising that the old accounts of the Kasuga Shrine, like *Koshaki* (dated 940) or *Kasuga Daimyōjin go-honji narabini go-takusenki* (dated 1175), should all contain notes on the Buddhist identities of the several deities. *Kasuga-sha shiki* (dated 1295) states (ST:71) that its list was "certified in Jōan 5 (1175), at the order of the Retired Emperor (Go-Shirakawa), by the Kannushi Ōnakatomi no Tokimori, the Shō-no-azukari Nakatomi no Nobutō, and others."

*Koshaki* (ST:9–11) and *Shun'ya shinki* (ST:183–87; earliest ms. dated 1437) also describe approved *suijaku* forms. In *Shun'ya shinki* these descriptions occur in a survey of *honji* and *suijaku* forms that the text identifies as *Fugenji-dono no yume no go-ki,* or "Lord Fugenji's record of his dreams." This gentleman is Konoe Motomichi (1160– 1233) who, as noted before, is said in *Genki* 4.3 to have "worshiped, in dream, the *suijaku mandara* that has become so popular." Since the *suijaku* forms in *Koshaki* and *Shun'ya shinki* are the same, they are apparently older than Motomichi—unless *Koshaki* really is no earlier than the mid-thirteenth century. (Even if it is, the connection with Motomichi may be fanciful or exaggerated.) In any case, the compilers of the *Genki* were clearly aware of all these forms.

*Koshaki,* which, in keeping with the date it claims, omits the Wakamiya, lists the *honji* as follows:

FIRST SANCTUARY: "Fukūkenjaku or, alternatively, Shaka Nyorai"
SECOND SANCTUARY: "Yakushi or, alternatively, Miroku"
THIRD SANCTUARY: "Jizō Bosatsu"
FOURTH SANCTUARY: "Ise Daijingū, [whose *honji* are] Dainichi Nyorai or, alternatively, Jūichimen Kannon"

*Kasuga Daimyōjin go-honji narabini go-takusenki* (ST:37–44) gives two similar lists, of which the first (ST:37–39) includes for each sanctuary a discussion of the complex iconographic features and significance of the *honji.* The Wakamiya is not included.

FIRST SANCTUARY: "Fukūkenjaku who resides on Fudaraku-sen in the southwest of Enbudai (Skt. Jambudvīpa)."
SECOND SANCTUARY: "A *suijaku* of Yakushi Nyorai [who] appears as Gozu Tennō"
THIRD SANCTUARY: "Jizō Bosatsu"
FOURTH SANCTUARY: "Dainichi Birushana Butsu"

The second list (ST:43), much more concise, give (1) "Fukūkenjaku Kannon"; (2) "Yakushi Nyorai"; (3) Jizō; (4) "Jūichimen Kannon"; and (5) for the Wakamiya, "Monjushiri Bosatsu."

*Shun'ya shinki* gives a list that, with its iconographic and other commentaries, closely resembles the first one just described for *Gotakusen ki.* It specifies (1) Fukūkenjaku; (2) Yakushi in the form of Gozu Tennō or, alternatively, Miroku; (3) Jizō; (4) Jūichimen Kannon or, alternatively, Dainichi; and (5) for the Wakamiya, Jūichimen Kannon or, alternatively, Monju Bosatsu.

It is clear that there were variant definitions of the *honji* for all five sanctuaries; indeed the variety to be found in both texts and art, throughout the history of the Kasuga cult, is greater still. One might note that although Dainichi and Amaterasu are often cited now as the type example of the *honji-suijaku* relationship, the *honji* of Amaterasu was often understood, as here, to be Jūichimen Kannon. *Hasedera engibun,* for example, explains why.

As to *suijaku* forms, *Koshaki* and *Shun'ya shinki* agree on the following portraits. All the figures are clearly standing, although this is not specified by the texts.

FIRST SANCTUARY: An old gentleman in his sixtieth year, wearing a dark gray over-robe *(ue-no-kinu);* lacquered shoes *(asagutsu);* a formal headdress *(kanmuri)* without *oikake* ("side-whiskers") or *ei* ("pendant tail"); and a sword with *hirao.* His arms are folded and he carries a *shaku* ("baton").

SECOND SANCTUARY: An old gentleman in his sixtieth year, without a beard *(Koshaki)* or with a long beard *(Shun'ya shinki).* *(Koshaki* is probably correct. The difference, that between *nashi* ["none"] and *nagashi* ["long"], looks like a copyist's error.) He too wears a dark gray over-robe; lacquered shoes; a formal headdress without *oikake;* and a sword with *hirao.* In his left hand he carries a *shaku,* the tip of which he touches with his right hand.

THIRD SANCTUARY: A monk wearing a *nōgesa* (a kind of "stole" worn by high-ranking monks) and straw sandals *(sōkai).*

FOURTH SANCTUARY: A beautiful lady like Kichijōten, wearing an ornamental crown *(kazari hōkan).* Her arms are folded.

WAKAMIYA: (In *Shun'ya shinki* only) A boy with his hair

in loops *(binzura)*. His palms are pressed together in *gasshō*.

Two *Kasuga mandara* in which these forms appear as described, with their *honji* and in the company of the shrine's principal *massha*, are reproduced in Nara Kokuritsu Hakubutsukan (1964:pl. 15, 16). One (pl. 16), owned by Hōzanji and dated to the Kamakura period, does not show the shrine or its landscape at all, but consists entirely of *honji* and *suijaku* figures.

It is interesting to note as well two dreams that yielded rather different portraits, even though there is no reason to believe that they were influential. Hakusen (1779: *kan* 5) included them in his eighteenth-century study of Kasuga. In Tenshō 15.8, the Kasuga shrine servant Morikiyo dreamed that a shrine priest *(kannushi)* opened the doors of the four main sanctuaries, so that Morikiyo could see within. (1) The First Sanctuary was a gentleman wearing a *kazaori eboshi* and a light yellow-green hunting cloak *(kariginu)*. He was seated. (2) The Second Sanctuary was a monk wearing a red robe, and with a brown cotton wrap around his neck. A boy stood to his right. (3) The Third Sanctuary was a seated gentleman wearing an *eboshi* and a light yellow-green robe. A boy stood to his right as well. (4) The Fourth Sanctuary, whose face was invisible, wore a yellow-green, figured robe. A boy with painted eyebrows, and with his hair in *binzura,* stood to her right. Two days later Morikiyo dreamed that he stood at the northeast corner of the *haiden* before the Wakamiya. The doors of the Wakamiya opened, and he saw within (5) Monju mounted on a lion, and looking over his shoulder to his left. Around him, in the four directions, stood the Shitennō ("Four Celestial Kings"), and behind him Jizō Bosatsu.

## *HONJI* OR OTHER SINGLE FIGURES THAT STAND FOR THE WHOLE SHRINE

All this diversity still does not exhaust the repertoire. Even the single figures who could represent the whole shrine are strikingly varied. The two major *honji,* Fukūkenjaku and Shaka, have already been discussed. Their standing demonstrates the senior position of the First Sanctuary.

*Fudō Myōō.* Fudō Myōō could also be a *honji* for the First Sanctuary, hence for the whole shrine. Susan Tyler (1987:192–95) has discussed this proposition and the startling passage in *Shun'ya shinki* that quotes a "secret oral teaching" as follows (ST:195):

> Fukūfunnuō [the wrathful form of Fukūkenjaku] is one in substance with Fudō. When Fukūkenjaku enters the samādhi of Fukūfunnuō, he manfests Kasuga no Daimyōjin and is therefore one in substance with Fudō.

According to *Gashūshō* by Shinkaku (d. 1180) (quoted in Mochizuki 1931–36 under "Fukūkenjaku"):

> Some say there are various original identities of Fukūkenjaku. One idea is that Dainichi changes into Miroku and Miroku changes in Fukūkenjaku. Another is that Dainichi changes into Jizō who changes into Fukūkenjaku. Fukūkenjaku changes into the King of Wrath [Fudō].

These ideas were acknowledged in an elaborate set of rites performed for a complete set of *honji-butsu* of the shrine (Fukūkenjaku, Yakushi, Jizō, Jūichimen, Jūichimen) on Kenkyū 5.7.8 (1194), and commissioned by Kujō Kanezane.

*Dainichi or Roshana.* Dainichi and Roshana cannot be distinguished from one another in connection with Kasuga. Perhaps one can see here influence from neighboring Tōdaiji. According to *Tōdaiji Hachiman genki* (ZGR:233b), the emperor even dreamed on Tenpyō 3.11.1 (731) that "the *honji* of Nichirin ["sun disk"] Dainichi Nyorai is Roshana Buddha." At Kasuga, Dainichi or Roshana never occurs as a *honji* for the whole shrine in art, but the idea appears in writing. The reason must be as suggested in chapter 5: the need to understand Kasuga as a pure expression of ultimate enlightenment. The following verse, written on several *Kasuga mandara,* is to be found also at the end of *Senjūshō* 1/1:

> The original substance, Roshana,
> perfectly enlightened for all eternity,
> in order to save sentient beings
> manifests the Daimyōjin.

The continuity between Shaka and Roshana, touched on in the previous chapter, appears to color the first paragraph of *Genki* 1.1 As to Dainichi, *Shun'ya shinki* (ST: 195) could not be more explicit: "Amaterasu Ōmikami is the Dainichi of the Taizō[kai]; Kasuga no Daimyōjin is the Dainichi of the Kongō[kai]. Mystically, in fact, Kasuga is the twofold, nondual Dainichi," In this passage, Mikasa-yama joins Mt. Fuji or the Ōmine range, among features of the Japanese landscape, as what some texts call a *kontai ryōbu no go-reizan,* a "sacred mountain where Kongōkai and Taizōkai conjoin."

*Jizō.* Jizō, the *honji* of the Third Sanctuary (Amenokoyane), and the only Kasuga *honji* seen in the *Genki,* had an enduring cult that needs no introduction here. Miyai Yoshio (1978:108) contended that from the late Heian period on, the name Amenokoyane (the Third Sanctuary) itself meant Kasuga. His evidence is inconclusive, and he appears to have exaggerated. The development in question took place, but only in the fourteenth century, as shown by *Sakakiba no nikki,* as well as the two Noh plays *Uneme* and *Saho-yama.*

The compassionate Jizō was obviously an attractive *honji* for the divine Fujiwara ancestor. However, *Jizō Bosatsu reigenki* 3 (ZGR 25b:58a–61a) presents so vividly another aspect of the matter that the material is worth reviewing here. The story concerns Matsudai Shōnin, who in the twelfth century spread the cult of Mt. Fuji and built a temple at Murayama, later the base of operations for the *shugendō* of the mountain. It is in two parts. The first, though not directly about Jizō, shows how the diverse forms of a deity resolve themselves in the deity's mountain itself—for instance, Mikasa-yama. Matsudai Shōnin could not understand why Mt. Fuji's *hottai* ("dharma body"), an emanation of Roshana, should be manifest not in male *(nantai)* but in female form *(nyoshin).* Having fasted and prayed for one hundred days, he heard a voice directing him to walk 108 paces toward the southwest and dig. There he exhumed a crystal miniature of Fuji, "and all his doubts were instantly dispelled."

The second part of the story presents an unforgettable encounter with Jizō. On his way to visit the *gongen* deities of Hakone and Yubashiri, Matsudai Shōnin came to Atami, which is dominated to the northwest by Higane-yama ("Mt. Sun Gold," 774m.). The landscape was then a volcanic "hell" very like the better-known hell of

Tateyama (*Konjaku* 14/7, 14/8). Matsudai was gazing at it, horrified at the sufferings of the beings there, when

it seemed to him that the wind *(oroshi)* blowing down from Higane sang Sanskrit sounds, and the waves on the sea below chanted *Shakujō*. He was deeply moved, and surprised too to see the smoke die down and the sea become calm. Going further into the valley he saw sentient beings as numberless as the sands of the Ganges, in agony amid the fierce heat that filled their world, and burning in searing fire, who were drinking water or milk and receiving comfort and aid. A monk was helping [them]. . . .

Presently the vapors parted and the monk rose with the clouds toward the peak of Higane. . . . Astonished by the sanctity of his vow and the sovereign efficacy of his deeds, Matsudai desired the blessing of contact with him. Approaching the monk with folded hands, he said: "I beg you, your grace, lay your hands upon me. It will be a blessing for my life to come. . . . For myself, my own practice being insufficient, I still fear for my own miserable person. I have not realized samādhi in this fleshly body, nor have I yet mastered flight. How can I relieve the sufferings of sentient beings by means of these powers of yours? In what realm do you dwell?"

Smiling, the monk appeared through the mist. "I am the lord of perfect, unsullied awakening in true, everlasting realization," he said. "Yet for the sake of sentient beings yet unsaved, I humbly mingle with the dust . . . and befriend the countless sinners there. . . . For one [sentient being] I enter the evil realms; for another I plead with the fiends of hell. Atami is a small corner of the hell of searing heat. . . . That is why I come down with the *oroshi* three times daily from the peak and care for those in agony. . . . Then I return to Higane-yama. . . . Though one has committed the five outrages, if he turns to me, confesses his faults, and does not repeat them, then I take on his sufferings and enter [for him] the nethermost hell. Such a one calls me Jizō."

Then he disappeared.

This remarkable story illumines perfectly the courtly Jizō of Kasuga and the Kasuga deity's hell in *Genki* 16.4. Coming as he does from the summit of Higane, and dwelling as he does in "perfect, unsullied awakening," etc., this Jizō is continuous with Roshana/Dainichi, just as in the passage cited above from *Gashūshō*. Therefore he is also continuous with Shaka, in the manner already discussed in connection with *Kasuga kōshiki* by Gedatsu Shōnin.

In fact, Gedatsu Shōnin himself contributed to the Jizō cult at Kasuga. This is clear from an account left by Ryōhen (1194–1252) in the year of his death, and quoted by Hakusen (1779: *kan* 5). Ryōhen was the master of Chisokuin at Tōdaiji. He wrote that in Kenkyū 6.9 (1195), Gedatsu Shōnin undertook a retreat at Kasuga and prayed to see the deity's own living form. During the night an old man came to him and said, "Go and get some sandalwood. I will carve you the Deity's living body." Gedatsu Shōnin brought the sandalwood, and the old man quickly carved a three-foot-tall Jizō. "I leave the eye-opening to you," he said, then vanished. Ryōhen noted that this image was now (1252) enshrined at Chisokuin, since Chisokuin was associated with Hossō studies. *Kōfukuji ranshōki* (DNBZa:322a) specifies that the image was made by Kasuga no Daimyōjin at Ryūge-juin, Gedatsu Shōnin's home at Kōfukuji. The story appears also in *Gaun nikken roku* for Bun'an 5.8 (1448).

Hakusen also quoted an account, written in 1611 by a former superintendent of Kōfukuji, that relates a visit to hell by the Kasuga priest Nakatomi no Suketsugu (1208–78). As is so common in Jizō stories (and in *Genki* 6.1 or 9.1), Suketsugu "died," then came back to life and told how he had found himself at Enma's court. A monk appeared and announced that, having served him so faithfully, Suketsugu deserved to be let go. Once released, Suketsugu questioned the monk, observing that he had served only the Daimyōjin, never the Buddha. The monk replied, "I am the Third Sanctuary of Kasuga, Amatsukoyane-no-mikoto. My *honji* is the Jizō of Chisokuin."

*Akadōji.* Just outside the south gate into the precincts of the present main shrine, a point of rock, surrounded by a low fence, pokes up through the gravel. This is *Akadōji shutsugen seki,* the "rock where Akadōji appeared." Akadōji ("Red Boy") has the form of a powerful youth with long, red hair who stands upon this rock, leaning on a staff or cudgel. He looks like an attendant *dōji* of a Buddhist divinity

—for instance, Kongara or Seitaka, the two principal *dōji* of Fudō. This being is the Kasuga deity.

A tradition whose source is difficult to determine has it that Akadōji first appeared in the ninth century. Certainly *Kasuga no Daimyō-jin shōsha ki* (1133) mentions him and his rock. However, his origins are unknown. He was genuinely popular in the Edo period, as shown by the many mass-produced paintings and prints of him that circulated then. The Edo-period cult of Akadōji clearly assumed that Akadōji was all the Kasuga sanctuaries, since Hakusen (1779) devoted part of *Kasuga-yama no ki* to demonstrating that, in fact, Akadōji was only the First Sanctuary.

Akadōji seems to have been an object of devotion even at Kōfukuji, for the sixteenth-century *Tamon'in nikki* (vol. 3:39) records a dream of Akadōji in action. When in his seventeenth year, Eishun, the diarist, became extremely ill. Among the things his teacher did to help him was to hang a picture of Akadōji ("a *honzon* owned by Rengejōin") in Eishun's room. That night Akadōji appeared to Eishun and advised him about how he should pursue his studies. A male and a female demon came before Akadōji, who beat them off with his staff. Then the demons prayed for mercy, and promised that they would not hurt Eishun any more.

*Anne and Nanda. Kasuga-sha sanjikkō saisho go-ganmon bun,* signed by Emperor Go-Fukakusa and dated Kōan 11.4.21 (1288), begins: "Kasuga no Daimyōjin is supremely illumined. He is originally a manifestation *(keshin)* of Anne (Skt. Sthiramati) and Nanda (Skt. Ānanda)"—two of the "ten great Hossō commentators."

*The Kongō hannya kyō.* Kujō Kanezane wrote in *Gyokuyō* (Jishō 5.int2.26 [1181]) of one Kakujō who came to see him just after a visit to Nara. Kakujō remarked, "According to the late Prelate Zō-shun, the true body *(mishōtai)* of Kasuga is actually the *Kongō hannya kyō.* I myself have seen this [in a dream] to be so." Kanezane then went on: "Hearing this, I no longer doubted that my own dream was true. [Zōshun's] words deserve the fullest credence. Now is the time when what I have been praying for all these years is surely to be realized." Moreover, a copy of the *Kongō hannya kyō* (Skt. *Vajracchedikā-prajñā-pāramitā-sūtra*) was discovered in this century inside a statue of Shishi Monju ("Monju on a Lion") originally from Daijōin. The frontispiece to the text is a beautiful painting of the Wakamiya as a boy of noble birth, standing against the landscape of Mikasa-yama, and with a monk and three shrine priests before him. The painting, the record of a monk's dream vision, is dated Bun'ei 10.8 (1273).

*Basanba-entei.* According to George Tanabe (1983:97, citing Tanaka Hisao, *Myōe,* p. 7), Basanba-entei (Skt. Vasanta-vayantī), the fifty-third *kalyāṇamitra* ("spiritual friend") in the *Kegon-gyō* was believed—undoubtedly by Myōe Shōnin—to be identical with Kasuga no Daimyōjin. The idea was probably familiar also to Gedatsu Shōnin, who alluded to the *Gaṇḍa-vyuha* in both *Kasuga kōshiki* and *Kasuga Daimyōjin hotsuganmon.*

*An ox.* Nakatomi no Sukekata reported in his diary for Bun'ei 2.8.15 (1265) the dream of a certain nun who lived in a noble residence in Kyoto. There lived near this nun an ox-driver who was also in the household's service. The nun dreamed that the man's ox was Kasuga no Daimyōjin. The diary entry suggests that the Kasuga priests were not much taken with this dream, but still felt obliged to go through the motions of discussing it. One is reminded of the black ox of Sekidera who, revealed by a dream as the Buddha Kashō (Skt. Kaśyāpa), became the object of a mass pilgrimage in 1025 (*Konjaku* 12/24).

*Nanda Ryūō.* Nanda Ryūō ("Dragon King Nanda") is one of the Eight Great Dragon Kings who gathered on Vulture Peak to hear the Buddha preach the Lotus Sutra. A fine statue of him at Hasedera is understood traditionally to be Kasuga no Daimyōjin. Dated 1316, the statue is immediately to the pilgrim's left of the temple's famous Jūichimen Kannon; on the right is a sixteenth-century statue of Uhō Dōji, a manifestion of Amaterasu. Clear authority for the identification with Kasuga no Daimyōjin is hard to find. However, a plaque identifies the statue as Kasuga no Daimyōjin to the modern visitor, and Yūgon of Hasedera noted the same tradition in the eighteenth century (Yūgon 1917:133–34).

*Other Dragons.* Kasuga no Daimyōjin's dragon aspect is attested otherwise by various lore, all connected with water. In the Noh play *Kasuga Ryūjin* (discussed in chapter 7), the Kasuga deity in dragon form inhabits Sarusawa Pond before the Great South Gate of Kōfu-kuji. This pond had long been associated with dragons. For example, there was said to be a dragon palace, inhabited by Zennyo Ryūō, under the Central Kondō of Kōfukuji. It was accessible through an entrance located under a *tsuki* tree on the slope between the Great South Gate and the pond (*Kōfukuji ruki,* DNBZa:306b). The monk who wrote *Saisai yōki nukigaki* actually reported, under the date Ōan 3.8.26 (1370), a monster sighted in Sarusawa Pond. That afternoon a whirlwind had lifted the water of the pond a dozen feet into the air, reminding the writer that on one dark night recently, a black body some twenty feet long had risen from the pond and "spewed forth a rainbow."

The most famous dragon legend of Kasuga begins in Sarusawa Pond where, according to *Kōjidan* 5, Zentatsu Ryūō once lived. In the reign of a certain emperor, however, a palace lady, disappointed in love, threw herself into the pond and drowned. (This legend is the basis for the Noh play *Uneme.*) The pond now being polluted with death, the dragon fled to Kōzen (*Genki* 16.4, n. 8) in the Kasuga hills, where a tiny pool has long been associated with dragons and rainmak-ing. Then someone threw a dead body into the pool. The dragon fled to Murō. This site is famous because of the beautiful Murōji, founded in the eighth century by the Kōfukuji monk Kenkei (Inokuma 1963:19). Its sacred character has to do with the dragon cave (*ryū-ketsu*) still honored there. The Zentatsu Ryūō of Murō is also known as Zennyo Ryūō. Nagashima (1944:238) quoted without attribution a document that says, "The Zennyo Ryūō of Murō-zan and Kasuga no Daimyōjin are one in substance, though different in name."

Were dragons ever seen at Kasuga? Hakusen (1779; *kan* 5) re-ported a dream that a Kasuga shrine servant had in Keichō 3.2 (1598). The man entered the shrine precincts and met there three dragon deities (*ryūjin*). One was an old monk, one a manifestation of Yaku-shi, and one a child dragon. They gave the dreamer the *mantra* and the *mudrā* of Yakushi, and told him to offer them daily at the shrine.

*A white fox.* On Tenshō 6.2.15, Eishun, the principal diarist of *Tamon'in nikki,* wrote down a sequence of four dreams. It is not clear that the fox in the third dream is precisely identical with Kasuga no Daimyōjin, but Kasuga is certainly present in all four.

On the night of the 11th, in front of my living quarters' store-house, Myōzen brought me what he said was a picture of Kasuga no Daimyōjin. I could see nothing of what the deity looked like. The night before last, south ... of the East Gate [of Kōfukuji] I saw the evening star and a bright moon rise over Hana-yama [the highest of the Kasuga hills]. Star and moon were the same size. Last night, northwest of the Godaiin [of Kōfukuji] there was a big stone like a wishing-jewel, and I touched it. It was warm. North of the stone lay three large foxes. I picked the white tuft off one's tail, and saw it was a big, white fox. "Wear red," the fox said, "when you bring me offerings." At dawn, then, I got twenty golden relics of the Buddha. As I write down this marvelous sequence of dreams, I shiver again with joy and awe.

## FINAL REMARKS

Wider investigation would surely turn up more forms and more dreams. And who knows how many have been lost? Some of those described here are formal or public, like Kanezane's *Kongō hannya kyō* or the Nanda Ryūō of Hasedera; while some, like the lady's ox or Eishun's white fox, are informal, even casual. All, however, proceed from the complex of knowledge, ideas, images, and beliefs available to those who upheld them; and despite their remarkable diversity, they all refer back to the Kasuga deity, who is difficult enough to disassociate from the Fujiwara clan, and impossible to separate from the place, Kasuga, where he is enshrined.

The notion of place, therefore, appears as fundamental. The religious understanding of all these people, from Kanezane to Eishun, is no doubt hard to grasp as a "creed" or a "philosophy." Any attempt to "systematize" their faith must ignore the *Kongō hannya kyō* and the white fox, on pain of lapsing into unintelligibility. Yet the sutra and the fox are not hard to understand. They are both voices of Kasuga, and their message for the dreamer is simply that he is, or has just been, in direct communication with the divine. But for the place and the dreamer's personal connection *(en)* with it, this communication could not happen at all. Given the connection, however, and the consequent possibility of this communication, an apparent chaos of beliefs, ideas, etc. acquires a heart—a "home"—which could hardly be easier to see. One glimpses here a mode of thought that deserves consideration in any appraisal of Japanese religion and the Japanese mind.

# 7

# Poems and Plays

In Kōan 6.6.25 (1283) the Kasuga deity presided over a poetry competition at the home of the "Former Regent" Mototada and his sons. The *Kanchūki* entry for that date says: "A fifty-round *uta-awase* was held at the Takatsukasa mansion before a picture of the Kasuga Shrine, to which were offered *go-hei*" (Kageyama 1962:86).

One of these sons was Fuyuhira, who wrote out scrolls 6, 7, and 8 of the *Genki*. Later, Fuyuhira had a dream. Kasuga no Daimyōjin appeared in the garden north of the same mansion and gave him a scroll. Fuyuhira commissioned a painting to commemorate the moment, and wrote on it a description of the dream. Dated Shōwa 1.9 (1312), the painting is now in the Fujita Art Museum. The inscription states that the dream occurred "some years ago." The painting shows a gentleman in formal court dress *(sokutai)*, seated in a carriage amid autumn grasses. A cloud decorously hides his divine countenance. Along the top of the painting, in a row, are the five Kasuga *honji*.

Discussing this work, Kageyama Haruki (1962:86–87) noted the *Kanchūki* passage and suggested that Fuyuhira, continuing the tradition of his house, had been praying for skill in poetry. Certainly Fuyuhira must have been very interested in poetry to record so meticulously in his diary (*Fuyuhira kō ki* for Shōwa 4.4.28 [1315] a long set of poems on the Lotus Sutra and the *Yuishiki ron* that various ranking courtiers and monks of Kōfukuji had just offered to the Kasuga Shrine.

Considering how well the Kasuga deity looked after the Fujiwara ladies and gentlemen of the court, it not surprising that he should have been able to guide them in poetry too. But most of the poems that Kasuga may have inspired, or improved, cannot be identified because they do not mention Kasuga at all. They treat all sorts of topics suitable for verse. The Lotus Sutra and *Yuishiki ron* poems of 1315 do not speak of Kasuga; nor do one hundred poems about rain *(Shadan dōei kiu hyakushu waka)*, dedicated to the shrine by the Kasuga priest Kunifuyu precisely in order to pray for rain. Fujiwara no Shunzei's *Shunzei no kyō bunji rokunen gosha hyakushu* (100 poems each on five shrines, written in 1190 and first conceived as a tribute to Kasuga) is generally the same. In this sense the deity's patronage of poetry was a little like his patronage of enlightenment: it transcended the particular.

On the other hand, hundreds of *waka* explicitly celebrate or appeal to Kasuga, which was one of the major *uta-makura* of the poetic tradition. This chapter will describe the main motifs of these poems. The approach is not chronological, but even the few examples chosen suggest that although the Kusaga deity is present in poems of the tenth century, a devotional mood became much more common in the late twelfth, with poets like Yoshitsune, Shunzei, Teika, and Jien. The earlier poems may be very pretty or clever, but some later ones (including many not included here) have a depth, or a sort of authority, not seen earlier. Few poems are cited from the *Man'yōshū* or from the *Man'yōshū* poets, since poetry then was a little different from what it became in more classical times. Poem numbers refer whenever possible to the first three volumes of *Shinpen kokka taikan;* otherwise, references are to *Heian waka utamakura chimei sakuin* (Katagiri 1972).

The chapter will close with a discussion of the four Kasuga Noh plays that appear in *Yōkyoku taikan: Uneme, Saho-yama, Nomori,* and *Kasuga Ryūjin.*

## THE KASUGA LANDSCAPE

Kasuga poetry (poetry that celebrates Kasuga) is founded, like Gedatsu Shōnin's Kasuga faith, upon the landscape of the place. As in the rest of classical Japanese poetry, the landscape features mentioned, the seasons with which they are associated, and the moods they evoke are defined by custom. Much of the poetry is conventional, and poems may differ from one another only by a word or two. Some are dazzlingly ingenious, some touching, some quite beautiful, and many rather close to greeting-card verse. *Heian waka uta-makura chimei sakuin* lists about 600 of them under three main headings: "Kasuga-yama," "Mikasa-yama," and "Kasuga-no." All in all, they leave an agreeable impression. Their sentiments are delicate, their images are lovely, and no tradition could be more thoroughly civilized than the one they represent.

"Kasuga-yama" and "Mikasa-yama" overlap in meaning. "Mikasa-yama" is the more specific term, since it designates only the hill upon which the Kasuga deity descended. "Kasuga-yama" may refer to the same hill or it may cover, more or less clearly, the several "Kasuga hills," including Hana-yama and Kōzen. In any case, both names evoke a mountain realm rather different from "Kasuga-no," the "Kasuga meadows." On Kasuga-no one may come across one's fellow human beings, or glimpse an entrancingly lovely girl; but on Kasuga-yama the wind sings the sovereign's eternal praise, while sun and moon speak of perfection and eternity. No poem alludes to the shrine as a set of man-made structures.

The mountain and the meadows are the Kasuga landscape proper: the landscape of *Kasuga no sato,* an expression poorly rendered in English by "the hamlet of Kasuga." "Hamlet" or "village" seems to insist too much on a cluster of houses. The French *pays* works better, for it evokes more clearly the whole landscape, or world, in which one has grown up. In other words, it conveys, like the idea of Kasuga in the cult and the poetry, a strong feeling of the place where one is at home, and which is therefore eloquent above all others. Kasuga had this value not just because of its association with the Fujiwara clan but also because of its venerable associations with the Nara court.

However, Mikasa-yama, Kasuga-yama, and Kasuga-no are not the whole landscape evoked by Kasuga poetry and the Noh plays. After all, one can look out from *Kasuga no sato* upon the Yamato plain and the hills or mountains that define its borders. Nearby, just to the north, is the low prominence of Saho-yama (now, alas, the site of the amusement park known as "Dreamland"); and between Saho-yama and Kasuga-no flows the Saho-gawa. Saho-yama, like Mikasa-yama, is an ancient *kamunabi,* and appears as such in the body of poetry devoted to it. *Man'yōshū* 10 (no. 1827) has the following:

From Mt. Hagai     *kasuga naru*
in Kasuga     *hagai no yama yu*
yonder over Saho,     *saho no uchi e*
crying, they fly,     *nakiyuku naru wa*
calling whom, the little birds?     *tare yobu kotori*

And *Kin'yōshū* 204 evokes the link between Kasuga and Saho in a manner more typical of Heian verse. The poem is by Minamoto no Tsunenobu (1016–97):

The Kasuga Hills:     *kasuga-yama*
moonbeams rising     *mine yori izuru*
spill from the peak     *tsukikage wa*
to the Saho river shallows     *saho no kawase no*
and shine as ice.     *kōri narikeri*

Being on the *east* side of the Yamato plain, the direction of sunrise, Saho and Kasuga both evoke spring. Saho-hime is particularly well known as the literary goddess of spring, but a poet at an *uta-awase* in 963 *(Ōwa sannen Koretada no kindachi haruaki uta-awase)* could write of "the Kasuga God who governs spring." The two places being linked, they inevitably complement one another. The unchanging pine is so prominent in Kasuga poetry that it is fair to define the Kasuga color as deep green. A few poems, like *Kokin rokujō* 1390, make the same point with moss. The spring of Saho, on the other hand, is the floating, insubstantial white garment celebrated in the play *Saho-yama:* the mist that clings to the hillsides in early spring.

Saho and Kasuga both have their fall colors, and these too are present in poetry, but they generally defer to a larger pattern. Since Kasuga is overwhelmingly of spring, and Saho too when paired with Kasuga, their autumn is muted. The counterpart spot that allows full celebration of fall is on the *west* side of the Yamato plain, toward the setting sun: Tatsuta-yama, another *kamunabi* and the home of the poetic goddess of fall, Tatsuta-hime. Tatsuta poetry may speak of spring blossoms, but its great theme is the brocade of red leaves carried down from Tatsuta-yama by the waters of the Tatsuta-gawa. The Noh play *Tatsuta* insists that Tatsuta-hime is these red autumn leaves.

Tatsuta does not appear in Kasuga poetry, but since it is the mirror-image of Kasuga, the larger poetic landscape of Kasuga includes it. In that sense the two Tatsuta Noh plays *(Tatsuta* and *Sakahoko)* belong to the same group as *Saho-yama,* etc. It is interesting to note that whereas evergreen Kasuga is distinctly male, white Saho and especially red Tatsuta are, poetically, female. This is another reason to acknowledge their poetic ties to one anther.

Invisible from Kasuga, far to the south, but present to the eye of the imagination, rise the noble peaks beyond Yoshino. They are not absent from the Kasuga landscape, any more than they were from the ambitions of Kōfukuji. For example, Akazome Emon *(Akazome Emon shū* 51) wrote to one who had just become a monk:

> Today I pluck            *kasuga-no ni*
> on the Kasuga meadows     *kyō no wakana o*
> new spring greens,         *tsumu totemo*
> yet still my love          *nao mi-yoshino no*
> goes to the Yoshino mountains.   *yama zo kanashiki*

## THEMES IN KASUGA POETRY: THE MEADOWS

Spring greens *(wakana)* provide the matter of countless Kasuga-no verses. On the 7th day of the 1st month of the year, especially in the time of the Nara court, ladies and gentlemen went forth into the meadows to pick new shoots amid the lingering snow. So in poetry a young man might glimpse a fair face among the gay company, and a fresh love be born; or a lord or lady might tenderly pick a basket of greens for an absent lover. The mingled shapes of meadow and unmelted snow *(yuki no muragie)* might look like the pickers' own long, waving sleeves. Of course not everyone on the meadows that day was as cheerful as the occasion. One might weep secret tears of unrequited longing, as his sleeves "wilted" *(shioru)* in a last flurry of spring snow; another, old already, might feel a jealous pang to see the youth of the *wakana,* unlike his own, renewed. Even this generally lighthearted *wakana* motif could evoke the thought that "new shoots on the Kasuga meadows are the blessings of the God" (Jien, *Shūgyo-kushū* 3066).

The "watchman of the signal fires" *(tobu hi no nomori)* is associated particularly with *wakana* because of *Kokinshū* 19, which calls to this rather mysterious figure, "Come out and look, how many days are left till we pick new greens!" No doubt the link between the shoots and the fires is the verb *moyu,* "sprout" or "burn": a wordplay that supports many a verse. But what were these fires? Fujiwara no Ietaka (*Minishū* 1179) playfully wondered whether they were fireflies, but actually no one seems to have known for sure. *Toshiyori kuden shū* cites only skeptically the explanation that they were signal fires lit on mountaintops in imitation of a classic Chinese practice. The watchman would then have been set to spot them. Perhaps, it is also said, they were fires lit to clear the fields in spring. At any rate, this nameless watchman could wander the meadows in poetry, looking into *nomori no kagami:* the "watchman's mirrors" that were (according once more to *Toshiyori kuden shū*) pools of water left in hollows of the meadows by the rain.

On the first day of the Rat *(ne no hi)* in the 1st month, ladies and gentleman went again into the fields to uproot young pines—a felicitous practice associated with wishes for long and happy life. Verses for the occasion speak seriously of prayers to the deity for "our Sovereign's thousand years" (*Horikawa hyakushu* 28); or evoke unbroken ages with "the little pines of Kasuga, whose branches interlace" *(Sanekata no Ason shū).* The pines may be sprinkled with snow, which then (by the familiar process of "elegant confusion") will look like blossoms—perhaps the "blossoms of a thousand reigns" of Fujiwara no Yoshitsune (*Akishino gessei shū* 1340). And on meadow or mountain, pines may be swathed in the mist *(kasumi)* that rises in spring. In *Kokin rokujō* 627 the poet looks across the Kasuga meadows, to find his love hidden by the mist. The "cloak of mist" of *Sahoyama* appears in this complex poem by Fujiwara no Teika (*Shūi gusō* 2130):

| | |
|---|---|
| Winds down the Mountain | *kasuga-no no* |
| sweep the Kasuga meadows' | *kasumi no koromo* |
| misty cloak afar, | *yamakaze ni* |
| tattered into curling glyphs | *shinobu mojizuri* |
| of the most secret heart | *midarete zo yuku* |

Later on, real blossoms grace the trees, and the shrine priests may add their own gay colors to a wholly uncomplicated picture. This verse is from an *uta-awase* of 921 *(Engi 21-nen Kyōgoku no Miyasun-dokoro uta-awase):*

| | |
|---|---|
| Swift and strong the God | *chihayaburu* |
| whose servants, mingling | *kasuga no nobe ni* |
| with blossoms at Kasuga | *kokimazete* |
| roam the meadows | *hana ka to miyuru* |
| and themselves seem flowers! | *kami no kine kana* |

## THEMES IN KASUGA POETRY: THE MOUNTAIN

Since Mikasa-yama and Kasuga-yama merge in poetry, they can be called simply "the mountain." In *Kasuga mandara,* a celestial orb rises over this mountain, and people wonder whether it is the sun or the moon. Most *mandara* of sacred mountains show both sun and moon. Kasuga poetry suggests that the orb, a cousin of the paradoxical "this shore" and "other shore," is sun and moon at once. As sun, it is the morning sun of spring. *Go-Toba no in shū* 190 has:

| | |
|---|---|
| The morning sun, | *mikasa-yama* |
| brilliant, rising | *izuru asahi no* |
| from Mikasa-yama | *hikari yori* |
| promises in light | *nodoka narubeki* |
| calm, everlasting spring. | *yorozuyo no haru* |

On the other hand, the full moon, in classical poetry, is of fall. Since spring and fall together sum up the round of the year, the orb's nonduality points to an eternal and blessed present. In this verse by Yoshitsune (*Akishino gessei shū* 83), sun and moon merge:

| | |
|---|---|
| The morning sun | *asahi sasu* |
| brilliant in a clear sky | *kasuga no mine no* |
| over the Kasuga hills, | *sora harete* |
| leaves a lingering sign: | *sono nagori naru* |
| the moon of an autumn night. | *aki no yo no tsuki* |

The play *Saho-yama* too speaks of "the spring sun shining with the moon" *(tsuki ni terisou haru no hi).* The nonduality of sun and moon might suggest also that of kami (sun, Ise) and buddhas (moon, India); or of emperor (sun, sovereign) and Fujiwara (moon, minister). These associations are perfectly natural in connection with Kasuga, though they are hard to document clearly.

The famous early poem by Abe no Nakamaro (*Kokinshū* 406), who from China gazed into the heavens and saw "the moon that rose over Mt. Mikasa," helped emphasize the moon. So did the influence of Buddhist imagery that associates enlightenment and the moon, as the verse spoken by the Kasuga deity through Gedatsu Shōnin in *Genki* 16.2 makes particularly plain. In *Kankoku shū* 219, the poet dreams under the Kasuga moon of the "radiant sky of enlightenment" *(satori no sora)*. Images of plenty, linked with harvest time and the moon, are present too, for the Kasuga moon may announce a thousand peaceful autumns (*Shigeie shū* 62) or promise comfort to "a pine in an unknown valley" (*Kin'yōshū* 537, Minamoto no Moromitsu)—that is, to a neglected courtier.

Fall often means sadness, separation, or a sense of loss, linked with the autumn imagery of moon, red leaves, cold rain *(shigure),* and the cry of the stag. These are not absent from Kasuga poetry, however bright the Kasuga spring may be. A poet with his hand stops a red leaf running down the Saho-gawa, and glances up for comfort at the moon over the mountain (Minamoto no Toshiyori, *Sanboku kika shū* 538); another contemplates the fallen Nara, no longer the imperial city, and takes comfort from the same moon (*Akazome Emon shū* 254). The cry of the stag is especially poignant, and of course especially meaningful at Kasuga where the god was present in his messenger. Kyōgoku Tamekane *(Tamekane no kyō shika hyakushu)* offered 100 poems on the stag (or deer) to the Kasuga Shrine. His work evokes the deer in all seasons. This poem by Jien (*Shūgyokushū* 2568) beautifully conveys the autumn mood:

> The stag's cry          *saoshika no*
> pierces one through:   *koe zo mi ni shimu*
> above Kasuga-yama,   *kasuga-yama*
> long awaited, autumn  *aki machietaru*
> in an evening sky.      *yūgure no sora*

These emotions, not unknown elsewhere, are prolonged especially in Kasuga poetry by the sorrow of one to whom life has not yet accorded sufficient recognition. Sanesada, in *Genki* 4.5 and 4.6, no doubt shared such feelings. The reasons for a Fujiwara to appeal to Kasuga for relief are obvioius. Poets who did so, including Fujiwara no Ietaka and Shunzei, often evoked the plight of something "buried," hence unseen or forgotten: the forgotten tree in the valley *(tani no umoregi);* the tree buried under snow *(yuki no umoregi);* plants buried under snow *(uzumoruru yuki no shita gusa);* or a smothered brook *(umoremizu).* And they prayed that divine favor bring them, or at least their posterity, into the light. Ietaka wrote *(Shinkokinshū* 1793):

| Kasuga-yama: | *kasuga-yama* |
| a forgotten tree | *tani no umoregi* |
| in the valley is dying; | *kuchinu to mo* |
| take our lord the news, | *kimi ni tsugekose* |
| wind in the mountain pines! | *mine no umoregi* |

And Shunzei *(Shinkokinshū* 1898), referring particularly to his progeny *(sue),* perhaps specifically Teika:

| On the Kasuga meadows, | *kasuga-no no* |
| down a weed-choked path | *odoro no michi no* |
| a smothered brook: | *umoremizu* |
| may your boon, o god, | *sue dani kami no* |
| at last free its waters! | *shirushi arawase* |

Other poems, or poets, may complain of being cut off from the spring radiance of Kasuga, or from the mountain's spring blossoms. The problem in every case is a feeling of not enjoying that which Mikasa-yama should so abundantly provide: favor, advantage, and protection.

Being the home, in fact the body of the Kasuga deity, Mikasa-yama has a special place in the Kasuga cult, and a special place in Kasuga poetry too. A page of Mikasa-yama poems may at first suggest another explanation, however: the rich possibilities for wordplay offered by the name Mikasa. It is true that many Mikasa verses are straightforward, as the sequence in *Genki* 3.2 shows. But some are so deliciously ingenious that one feels like applauding—not the mountain, but the poet or the tradition that encourages such tiny miracles of cleverness.

The occasion for all this ingenuity is that the *kasa* of Mikasa is also the word for "umbrella." Poems that pun this way on *kasa* usually take *mi* as an honorific prefix ("august umbrella"), although they may also use it as the stem of the verb *miru* ("see"). And since to put up an umbrella, or to hold an umbrella over one's head, is *kasa o sasu,* Mikasa-yama poems favor inflections of the verb *sasu.*

*Sasu* has a wider range of meaning than the one just mentioned, having to do with umbrellas. *Hikari sasu,* "radiating light," is an epithet for *asahi,* "morning sun"; but in this poem (*Sanka shū* 1178), Saigyō linked it discreetly with Mikasa-yama too:

| | |
|---|---|
| Mikasa-yama: | *hikari sasu* |
| radiant with light | *mikasa no yama no* |
| your morning sun | *asahi koso* |
| shines, a bright emblem | *ge ni yorozuyo no* |
| of ten thousand years. | *tameshi narikere* |

On the other hand, *kazu o sasu,* at an *uta-awase,* meant "give points" to a poem; and so a poet at an *uta-awase* in Ōwa 3 (963) wrote that "the Kasuga deity's Mikasa-yama scores points for fall" as well as spring. Since *sasu* can also mean "head for" a destination, Teika could celebrate in a pretty verse (*Shūi gusō* 1882) the gay sleeves of the courtiers who had "headed for Mikasa-yama" with the imperial envoy to the Kasuga Festival. Other meanings appear as well.

Nevertheless, the association of *sasu* with "umbrella" is pervasive. Mikasa-yama in many poems quite frankly shelters the poet from the rain of adversity that otherwise would touch him with sorrow. Among the sorrows of life, those of old age may be evoked with a play on *furu,* the verb for rain "falling" and for "growing old." But the best play is on the "rain" itself, since *ame no shita* means at once "under/in the rain" and "under the heavens" or "in all the world." ("In the rain" and "in the reign" make a nicely consonant pun in English.) A poem from an *uta-awase* of 1050 (Eijō 5.2.6, *Rokujō no saiin uta-awase* 7, by Musashi), evokes the Kasuga Festival to make the intended point:

| | |
|---|---|
| Mikasa-yama: | *mikasa-yama* |
| all my trust | *sashite zo tanomu* |
| goes to Him we feast today, | *kyō matsuru* |
| the God of Kasuga | *kasuga no kami o* |
| in this world of ours/under the rain. | *ame no shita ni wa* |

And Kujō Kanezane (*Shinkokinshū* 1897) gave voice to much the same thought:

| | |
|---|---|
| Could we not trust | *ame no shita* |
| —surely you know?— | *mikasa no yama no* |
| in this world of ours/under the rain | *kage narade* |
| Mikasa-yama, | *tanomu kata naki* |
| we would have nowhere to turn. | *mi to wa shirazu ya* |

So one is not surprised to find a mood of desolation expressed by Kanezane's brother Jien (*Shūgyoku shū* 154) in terms of being far from Mikasa-yama. The poem alludes moreover to the one Nakamaro had written long ago in China:

| | |
|---|---|
| Now I am gone | *sashi-hanare* |
| far from the sheltering | *mikasa no yama o* |
| Mikasa-yama, | *ideshi yori* |
| I am wet with endless rains | *mi o shiru ame ni* |
| acknowledging my lot. | *nurenu ma zo naki* |

Another emblem of lament or triumph for a Fujiwara is wisteria (*fuji*), which grows wild in the Kyoto-Nara area, and which has always been linked with the Kasuga deity's people. Kasuga and Kōfukuji insisted that wisteria grows on the trees of Kannon's paradise (see chapter 4, under "The Nan'endō"), and the shrine precincts in season were perfumed with wisteria. The rich clusters of blossoms swaying in the breeze gave rise to the common image of "wisteria billows" (*fujinami*), which could refer directly to the generations of the Fuji-wara, especially to the dominant "northern house" (*kita no fujinami*). *Shinkokinshū* 1854, already discussed in chapter 4, celebrates the building of the Nan'endō:

| | |
|---|---|
| Now their hall stands | *fudaraku no* |
| on the southern shore | *minami no kishi ni* |
| of Fudaraku, | *dō tatete* |
| how they shall flourish, | *ima zo sakaen* |
| the wisteria billows of the north! | *kita no fujinami* |

The "latest leaves of the wisteria" (*fuji no sueba*) were therefore the present Fujiwara generation, and usually one suffering member of it in particular. A verse in the *Heike monogatari* version of *Genki* 4.3

(spoken by a supernatural emissary from Kasuga) describes them as "dying" *(kareyuku),* and urges them to trust in "the spring sun," namely Kasuga. Teika *(Shūi gusō* 81) addressed this appeal to the mountain:

| | |
|---|---|
| Kasuga-yama: | *kasuga-yama* |
| again wisteria billows | *tani no fujinami* |
| deck the trees of the valley— | *tachikaeri* |
| ah, that I might know | *hana saku haru ni* |
| a blossoming spring! | *au yoshi mo gana* |

Happily, some poets *did* feel they were in bloom. One *(Suetsune shū* 66) acknowledged the wisteria's glorious flowering that made him (he wrote) an old pine covered with blossoms.

It is especially the pine, at least in literature, that supports the wisteria's fragrant profusion. The Noh play *Fuji* develops the image. Since perennial wisteria is the Fujiwara, the evergreen pine often stands for the imperial line, and this value is not absent from Kasuga poetry. (After all, the Fourth Sanctuary was Ise.) But at Kasuga the pine is above all the deity. It is as though every pine on the Kasuga meadows and hills is a *yōgō no matsu.*

The interlaced branches of the pines on the heights *(mine no matsubara),* like those on the meadows, could demonstrate the deity's pledge to keep the succession of happy generations unbroken (Shunzei, *Chōshū eisō* 538). Even as tiny seedlings *(futaba yori)* the pines of Kasuga-yama are "worthy of trust" (Yoshinobu, *Shūi shū* 267). Moreover, the pines of the peak nurture and protect even the sun and moon, which rise through them. Teika wrote *(Shūi gusō* 2085):

| | |
|---|---|
| Kasuga-yama: | *kasuga-yama* |
| the moon rises | *mine no ko no ma mo* |
| through your trees, | *tsuki nareba* |
| and to left and right | *hidari migi ni zo* |
| the God mounts guard. | *kami no mamoran* |

And Fujiwara no Yoshitsune *(Akishino gessei shū* 1394):

| | |
|---|---|
| Immaculate, | *kumori naki* |
| the light of a thousand reigns | *chiyo no hikari wa* |
| rises from the pines | *kasuga-yama* |

of Kasuga-yama:          *matsu yori izuru*
the morning sun.         *asahi narikeri*

No wonder *Genki* 1.1 has "the winds of Mikasa-yama proclaim the Eternal Name." Stirred by these winds, the mountain pines sing the everlasting order of the Fujiwara world. Teika celebrated their voice (*Shūi gusō* 783):

Kasuga-yama:                      *kasuga-yama*
in the blowing wind               *mine no matsubara*
the pine forest on the peak       *fuku kaze no*
sings aloud to the heavens,       *kumoi ni takaki*
its voice eternity.               *yorozuyo no koe*

## THE KASUGA NOH PLAYS

Compared to the poetry or to the stories of the *Genki,* all four Kasuga plays are *late.* Chronologically this is obvious, of course. They belong to the fifteenth century—on the average, a century later even than *Sakakiba no nikki.* What makes the point worth making, however, is their relationship to earlier material. Some writers have assumed that Noh plays speak somehow with the voice of direct religious and ritual experience. Yet this is not quite true. The texts we have were carefully designed to support performances that would please an audience. That is to say, they are concerned less with myth or ritual than with effective theater. Not that they have nothing valid to say about religion, far from it; but their religious messages, if any, should not be confused with the motifs used to convey them.

Excellent as they are, the Kasuga plays—and after all, it was above all Kasuga and Kōfukuji that nurtured early Noh—display a great deal of artifice. For example, *Uneme* appeals to an apocryphal legend that Mikasa-yama was once bare of trees, and in any case appropriates to the Kasuga Shrine another legend (that of the *uneme* lady herself) that originally had nothing special to do with it; *Nomori* features a stage demon beside a pond on the Kasuga meadows that never existed; and the divine lady of *Saho-yama* is as literary as a renaissance Primavera. *Kasuga Ryūjin,* for its part, demonstrates perfectly the danger of taking a Noh play for a primary religious document. However convincing its oracles and its dragon king may sound, they are inventions derived from earlier materials and motifs.

*Uneme.* The word *uneme,* so archaic that the play defines it for the audience, means a lady in service at the imperial palace. This *uneme* (according to *Yamato monogatari* no. 50) fell in love with "the Nara Emperor," and when he failed to respond as she had hoped, drowned herself in Sarusawa pond. The emperor then went to the pond and grieved to see a girl once so fair now lifeless, the sport of the waters *(mokuzu).* In the play, a monk comes from Kyoto to see the sights of Nara and goes straight to the Kasuga Shrine. There he meets a young woman planting trees. She tells him the shrine's history, then invites him to see Sarusawa pond and asks him to pray. She has in mind the unhappy *uneme,* whose ghost she at last admits she is. The major scene of the play ignores her death, displaying her instead (as other lovely ladies are displayed in other plays) as a radiant embodiment of music and dance. The play has taken a romantic old story, much older than the indissoluble marriage of temple and shrine, and updated it to celebrate an idealized pattern (a stereotyped pattern, in fact, however appealing it may be). The closing passage evokes "the Realm at peace, the Four Seas calm," just like *Genki* 1.1. *Uneme,* like *Saho-yama,* identifies Kasuga principally with Amenokoyane and Jizō.

*Saho-yama. Saho-yama* is a spring rhapsody for the stage. It takes place on the first *saru* day in the second month of the year: the day of the spring Kasuga Festival. The poetic seed of the play is a verse by the lady Ise (*Kokinshū* 926):

| | |
|---|---|
| Neither cut nor sewn, | *tachinuwanu* |
| the dress, and inside it, | *kinu kishi hito mo* |
| not a soul— | *naki mono o* |
| why should the maiden of the mountain | *nani yama-hime no* |
| hang her gown to air? | *nuno sarasuran* |

Ise wrote this beneath the waterfall at Ryūmonji, near Yoshino, but the poem does beautifully for the mists of the Kasuga spring.

The play's *waki* is one Fujiwara no Toshiie, who sets out from Kyoto on pilgrimage to the Kasuga Shrine. Gazing out from Kasuga, he notes clouds clinging to the flanks of Saho-yama. When a companion tells him they are not clouds, but simply gowns hung out to air, he wants a closer look. So he climbs the hill. Several maidens greet him, and their leader (the *shite*) shows him her luminous, infinitely fragrant gown. Not cut, not sewn, not woven, a "feather cloak trailing down the wind," it resembles the angel's cloak in *Hagoromo*. In fact, it is a cousin of several other seamless expanses, all of which are magical and speak of blessedly unbroken continuity: the Kasuga moss, the interlaced pines of Kasuga-yama, and the brocade of red fall leaves on the waters of the Tatsuta-gawa.

Having proclaimed that the lady of Saho-yama rules spring, the *shite* now lauds the hill's fall too, and its perfection in all seasons. Her praise of Saho-yama merges into a celebration of Kasuga and the glory of Amenokoyane. At last the light fades, she invites the *waki* to witness "an entertainment under the moon for the deity of Saho-yama," and disappears. In the play's last scene she returns to dance, in her own honor, the resplendent *kagura* of the Kasuga Festival.

*Saho-yama* is the precise counterpart of *Tatsuta,* which ends just the same way. Both plays enlarge elaborately on classic poems, and develop their theme into something like a superb *mandara* painting for the imagination.

*Nomori.* The old story developed in *Nomori* (told in *Toshiyori kuden shū, Shūchū shō,* and other collections of materials on poetry) seems originally to have had no necessary connection with Kasuga, since the place is unnamed. A *nomori,* asked by an ancient emperor (Yūryaku or Tenchi) to look for the emperor's lost hawk, finds the hawk— perched on a high branch—by looking into the sort of pool-mirror already mentioned. The "watchman of the signal fires" being a Kasuga figure, it is not unnatural to place this *nomori* too at Kasuga. Note, however, how thoroughly Kasuga (that is to say, Kōfukuji) annexed the *Uneme* and *Saho-yama* motifs as well.

Having described the pool-mirror(s), *Toshiyori kuden shū* says this mirror is also one that reveals the secrets of the heart. All people were therefore greedy to look into it (like the *waki* in the play), and so fearing to lose the mirror, the *nomori* buried it under a mound. In the play, this mound is the home of a *nomori,* the *shite,* who is actually a demon. The *waki* is a *yamabushi* who asks the *nomori* about a "body of water that must have some story to it"—a rather unlikely elevation of a puddle into a *meisho* ("famous place") of Nara. Upon the already suggestive original material, *Nomori* builds a good story and a superb complex of poetic and philosophical paradoxes, generously ornamented with Kasuga-Kōfukuji rhetoric ("The hues of spring, in Mercy's Works Complete, mantle Mikasa-yama; winds of Fivefold-Consciousness-Only fall visit Kasuga village," etc.). The paradoxes play with outside and inside (the two aspects of the mirror); "I" and the cosmos (the hawk and the *waki*'s "true face"); social high and low (the *nomori* and the emperor); spiritual high and low (supreme knowledge and hell); past and present (the play and the old story); and others too. It is a witty play.

*Kasuga Ryūjin.* This rendering of the material covered also in *Genki* 17.1–18.4 is particularly deceptive because it sounds like a rather straightforward dramatization of a presumably similar original story. Instead, *Kasuga Ryūjin* is totally unlike its sources. The least that can be said is that, as in the case of *Uneme, Saho-yama,* and *Nomori,* the playwright has gathered to the Kasuga Shrine what did not wholly belong to it. Myōe Shōnin, the *waki,* hears from the Kasuga deity not in Kii but at Kasuga where he goes to bid the deity farewell. The medium is not his aunt but Tokifū Hideyuki, a composite character made up from the two priests who accompanied Takemikazuchi to Kasuga from Kashima. (The play reads the second name as "Hideyuki" even though "Hidetsura" is traditional in the Ōhigashi house.) The deity is not the "this old man" of *Kasuga Daimyōjin gotakusen ki* but a dragon. Moreover, the final vision of *Kasuga Ryūjin,* a gloriously festive celebration of the deity, has about the same relationship to the material of *Genki* 18.1 and its sources as the play *Saho-yama* to Ise's poem.

The significance of the dragon is particularly tricky. Gorai Shigeru (1977, 1978b) took him as the aboriginal Kasuga divinity, prior to Takemikazuchi and the rest, and went on to identify him with the Wakamiya. No doubt there is a connection between any dragon god and water, and between the Wakamiya deity and water. But is the dragon of *Kasuga Ryūjin* really an authentic form of the Kasuga deity in any sense?

Of the various manifestations of the Kasuga dragon discussed in chapter 6, none are explicitly connected with the Wakamiya, though of course they do not exclude it. Certainly none of them ever take center stage on behalf of Kasuga the way the one in the play does. Moreover, no dragon is to be seen anywhere in the documents that describe the deity's visitations vouchsafed to Myōe. On the other hand, many Noh plays feature deities in dragon form. Just as the *Kokinshū* greatly restricted the variety of plants, creatures, themes, etc. treated in the *Man'yōshū*, the conventions of Noh reduced still further the variety allowed by the *Kokinshū* tradition. The world of Noh is a world of magnificently ornamented, elementary types. As to deities, the profusion of forms present in the *Genki* and in the rest of Kasuga lore (not to mention the lore of other shrines) would be wholly out of place in Noh. By the fifteenth century, a dragon was an elementary representation of a deity. It therefore seems likely that the dragon of *Kasuga Ryūjin* says less about the Kasuga deity than about the conventions of Noh.

Considering the clear connection between some *Genki* stories and *Senjūshō*, it is interesting that the deity in *Kasuga Ryūjin* should advance arguments not found in the earlier material but present in *Senjūshō*. According to the *ai* (a Kasuga *massha* deity), the deity is deeply disturbed to contemplate the terrible dangers of the journey to India, and insists that since Buddhism is presently dead in India, there is no point in Myōe going at all. These two issues are raised in *Senjūshō* 4/8 and 6/1. The first story tells how a monk from Miidera wanted to go to India, but in Kyushu was turned back by an oracle from Hachiman. Hachiman objected that since Buddhism was dead in India, there was no reason to risk so dangerous a journey. The second story describes Hsüan-tsang's disappointment with India in terms that recall both the first story and *Kasuga Ryūjin*.

## FINAL REMARKS

No doubt there is more to Kasuga literature than the above few poems and plays, the *Sakakiba no nikki* (which follows in chapter 8), and the *Genki* text itself. However, the examples discussed here are enough to confirm what is already clear from the history of the shrine, the temple, and the Kasuga cult: the Kasuga-Kōfukuji world (that is to say, in the language of the time, "the Southern Capital") was a rich center of culture founded upon hallowed traditions, high prestige, and imposing might. Even in its decline, this world, led by the Kasuga *sakaki,* could foster what was to emerge as Noh. Nagashima Fukutarō (1944:291–305) described how Ichijō Kanera took refuge from the Ōnin war at Daijōin, as a guest of his son Jinson, and lived a luxurious life there with all his entourage. (Jinson once groaned in writing about the resulting expense.) Kanera's stay established *renga* in Nara, and the Southern Capital remained a center of *renga* activity through the sixteenth century. Its *waka* tradition too remained alive.

The Kasuga priests naturally practiced the art of poetry, and the best poets among them belonged to the Chidori (Wakamiya) line. Nakatomi (Chidori) no Sukesada (1198–1269), a major *Man'yōshū* scholar of Kamakura times, was also known as a poet and calligrapher. A convenient biography of him and his son Sukekata (1221–82) can be found in Rosenfield (1973:307). Sukekata too engaged in *Man'-yōshū* studies. His son Sukeharu (1245–1324), the sixth chief priest of the Wakamiya, became particularly well known as a poet. Nagashima (1944:288) quoted this verse of his, inspired by the Mongol threat:

| | |
|---|---|
| Waves thundering in | *nishi no umi* |
| from the western sea, | *yosekuru nami mo* |
| take care! | *kokoro seyo* |
| This is the Isle of Yamato | *kami no mamoreru* |
| guarded by the Gods! | *yamato shimane zo* |

Sukeharu's son Sukeomi was not yet thirty when a poem of his was included in *Shin gosenshū*—listed as "anonymous." Sukeomi was so put out that he wrote an elegant and pointed complaint (*Gyokuyōshū* 2453, quoted in Nagashima 1944:289). He evoked the plight of the plover *(chidori)* who, having left his footprints (verses) on Waka shore (the registers of recognized poetry), cries and cries that his name should still be unknown. This retort made him and his house famous, and verses of his were included in several later imperial collections.

# 8

# The Sakaki Leaf Diary

In Jōji 3.12 (1364), fifty-five years after the *Genki* was finished, the Kasuga *sakaki* came again to Kyoto, as so often in the past, to demand justice. Shiba no Takatsune (1306-67), a warlord allied with the Ashikaga, and the constable *(shugo)* of Echizen province, had for some years past appropriated the entire revenue from the great Kawaguchi estate (see *Genki* 2.1). As a result the Yuima-e could no longer be held and, if *Taiheiki* is to be believed, monks at Kōfukuji were starving. The enraged Kasuga and Kōfukuji forces, demanding the estate back, planted the sacred tree before Takatsune's residence. Then an imperial envoy arrived and accompanied the *sakaki* to the Chōkōdō, which by then was its customary station in Kyoto. *Taiheiki* 39 *("Shinboku nyūraku no koto, tsuketari rakuchū hen'i no koto"* and *"Shinboku go-kiza no koto")* tells the story in detail as an episode of those tumultuous times.

Another sort of telling is to be found in *Sakakiba no nikki* ("The Sakaki Leaf Diary," 1366) by the then regent and head of the Fujiwara clan, the celebrated man of letters Nijō Yoshimoto (1320–88). Yoshimoto had addressed personal prayers to Kasuga in the past; and in 1363, in particular, he had prayed successfully to the deity for reappointment as regent *(kanpaku)*, replacing Konoe Michitsugu (Kido 1987:77–79). His *Sakakiba no nikki*, a devotional work that is clearly a gesture of thanks, sums up the Kasuga cult in the fourteenth century. More vividly still than the *Genki*, it evokes mingled decline and lingering vigor.

*Sakakiba no nikki* is not a "diary" at all but a thoroughly literary composition in which Yoshimoto assumes the persona of a nameless old man from the vicinity of Nara. Distressed by recent, gloomy events, the old man comes up to Kyoto. He is present when, suddenly, the Daimyōjin's demand is met; he witnesses the sacred tree's triumphal departure on the return journey to Kasuga (a pageant in which Yoshimoto himself played a key role); and finally he overhears an ancient monk from Kōfukuji wax eloquent to a still more ancient shrine servant about the might, wisdom, and compassion of the deity. The ancient monk does not need to remind his listener—because the "old man" has already reminded his reader—of how the Daimyōjin dealt personally with Takatsune ("the Lay Monk Dōchō"). Already in Jōji 3.10, Takatsune's residence burned to the ground; and, as *Taiheiki* observes, "absolutely everyone agreed that Kasuga no Myojin's curse had done it."

Actually, Takatsune soon rebuilt his mansion elsewhere in the city, but then fell out with his colleagues and the shogun Yoshiakira (1330–67), and was obliged to withdraw back to Echizen. While he was still in favor, no one could or would do anything about the Kasuga complaint. As a result the *sakaki* languished at the Chōkōdō for a dreary two years and nine months. But at last Takatsune himself, in Echizen, gave in, and Kawaguchi was restored to Kōfukuji. The *sakaki* started back on Jōji 5.8.12 (1366). *Sanne jōikki* shows that the Yuima-e was held that year for the first time since 1355.

Most of the events in *Sakakiba no nikki* occur at the Chōkōdō or the Rokujō Palace (Rokujkō-dono). The Rokujō Palace, built in the late twelfth century for Retired Emperor Go-Shirakawa, then passed to Go-Shirakawa's sixth daughter. According to *Kyōto-shi no chimei*, its subsequent history is unclear, except for the fact that it burned down more than once. *Taiheiki* does not mention it, at least not in connection with this affair, but *Sakakiba no nikki* suggests that it was the residence of the regent and head of the clan. If not, it is hard to see why the *sakaki* should on this and other occasions have been taken to the Chōkōdō, the chapel on the grounds of the Rokujō Palace.

This chapter is obviously not a full-scale study of *Sakakiba no nikki*. The translation below is meant only to accompany, and complete, the preceding chapters and the study of the *Genki* itself. The little glosses in parentheses are in the original.

## The Sakaki Leaf Diary

This old man has lived many years at Saho in Kasuga village near the Nara Capital, having property there. That ancient and noble city flourished brilliantly, reign after reign, thanks to a deep trust in Mikasa-yama, but then fell on less happy times.

In the winter of the year before last,[1] the Sakaki journeyed to the Capital. Above the Mountain, now deserted by the God, shone a moon of forlorn reproach. The stag's cry in the forest, the rivulet's trickling murmur beneath the moss—all these voices spoke only of desolation. And perhaps their complaint was heard, for this spring many people were ill, while others had alarming dreams. Those with a little wit groaned that the divine curse was upon them. The heads of deer lay scattered in street and avenue, and an eyeless, noseless [human] head appeared, no one knew from where, in the garden of the Rokujō Palace. These were troubling events indeed.

They say the mind of the Gods is very like our own. The Kasuga God does not send instant chastisement, but surely there has never been a time when those who offend the Divine Will have not come in the end to grief. So during the Tokuji years,[2] when the Daikakuji Cloistered Emperor (Go-Uda) ordered the progress of the Sakaki stopped, there promptly came—or so they say—an oracle, and the God spoke a most distressing verse. And soon the oracle's meaning was made plain by events. Now, too, people were wondering what was to come next. Perhaps they realized that what had befallen the Lay Monk Dōchō might happen again, today or tomorrow. Surely selfish willfulness had caused all the trouble. Such, at least, was the whispered speculation, and one had to agree that there was reason for it.

This old man set out on a journey hateful to one already so near the summit of great age, and made a pilgrimage to the Chōkōdō. His thoughts went to the God, lodged in this unaccustomed, temporary dwelling, and he could not keep himself from weeping. Yes, the God's own Shrine was fine and lively, but here the ruinous old temple hall was falling to pieces, and the eaves, which let even moonlight through, were thick with *shinobu-gusa*.[3] Fading insect cries sounded here and there among the dying weeds of the neglected grounds, evoking poignantly the sadness of an autumn evening at the Shrine in the Fields.[4] Within makeshift shelters and screens, forty or fifty Shrine priests huddled together against the gathering chill of the night air.

What an endless stay, so far from home! The God's complaint, these three years, had gone unheard. And when, then, would human sorrows—those of His people—resolve themselves into smiles? Lately this old man, praying before the Sacred Presence in the Nan'endō, had said bitterly, "All this can only end in disaster." Events had shown that the Divine Oath, voiced in the oracle, was not without power.

But in one night the turmoil in the Capital was over, and Nara's complaint received full satisfaction. The Divine Presence had suffered not the slightest indignity. His return to Kasuga was set for the 12th day of the 8th month, and the Capital was abuzz with the glad news. Now the clouds that had veiled the heavens dispersed, and the rank weeds that once choked the heart were gone as though they had never been.

In two or three days, some ten or twenty thousand *shuto* and shrine servants came up to the Capital. They filled all the roads and gathered at Nunobiki.[5] On the day itself, the Capital was bursting. Sightseers, doddering old men, servant girls, menials, and strolling entertainers, all raced as fast as their legs could carry them to the Rokujō Palace.

The *shuto* assembled at Rokujōin.[6] At nightfall it began to rain, which for a time broke the happy mood. Then sensible people recalled that in Kōan and Shōwa[7] the weather had been just the same, but that when the moment had come for the Sakaki to set off, the sky had cleared beautifully. Surely this time would be no different.

When the senior nobles took their places, enough rain was still falling to wet their robes. But then the rain stopped, though the sky remained overcast, and this sign was received by one and all as revealing the God's august wish. At the hour of the Dragon,[8] Tsugufusa, the Kangakuin Adviser, made his way to the Chōkōdō to report on how things were going. The *shuto* and shrine servants finally gathered and lined up in serried ranks over six or seven *chō*, starting in the Rokujō Palace grounds. At the hour of the Snake[9] the Deputy Superintendent, Provisional Grand Prelate Kaiga, led thirty or forty ranking monks to the north side of the east garden. The *shuto* were closely packed along the east side. Precisely at the hour of the Snake, His Excellency the Regent arrived. The group of Shrine priests then came together in front of the gate. However, the cortege was not yet ready, and so His Excellency first entered the Chōkōdō, summoned Tsugufusa, and gave him various orders. The Daijōin Prelate, and others after him, were sent to deliver them.

At the hour of the Horse,[10] Their Excellencies the Minister of the Left (Fuyumichi), the Kujō Major Counselor (Kimimoto), the Ichijō Major Counselor (Fusatsune), and the Superintendent (Chūkō) arrived and took their places among the senior nobles along the south side of the east garden. With everything now ready, His Excellency the Regent took his own place. All the Nara monks stepped down from their seats and prostrated themselves to him—no doubt a special tribute to the present Head of the Clan.[11]

The seats of the Ministers and other nobles were just one mat each, with a Korean border, while the Regent's seat was two mats, one laid upon the other. This was apparently to mark the transcendent rank of the Head of the Clan—a lord who had been present also in Ryakuō,[12] as Palace Minister. This time, pleased with the present Palace Minister's advice, he presented the gentleman with a robe.

Next the Daijōin Prelate appeared with his attendants in glittering array. The Departure was now at hand, and the *shuto* formed their ranks. The God's discontent had been entirely dispelled. The Regent, and all the people of the Clan below him, joined the sacred cortege. The might of our God surpasses that of all others, and promises endless prosperity to both the courtly and the military houses.[13] On that, all are agreed.

Now the musicians advanced from the north side of the garden, playing *Ranjō*. As the Sacred Treasure of Furu[14] descended the eastern steps, the Regent and all his gentlemen stepped down from their seats and knelt. Once Furu had passed by, the Kasuga Sakaki and the True Bodies[15] of the Five Sanctuaries came forth. The priest-bearers' faces were covered. Then the musicians began *Genjōraku*. The warning cries[16] were eerily impressive. The Regent and his nobles, and the monks themselves, all touched their foreheads to the ground and prostrated themselves full-length. The senior nobles resumed their seats when the Sakaki reached the middle gate, then one by one joined the cortege.

The composition of the cortege is always the same, but I note it here as I myself witnessed it. First came several scores of page boys in red, in twin files, carrying white staffs; then several hundred white-robed shrine servants bearing sakaki branches; then the Sacred Treasure of Furu no Daimyōjin, accompanied by several hundred shrine servants; then several hundred yellow-robed shrine servants; then the True Bodies. The priest-bearers wore formal dress,[17] with the cloth of their hoods hanging loose. Several hundred shrine servants followed them. The musicians in the cortege played on and on.

The Regent wore white over green, with *itogutsu* shoes. Ten attendants preceded him, since he feared [direct contact with] the sacred procession. One or two courtiers held his train, and four more attendants followed him.

Next came the Minister of the Right (Sanetoshi), with a courtier (the Commander of the Palace Guards) and two attendants; then the Imadegawa Major Counselor (Kiminao); then the Kazan'in Major Counselor (Kanesada). Their costumes glowed with color. The Kujō Major Counselor and the Ichijō Major Counselor followed, with the Bōjō Middle Counselor, the Shijō Middle Counselor, and the Superintendent behind them. One had seen all this before, yet their entourage still looked wonderfully imposing. Next came the Saionji Middle Counselor, the Shijō Consultant, and the Tōin Consultant and Middle Captain.

The courtiers followed. Lord Tadayori held the Regent's train, while Lord Suemura accompanied the Minister of the Left, Lord Chikatada the Regent, and Lords Tsugufusa and Motonobu the Ichijō Major Counselor. Nobukata, Sukeyasu, Nakamitsu, Muneaki, Tameari, and Kanetoki were with the Kujō Major Counselor. Next came the senior monks, then the Deputy Superintendent and the rest of the ranking monks, among whom walked the Daijōin Prelate, looking very dignified.

Now came the press of ten or twenty thousand *shuto*, blowing conches. It was terrifying how they threw stones at the viewing stands, on next to no provocation, but apparently this is the way they always behave. Normally, of course, some people watch events like this one from their carriages, but in this case the practice had been forbidden. The police had been informed accordingly. Unfortunately, however, two or three carriages were nonetheless standing along the route. I hear the *shuto* ruthlessly demolished them. One wonders who their occupants can have been. What awful conduct!

It seemed to an ordinary onlooker that the number of senior nobles participating was not as great as on past occasions of this kind. Still, it was not unimpressive.

At the hour of the Monkey[18] the sky cleared, and the late afternoon sun on the Sakaki displayed the mirrors just as they must have looked long ago, on Kagu-yama.[19] The sight was unspeakably awe-inspiring, and the warning shouts of the shrine servants, too, filled one with eerie intimations. I have seen the gleaming sacred cars[20] at Festival time, but now the intensely green, spreading Sakaki branches seemed the Mikasa Grove[21] itself. The sight inspired holy dread, till all one's hair stood on end. The least serving girl wept to hear the music, which never paused as the cortege moved on. It was a joy to watch today, with my hand to my forehead [to shade my eyes]. Our Regent and Ministers shared the same gladness as they strode along the avenue. Yes, it was all quite wonderful!

There was no viewing stand for the Retired Emperor this time, so the noise and commotion were tremendous. But the Shogun (Yoshiakira) was watching from a viewing stand he built at Sixth Avenue, and everyone took more care as they passed him. Magnificently decked out, the Shogun and his entourage gave further luster to the scene. The fact that all consultations with him today went so smoothly can only strengthen his prospects for good fortune in war. [ . . . ][22]

This old man had come a very long way already, having reached the Rokujō Palace that morning at the hour of the Rabbit.[23] I was resting a while at a back door, exhausted, when I heard a shrine servant who looked at least ninety, and a monk over eighty (apparently a temple official), talking together. They were telling each other stories about all the inspiring events of the Shrine, since the earliest times. I do not hear very well any more, so I could not catch everything they said, but I noted down what I could.

This is what the monk said. "It's quite wrong to think that our Kasuga no Daimyōjin is just like any other deity. After all, He sees to the running of this land of ours. That's because the Grand Shrine of Ise, Hachiman, and the Daimyōjin of Kasuga—those three—select both our Sovereign and his Ministers according to their merit. Hachiman Daibosatsu is Emperor Ōjin, so the Human Sovereigns appear much later on as Gods.

"It was Ise and Kasuga's idea to establish our Central Land of Reed

Plains. There lived in the Heavens, of old, a divinity named Taka-sumera-musubi-mitama-no-mikoto who did not descend to earth, but simply ruled all things from on high. He brought up the August Grandson of the Great Heaven-Illumining Deity; and when He sent Him down to this Land of Reed Plains, the Heaven-Illumining Deity gave Her Grandson three treasures. These were the Eight-Span Mirror (now in the Naishidokoro); the Yasaka-ni-no-magatama (now in the Imperial Seal Chest); and the Kusanagi-no-tsurugi (now the Imperial Sword). Having received these three, He had Amenokoyane-no-mikoto accompany him down to Mt. Takachiho in Hyūga province of Tsukushi.

"The Gods praised Amenokoyane-no-mikoto as having a form like the sun, a mind like the sea, and virtue like the earth. So the Great Heaven-Illumining Deity made him a solemn promise, saying, 'My descendants shall rule over this Central Land of Reed Plains. Yours, generation after generation, shall take in hand the affairs of government, shall set their couches side by side with those of mine, shall dwell in palaces equal to those of mine, and so shall assist my own descendants.' No rift has ever, since that time, divided Sovereign from Minister, no more than a barrier parts fish from water. The two are as mutually responsive as wind and cloud.

"This, then, is when [Amenokoyane-no-mikoto] began to protect our land and assist our Sovereign. He is the present Third Sanctuary of Kasuga, and the ancestor of the Regents. So even in these latter times, no one not descended from the Grand Shrine of Ise has ever attained the imperial dignity—an outstanding proof that ours is a divine land. In China, persons of the most varied extraction have risen to that height—in fact, I hear that now a Mongol sits on the throne. Since even ordinary people keep their promises, how much more trustworthy is the promise a God made to a God! Why, it is like Heaven and Earth themselves. The Wise Kings and Wise Ministers of our land enjoy special blessing. And if strange, rebellious ministers are instantly banished afar, we have no power to thank for that but the Daimyōjin of Kasuga.

"After the Kamakura Major Captain of the Right, in Juei, sank the Imperial Sword in the Western Sea,[24] he became in recompense the protector of the Imperial House, and quelled the enemies of Realm and Court. When he raised a righteous host in Jishō 4,[25] at the very start of his rise, he offered land to the Grand Shrine; and after that he saw all his ambitions fulfilled. That's why in Yamato, alone of all the provinces, he appointed not a single steward, but instead offered the province to the Kasuga Shrine. In this he displayed true understanding of the events of the Age of the Gods, and a sound grasp of current affairs.

"Hachiman and Kasuga, having both sworn to dwell on an upright head, forever protect the posterity of those who have brought peace to the realm. Obviously those who merit the name of Sage, but even those too who deserve simply to be called Wise, don't look first to their own advantage; and no doubt that's why the land subsides into peace [in their presence], and why the people [under their reign] are untroubled. It's just the same as when the Buddha came into our world and took pity on all sentient beings. They say He taught in the sutras that after His passing He would become a great God in Enbudai,[26] and would guide sentient beings everywhere. I shouldn't talk about things I don't really know, but that's what my old teachers used to say. And since Kasuga no Daimyōjin, especially, has Jizō Bosatsu for His *honji,* the compassion He offers people is bottomless. The late Posthumous Minister of the Left (Takauji) believed this deeply, and wrote it every day, and so was naturally attuned to the Divine Will. Surely that's why he was able to take the realm in hand for himself and his successors. How extraordinary it all is, when you think about it!"

He went on like this for some time, but I am forgetful in my old age, and must have left out a lot of what he said. Then the shrine servants began to clear out everyone who did not belong there, and to curtain off the spot. Since they were rather rough and frightening about it I left immediately, but I am sure the subject was still far from exhausted.

1. 1364.

2. 1306–7.

3. A plant well known, especially in poetry, to grow in the neglected thatch of old buildings, and to encourage fond memories *(shinobu)* of the past.

4. An allusion to a passage in the *Tale of Genji.*

5. Perhaps a spot near Kiyomizudera, whose waterfall (Otowa no taki) was also known as Nunobiki no taki.

6. A mansion that once belonged to the poet and religious official Ōnakatomi no Sukechika (d. 1038), and which had a famous garden.

7. 1278–88 and 1312–17.

8. Ca. 7–9 A.M.

9. Ca. 9–11 A.M.

10. Ca. 11 A.M.–1P.M.

11. Exactly the same thought is expressed in the *Taiheiki* account, which in other ways too is very like *Sakakiba no nikki* here. There is clearly a close connection between some parts of the two texts.

12. 1338–42.

13. The Fujiwara and the Ashikaga.

14. The deity of Isonokami, who always accompanied the Kasuga deity on *shinboku dōza* expeditions.

15. *Mishōtai:* mirrors, perhaps incised with an outline drawing of the corresponding *honji,* hung in the branches of the sacred tree.

16. *Keihitsu,* warning cries made ceremonially by members of the procession to clear the road and, no doubt, to turn away all evil powers.

17. *Sokutai,* the costume for formal court occasions, and the one most commonly worn by the Kasuga deity in dreams.

18. Ca 3–5 P.M.

19. An allusion to the famous story briefly described in *Genki* 1.1, n. 7.

20. *Mikoshi.* The festival is the *Kasuga matsuri,* discussed in chapter 3 under "Rites, festivals, and offerings."

21. *Mikasa no mori* is not a actually a place-name, but evokes images of the deity's presence in a primordial sacred grove.

22. I cannot make out one short sentence.

23. Ca. 5–7 A.M.

24. Minamoto no Yoritomo's forces finished the Taira at Dannoura in 1185, and the imperial sword was believed to have gone to the bottom of the sea with the child emperor Antoku.

25. 1180.

26. Skt. Jambudvīpa, the continent where humans live.

# Part Two

# The Miracles of the Kasuga Deity

Contents

Graduate Kyōei
The Daijōin Grand Prelate
The Kii Superior
Shōzō
Scroll 16 (The Former Regent)
The Venerable Gedatsu
Shōen
Scroll 17 (Grand Prelate Ryōshin, Ichijōin)
The Venerable Myōe
Scroll 18 (as above)
(as above)
Scroll 19 (Lord Fuyumoto)
The Sacred Mirrors in the Shōan Era
Scroll 20 (as above)
The Spirit Fires of the Kagen Era

*Paintings:* Ukon no Taifu and Shōgen Takashina no Takakane, Director of the Office of Painting.[1]

*Text:* The Former Regent and his three sons,[2] zealous to honor the Deity, vowed that in order to ensure the efficacy of their work,[3] no outside brush should be involved.[4] The material was selected by Hōin Kakuen,[5] in consultation with the two former Major Grand Prelates Jishin[6] and Hanken.[7]

## {Prefatory Note}

As a descendant of the Fujiwara ancestors, I place my trust entirely in the protection of this Shrine. Unable to restrain my zeal to honor the Deity, I have gathered this collection together to the best of my ability, so as to increase the faith of all men. Now that the work is in its final form, I have only to add these words. After I conceived this gesture of devotion, great good fortune blessed my house, and by this I knew that my plan had met with divine approval. May those who come after me be inspired by it to ever greater reverence and faith!

Engyō 2.3 (1309)

## The Minister of the Left (cipher)

1. Takakane (fl. 1309–30) may also have painted the first three scrolls of *Ishiyama-dera engi emaki*, as well as parts of *Hossō-shō hiji ekotoba* and *Genjō Sanzō emaki*. "Ukon no Taifu" indicates that he held the fifth rank and was an officer in the right inner palace guards. "Shōgen" is a title applied to third-level officers in various agencies including the guards. The office of painting *(edokoro)* was an agency of the imperial household. Takakane held there the title of *azukari*.

2. The "Former Regent" is Fujiwara (Takatsukasa) no Mototada (1247–1313), the son of Takatsukasa no Kanehira. He was regent *(kanpaku)* 1268–73. As indicated by the "Contents," he copied out scrolls 1–5, 9–13, and 16. (2) Fuyuhira (1275–1327), Mototada's eldest son, was regent *(sesshō)* 1308–11. He copied out scrolls 6–8. (3) The second son, Fuyumoto (1275–1309), who copied scrolls 14 and 15, died on Engyō 2.6.29 just before the *Genki* was dedicated. He was a provisional major counselor at the time. (4) Ryōshin (1277–1329), the fourth son, was head of Ichijōin, and by 1309 held the rank of major grand prelate. He served four times as superintendent: nine months in 1307, about two years in 1310–12, one year starting in 1316, and about three years in 1323–26. Ryōshin copied out scrolls 17 and 18.

3. *Kechien no tame:* to strengthen, by their gesture, the bond between the deity and his people, the Fujiwara clan.

4. In other words, that no part of the text should be written out by a non-Fujiwara. This decision recalls, for example, the prohibition against non-Fujiwara going beyond the Chakutō-den at the time of the Kasuga Festival (Miyai 1978:95–96).

5. Kakuen (1277–1340), a son of the chancellor Saionji Sanekane, was therefore a younger brother of Kinhira. He was the head of Tōbokuin, an important subtemple founded by a son of the Takasue mentioned in *Genki* 7.4, and which was allied with Ichijōin (Nagashima 1944:172). Kakuen was superintendent twice, in 1319 and 1336.

6. Jishin (1257–1325) was a son of Ichijō Sanetsune, and so a grandson of Kujō Kanezane. The head of Daijōin, he was appointed superintendent six times (1281, 1286, 1291, 1294, 1300, 1323), though his longest term was less than two years and his shortest only a few days.

7. Hanken (1247–1339), the son of Hōin Sonken, succeeded to his father as head of Sanzōin, a Kōfukuji subtemple founded by Zōshun. He was also the adopted son of Fujiwara (Nakamikado) no Munemasa (1217–69), who held the third rank and served as consultant *(sangi)*. Hanken was superintendent five times (1299, 1302, 1307, 1313, 1327) but was never in office much longer than half a year.

## *1.1 (No Title)*

In Kasuga no Daimyōjin the Nyorai of the full moon's bright orb has tempered the effulgence of His eternal enlightenment;[1] in Him the perfectly awakened Satta, the Cloud of the Teaching, has veiled the radiance of His inner realization of the Source.[2] Being a God purely devoted to the Realm, He vigilantly protects the peace and calm of the Four Seas.

When the Celestial Scion and Sovereign Lord[3] first entered the Central Land of Reed Plains, evil deities blocked His way, but Heaven hurled down a jewel-sword and slew them.[4] When Ōnamuchi no Mikoto and Kotoshironushi no Mikoto endangered Amaterasu no Ōmikami,[5] Futsunushi (Katori) and Takemikazuchi no Mikoto (Kashima) went to suppress the rebels, who then surrendered the spear of sovereignty over the land.[6]

When [Amaterasu no Ōmikami] pushed open the door of the Celestial Rock Cave, She illumined the darkness that had engulfed the world, and so relieved the people's distress.[7] This means that She and [Ameno]koyane no Mikoto are conjoined in profound union, and likewise that the Grand Shrine of Ise is manifest in the Fourth Sanctuary.[8] Therefore the flow of the Mimosuso River bears aloft the Countenance of a Thousand Autumns, and the Imperial Seat is secure;[9] while the winds of Mikasa-yama proclaim the Eternal Name, investing with great dignity the bond between [the Emperor and] the Regent.[10]

The source of this bond is as follows. Anciently in our Realm, demons and evil deities warred incessantly with one another, leaving neither town nor country at peace. Moved to pity, Takemikazuchi no Mikoto descended from Heaven[11] onto Shiogama shore in the province of Mutsu,[12] and the evil deities, awed by the divine majesty, either fled or surrendered. Then He moved from the [miscreant] deity's shrine to Kashima, both being in Hitachi province.[13] At last in the spring of Jingo-keiun 2, He went on to Mikasa-yama in order to protect the Hossō Teaching.[14] There He sports among the triple-nature, fivefold spring blossoms, and delights in the eight-gate, double-awakening autumn moon.[15]

Akitsusu[16] has many mountains and plains, but their moonlight does not equal Mikasa-yama's; nor are their blossoms as deliciously fragrant as the ones on the Kasuga meadows.[17] "Come and enjoy these blossoms and this moon," said Takemikazuchi no Mikoto to the two Gods of Katori and Hiraoka; and so they appeared there in the winter of the same year. The power of this divine presence has lived on ever since, and each day brings fresh boons. Hence all its wonders ever recorded or witnessed, in past or present, have been included here without emendation, and modestly depicted also in paintings. The work's only aim has been to foster heartfelt devotion.

COMMENT. The notes to this rather elliptical introduction will acknowledge some of the comments made on it by Tayasu Munetake (1715–71), who commissioned the copy of the *Genki* now known as the *Kasuga-bon*. Munetake could not bring himself to leave it in its place at the head of the work, and relegated it instead to a separate scroll that includes his own remarks. He found the passage "exceedingly unfortunate" *(hanahada tsutanashi)*, and riddled with errors.

1. In other words, the Kasuga deity manifests locally, for the benefit of sentient beings, the Buddha's eternal enlightenment; and his first concern is the welfare of the realm ("the Four Seas"). Nyorai (Skt. Tathāgata) is the title of the Buddha, while Satta (Skt. Sattva) means an exalted being.

2. *Naishō honji. Naishō* ("inner realization") is discussed in the tenth fascicle of the *Jōyuishiki ron. Honji* suggests *honjishin* (Skt. *dharmakāya*), the enlightenment that is the source and fruition of all things; but here it refers also to the "original ground Buddhas" *(honji-butsu)* of the Kasuga deity. According to the opening passage of *Shasekishū*, "The Celestial Rock Cave is the Tosotsu Heaven, also known as the High Plain of Heaven. . . . Tosotsu means the dharma-realm *(hokkai)* of inner realization *(naishō)*. . . . [The Buddha Dainichi] came forth from the Capital of Inner Realization and manifested his trace in Japan." Moreover, Gedatsu Shōnin in *Kasuga kōshiki* (p. 217) contrasted *naishō honji* with *gegen no gyōsō* ("the aspect of outwardly manifested works"), an expression that recalls the Kasuga deity's "bosatsu name" (see *Genki* 1.2); and he named the *naishō honji* as Shaka, Yakushi, Jizō, Kannon, and Monju—his preferred list of the five Kasuga *honji*. The language in this passage all points to Dainichi and especially Shaka, in keeping with the interpretation favored by Gedatsu Shōnin.

3. Amatsuhiko-ame-no-sumeramikoto. Probably Ninigi, the grandson of Amaterasu. *Kasuga go-ruki* takes him to be Ninigi, since a note at this place in the text reads, "This deity reigned 318,542 years in Hyūga province." Tayasu Munetake assumed the same thing, but he objected to this unheard-of designation for Ninigi, and pointed out that nothing in *Kojiki* or *Nihon shoki* connects Ninigi with a story about Heaven hurling down a sword. The other possibility is Emperor Jinmu.

4. Although Ninigi "entered the Central Land of Reed Plains" (Japan), the only similar event in the mythology happened instead to Jinmu. According to *Nihon shoki*, Jinmu was proceeding northward from Kumano to Yamato when "the Gods belched up a poisonous vapor" that immobilized Jinmu's army. Then one Takakuraji dreamed he heard Amaterasu telling Takemikazuchi to go down to the Central Land of Reed Plains and quell the disturbance. Takemikazuchi replied that he would send down his sword, then told Takakuraji that he would place this sword in Takakuraji's storehouse. "Do thou take it and present it to the Heavenly Grandchild," he added. Takakuraji did so, and Jinmu was able again to advance. (*Nihon shoki*, NKBT:1:194-95; Aston 1972:115.) *Kojiki* has a similar account. But if Jinmu is meant, why does the next sentence refer to a long time before Jinmu—in fact, to a time before Ninigi's own descent?

5. For Ōnamuchi and Kotoshironushi, see n. 6. *Nihon shoki* and *Kojiki* say nothing about their ever having "endangered" the Sun Goddess Amaterasu; nor does such a Kasuga document as *Koshaki*. Munetake maintained that the idea was nonsense. Since Amaterasu never descended to earth at all, this sentence may simply telescope Amaterasu and her claim of ultimate dominion over the land.

6. *Nihon shoki* (NKBT:1:138-39; Aston 1972:68–69). Ōnamuchi ruled the Izumo region. When Takemikazuchi and Futsunushi went down to obtain his allegiance to Ninigi, Ōnamuchi consulted his two sons. Kotoshironushi, the elder, consented; but the younger one refused and was slain by Takemikazuchi.

7. *Nihon shoki* (NKBT:1:112 ff; Aston 1972:41). Angered by the behavior of her brother, Susanoo, Amaterasu had hidden herself in a cave so that the world was plunged in darkness. Amenokoyane played a major role in getting her to come out again.

8. Munetake found the meaning of this sentence absurd, although it is perfectly normal for the Kamakura period.

9. The Mimosuso River flows past the Inner Shrine at Ise. The idea that its eternally renewed waters bear aloft the Countenance of a Thousand Autumns (the emperor's eternally renewed face) evokes the image of the moon reflected in water. The metaphorical role of the river in this passage seems to be that of the Fujiwara clan.

10. Classical poetry alludes to the pines of Mikasa-yama as emblems of timelessness, sometimes of the imperial glory, and sometimes of generations of the Fujiwara. The "Eternal Name" proclaimed by the wind blowing through them is that of the endlessly renewed imperial line.

11. *Nihon shoki* (NKBT:1:138; Aston 1972:68) mentions the uproarious disorder that reigned in the Central Land of Reed Plains before Ninigi's descent; and it describes how Takemikazuchi and Futsunushi descended to Izumo, received the submission of Ōnamuchi, destroyed the "evil deities," and returned to Heaven to report on their mission. On the whole, though, Futsunushi's role is stressed more than that of Takemikazuchi, whereas here Takemikazuchi alone is mentioned.

12. *Nihon shoki* gives several variant accounts of the two gods' expedition. In one (NKBT:1:151; Aston 1972:81), after Ōnamuchi's surrender, "Futsu-nushi no Kami appointed Kunado no Kami as guide, and went on a circuit of pacification. Those rebellious to his authority he put to death, while those who rendered obedience were rewarded." Their "circuit" may well have taken them to Shiogama, but the place is not mentioned. *Shun'ya shinki,* however, states (ST:188) that Kashima, Katori, and Sakado, three brothers, descended from the sky onto Shiogama shore in Mutsu. Herbert (1967:351) reported a tradition that "Take-mika-dzuchi and Futsu-nushi, in their tour of pacification around the country, took with them as a guide, not Funado [or "Kunado"] but Shio-tsuchi-no-oji-no-kami," the local Shiogama deity; and that "the three Kami stopped at eighteen different places in Japan, and that the last one, where their journey ended, was precisely Shiogama." The Shiogama Shrine honors Takemikazuchi and Futsunushi.

13. According to *Nihon shoki* (NKBT:1:135/on 1972:65), before Takemikazuchi and Futsunushi were sent down to suppress the unruly deities, another divinity, Ame-no-waka-hiko, was charged with the same task. However, Ame-no-waka-hiko married

an earthly deity, settled down, and never carried out his mission. Finally the heavenly deities sent down a pheasant to find out why he had not returned. Ame-no-waka-hiko shot the pheasant and his arrow continued on up to heaven, whereupon Takamimusubi (or Amaterasu) hurled the arrow back and killed him. There is no mention in all this of Takemikazuchi or Kashima. However, the *Koshaki* version of the story is quite different.

*Koshaki* (ST:4) claims that Susanoo was conspiring with "the evil deities of Kashima" to make trouble, and that Takemikazuchi proposed to Amaterasu that the rebels should be suppressed. Accordingly Amaterasu sent down Ame-no-waka-hiko, with the same results as above. When the miscreant's arrow reached heaven, Takemikazuchi got permission to go down to earth himself. He descended riding a heron, accompanied by eight dragon deities in the form of eight cranes, and on arrival killed all the rebels. When he returned to heaven, the pleased Amaterasu told him that his descendants would "ride in a golden phoenix carriage," and gave him Kashima as his domain.

The *Koshaki* version certainly explains Takemikazuchi's presence at Kashima. But what can "He moved from the [miscreant] deity's shrine *(ato no yashiro)* to Kashima, both being in Hitachi province," refer to? Perhaps this shrine is that of Ame-no-waka-hiko, whom Takemikazuchi had just killed. The shrine would have been Ame-no-waka-hiko's *ato,* that is, the spot or "trace" infused with his presence. In *Koshaki,* at least, Ame-no-waka-hiko had clearly settled in Hitachi, near Kashima.

14. The date is 768. Mikasa-yama is the name of the sacred hill at Kashima, and the name was transferred from there to Kasuga, as *Koshaki* points out.

15. These epithets for the blossoms and moon are all technical terms in Hossō philosophy. (1) The "three natures" *(sanshō)* are the three categories into which Hossō thought divides the fundamental character of all things. They are expounded in the *Yuishiki sanjūron* (Skt. *Triṃsikā-vijñapti*) by Seshin (Skt. Vasubandhu), the basic Hossō text. The significance of each is being *(u),* nonbeing *(mu),* and provisional reality *(kejitsu).* (2) "Fivefold" is an abbreviation of "fivefold consciousness-only" *(gojū yuishiki),* the five levels of meditation on the principles of consciousness-only, the basic concept of Hossō thought. (3) The "eight gates" *(hachimon)* are the eight headings under which Shōkatsurashu (Skt. Saṃkarasvāmin), in his *Inmyō nisshōri ron* (Skt. *Hetuvidyā-nyāya-praveśa*) explained the content of Jinna's (Skt. Dignāga) *Inmyō shōrimon ron* (Skt. *Hetu-vidyā-nyāya-dvāra*). Jinna's treatise is a fundamental text of the school of logic based on the *Yugashiji ron* (Skt. *Yogācāra-bhumi*) by Mujaku (Skt. Asaṅga). (4) Shōkatsurashu divided the "eight gates" into two modes of awakening *(nigo):* "self-awakening" *(jigo)* and "awakening to others" *(gota).*

16. Japan.

17. Kasuga-no, the slightly sloping, still uneven ground at the foot of Mikasa-yama, east of Kōfukuji and south of Tōdaiji.

SIGNIFICANT VARIANT. Instead of "went to suppress the rebels, who then surrendered the spear of sovereignty over the land," *Kasuga go-ruki* has an apparently corrupt passage that could be translated, "extracted a deed of title to the land from the two deities." The "deed of title to the land" is *saribumi,* a medieval legal term. *Nihon shoki* specifies a spear.

## 1.2 The Jōhei Oracle

On the 25th day of the 7th month of Jōhei 7, at the hour of the Boar, the Shrine groaned and shook in the wind; and at the hour of the Rat, a Tachibana lady[1] who was then before the Sanctuaries uttered a cry. She called in the Shrine Guards, the Overseer,[2] and the other priests, who gathered respectfully before her. She also summoned Shōen,[3] a Kōfukuji monk who since the 23d of the same month had been chanting Sutras at the Shrine. Then the God gave this oracle: "I am already a Bosatsu, but the Court has not yet given me any Bosatsu Name."

At this, Senryō, a monk who practiced upon the Tendai Mountain,[4] said, "What Bosatsu Name should we give you?"

The God replied, "Jihi Mangyō Bosatsu."[5]

The Chancellor, the Ministers of the Left and Right,[6] and all the Nobles murmured together. "It was up to us to decide that," they said.

[FIGURE 1.2: Monks and laymen gathered before the Sanctuaries, listening to the oracle.]

DATE. Jōhei 7.2.25 (937). The hour of the Boar is ca. 10 A.M.; the hour of the Rat, ca. midnight.

EARLIER OCCURRENCES OF THE MATERIAL. *Kasuga go-honji narabi ni go-takusen ki* (1175) tells this story in the same way. The oracle is also mentioned in *Kasuga kōshiki* and *Kasuga Daimyōjin hotsuganmon* by Gedatsu Shōnin.

1. Perhaps an official medium at the shrine. Powerful in the eighth and early ninth centuries, the Tachibana clan had sunk into relative obscurity, and by the mid-tenth century supplied only minor officials to the court. However, their close connection with the Fujiwara founders Kamatari and Fuhito made a Tachibana presence at the shrine quite natural (Koresawa 1963:12). The medium in 17.1 was also a Tachibana.

2. Shrine guards *(shinden-mori)*, the senior among the "yellow-robe" shrine servants *(jinnin)*, were permanently stationed at the shrine. The overseer *(azukari,* later *shō-no-azukari)* was at this time the highest-ranking Kasuga priest, although a high priest *(kannushi)* of comparable standing joined him after 965 (Nagashima 1944:13). The title *shō-no-azukari* dates from the time of Norikiyo (974–1052) *(Ōhigashi-ke shikan keifu)*.

3. Shōen (891–966) was the lecturer for the Yuima-e in 949.

4. Senryō is not otherwise known. Mt. Hiei, just northeast of Kyoto, is the stronghold of Tendai Buddhism.

5. This title means "Bodhisattva Complete in Mercy's Works." Hachiman in 783 was the first Japanese deity to claim a "Bosatsu Name."

6. In 937 the chancellor was Fujiwara no Tadahira (880–949); the minister of the left was Fujiwara no Nakahira (875–945); and the minister of the right was Fujiwara no Tsunesuke (880–938).

## 1.3 The Bamboo Grove Hall

In the village of Yama, in Heguri county of Yamato Province,[1] there is a sacred place named Chikurin-den [Bamboo Grove Hall] where Kasuga no Daimyōjin appeared.

Of old, Fujiwara no Mitsuhiro, an Assistant Keeper of the Right Imperial Stables,[2] lived at Kichinan-den[3] in Hirose county.[4] Every night he saw a spot shining on the north bank of the Yamato River. A noble lady came there, and told him that this was where his descendants would flourish.

"Who are you, and where are you from?" Mitsuhiro asked.

The lady said:

I make my home          *waga yado wa*
south of the Capital     *miyako no minami*
in the floating cloud palace  *shika no sumu*

on Mikasa-yama,     *mikasa no yama no*
the haunt of deer.[5]    *ukigumo no miya*

Then she vanished.

[FIGURE 1.3: Mitsuhiro kneeling before the lady, who is seated at the edge of a bamboo grove. In the background, the river.]

This dream inspired Mitsuhiro to begin building on the 25th day of the 2d month of Tenryaku 2. Then, after informing Emperor Murakami, he moved in on the 16th day of the 6th month of the same year.

DATE. Tenryaku 2 (948).

1. Now Meyasu, a locality in eastern Ikaruga-chō in Ikoma-gun, Nara-ken. *Kasuga genki ekotoba kikigaki* identifies Chikurin-den with the Meyasu Shrine, on the north bank of the Yamato River. The spot is two or three kilometers south of Hōryūji. In the Kamakura period, Meyasu was also an estate belonging to Daijōin.

2. Unknown. His title, *uma-no-jō,* indicates that he was a third-level officer and probably held the lowly seventh rank.

3. Unknown.

4. Hirose county was the present Kawai-chō in Kitakatsuragi-gun, Nara-ken, south of the Yamato River.

5. The "palace" is probably the Kasuga Shrine, although it could be interpreted as the present Hongū Jinja at the top of Mikasa-yama, where Takemikazuchi descended on first arriving at Kasuga. In *Kasuga ruki* only, the third line of the poem reads *shika zo sumu,* in Kasuga poetry a common pun on "deer live" and "I live thus." A particularly famous example occurs in *Kokinshū* 982.

## 1.4 (No Separate Title)

Later, in Shōryaku 3, Fujiwara no Yoshikane[1] dreamed that a noble lady flew down to the bamboo grove southwest of the house.

"I am Kasuga no Daimyōjin, your Clan God," she said. "I have come to live here because your house is so high and your bamboo grove so thick that the place is like the Bamboo Grove Garden.[2] As

[FIGURE 1.4 (2): Carpenters and laborers at work building Mitsuhiro's new residence; the lady floats in the bamboo grove outside the house, Yoshikane and his wife being asleep within.]

long as the bamboo grows fine and strong, your descendants will prosper."

Yoshikane immediately erected a shrine and worshiped the God, and he wrote a pledge that this sacred bamboo should never be cut. They say the bamboo now grows very tall there, so that the spot is just like the Ryō Garden.[3]

DATE. Shōryaku 3 (992).

1. Apparently the heir of Mitsuhiro, but otherwise unknown.

2. Chikurin'en. Possibly an allusion to the bamboo grove near the royal palace in which Karanda (Skt. Kalanda) built a monastery for the Budda. The monastery was named Chikurin Shōja (Skt. Veṇuvana).

3. Ryōen (Ch. Liang-yuan), a famous garden made by King Hsiao of Liang to entertain guests. It appears in Chinese poetry.


## 1.5 The Imperial Pilgrimage to Kinpusen

In the 7th month of Kanji 6, Retired Emperor Shirakawa[1] made a pilgrimage to Kinpusen.[2] On the mountain[3] he suddenly looked ill, and his attendants paled. Then the Dragon Visage turned very wroth.[4]

"I am the old man who lives by Kasuga-yama," he said. "This excursion of yours is rather a waste of time. And why did you not take advantage of it to visit my own modest home?"

Looking around, he saw that Major Counselor Morotada,[5] Master of the Empress's Household Masazane,[6] and others were with him. "Ah yes," he exclaimed, "you Genji are doing very well, aren't you!"[7] Those present were frightened and left him.

When he came to himself he was deeply embarassed, and wondered whether perhaps he should turn back. But instead he sent a sacred horse[8] to the Kasuga Shrine, with a special prayer; and then had Lord Masafusa, the Major Controller of the Left,[9] compose a declaration promising that His Majesty would bring the Shrine a complete copy of the Canon.[10] When this was done, he recovered completely, and finished his pilgrimage.

[PICTURE: A nobleman's mansion. Masafusa, seated before Shirakawa writes the declaration.]

# THE MIRACLES OF THE KASUGA DEITY

DATE. Kanji 6.7 (1092). A "shrine record" (*Nara:* 118) specifies that Shirakawa set out on Kanji 6.7.2. After a lacuna of about two lines, the record mentions the deity's display of irritation, and states that Shirakawa's prayer, and the horse, were offered to the shrine on Kanji 6.7.9.

RELATED MATERIALS. Shirakawa's pilgrimage to Kinpusen is mentioned without details in many documents, including *Chūyūki, Go-Nijō no kanpaku ki, Fusō ryakki, Hyakuren-shō,* and *Genkō shakusho. Kōfukuji ryaku nendai ki* includes an abbreviated version of this story. *Kasuga Gongen genki shō* gives a version that may be roughly contemporary with the *Genki,* but the brief text is poor, and diverges widely from the *Genki* telling.

1. Shirakawa (1053–1129, r. 1072–86), who initiated *insei* government, became a monk in 1096. He made many pilgrimages to holy sites.

2. The chief peak in the Ōmine range, now identified on maps as Sanjō-ga-take (1719 m.), and the most important *shugendō* center in Japan. Other illustrious pilgrims there were Emperor Uda in 900 and Fujiwara no Michinaga in 1007. By 1092, Kōfukuji claimed Kinpusen as a dependency *(matsuji),* and a year after Shirakawa's visit the two fought a brief war that resulted in the appointment of a Kōfukuji monk as *kengyō* (senior monk) of Kinpusen. (*Hyakurenshō* for Kanji 7.10.21; *Chūyūki* for Kanji 7.10.27, 7.11.3, 7.11.17, 8.3.6.)

3. According to *Kasuga Gongen genki shō,* this happened not on Kinpusen but at Hiuchi-saki, a locality on the south bank of the Yamato River, near present Gojō-shi. If so, Shirakawa would have had to make a wide detour to pass through Hiuchi-saki on his way to the mountain. On the other hand, he had passed there quite naturally on Kanji 2.2.23 (1088), on his way to Mt. Kōya (*Nara-ken no chimei,* "Hiuchino-mura").

4. "Dragon Visage" *(ryūgan)* is the proper term for an emperor's face. According to *Kasuga Gongen genki shō,* Shirakawa seemed at first to be dead.

5. Minamoto no Morotada (1054–1114). Two of Morotada's brothers, Toshifusa and Akifusa, appear in 3.1. A major counselor *(dainagon)* belonged to the council of state *(daijōkan),* and ranked just below the ministers of state.

6. Minamoto no Masazane (1059–1127), the eldest son of Akifusa. Masazane went back to Kinpusen in 1103 and 1116. The master of the empress's household *(chūgū no daibu)* was an important figure at court.

7. See chapter 4, under "The Nan'endō," for a discussion of this utterance.

8. Such horses *(jinme)* were commonly offered to shrines by wealthy patrons. According to *Yamato shiryō* (1:152), Shirakawa also gave the shrine the robe he wore on his pilgrimage.

9. Ōe no Masafusa (1041–1111), a famous scholar, wrote *Honchō shinsenden* and other works. *Gōdanshō* is a record of his conversations taken down by Fujiwara no Sanekane, the great-grandfather of Gedatsu Shōnin. A major controller of the left *(sadaiben)* was an official of the fourth rank, responsible to the council of state.

10. A complete set of the Buddhist scriptures.

## 2.1 The Imperial Pilgrimage of the Kanji Era

In the 3d month of Kanji 7 he made a pilgrimage to the Kasuga Shrine, as he had vowed to do the year before. He brought a dancer with him, and made sure the rites were done as beautifully as possible. The Palace Minister[1] and those under him did *Katamai,*[2] while the Minister of the Left[3] joined the musicians. The precedents were most encouraging,[4] and the Divine Will must surely have been pleased.

Later on, during the Kōwa era, he had the Canon copied, built a Sutra Repository for it at the Shrine, and assigned a hundred monks to read the sacred texts.[5] He also ceded to the Shrine in perpetuity the Kawaguchi estate in Echizen province, as an endowment to support his gift.[6] Everyone apologized for having been afraid on that other day.[7] Ever since, each imperial generation has shown matchless devotion, and there have been many imperial pilgrimages to the Shrine.

Some years before, Lord Korefusa[8] had secretly prepared a plaque that read "Go-kyōzō,"[9] having been instructed to do so in a dream. When an oracle revealed the plaque's existence it was called for, and affixed to the Sutra Repository's south gate. They say it is still there.

[FIGURE 2.1: Part of a long scene showing Shirakawa before the shrine, with dancers and musicians; outside, groups of monks, priests, courtiers, and guards.]

DATES. (1) Kanji 7.3.20 (1093) as reported in *Sōgō bunin,* and in *Chūyūki* under that date. *Chūyūki* agrees entirely with the first paragraph of 2.1, but provides more details. Among those who accompanied Shirakawa were the Morotada, Masazane, and Masa-fusa of 1.5, and the Akisue of 2.2. However, *Chūyūki* says nothing about the Canon or the plaque, either in this entry or in later ones.

(2) *Kōfukuji ryaku nendai ki,* under the date Kanji 7, says Shirakawa brought the Canon with him, but the Kōwa era (1099–1104) seems more plausible. Fukuyama (1961:8) specified 1100.

(3) Korefusa probably wrote the plaque after 1088, when he was appointed deputy governor-general of Dazaifu.

RELATED MATERIALS. *Koshaki* includes the story about the plaque, noting that Korefusa was in Kyushu when the deity spoke to him through a woman of his household, and that the purpose of the plaque became plain "several years" later. The versions in *Jikkinshō* 10/68 and *Kokonchomonjū* 7/8 are less detailed than *Koshaki.*

REMARK. According to Fukuyama (1961:8), another Canon written in gold, begun by Tadazane (see 3.1, n. 1) and completed by the wife of Fujiwara no Motozane, was offered to the shrine in 1178.

1. Fujiwara no Moromichi (see 2.3, n. 1). The palace minister was the lowest-ranking of the ministers of state.

2. This name designates the dance *Motomego-mai* when it is done alone. (When done with *Suruga-mai,* the pair are called *Moromai.*)

3. Minamoto no Toshifusa (see 3.1, n. 2).

4. It is unclear what these precedents are.

5. This "reading" is *tendoku:* a method of reading long texts expeditiously by voicing the chapter headings but otherwise simply fanning through the pages. Shiraka-wa's gift amounted to an elaborate form of *hosse* ("offering of the Teaching"), the chanting of Buddhist scriptures as an offering for Shinto deities.

6. This important estate, often mentioned in Kasuga or Kōfukuji records, came to be administered by Daijōin. By the 1360s, according to *Taiheiki* 39, it was supporting not Shirakawa's gift so much as the Yuima-e of Kōfukuji (see ch. 8).

7. In 1092, on the way to Kinpusen.

8. Fujiwara no Korefusa (1031–?), a distinguished calligrapher. As a middle coun-selor of the senior second rank, he was appointed deputy governor-general of Dazaifu *(Dazai gon-no-sotsu)* on Kanji 2.9.28 (1088), and resigned on Kanji 8.2.25 (1094).

9. The name on the *gaku* ("plaque") put over the entrance to a building should be written by a distinguished calligrapher. Perhaps it can be said that affixing the *gaku* to a building is a little like the "eye-opening" for a new Buddhist image. "Go-kyōzō" means "Sutra Repository."

## 2.2 Kōfukuji Goes to War in the Eikyū Era

In Eikyū 1 the monks[1] of Enryakuji burned Kiyomizudera to the ground. Kōfukuji was furious, since Kiyomizudera is its dependency,[2] and the Kōfukuji monks set forth to war. The Court sent troops to stop them. Undaunted by the imperial authority, however, the monks joined battle with these troops at Kurikoma-yama.[3] The Retired Emperor,[4] outraged, declared that the Southern Capital[5] was to be punished.

At this point Akisue,[6] the Master of Palace Repairs and an officer in the Retired Emperor's Household, dared to observe: "It is to Kasuga no Daimyōjin's supernatural help that you owe all your good fortune, My Lord. How could you forget Kasuga's divine virtue?"

"What do you mean?" asked His Majesty.

"When you were young, My Lord," Akisue replied, "the ceiling of your residence shook, greatly startling you. Then a voice said, 'By the will of the Grand Shrine of Ise I guard the Imperial Person. I am the Daimyōjin of Kasuga.' Your Majesty should show more gratitude."

The Retired Emperor did not answer, but in the end he called off the campaign against Kōfukuji.

[PICTURE: The battle]

DATE. Eikyū 1 (1113).

BACKGROUND. Ensei, the newly appointed superintendent of Kiyomizudera, was affiliated with Mt. Hiei. According to *Kōfukuji ryaku nendai ki*, Kōfukuji's protest march on the Capital began on Eikyū 1.3.20, and on 3.22 the Kōfukuji monk Eien was appointed in Ensei's place. Then on 3.29 Enryakuji burned Kiyomizudera down. It was on 4.29 that Kōfukuji fought the imperial troops at Kurikoma-yama. Meanwhile the monks of Enryakuji came down into the Capital as far as Gion. The Retired Emperor wanted to punish Kōfukuji, but Akisue persuaded him to desist. *Chūyūki* (cited by Kuroda 1980:61) has this comment during the quarrel: "The Buddha's Law, the Kingly Law, the Tendai and Hossō are all three about to end."

1. The forces of both temples are here called *shuto*.

2. Enryakuji is the Tendai establishment on Mt. Hiei. Kiyomizudera, dangerously close to Enryakuji's territory, was officially a Hossō temple and a dependency of Kōfukuji. On the other hand. Tōnomine (the site of the mausoleum of Kamatari), dangerously close to Kōfukuji territory, was a dependency of Enryakuji. The result was repeated destruction of both.

3. An area of low hills just southeast of Uji, along the regular route between the Capital and Nara.

4. Shirakawa.

5. In the writings of this period, "Southern Capital" (Nara) often means simply "Kōfukuji."

6. Fujiwara no Akisue (1054–1123), the great-grandfather of Takasue (see 7.4).

Sanesue, his adoptive father, became the father-in-law of Emperor Go-Sanjō and the grandfather of Emperor Toba. Akisue's own mother was Shirakawa's favorite wetnurse, so that his relationship with Shirakawa was old and close. Besides the positions mentioned in the text (he was actually superintendent of Shirakawa's household), he served as governor of six different provinces. His six daughters all married ranking courtiers closely connected to Shirakawa and Toba. Akisue was also well known as a poet. The master of palace repairs (*shuri no daibu*) was the second-in-command of this office.

## 2.3 The Nijō Regent

When the Nijō Regent[1] forgot his sword on withdrawing from duty at the Palace, a lady-in-waiting went back in to get it for him. She found the Regent seated just as he had been before, smiling, with the sword beneath one knee. He would not let her have it. Confused, she went out again, only to hear His Excellency calling from inside his carriage, "Why haven't you brought me my sword?" Back in she went, sorely flustered now, and there was the Regent once more.

The people of the time said that Kasuga no Daimyōjin must have appeared that way because He kept as close to the Regent as his own shadow, and protected him. Certainly, this great lord was deeply devoted to the Shrine and the Temple.[2] If a messenger came from the Temple, he would not touch his food until he had learned what the matter was.

[PICTURE: The regent (the deity) seated cross-legged, with the lady-in-waiting facing him.]

DATE. Between Kahō 1.3.9 (1094) and Kōwa 1.6.28 (1099), when Moromichi was regent.

1. Fujiwara no Moromichi (1062–99), the son of Morozane and the father of Tadazane. Moromichi and his father were both regent during Shirakawa's rise to supreme power at court.
2. The Kasuga Shrine and Kōfukuji.

## 3.1 The Horikawa Minister of the Left

In his youth the Chisokuin Regent[1] married the daughter of the Horikawa Minister of the Left.[2] Since he did not like his wife, perhaps because she was much older than he, the result was a situation distressing to all. The Minister was very pleased when she conceived.

The birth caused great excitement, but alas, the baby died. This so upset the women of the Minister's household that they hid the truth from him and arranged to bring in the newborn son of a *hōshi*,[3] whom they treated as the lady's own.

The Minister was preparing to celebrate magnificently the nightly rite[4] when he suddenly looked ill, and Kasuga no Daimyōjin possessed him. "Yes, I must see my son-in-law, the Major Captain,"[5] he declared.

Greatly surprised, his son-in-law received him.

"Do you believe this new son you're so taken with is *yours?*" asked the Minister. "He certainly is not. They brought in some nobody's child and passed it off as yours. You must have nothing to do with it. It seems to me that you already have a son who can succeed you as Head of the Clan." (No doubt he meant Lord Hosshōji,[6] born to the daughter of his younger brother Akifusa,[7] the Minister of the Right.) He repeated all this several times before coming to himself.

The Minister had no idea that he had said anything of the kind, but those present told him every detail. Overwhelmed by this shame that had come upon him in his old age, he refused thereafter to live under the same roof as his wife or daughter. As to the Major Captain, he had never cared for his wife in the first place, and so stopped seeing her entirely.

[FIGURE 3.1: The Minister talking to his son-in-law.]

People felt this had been a very sad and strange oracle to get from the Daimyōjin.

DATE. Ca. 1098. Tadazane's diary does not mention this event. However, Tadamichi, Tadazane's son by the daughter of Akifusa, was born in 1097; and while Tadazane held the post of major captain of the left 1094–1103, he was appointed minister of the right in 1099.

1. Fujiwara no Tadazane (1078–1162), the eldest son of Moromichi, and the father of Tadamichi and Yorinaga. *Kugyō bunin* and *Sonpi bunmyaku* mention no marriage to the lady of this story. Tadazane became head of the clan in 1099, then regent; he was appointed chancellor in 1122. That same year he refused to let his daughter become one of the Emperor Toba's consorts, which made Retired Emperor Shirakawa so angry that Tadazane had to retire to Uji. He was replaced by Tadamichi. Eventually Tadazane returned to active life, but then became involved in—in fact, promoted—rivalry between Tadamichi and Yorinaga. Having backed Yorinaga, he found himself linked with the losing side in the Hōgen disturbance, after which he retired for good to Chisokuin, a Tendai temple just north of the Capital, probably near Urin'in. A record of his sayings *(Chūgaishō)* survives, together with his diary *(Denreki)* for 1097–1118. Tadazane gave the Kasuga Shrine its West Pagoda in 1116.

*Genki* 4.1 and 4.2 both link Tadazane with supernatural manifestions, and so do several stories found elsewhere. *Hie Sannō rishōki* 4 tells how Tadazane himself was possessed by Sannō Jūzenji; *Kokonchomonjū* no. 265 relates how Tadazane had the Dakini rite performed in order to assure his appointment as regent, and how he dallied with a fox deity; while *Kokonchomonjū* no. 13 tells how the Kasuga deity addressed him through his own wife.

2. Minamoto no Toshifusa (1035–1121), a son of the chancellor Morofusa and a daughter of Fujiwara no Michinaga, and a brother of Morotada and Akifusa. He became minister of the left in 1083. *Kyōkunshō* says that at his death, Toshifusa heard heavenly music and was welcomed into the Inner Sanctum of the Tosotu Heaven; however, *Goshūi ōjōden* describes his end as a pious Amida Devotee.

3. A quasi-monk who had not taken monastic vows and who in most respects still led a lay life. A *hōshi* could marry, eat meat, etc.

4. Probably the first of the celebratory banquets given on the third, fifth, seventh, and ninth nights after the birth of a child.

5. Tadazane.

6. Fujiwara no Tadamichi (1097–1164), the son of Tadazane, the brother of Yorinaga, and the ancestor of the Konoe and Kujō lines. First named regent in 1121, he became chancellor in 1129. Tadamichi was in sharp political rivalry with both his father and Yorinaga. After becoming a monk in 1162, he retired to Hosshōji, the great Tendai temple founded in 925 by Fujiwara no Tadahira. Tadamichi was a respected poet and an influential calligrapher. His personal *waka* and *kanshi* collections both survive.

7. Minamoto no Akifusa (1037–94), brother of Toshifusa and Morotada, father-in-law of Tadazane, and father of Ryūkaku (see 14.2–4). He became minister of the right in 1083. A distinguished poet whose work appears in several imperial collections, he is also a leading candidate for recognition as the author of *Ōkagami*. One daughter, Kenshi, was the consort of Shirakawa. Another, Shishi, was Tadamichi's mother; she appears also in 3.3.

## 3.2 The Kashima Poems

In the tenth month of Eikyū 2, while Lord Chisokuin was Head of the Clan, the Governor of Hitachi[1] rebuilt the Kashima Shrine. He then made a record of what the Shrine looked like,[2] and sent it to a lady of the Regent's household whom he had been visiting. The Regent, having seen it, gave the lady his fan.[3] She was delighted, and replied with this verse:

| | |
|---|---|
| Mikasa-yama: | *mikasa-yama* |
| the wind among your pines | *matsu fuku kaze mo* |
| blows peacefully, while I, | *nodokekute* |
| awe-inspired, lift my gaze | *chitose no kage o* |
| to your ageless form. | *aogimiru kana* |

The Regent answered:

| | |
|---|---|
| Mikasa-yama: | *mikasa-yama* |
| since you are the Lord | *sashite tanomeru* |
| I deeply trust, | *kimi nareba* |
| I shall gaze in peace | *chitose no kage o* |
| upon your ageless form. | *nodokeku ya min* |

The Governor saw these verses and presented them to the Kashima Shrine with one of his own:

| | |
|---|---|
| Ah, the missives of our Lord | *chitose made* |
| who sits in majesty | *kakete zo mamoru* |
| over us of the Clan, | *ujibito no* |
| mounting enduring guard | *kōbe to imasu* |
| through eons ageless! | *kimi no tamazusa* |

These poems were laid in the main sanctuary. That night the Chief Priest, Nakatomi no Norisuke,[4] received the revelation of the following verse:

Mikasa-yama:          *mikasa-yama*
from the Isle of Deer,   *kasegi no shima ni*
where I reside,        *sumai shite*
I see such rare witnesses *kaku mezurashiki*
to my enduring glory![5]  *ato o miru kana*

[FIGURE 3.2: The regent and the lady sitting face to face with the fan between them. A written text lies before the regent.]

DATE. Eikyū 2.10 (1114).

POSSIBLE SOURCE. *Kasuga go-sha go-honji narabi ni go-takusen ki* contains this sequence of poems, introduced much as they are here. The document notes that the governor of Hitachi was moved to write the description of the Kashima Shrine by his joy on learning that his rebuilding of the shrine had earned him reappointment. Tadazane mentioned nothing like this incident in *Denreki*.

1. Fujiwara no Sanemune, according to Miyai (1978:151).

2. Apparently a written description rather than a picture. The text has *arisama o kiroku shite,* while *Kasuga go-sha go-honji narabi ni go-takusen ki* has *teitaraku o kiroku shi.* The painting for 3.2 shows a text lying before Tadazane.

3. A gesture of thanks.

4. Unknown. "Chief Priest" is *ōnegi.*

5. "Isle of Deer" *(kasegi no shima)* is simply the literal meaning of the characters normally used to spell "Kashima." Mikasa-yama is the name of the sacred hill at both Kashima and Kasuga.

## 3.3 Sanetsune

The Kasuga Overseer Sanetsune[1] was Hidetsura's successor in the sixth generation.[2] He had been under arrest for several days, on order from the outraged Lord Chisokuin, when Lord Chisokuin fell ill.

At first the Regent suffered from a fever every other day, as though he had an ague; but in time the fever came upon him daily. Zōyo, the Grand Prelate of Ichijōji,[3] was among the healers His Excellency summoned. When the fever arose as usual, despite his prayers, Zōyo dedicated to His Excellency all the merit he had gained from having practiced the *goma* of Fudō, so as to abolish every sin, during his three thousand days at the Nachi waterfall.[4] Then he begged the Great Holy One[5] for help, and His Excellency began to look much better. The fever seemed to be gone. Zōyo was rewarded before he withdrew.

[PICTURE: A view of Tadazane's mansion, with a monk praying.]

The next day the fever arose again at the usual hour. Having now been ill for a long time, His Excellency was very weak, and the new attack was more severe than ever. At last his breathing became so feeble, and the color of his nails so bad, that he seemed to be dying. The whole household was naturally aghast. Grand Prelate Zōyo was summoned again, and despite his ignominious failure, he came.

Zōyo went to His Excellency, looked into his eyes, then drew far back and bowed very, very low. "No words can describe my incompetence," he said. "The healer's first duty is to grasp the nature of the disorder. He must discriminate between the curse of a living person and that of someone deceased, and discern whether a great or a minor divinity is at work; and it is upon this understanding that he must found all his prayers and protective rites. But I was inattentive, and missed the truth. This is extremely serious. Clearly, a very great God has come down upon you. It was an awful blunder for a fool like me to have prayed on your behalf."

By "a very great God," he meant the God of Kasuga.

His Excellency summoned Sanetsune, in case it was his holding Sanetsune under arrest that had provoked the divine displeasure.

[PICTURE: Another view of the residence, with Tadazane lying ill in an inner room.]

Sanetsune accordingly appeared: a bent old man over seventy, with white hair and eyebrows, who came tottering in wearing a rumpled white robe.[6] He might as well have been an ancient of Shōzan[7] in days of yore, and was obviously old and venerable—the mere sight of him made that plain. Lord Hosshōji[8] gave him a direct audience.

"Well," said Lord Hosshōji, "how many days is it now that you have been confined?"

He had not finished speaking before Sanetsune burst into tears and hung his head. "This is already the one hundred and thirtieth day," he replied after a pause.

"What have you been thinking about all this time?"

The weeping Sanetsune took a moment to answer. "This and only this," he said at last. "My mother and father told me that for the first six months after I was conceived, they went every day on pilgrimage —and I therefore with them—to the Daimyōjin; and that after I was born, they had my wetnurse take me every day, in her arms, to walk on the Mountain.[9] As an adult I have gone before the Daimyōjin every day, except when I was ill, and each time have sat against the Shrine fence.[10] But for one hundred and thirty days now, ever since My Lord placed me under arrest this spring, I have drifted on the waves of my seventy years and more, separated from the Daimyōjin. Old as I am, I am not ill, but still, each breath I draw may be my last; and how much more so now, in the stifling heat of summer! It is really more than I can bear. If I pass away here in the Capital, I will never go home, and will never worship the Daimyōjin again. That thought is so painful that I grieve over nothing else, day or night." Here he broke off and sobbed aloud.

Lord Hosshōji was in tears himself as he relayed all this to the Regent.

"I do feel sorry for him," Lord Chisokuin said. "Let him pray to the Daimyōjin and heal this sickness of mine."

At a word from Lord Hosshōji, Sanetsune faced south and, with tears in his eyes, wrung his hands in supplication. "Please, my Dai-myōjin," he prayed, "heal His Excellency's affliction, and set my face once more toward your Mountain!"

Even as he spoke, Lord Chisokuin recovered completely. Deeply moved, he had Lord Hosshōji present Sanetsune with a sword, and Her Ladyship[11] sent him a robe. Sanetsune then withdrew, with two gentleman leading him by the hand.

Sanetsune received Daigō in Harima province[12] as a fee for his prayers.

PICTURE: Sanetsune weeping as he talks with Tadamichi; Sanetsune praying; Sanetsune leaving between two gentlemen.]

DATE. 1110 (Tennin 3 or Ten'ei 1). According to Ōhigashi Nobuatsu (1972, "Nobu-tsune"), Tadazane relieved Sanetsune of his post as Kasuga Overseer in Tennin 3; while in *Denreki,* Tadazane recorded sentencing Sanetsune on Ten'ei 1.3.17. If Sane-tsune was imprisoned at the time, he must have prayed for Tadazane at about the beginning of Ten'ei 1.int7. However, as explained below, *Denreki* does not confirm any such date.

BACKGROUND. Ōhigashi Nobuatsu (1972), confirmed by *Denreki* for Ten'ei 1.3.17, states that Sanetsune was suspected of having passed off as his own a son of his wetnurse, and of having brought up this non-Nakatomi boy as his successor, Nakatomi no Nobutoshi. An oracle from the Kasuga deity, recorded in *Koshaki* and discussed in chapter 3, suggests the seriousness of the charge. In the end, Nobutoshi was recog-nized as Sanetsune's son. Sanetsune was reinstated in Tenin 3.9 (Ten'ei 1.9).

POSSIBLE SOURCE, RELATED MATERIALS. See the extended discussion below under "Significant Variants."

1. Nakatomi (Ōhigashi) no Sanetsune (1038–1123). Appointed overseer in 1091, Sanetsune resigned in favor of his son, Nobutoshi, in 1115. In 1122 he was reap-pointed, and died the next year. Although Ōhigashi Nobuatsu (1972) read his name "Nobutsune," *Kasuga genki ekotoba kikigaki* gives *sane* for the first character. *Denreki* supports this reading. In the entry for Ten'ei 1.3.17, Tadazane wrote Sanetsune's name correctly, with the character normally read *nobu,* perhaps because he had just seen the name written in a communication from the Kasuga Shrine. However, on Eikyū 2.2.17 (1114), when recording a visit from "the Kasuga Overseer Sanetsune," Tadazane mistakenly, but understandably, used for *sane* the second character of his *own* name.

2. Nakatomi no Hidetsura (713–807) came with Takemikazuchi from Kashima to Kasuga, together with Tokifū. He is the ancestor of the Ōhigashi line of Kasuga priests. However, *Ōhigashi-ke shikan keifu* lists the sixth generation as Arichika (1017–92) and the seventh as Aritada (1074–1119), Arichika's son, who is described as having become the head of the family in 1110. It says that the overseer Arichika ceded his post to his nephew Sanetsune on Kanji 5.10.25 (1091), because of illness; and that on

Ten'ei 1.int7.29 (1110), Aritada, the deputy overseer, became the overseer. In Ten'ei 1.9, Sanetsune was pardoned and reappointed overseer, and Aritada stepped down. Kondō Kihaku (1958:84) cited evidence from the colophon to a sutra manuscript at Hōryūji to show that Sanetsune was indeed overseer in Eikyū 4.1 (1116). However, the shadow that darkened his career excluded him from his family lineage.

    3. Zōyo (1032–1116), a grandson of the regent Michitaka, was a famous healer and *shugendō* adept. He served as the head monk of Miidera, Enryakuji, and other great temples. Zōyo was the first *kengyō* of Kumano and founded Shōgoin in Kyoto, still the headquarters of Honzan-ha (Tendai) *shugendō*. In 1091 he moved to Ichijōji, in eastern Kyoto. *Shingonden* 7 narrates a series of wonders he performed, and *Uji shūi monogatari* 5/9 gives a delicious account of his colorful manner of living. "Grand Prelate" (*sōjō*) was the next-to-highest eccesiastical (*sōgō*) rank.

    4. Since the longest period of sustained practice recognized in *shugendō* is 1000 days, Zōyo had apparently done three 1000-day retreats. The Nachi waterfall, one of the three Kumano shrines, was a major center of such ascetic practice; and the wrathful Fudō is a common object of devotion in *shugendō*. *Goma* (from the Skt. *homa*) is a fire rite most commonly associated with Fudō. Zōyo, like other ascetics, practiced it to achieve *metsuzai* ("destruction of sins.").

    5. I.e., Fudō.

    6. Sanetsune had on *jōe* ("pure raiment"), white clothing worn by persons who are in special contact with the sacred.

    7. Shangshan, a mountain in Shensi province in China, where four ancient, white-haired advisers to the Ch'in court took refuge when the dynasty fell. According to *Shih-chi*, they were eventually persuaded to come forth and serve the Han court. *Kara monogatari* 17 also tells the story.

    8. Tadamichi (see 3.1, n. 5).

    9. Mikasa-yama.

    10. Literally, "I have never failed to warm the Shrine fence."

    11. Shishi, the second daughter of Minamoto no Akifusa (3.1, n. 7). *Kokonchomonjū* no. 13 tells how once, when a distressed Tadazane prayed to the Kasuga deity, the deity possessed this lady in order to assure him, "You will come into your own again."

    12. According to *Koshaki,* an estate worth 500 *koku.*

SIGNIFICANT VARIANTS. In the original *Genki* text, the names Sanetsune and Zōyo have been written over erasures. *Kasuga go-ruki* speaks instead of Sukefusa and Gyō-son. Its version of 3.3 begins in this manner:

> The Kasuga Overseer Sukefusa was the first Chief Priest of the Wakamiya. Being a seventh-generation descendant of the Tokifū who served[Takemikazuchi] on the way from Kashima, he was in touch with the God; so that even on two occasions when Sukefusa was ill or off duty, the Daimyōjin appeared to him at his home in Tatsuichi. At present [Sukefusa] has appeared as a deity, and dwells upon the Mountain. This Sukefusa had been under arrest for several days, on order from the outraged Lord Chisokuin . . .

An original note inserted beside "Kasuga Overseer Sukefusa" says, "This is Sanetsune. He was not a Chief Priest of the Wakamiya." Otherwise, the two texts are the same.

# THE MIRACLES OF THE KASUGA DEITY

*Nakatomi (Tatsuichi) no Sukefusa.* Sukefusa is variously reported to have been born in 1069 (the *kaisetsu* in *Kasuga-sha kiroku,* vol. 1) and 1078 (Ōhigashi Nobuatsu 1972); he died in 1152. He was the Kasuga overseer when the new Wakamiya sanctuary was established in 1135, and he founded the Chidori line of Wakamiya priests. Koretada (d. 1004), who first saw the Wakamiya, was Sukefusa's great-grandfather. In 1178, at the direction of an oracle, Sukefusa's spirit was enshrined in the Tsugō Jinja, within the sacred fence of the Wakamiya *(Kōfukuji ranshōki).* The shrine is still there.

*Gyōson.* Gyōson (1052?–1132, an adopted son of Michinaga's second son Yorimune, was, like Zōyo, a famous ascetic and healer. He too served as abbot of Enryakuji. Gyōson's winter retreat in Shō-no-iwaya in the Ōmine mountains, and the verse he left at the cave, are particularly well known *(Kokonchomonjū* no. 52; *Senjūshō* 8/32). He was called the Byōdōin Grand Prelate.

*A possible source in Koshaki. Koshaki* supports *Kasuga go-ruki.* It contains an account of the incident that could be the source for both the *Kasuga go-ruki* and the *Genki* texts. The account starts: "The Overseer [blank] was a descendant of Tokifū . . ." Two characters in the blank have been erased, but they must have been those for Sukefusa, since Sukefusa and not Hidetsura was descended from Tokifū. The text then goes on to speak of Gyōson, not Zōyo. Unfortunately, there is a large gap in the *Koshaki* version of the story. The narrative breaks off just after Gyōson has diagnosed the real trouble as being the deity's displeasure, and has had his diagnosis confirmed by a yinyang master. It resumes as the old man is telling how he used to be taken to the shrine as a child. When the old man (whose name has again been erased) prays, Tadazane feels a cool breeze and recovers.

*A completely different version in Shingonden.* An entirely different version occurs in the *Shingonden* account of Gyōson. This work by the monk Eikai (1268–1348) dates from 1325, and so is roughly contemporary with the *Genki.* The text is as follows.

> The same gentleman [Tadazane] suffered from an ague, and although healers came from Hiei and Miidera to pray for him, their intervention had no effect. Grand Prelate Zōyo twice worked his rites on [Tadazane's] behalf, but the ague kept coming back. When Grand Prelate [Gyōson] worked his rites, on the order of Retired Emperor [Shirakawa], the Regent lay with his head on Gyōson's lap. [Gyōson] prayed by intoning with great intensity the *Senju-kyō* ["Sutra of Thousand-Armed Kannon"]. That day the ague did not return, and His Excellency had the two Chamberlains of the Fifth Rank, Minamoto no Morimasa and Fujiwara no Nagazane, present Gyōson with a fine horse.

Both Zōyo and Gyōson appear here, but Gyōson's role corresponds to that of Zōyo in *Genki* 3.3. *Shingonden* naturally fails to mention any subsequent lapse, since its account of Gyōson is entirely laudatory. (The *Shigonden* account of Zōyo contains nothing remotely like this story.) Fudō could have been invoked by either monk.

*The testimony of Tadazane's diary. Denreki* gives no comfort to either side, nor does it support the other aspects of 3.3 very well either. On Ten'ei 1.3.17, Tadazane assessed Sanetsune a fine and imposed on him the punitive purification known as *chūbarae;* and the next day he sent offerings to Kasuga because of the pollution Sanetsune was alleged to have caused. However, if Tadazane had been outraged enough, he could have imposed a stiffer sentence, since there existed two grades of punitive purification more severe than *chū-barae*.

On Ten'ei 1.4.1 Tadazane mentioned not feeling well, and continued in poor health for several weeks. He tried eating leeks, called in various monks for various rites, and on 1.4.21 even consulted a physician. Eventually he began swallowing ashes from the "Six Character Rite" *(rokuji hō)*. But on 1.5.16 he went to wait on the emperor, and seems to have recovered thereafter. On 1.7.27, he decided to make a pilgrimage to Kasuga, though without specifying the date. On 1.int7.5, he sent preparatory offerings to the Kasuga, Ōharano, and Yoshida shrines. Then a cough started going around. Tadamichi got it, and so did Tadazane's daughter Taishi.

On 1.int7.26, Tadazane felt unwell, and left the palace to go home. He had various Buddhist observances performed, by monks and by the members of his own household. On 1.8.2, being definitely ill, he had Zōyo come and pray for him all day. When his condition improved (apparently his usual fever did not arise), he gave Zōyo a horse. Then he felt so much better that he sent Tadamichi after Zōyo with an ox.

Alas, on 1.8.8, Tadazane felt obliged to resign as regent because of his illness. On 1.8.10, he had Gyōson come and pray all day, as Zōyo had done. Since this seemed to work, he gave Gyōson a horse also. However, he was soon ill again. On 1.8.17, the emperor declared a special amnesty to help Tadazane, who called in more monks. His household too was praying.

Perhaps it was Ise, not Kasuga, that helped. On 1.8.20, Tadazane noted that offerings had been made for him on that day to Ise, and that that evening he had no fever. He and others concluded that the offerings to Ise had worked. In fact, the next day, he felt it unnecessary to call in a monk as usual. After that he stopped mentioning being ill. Then on 1.9.30, he remarked that he had not called in any monks that month, despite being unwell; and he noted taking a bath that day for the first time in ages, since a yin-yang master had declared the day to be a fortunate one. Finally, on 1.10.23, he returned to serve at the palace for the first time since his illness began.

*Conclusion.* "Sukefusa" is certainly an error since *Denreki* speaks of Sanetsune, and since in any case Sukefusa was then too young to be the old man in the story. However, after the initial entry about Sanetsune, *Denreki* does not allude to him again. As for Zōyo and Gyōson, *Denreki* mentions them once each, in very similar entries. The thousand-day retreats at Nachi no doubt favor Zōyo. Both Zōyo and Gyōson were senior monks in 1110, but Zōyo was the older by twenty years; and above all, Zōyo's association with Kumano is famous. Tadazane's two illnesses in *Denreki* are no help. One lasted from Ten'ei 1.4.1 to about the middle of Ten'ei 1.5, long before Sanetsune could have intervened for him. The second began on Ten'ei 1.int7.26, after Sanetsune would have intervened, and the worst part of it ended ca. Ten'ei 1.9.30. To be sure, Ōhigashi Nobuatsu (1972) has Sanetsune reappointed in Ten'ei 1.9, but this date does not agree with *Genki* 3.3.

*Why the confusion?* But apart from discrepancies in chronology, why should this confusion about the actors have arisen? Perhaps, on the one hand, it comes from a simple, initial error. On the other hand, *Denreki* offers so little evidence to decide the issue that one suspects the whole story of having been fabricated after the fact. If so, it must have been intended to make a point, perhaps a political one. The two sets of actors would then represent rival factions vying for credit. Concerning the two Kasuga priests, Sanetsune and Sukefusa belonged to two different priestly houses. Moreover, Sukefusa, who presided over the establishment of the Wakamiya's own sanctuary in 1135, seems to have been highly influential, and to have taken part in delicate political maneuvering involving Kōfukuji and the court. Kondō (1958:84) summarily explained the whole affair as a matter of Ōhigashi-Tatsuichi rivalry, although he suggested no motive. (Since Sukefusa is involved, one can more easily imagine Tatsuichi-Ōnakatomi rivalry having to do with Tokimori [4.1, n. 4].) As for the two monks, Zōyo was linked especially to Miidera, which by the late twelfth century was a traditional ally of Kōfukuji; while Gyōson was more identified with Enryakuji. Still, one can only conclude in the end that the matter remains obscure.

## 4.1 Tengu Invade Higashisanjō

While Lord Chisokuin was living at Higashisanjō,[1] he dreamed that he had summoned a holy monk and was listening to the Esoteric Teaching when there came forward, besides the monk, two or three *hōshi* whom he did not recognize. He wondered who they were. Then he noticed that they had bird beaks instead of mouths, and realized they were *tengu*.[2]

"How did such creatures get into Higashisanjō?" he said. "Is the Deity Tsunofuri not here?" As he spoke, the Kasuga priest Tokimori[3] entered the room. At the sight of him the *tengu hōshi* all fled and disappeared.

The Deities Tsunofuri and Hayabusa are followers of Kasuga, and dwell at the Shrine.[4]

[PICTURE: Tadazane lying asleep, with his dream-self sitting facing the monk. Tokimori has just arrived and the *tengu* are fleeing.]

DATE. Between 1131 and 1156? Tadazane probably moved to Higashisanjō after 1099, when he became head of the clan. However, if Tokimori was living at the time, the dream must have occurred after 1131, when Tokimori became Kasuga overseer. Tadazane retired to Chisokuin in the aftermath of the Hōgen disturbance (1156).

RELATED MATERIAL. *Tamon'in nikki* for Tenbun 12.7.1 (1543) records a very similar, undated story. Once the emperor was receiving the Buddhist precepts in the palace when, in broad daylight, a horde of *tengu* appeared in all sorts of horrific shapes. His Majesty asked who the deity on guard *(ban no kami)*. was. On being told that it was Tsunofuri no Myōjin, he heard the rustling of a shrine priest's robe, and realized that the deity had arrived. The *tengu* vanished.

1. Higashisanjō (or Tōsanjō) was a palace built originally by Retired Emperor Uda

(r. 887–97). In time it passed to Senshi, the Fujiwara mother of Emperor Ichijō (r. 986–1001), and thence became the traditional property of the head of the Fujiwara clan. Tadazane ("Lord Chisokuin") gave it in succession to his two sons Tadamichi and Yorinaga, who both held this title.

2. Magical, troublesome creatures who usually live in the mountains but may also appear in town. Their forms include birds of prey such as the kite or the kestrel. In medieval times they especially enjoyed pestering monks and Buddhist establishments.

3. Ōnakatomi (Nakahigashi) no Tokimori (1097–1180), apparently a prominent figure whose name appears in many Kasuga records. He became overseer in 1131 and was in and out of the office several times after that, until the end of his life. Ōhigashi Nobuatsu (1972) quoted the diary of Nakatomi no Sukeharu (1245–1324) as follows: "The Tsubakimoto Shrine behind the Main Sanctuaries is [Tokimori's] spirit." However, the other records (see n. 4, below) suggest that this shrine may be older than Tokimori.

4. Tsunofuri and Hayabusa are deliciously confusing. They were, jointly, the local protector deity of Higashisanjō, but each was a separate *massha* of the Kasuga Shrine. *Kasuga Daimyōjin suijaku shōshaki* identifies Hayabusa with "Kurikara no Myōjin," and states that Tsunofuri is the deity of the Tsubakimoto-sha—the one that Sukeharu (see n. 3, above) identified with the spirit of Tokimori. Other Kasuga documents give different, conflicting testimony. As for Higashisanjō, Tadazane himself noted in *Chūgaishō:* "The Tsunofuri and Hayabusa no Myōjin of Higashisanjō are the aftersoul[s] of an Emperor [Emperors?] whose name[s] I do not remember. The Emperor is a later embodiment of it/them" (quoted in n. 3 to *Konjaku* 19/33, NKBT vol. 4).

Tsunofuri-Hayabusa were enshrined at the northwest corner of Higashisanjō, and could do surprising things. The "Toribeno" chapter of *Eiga monogatari* has them laying a curse on Senshi; and *Konjaku* 19/33 tells how they enticed a monk up a tree by their shrine. At the top of the tree, the monk found a beautiful palace whence he saw a mandala-like vision of all the annual ceremonies of the court.

As the deity of the Tsubakimoto-sha, Tsunofuri is still present at Kasuga, and the name lives on in the names of two districts of modern Nara. Hayabusa seems to have disappeared from Kasuga, but oddly enough there is a Hayabusa Jinja in present Tsunofuri Shin'ya-chō. Even more curiously, this tiny sanctuary is now dedicated to the Munakata deities.

## 4.2 The Oracle at the Time of the Pilgrimage to Kasuga in the Eikyū Era

Governing the whole realm as he did, in his capacity as Regent, Lord Chisokuin had reached in his lifetime the pinnacle of glory; and having passed four decades, he feared the approach of the long night.[1] Wishing "to withdraw now that fame was won,"[2] he made a pilgrimage to the Kasuga Shrine to announce his decision to leave the world, and to bid the Deity farewell.

While he was there, a boy in his eleventh or twelfth year suddenly assumed an august appearance. " 'Although one contemplate phenomena and noumena,' " the boy said, " 'none of these are separate from consciousness. However, within this consciousness there are objects and there is mind, because when mind arises, objects come into being within it.' Ah, how fine!"

Realizing that this was no ordinary event, the Regent signified his awe.

"I am the Third Deity of Kasuga,"[3] the boy declared. "Your visit on this occasion gives me special pleasure. You see, you have no common purpose in mind, but intend to cast off your finery, and this makes me so happy that I am weeping for sheer joy. I am giving you this oracle just to let you know. Never forget impermanence, but keep it always present to mind, and be quite sure that that is what will please me.

"Now, since you have two sons, both shall be Head of the Clan. Lord Tadamichi is upright in his conduct of public affairs, his calligraphy is beautiful, and he is expert in poetry and music. Certainly he is to be acknowledged a fine gentleman. However, I do not care much for him because he has no interest in the Buddha's Way. Yorinaga,[4] his younger brother, is versed in the classics, disposes shrewdly of administrative matters, and instantly discerns people's strengths and weaknesses. No doubt later generations will remember him with deep respect. He neglects to serve the Gods and Buddhas, however, and is likely to bring grief upon the temples of the Clan. That is why I do not abide with him." And with these words the Deity ascended.[5]

The passage "Although one contemplate phenomena and noumena" occurs in the *Yuishiki shō* of Jion Daishi.[6] It expresses the profoundly subtle principle of consciousness-only: that the myriad dharmas are not apart from the one mind, and not outside the field of the mind.

[PICTURE: Tadazane before the Kasuga sanctuaries, being addressed by the boy.]

DATE. Probably 1116 (Eikyū 4), though Tadazane, born in 1078, had not yet quite "passed four decades." According to *Denreki,* Tadazane's only formal visit to Kasuga during the Eikyū era took place on Eikyū 4.3.5. His announced purpose was to dedicate the pagoda that he had built for the shrine, though he might at the same time have entertained private thoughts of leaving the world. Tadazane recorded the details of the ceremonial procecure followed, but nothing about the subject of 4.2. Otherwise, he had been to Nara only on Eikyū 4.1.14 and 4.int1.25, on personal visits. (He stayed at "Sahota," the villa of his uncle Kakushin of Kōfukuji.) *Kōfukuji ryaku nendai ki* states that Tadazane resigned as regent and head of the clan in Hōan 2.1 (1121), although he did not actually become a monk until 1140.

POSSIBLE SOURCE. *Senjūshō* 6/6 tells this story in language so similar to the *Genki*'s that the Genki must have drawn upon it or a common source.

1. *Kyūya no yami,* the darkness of the forty-nine days after death, during which the soul wanders in the bardo (Jap. *chūu,* the "intermediate state") before its karma compels it to animate another body.

2. A phrase from the *Tao-te-ching:* "To withdraw after fame is won is the way of heaven."

3. Amenokoyane, whose *honji* was Jizō.

4. Fujiwara no Yorinaga (1120–56).

5. The normal expression to indicate the end of a divine possession.

6. Jion Daishi is the posthumous title of K'uei-chi (Jap. Kiki, 632–82), a distinguished disciple of Hsüan-tsang (Jap. Genjō), and the actual founder of Hossō in China. *Yuishiki shō* is an abbreviated title for *Jōyuishiki ron besshō* (Ch. *Ch'eng-wei-shih-lun-p'ieh-ch'ao*), K'uei-chi's record of his master's oral teachings on the *Jōyuishiki ron* (see 8.2, n. 4).

## 4.3 The Fugenji Regent

Since his Excellency the Fugenji Regent[1] was at one with the Heike, he started westward with them when, in the Juei era, Lord Munemori and all his clan set out for the Western Seas.[2]

He had accompanied His Majesty[3] as far as the crossing of Gojō and Ōmiya[4] when he saw a shrine servant in a yellow robe beckoning to him from behind, and stopped his carriage. The shrine servant was no longer to be seen. When he went on again, the beckoning servant reappeared. After this sequence had repeated itself two or three times, it occurred to His Excellency that Kasuga no Daimyōjin must be giving him a message. He therefore turned the shafts of his carriage to the north and went no father. It is extraordinary that when he drove back through the throng of warriors surrounding him, none raised any objection.

Deer would lick His Excellency's face when he came before the Kasuga Sanctuaries, perhaps because His Excellency always pleased the Deity. Moreover, they also say that he worshiped, in dream, the *suijaku mandara* that has become so popular. [5]

[PICTURE: Motomichi's carriage and escort among the fleeing warriors.]

DATE. The morning of Juei 2.7.25 (1183).

RELATED MATERIAL. *Heike monogatari* 7 *(Shushō no miyako-ochi)* tells nearly the same story. Motomichi sees not a shrine servant beckoning to him from behind but a boy with his hair in *binzura,* and with the characters for Kasuga *(haru* and *hi)* on his sleeves, running before the carriage. The boy advises Motomichi, in verse, to trust in Kasuga.

    1. Fujiwara (Konoe) no Motomichi (1160–1233), the son of Motozane and nephew of Kujō Kanezane. He was adopted by Seishi, the daughter of Taira no Kiyomori, and thanks to Kiyomori became palace minister and then regent for the child-emperor Antoku. After the flight of the Taira he became closely allied with Retired Emperor Go-Shirakawa, against Minamoto no Yoritomo and Kanezane (Yoritomo's ally at court). Dismissed as regent in 1186, at Yoritomo's insistence, he regained the post in 1196 when Yoritomo brought about the dismissal of Kanezane. Motomichi had a residence near Fugenji, then a dependency of Kōfukuji, in modern Tsuzuki-gun, Kyoto-fu, between Kyoto and Nara.

    2. Taira no Munemori (1147–85) was the eldest son of Kiyomori, and the senior Taira after Kiyomori's death in 1181. He fled Kyoto in 1183, as the Minamoto approached the city.

    3. Emperor Antoku with whom the Taira fled, and who drowned at Dannoura in 1185.

    4. Gojō ("Fifth Avenue") runs east and west. Ōmiya here is Higashi Ōmiya, the north-south avenue that ran along the east side of the palace compound.

    5. Motomichi was credited with having seen, in a dream or series of dreams, a full set of Kasuga *honji* and *suijaku* forms. This set then became the basis for many *Kasuga mandara*. The *Yamato shiryō* entry for "Tsugō Jinja" says that Motomichi had these dreams during the Juei period (1182–85), and that the Tsugō Jinja contained, or contains, a painting of them. *Shun-ya shinki* identifies this set of forms with Motomichi. On the other hand, *Kasuga shiki,* dated 1295, does not mention Motomichi. Instead it notes that the same list of *honji* and *suijaku* forms was "certified in Jōan 5 (1175), at the order of Retired Emperor [Go-Shirakawa], by the priest Ōnakatomi no Tokimori, the Overseer Nakatomi no Nobutō, and others." An entry in Kanezane's diary *Gyokuyō* for Juei 3.5 (1184), the earliest written reference to a *Kasuga mandara,* does not make clear just what the picture showed.

## 4.4 *The Sanjō Palace Minister*

When the Sanjō Palace Minister[1] was gravely ill, he sent Grand Prelate Kyōen of Shōrin'in[2] and Hokkyō Kōen[3] to the Kasuga Shrine to pray for him. Starting back to the Capital at dawn, after many days spent in seculsion at the Shrine, they came to the Worship Hall[4] of the Wakamiya. A shrine maiden[5] dancing there came into the open, picked the two out of the crowd, and spoke to them. "I really should grant your prayer," she said, "but although he has risen high as a member of the Clan, he has neglected to worship Me, and this displeases Me greatly. That is why I have now called back his life."

The astonished pair continued their journey immediately. On the way they met a messenger from the Capital, who announced the gentleman's demise.

FIGURE 4.4: The two monks in palanquins, on their way to the Capital, meet the messenger.]

DATE. Eiryaku 1.6.6 (1160), the date of Kinnori's death.

1. Fujiwara (Saionji) no Kinnori (1103–60), the eldest son of major counselor Saneyuki and a daughter of Akisue (see 2.2). *Kasuga genki ekotoba kikigaki* identifies "the Sanjō Palace Minister" tentatively as "Lord Sanefusa." However, Fujiwara no Sanefusa was alive in 1196, while Kyōen died in 1179.

2. Kyōen (1099–1179), a son of Minamoto no Toshishige, was appointed superintendent of Kōfukuji in 1175. He was head of Shōrin'in, a subtemple found by Hanshun (1038–1112).

3. Unknown.

4. *Haiden,* one of the two principal structures at a shrine, the other being the *honden* ("main hall"). The *haiden* of the Wakamiya includes a space for *kagura* dancing.

5. *Miko.* The Wakamiya, unlike the main Kasuga sanctuaries, had a regular staff of *miko* who danced *kagura* and gave oracles.

## 4.5 The Gotokudaiji Minister of the Left

The Gotokudaiji Minister of the Left[1] had resigned as Major Counselor and been in retirement for a dozen years[2] when his son, Kinmori,[3] went to Kasuga as the Festival Envoy.[4] He secretly rode with Kinmori in Kinmori's carriage.

He was at the Wakamiya, unrecognizēd among the servants in Kinmori's train, when the time came for the shrine maidens to perform *kagura* before the Sanctuary. The Deity then gave this oracle: "I am delighted to have you here, and shall make sure you are rewarded."

"Who is this message for?" someone asked.

"This gentleman here," said the Deity, pointing to the incognito Major Counselor.

Soon after his return to Kyoto, he was restored to his Major Counselor post, and within the same year he was appointed Major Captain.

[PICTURE: The scene at the Wakamiya.]

DATE. Probably Angen 3.2 (1177), the time of the Kasuga Festival. Sanesada was reappointed major counselor on Angen 3.3.1, and named major captain of the left in Angen 3.12.

RELATED MATERIALS. The story appears in *Ima kagami* 6, and in *Kokonchomonjū* no. 20. These versions omit Sanesada's son.

BACKGROUND. Although the *Genki* hints that Sanesada was disinterested, the full account in *Kokonchomonjū* ruins this impression. The tedious details are as follows.

When Sanesada was a middle counselor, in Ōhō 2.2 (1162), a fellow middle counselor named Sanenaga was promoted over Sanesada to the junior second rank. Sanesada took this hard, and refused to serve at court on the same days as his rival. He received the same promotion in Ōhō 2.8, but still resented Sanenaga's seniority. Both were promoted to major counselor in Chōkan 2 (1164), but Sanesada remained unappeased, and in Eiman 1.8 (1165) he resigned his post. Very exceptionally, however, he received at the same time a promotion to the senior second rank. This time it was Sanenaga who was put out.

In 1177, thanks to Taira no Shigemori's promotion to palace minister, a major counselor post became vacant and was awarded to Sanesada. Shortly afterwards, Shigemori also resigned as major captain of the left. Sanesada vowed that if he got this post as well, he would make another pilgrimage—this time to Itsukushima, the ancestral shrine of the Taira. Having been successful, he went to Itsukushima in Jishō 3.3 (1179). This is hardly something the *Genki* would have mentioned.

1. Fujiwara (Gotokudaiji) no Sanesada (1139–90), a poet and musician especially expert at *kagura*. Sanesada eventually became palace minister, minister of the right, and, in Bunji 4 (1188), minister of the left. It was Sanesada whom the poet Saigyō served before becoming a monk. He may be the "Lord Tokudaiji" represented in *Senjūshō* 5/15 as being adept at making living people out of bones.

2. He resigned in Chōkan 3 (1165).

3. 1162–86. Kinmori died of a fall from a horse.

4. The imperial envoy to the Kasuga Festival, which after 1135 was held annually on the first *saru* ("monkey") day in the second month. The envoy was normally a member of the imperial guard.

## 4.6 (No separate title)

He was Palace Minister and Major Captain of the Left when Kiso-no-Kanja Yoshinaka's[1] lawlessness prevented him from continuing as a Minister of State. Bitterly disappointed, he prayed day and night to the Daimyōjin. Then he dreamed that a monk wearing an over-robe[2] came to him and said, "You must proceed to the Antechamber[3] immediately."

Puzzled at the messenger's guise, Sanesada asked who he was.

"A junior official[4] of Kōfukuji," the messenger replied.

"No longer being in office, I certainly cannot go to the Antechamber. Besides, a Minister of Sate is customarily called to service by a Secretary.[5] A junior official of Kōfukuji is a most unsuitable messenger. No I cannot possibly go."

The same messenger came back again. "The Ministers of State and all the nobles below them have repaired to the Palace, where they are now considering the affairs of the Realm." he insisted. "You *must* hurry to join them."

Sanesada realized when he awoke that this had been no ordinary dream, and he took the opportunity to mention it when, the following day, he visited the palace of the Senior Grand Empress.[6]

"Perhaps you are to be reappointed," Her Majesty suggested.

Extraordinary to relate, he was reappointed Palace Minister two or three days later.

[PICTURE: The monk arriving at Sanesada's residence, with Sanesada peering out at him.]

DATE. Sanesada was restored to office on Juei 3.1.12 (1184).

BACKGROUND. The Taira fled Kyoto with Emperor Antoku on Juei 2.3.25 (1183), just before the arrival of Yoshinaka's troops. Yoshinaka's choice of a new emperor did not please Retired Emperor Go-Shirakawa, and various other demands and actions of his aroused resentment in Kyoto. Angered, Yoshinaka then intervened violently in the affairs of the court. Sanesada was relieved of his post on Juei 2.11.21. Yoshinaka was driven from Kyoto and killed on Juei 3.1.20, a week after Sanesada's reinstatement.

1. Minamoto no Yoshinaka (1154–84), the warlord who in 1183 captured Kyoto from the Taira.

2. *Ue-no-kinu,* the outer robe worn by a civil official on duty at court, normally over the "formal dress" *(sokutai)* costume.

3. *Jin,* the place in the palace compound, by the Shishinden, where the nobles gathered for ceremonies and councils.

4. *Geshoshi,* one of a number of junior officials directly under the superintendent.

5. *Geki,* a secretary to the council of state.

6. Fujiwara no Tashi (1140–1201), Sanesada's full sister by blood, although she had been adopted by Fujiwara no Yorinaga. Tashi became Konoe's empress in 1150, then grand empress *(kōtaigō),* then senior grand empress *(taikōtaigō)* after Konoe's death in 1155. She was so beautiful that Nijō insisted on making her his empress too in 1160—something unprecedented.

## 5.1 Lord Toshimori

Lord Toshimori, the Provisional Master of the Grand Empress's Household,[1] lived a long time in obscurity, having been left an orphan by his father. He was pondering how to establish himself when he had a visit from the Kasuga priest Tokimori, and discussed the matter with him. Tokimori recommended monthly pilgrimages to the Kasuga Shrine, and Toshimori took his advice.

[PICTURE: Tokimori at Toshimori's house; Toshimori setting off to Kasuga.]

For years he never missed a single pilgrimage, until he was named Governor of Sanuki. In due course he gained the respect of all, was called into the Retired Emperor's intimate service, and became the Assistant Director of the Grand Empress's Household.[2] His house grew rich in consequence, and his reputation rose wonderfully high. He attributed all this entirely to the blessings of the Daimyōjin, whom he served with ever-increasing zeal.

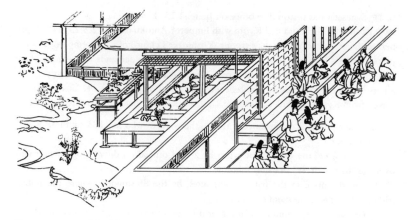

[FIGURE 5.1: Toshimori's prosperous mansion and garden. The gate and approaches to the mansion are crowded with visitors.]

Once when he was on pilgrimage at the Shrine, a quiet night rain was dripping pleasingly from the pines. Feeling unusually at peace, he was deep in reflection on the vanity of coming here in search of worldly gain, when he heard an awesome voice over by the Sanctuaries saying, "The path of enlightenment too is the path of my Mountain." He shed tears of joy, and would wet his sleeves again long afterward, remembering.

[PICTURE: Toshimori dozing at the shrine.]

As the years passed, the fortunes of Toshimori's house gradually declined. All was quiet before his gate, and a visitor's horse was seldom to be seen. Then he understood that glory and obscurity each have their portion, and prosperity and decline each their time; and so he gave no more thought to anything but the life to come. Until the very moment of his death he entrusted himself to the Daimyōjin's protection. Someone in fact dreamed of hearing that the Lay Monk of the Third Rank was on his way to Rebirth.[3] The dreamer saw a purple cloud floating in the air, and a lotus throne growing from Toshimori's house. On the throne sat a child of three, accompanied by a yellow-robed shrine servant. And there came a voice saying, "Kasuga no Daimyōjin has commanded that a servant shall go with him."

Three years later, Toshimori did indeed achieve Rebirth. The three-year-old child had meant that he was to do so in three years. There were many auspicious signs too when at last he passed away, and they say that people knew of the event from dreams.

[PICTURE: Toshimori, dressed as a monk, rising upward on a cloud. A shrine servant follows him.

DATES. Born in 1120, Toshimori in 1151 held the fourth rank *(Kasuga mōde burui ki)*; rose to the junior third rank in 1163; was named provisional master *(gon-no daibu)* of the grand empress's household in 1166; achieved the senior third rank in 1167; became a monk in 1177; and died ca. 1180 *(Kugyō bunin)*.

RELATED MATERIALS. *Ima monogatari* tells briefly how Toshimori heard the deity speak the words quoted by the *Genki,* and how he achieved rebirth. It specifies that Toshimori was passing Kasuga-yama at the time, and that the voice spoke "from a high branch."

ANOTHER STORY ON THE "PATH OF MY MOUNTAIN" THEME. *Shaksekishū* 1/2 tells how Gedatsu Shōnin traveled in dream to the Outer Shrine of Ise, went straight up a path to the top of the hill south of the shrine, and found there a pond filled with lotuses. He was told that these were for the priests of the shrine who achieved rebirth. In other words, the top of the little hill was paradise.

1 Fujiwara no Toshimori (1120–ca. 1180) was the son of Akimori who had served Retired Emperor Shirakawa. The *Kugyō bunin* entry under Toshimori's name for Eiman 2 (1166) notes his appointment as *Kōtaigō no miya no gon-no-daibu;* then from Nin'an 2 (1167) on describes him, like the *Genki,* as *Ōmiya no gon-no-daibu.*

2. The text says that Toshimori served the retired emperor *(in),* who must have been Go-Shirakawa; then in the same sentence states simply that he was appointed *nen'yo.* A *nen'yo* was the assistant director of a household such as the retired emperor's or the regent's. One would assume that the retired emperor's household is meant, except that as explained in n.1 above, Toshimori clearly belonged to the household of the grand empress. This lady was probably Kenshunmon'in (Taira no Shigeko, 1142–76), who became Go-Shirakawa's consort in 1167, though she was not actually appointed grand empress until 1168.

3. Rebirth *(ōjō)* means birth into the paradise of Amida, a happy event often announced to the living by miraculous signs. The "Lay Monk of the Third Rank" is Toshimori. A lay monk *(nyūdō)* was a gentleman who had retired to "enter the path" of Buddhism, but who generally remained at home and led the life of a leisured, though perhaps pious layman.

SIGNIFICANT VARIANTS. (1) The phrase "was dripping pleasingly from the pines" translates *shōro maikudarikereba* from the Kadokawa text. *Gunsho ruijū* has *shadan sekisekitarikereba,* "the Shrine was still"; while the Yōmei Bunko text has *shōzen sekiseki-tarikereba,* "the pine fence was still."

(2) Instead of "the path of my Mountain," the Kadokawa and Yōmei Bunko texts

have "the path of my heart." This is an error. Someone, perhaps even Mototada who wrote out the original, has mistaken the character *yama* for the character *kokoro*. Not only does the *Ima monogatari* version, like *Gunsho ruijū* and *Kasuga go-ruki*, have *yama*, but *Genki* 20.2 has the passage, "Surely that is why the Venerable Myōe revered the Mountain as Vulture Peak, and why He told Lord Toshimori that it is the path to enlightenment."

## 5.2 Lord Sueyoshi

Lord Sueyoshi,[1] of the Senior Third Rank, was Lord Toshimori's son. Ever since his father's day he had greatly revered the Daimyōjin, and had gone each month to Kasuga on pilgrimage. One night he dreamed that a monk came to him, very swarthy and frightening to look at. The helpless Sueyoshi's hair stood on end as the monk approached. Just then there was a noise of someone outside. To the servant who went to find out who it was, the visitor identified himself as a messenger from the Kasuga Shrine. The monk paled at the sound of the man's voice, and fled. Sueyoshi awoke in a sweat and related the dream to his attendants. Evidently a *tengu* had come, and the Daimyōjin had seen him and driven him off. It was a signal blessing.

[FIGURE 5.2: Sueyoshi and his wife lie sleeping while the monk flees. The messenger stands outside.]

DATE. Probably after 1180, the last known date for Toshimori.

1. Fujiwara no Sueyoshi (d. ca. 1211). He was named to the junior fifth rank, lower, in 1158; reached the junior third rank in 1183; and became a monk in 1210.

## 6.1 Koma no Yukimitsu

Koma no Yukimitsu[1] was a dancer at Kōfukuji. He had learned the dance *Katen*[2] from his father in his sixteenth year, and several times since then had danced it secretly, as an offering, before the Shrine.

Once when Yukimitsu was very ill, he stopped breathing and found himself at Enma's court.[3] Just then a majestic-looking gentleman arrived, and King Enma welcomed him effusively. "This man is deeply devoted to me," said the gentleman to Enma, "and has been so ever since his sixteenth year. I should like you to release him to me."

King Enma obeyed, and the gentleman led Yukimitsu from the palace.

Yukimitsu was amazed. "My Lord," he said, "your generous kindness alone has procured me this pardon. But who are you?"

"I am Kasuga no Daimyōjin," the gentleman replied. "Would you care to see Hell?"

"Yes, please," said Yukimitsu.

Kasuga no Daimyōjin took Yukimitsu straight off and showed him Hell. The torments there were quite indescribable. After seeing them all, Yukimitsu asked how he could possibly avoid such retribution.

"Be filial to your father and mother," the Daimyōjin instructed him. "Filial piety is the highest virtue. If you cultivate it, you will not fall into Hell."

[PICTURE: Yukimitsu dancing before the shrine; kneeling naked before Enma; and being led by the deity to see hell, which is vividly depicted in several scenes.]

DATE. Ca. 1130-50, since Yukimitsu lived 1090–1152 and this story clearly refers to his later years.

POSSIBLE SOURCE. This story appears in nearly identical form in *Kyōkunshō* 1, where the author Chikazane (see 7.3,n. 7) attributes it to a *Miyashiro no genki,* now lost, written by Gedatsu Shōnin.

1. 1090–1152, probably the son of Koma no Yukitaka *(Kyōkunshō)*.
2. A dance of the left, usually performed by four unmasked dancers. Chikazane in *Kyōkunshō* 1 makes it clear that *Katen* was an extremely felicitous dance.
3. Enma, the king of hell, judged the dead, aided by a whole staff of officials, bailiffs, etc. He looked like a Chinese magistrate.


## 6.2 Lord Chikamune

When Middle Counselor Chikamune[1] was the proprietor[2] of Izumi province, there was a disturbance in which some Kasuga shrine servants were involved. Chikamune seized a shrine servant, rolled him up in a blind, and beat him so severely that he killed him. Kōfukuji submitted a report on the incident, with the result that Chikamune's son,[3] the Governor of the province, was exiled, and Chikamune was relieved of his proprietary rights.

Perhaps the Daimyōjin was not yet satisfied, however, for in the 7th month of Shōji 1, Chikamune came down with an ague and suffered for days while his condition only worsened. Finally he summoned a healer, a monk from the Mountain known as Sanmi no Azari,[4] to pray in his behalf.

Sannō Jūzenji[5] possessed the medium and announced, "It is not because of fixed karma[6] that this man is ill, nor is King Enma insisting on calling him to his palace because he has accomplished no great good.[7] No, he is being summoned because Kasuga no Daimyōjin has rejected him. He has no more than a day or two to live. Do not pray on his behalf. Leave him immediately." Realizing that his efforts were useless, the healer withdrew.

The illness grew steadily worse until on the 27th of the 7th month, Chikamune died. Someone then dreamed that three shrine servants ran past his gate. "What is going on?" the dreamer demanded to know. The shrine servants replied, "We are messengers from Kasuga no Daimyōjin, come to fetch the Taira Middle Counselor." Not only that, but the gentleman who lived across the street from Chikamune dreamed he saw some shrine servants break violently into Chikamune's house.[8] In other words, even though the Daimyōjin's curse did not fall immediately, it inevitably struck at last. How then could those who serve Him faithfully go in the end unrewarded?

# THE MIRACLES OF THE KASUGA DEITY

[PICTURE: The scene at Chikamune's mansion as the healer and medium go about their business.]

DATE. The incident occurred in the 9th or early 10th month of Kenkyū 9 (1198). Chikamune died on Shōji 1.7.27 (1199).

BACKGROUND. A dispatch from Kōfukuji to Kamakura (*Kōfukuji chōjō*, document no. 1009 in *Kamakura ibun*, vol. 2), drafted by none other than Gedatsu Shōnin, provides the background of this affair. The dispatch is dated Kenkyū 9.11.1 (1198). It appears that in connection with preparations to entertain Retired Emperor Go-Shirakawa, when he passed through Izumi on his way to Kumano, outrageous corvée labor was levied on the inhabitants of Kōfukuji and Kasuga estates in the province; and that the authority responsible was the proprietor of the province, Taira no Chikamune. During that time, a servant *(shichō)* on the Tanikawa estate, belonging to Kōfukuji, was rolled up in a blind, and scalding water was poured over him, causing him extreme suffering. The other people of the estate only barely managed to save his life. (The text does not make it quite clear whether Chikamune was directly responsible for the outrage.) Kōfukuji was preparing a protest when, on the Haruki estate belonging to Kasuga, a shrine servant (or perhaps several shrine servants) was likewise rolled up in a blind, and the local Kasuga *sakaki* seized and burned. When the local people tried to intervene, more sacred *sakaki* were burned. The dispatch also cites, without details, other outrages perpetrated on the Ikeda estate. It expresses the highest degree of indignation at such sacrilegious affronts to the Kasuga deity's dignity.

By the time Kōfukuji sent this communication to Kamakura, the affair had already become very serious. *Kōfukuji shinboku dōza chōjō*, dated Kenkyū 9.10.8, cites "the recent burning of the sacred tree and maltreatment of shrine servants in Izumi province,[11] and announces an expedition *(shinboku dōza)* to press the grievance, set for Kenkyū 9.10.20. However, according to Uwayokote Masataka (1975:51), Yoritomo forbade this action, informing Kōfukuji that he would send troops, led by himself if necessary, even if this meant bloodshed among the monks.

A document dated to the 6th month of 1213 (*Fukuchiin-ke monjo* no. 18) alludes to the incident of 1198, but states that although the shrine servant (or servants) was treated harshly, no one was killed. The document is a long complaint about the death of a Kasuga shrine servant, written by "the Kasuga shrine servants residing in the village of Ikeda in Izumi province." The death in question followed the punishment of five villagers—who were also shrine servants—suspected of concealing some of their paddy fields.

Fujiwara no Teika's diary, *Meigetsuki,* often mentions Chikamune. The entry for Shōji 1.7.25 (1199) says:

Lord Taira no Chikamune, the Middle Counselor of the Second Rank, died today. They say he had recently been ill. He was in his sixty-fifth year. Last year the monks of Kōfukuji made a complaint against him, and he was dismissed as the proprietor of the province of Izumi. Shortly thereafter His Majesty was gracious enough to award him Kaga. Chikamune was then granted the Senior Second Rank despite the fact that his son was in exile. Did this violate the divine will, I wonder? The grant was made immediately after he was awarded Kaga. One has to call it awesome good fortune.

The remark about "divine will" suggests that people were already attributing Chikamune's death to the wrath of the Kasuga deity. At any rate, the next day (the 26th), Teika noted, "The report about Chikamune was wrong. He is still alive." However, Teika's entry for the following day has, "Lord Chikamune passed away at noon. This is firm."

The poet and diarist Ukyō no Daibu noted Chikamune's death, without further comment, and addressed to Chikamune's son Chikanaga (?–?) a long series of poems of condolence (*Kenreimon' in Ukyō no Daibu shū*) nos. 334–46.

1. Taira no Chikamune (1144-99), a son of the posthumous minister of the left Taira no Tokinobu. He was appointed middle counselor *(chūnagon)* only in Shōji 1.6 (1199), just before falling ill.

2. *Chigyō shikeru hodo ni.* According to Peter J. Arnesen (1982:94): "By the early part of the twelfth century the Heian court had begun to assign proprietary provinces to members of the upper nobility for periods as long as four to eight years. . . . The man who was assigned to such a province thereby acquired the right not only to designate who should be its governor, but also to share with the latter at least part of the proceeds of the province's public domain." Chikamune had obviously chosen the governor, his son Munenobu, himself.

3. Taira no Munenobu (1177–1231), Chikamune's third son. Appointed governor of Izumi in 1194 (he was rather young), he was dismissed in 1198 (Kenkyū 9.10.1) because of this incident, then (according to *Kugyō bunin*) exiled to Harima, although *Kasuga genki ekotoba kikigaki* says he was exiled to Sanuki. He was recalled in 1201, and reinstated the next year as a minor counselor *(shōnagon).* He was given the junior third rank in 1228.

4. Unidentified. "The Mountain" is Mt. Hiei. "Sanmi" means that he held the third court rank before entering religion. "Azari" (or Ajari) was a title conferred on certain ranking esoteric adepts, who were often healers.

5. One of the sanctuaries of the Hie Shrine complex below Mt. Hiei.

6. *Jōgō:* karma fixed by one's actions before one came into this present life.

7. *Daizen:* action that constitutes good karma.

8. Sometimes shrine servants really did break into and lay waste the house of someone who had offended the shrine and who remained adamantly unrepentant. They arrived carrying the divine *sakaki,* making it perfectly clear that it was the deity who was punishing the offender.

## 6.3 A Snake Swallows the Heart Sutra

At the spot at Kasuga known as Rokudō,[1] some children beat a snake that had swallowed a copy of the Heart Sutra,[2] and made it disgorge the book. Their ringleader immediately became very ill. When *gohō* divination[3] was done, the Daimyōjin came down and declared: "Someone who honored me has fallen, because of a single evil attachment, into the realm of snakes. To save him I got him to swallow the Heart Sutra, hoping in this way to spare him being rewarded with the Evil Realms.[4] Then this child beat him until he spat it out. I am greatly displeased, and so have punished the child. He will live if you read through the whole *Daihannya-kyō*."[5]

The reading was done right away, and the child recovered.

[PICTURE: The snake with the scroll in its mouth, surrounded by its attackers; the boy lying sick.]

AN ANALOGOUS STORY. An analogous incident appears in *Ōkagami* (McCullough 1980:182): "Fukutarigimi [an unmanageable boy, the son of Fujiwara no Michikane] died after he made the mistake of tormenting a snake, which cursed him and made a tumor grow on his head."

1. Presently a spot on the main avenue to the shrine at the entrance to the "Man'yō Garden." A rivulet flows under the path there. The name means the "six realms" of reincarnation. *Senjūshō* 5/14 describes the place as follows (tr. Moore 1982:188): "I gradually made my way into the shrine grounds where stood a grove of tall, luxuriant cryptomeria, traversed by six paths like the six-forked crossroads of the afterworld."

2. The *Hannyaharamitta shingyō* (Skt. *Prajñāpāramitā-hrdaya-sūtra*): a short summary of the *prajñāpāramitā* literature, widely used in Mahāyāna Buddhism.

3. See chapter 5, under "The Fourth Sanctuary as *gohō*."

4. *Akushu*. The less desirable realms of incarnation: hell, hungry ghosts, beasts, and ashuras.

5. The *Mahāprajñāpāramitā-sūtra*, or "Greater Sutra on the Perfection of Wisdom," translated by Hsüan-tsang in 659. It was read regularly for the Kasuga deity, as for other deities.

## 7.1 Lord Tsunemichi

Lord Tsunemichi[1] was Head Chamberlain[2] when, at the beginning of Emperor Juntoku's reign, he came to wear deep mourning.[3] His office was then reassigned, since someone in deep mourning could not very well hold it.[4]

Three years later there was still no sign that Tsunemichi would get his post back. He was so upset that on the 6th day of the 1st month of Kenryaku 2 he began a retreat at Kasuga, stationing himself in the evening under the Rōmon to sing *kagura*[5] and play the flute all through the night.

During the night of the 10th of the 5th month, the Retired Emperor[6] dreamed that someone unknown to him approached him and asked, "Why do you not return Lord Tsunemichi to the office of Head Chamberlain?"

His Majesty woke up and asked Kyō-no-nii[7] whether Tsunemichi were present. The lady replied that he had not been seen for some time.

"Ah," thought the Retired Emperor, "the fellow must be on retreat at Kamo[8] or somewhere, praying."

"Then look for him," he ordered.

Kyō-no-nii sent someone to do so, and reported that lately Tsunemichi had been on retreat at Kasuga.

"Sure enough," remarked His Majesty, "the Gods do not proceed as we simple humans do!" He commanded that Tsunemichi be reinstated the following day.

On the 11th, the messenger reached Kasuga with the news. Tsunemichi was beneath the Rōmon at the time. "Monks of the Temple!" he cried. "Listen! I am happy now, for suddenly I have my boon!" And he withdrew, struggling to keep back his tears. Everyone near the Rōmon, including the monks, praised as unrivaled the blessings of the Daimyōjin.

After that, Tsunemichi chanted "Namu Daimyōjin" constantly, day and night. He rose to be a Major Counselor of the Senior Second Rank. Even as he lay dying his devotion never wavered. No doubt the Daimyōjin watched over him in his next life as well.

[PICTURE: Tsunemichi playing his flute under the Rōmon; the messenger delivering the good news to Tsunemichi, in the presence of three monks.]

DATE. Kenryaku 2 (1212).

1. Fujiwara no Tsunemichi (1176-1239), the eldest son of Fujiwara no Yasumichi and the daughter of Takasue (see 7.4). *Kugyō bunin* confirms that he reached the senior second rank, as well as the post of provisional major counselor.

2. A head chamberlain (there were two *Kurōdo no tō*) was in charge of daily affairs in the emperor's private secretariat. The post was highly advantageous, and normally led to greater things.

3. *Jūbuku*, mourning for a parent—probably Tsunemichi's father who became a monk in 1209, though his death date is not recorded.

4. Because he was polluted by his association with death.

5. The Rōmon, also known as Chūmon ("Middle Gate"), is the south gate in the gallery directly before the four main sanctuaries, between the *heiden* and the sanctuaries. *Kagura* is the music and dance offered at shrines.

6. Go-Toba (1180–1239, r. 1183–98).

7. Kenshi (1155–1229), Go-Toba's wetnurse; the daughter of Fujiwara no Norikane; and the wife of Gedatsu Shōnin's father, Fujiwara no Sadanori. She was a powerful figure at Go-Toba's court.

8. A complex of two great shrines in northeast Kyoto, along the Kamo River. They protect Kyoto and are closely associated with the imperial house.

## 7.2 Kairen-bō's Dream

The nun Kairen-bō was the mother of a Kōfukuji monk named Sonpen (a Personal Attendant).[1] She dreamed that she was told, "Chant the invocation 'Namu Daimyōjin.' Other invocations manifest the virtue of only one Buddha or Bodhisattva. One saying of 'Namu Daimyōjin,' however, makes manifest the power of all Five Sanctuaries, and so its benefits are vast."

[PICTURE: Kairen-bō lying asleep at home, dreaming.]

DATE. Perhaps ca. 1225–29, the period when Jisson, Sonpen's patron, was superintendent.

MATERIALS ON NAMU DAIMYŌJIN. (1) *Tamon'in nikki* 43 (vol. 5:45) records the following oracle, to which it attributes the dubious date of Tenpyō-Shōhō 1.4.8 (757).

What should the people and clansmen of this Shrine consider throughout all future generations to be their treasure? Let them take no account of riches. . . . They must consider only that the Great Deity [or Deities] Manifest Below (*ōkami suijaku*) is their treasure. One who calls My Name in an instant of thought will not do so in vain. In this life he will have countless benefits according to his own wishes, and in the next life he will receive a good birth, and enjoy great happiness.

(2) Jinson (*Daijōin jisha zōjiki* for Meiō 7.12.1[1498]) raised in his diary the issue of the conflicting theories about the *honji* of the Kasuga sanctuaries. After acknowledging that the matter was vexingly complex, he wrote, "All these [theories] are resolved in the invocation 'Namu Kasuga no Daimyōjin.' It is like the light of many lamps illumining a single room."

(3) *Senjūshō* 5/9 tells how grand prelate Shinpan of Kōfukuji left his temple and took up the life of a wandering ascetic. At last, at a spot below Mt. Miwa, he faced

east, chanted "Namu Kasuga no Daimyōjin," and "passed away as though falling asleep."

1. Kairen-bō is unknown. Sonpen appears in a list of *daibōshi* who attended the Yuima-e of 1224 (Hiraoka 1958–60, vol. 1:313); and *Kōfukuji bettō shidai* ("Jisson") records that in 1229 Jisson delegated his administrative duties *(bōmu)* to graduate *(tokugō)* Sonpen. "Personal Attendant" *(jijū)* means that Sonpen personally attended the superintendent.

## 7.3 Chikazane and Ryōō

On the 2d day of the 1st month of Kenpō 5, at the hour of the Tiger,[1] Hanken, a Superior at Kōfukuji,[2] dreamed that he went to the Kasuga Shrine. Looking toward the Sanctuaries from beneath the wisteria in front of the *heiden,*[3] he noticed an extraordinarily tall young man in his late teens standing under the Rōmon. As Hanken watched the young man, a gentleman in formal dress[4] approached from the western end of the Shrine fence, joined Hanken under the wisteria, and said to him, "He has told Chikazane[5] to do *Ryōō*[6] for him, but Chikazane has replied that he cannot because no baton[7] has been handed down to him. Make a baton for *Ryōō,* give it to Chikazane, and have him dance *Ryōō* before the Shrine."

Hanken respectfully agreed. "But whatever you may tell *me,*" he observed, "I doubt that Chikazane himself will listen."

"Well," rejoined the gentleman, "if Chikazane resists, then He will have to devise something else."

The young man beneath the Rōmon spoke. "Now you know my will," he said. "Go quickly." His voice echoed loudly from the Mountain.

No further argument was possible. Hanken (in his dream) left by the Keigamon.[8] Then he woke up.

[PICTURE: Hanken at the Rōmon; the two divine presences are shown with their faces covered by tree branches.]

Hanken soon found out how the baton at Zenjōin[9] was made, and copied it. He put the new baton in a brocade bag and sent it to Chikazane with a note explaining his dream and the model he had used. Chikazane arranged with the musicians to dance *Ryōō* at the Shrine, using this baton, on the 16th of the 2d month of the same year. He did all the secret pieces such as *Ranjo, Saezuri,* and *Kōjo.*[10] Apparently Kagemoto played the flute,[11] Tadaaki the *shō,*[12] and Kagekata the great drum.[13] This was a wonder indeed.

[PICTURE: Chikazane dancing *Ryōō.*]

DATE. Kenpō 5 (1217).

POSSIBLE SOURCE. Chikazane himself told exactly the same story in *Kyōkunshō* 1, down to the list of musicians and of pieces performed. He also noted that the baton Hanken copied was the property of his (Chikazane's) grandfather, Mitsuchika; and that it was deposited at the "Zenjōin Palace." Thus Hanken's model actually belonged to Chikazane's line, but Chikazane had not yet been given it.

RELATED MATERIALS. The story appears, differently told, in the *Jizō engi* owned by the Freer Gallery (Kondō 1958:88).

1. Ca. 4 A.M.

2. "Superior" *(jishu),* a monastic rank, suggests that Hanken was a member of the temple council *(gōsho,* as here, or *sangō);* however, his name does not appear in *Kōfukuji sōgō bunin,* for this date or anywhere near this date. (There were other *jishu* at this time named Hanzō and Hangon.) This Hanken should not be confused with the Hanken who was consulted about the compiling of the *Genki.*

3. The structure, within the main sanctuary precincts, from which the ordinary pilgrim greets the sanctuaries. Hanken was between it and the Rōmon.

4. *Sokutai,* the normal costume for court ceremonies. One who wore *sokutai* normally carried a ceremonial baton *(shaku).*

5. Komo no Chikazane (1177–1242), a musician and dancer at Kōfukuji, and the author of *Kyōkunshō* (1233), an essential treatise on *bugaku.* There is presently a small shrine to him (the Hyōshi Jinja) at the northeast corner of the Noboriōji-Yonbanchō intersection in Nara, near the Nara National Museum. It is absent from lists of Kasuga *massha* dating back to 1133, but according to *Kōfukuji ranshōki,* a shrine with a similar name (perhaps read Komako Jinja) was built in 1081. The text quotes from the diary of Koma no Mitsutoki (1087–1159), who wrote that in accordance with a sacred dream, he buried beneath the sanctuary a *Ryōō* mask that was a family treasure.

6. A *bugaku* dance said variously to have originated in P'o-hai (modern Manchuria) or in India. The two completely different versions of its story line both have to do with a dragon-visaged being triumphing in battle. The mask is fierce and surmounted by a dragon. *Ryōō* was often danced to bring rain. Chikazane discussed it in detail in *Kyōkunshō.*

7. *Bachi,* the baton that *bugaku* dancers hold for certain dances. *Kyōkunshō* contains a section on the *Ryōō* baton.

8. A secondary gate to the main Kasuga sanctuaries, on the west side of the *kairō* enclosure. It was generally reserved for members of the Fujiwara clan.

9. A subtemple of Kōfukuji, founded by Jōgen (d. 1158) of Gangōji, on the site of the present Nara Hotel. Jōgen ceded Zenjōin to his disciple Raijitsu of Daijōin, and thereafter the head of Daijōin was also by tradition the head of Zenjōin. Since Zenjōin

escaped the great fire of 1180, all the *honzon* of Kōfukuji that had been saved from the fire were deposited there; and for years afterwards, all important Kōfukuji ceremonies except the Yuima-e were held there. (The Yuima-e was held in the Jikidō.) Zenjōin burned down in 1451 and was not rebuilt.

10. *Ranjo, Saezuri,* and *Kōjo* are all passages from the full form of *Ryōō. Kōjo,* an extremely "secret" piece, was seldom done and is now no longer performed. It required a special mask.

11. Ōkami no Kagemoto (1200–50), a professional *gagaku* musician and the son of Kagekata. His flute was probably a *ryūteki,* a bamboo pipe with seven holes, about a foot long and wrapped in cherry bark.

12. A professional *gagaku* musician. *Kyōkunshō* mentions him playing the *shō* in 1222. The *shō* is a reed instrument composed of seventeen pipes of varying lengths that are blown through a common air chamber.

13. Ōkami no Kagekata (1168–1224), a professional musician and the father of Kagemoto. *Bugaku* requires a pair of great drums *(taiko),* though only one is played for each piece. The famous pair at Kasuga is huge.

## 7.4 The Dream of the Lady in Lord Takasue's Household

Gojō-no-Tsubone, a lady in the household of Lord Takasue, the [Deputy] Governor-General of Dazaifu,[1] dreamed that she saw on the bank of a great river a *sotoba*[2] bearing this inscription:

Those with heavy karmic impediments[3]
will have, thanks to Mikasa Daibosatsu[4]
the Compassionate Lord, the Great Guide,[5]
Rebirth in the Land of Bliss.

[PICTURE: The lady asleep; then standing in her dream before the *sotoba.*]

DATE. Ca. 1180, if one assumes that Takasue then actually bore the title mentioned.

1. Gojō-no-Tsubone is unknown. Fujiwara no Takasue (1126–at least 1182) was a great-grandson of Akisue (see 2.2). He served Retired Emperors Toba and Go-Shira-kawa, Kenreimon'in, and Takakura. In 1179 he was appointed deputy governor-general of Dazaifu *(Dazai gon-no-sotsu).* (The *Genki* text has just *Dazai no sotsu,* but this means *gon-no-sotsu,* for by this time the governor-general himself was almost always an imperial prince who stayed in the Capital.) Illness forced him to become a monk in 1182. Engen (1175–1250), one of his sons, was head of Ichijōin, and superintendent in 1232–33 and 1249–50.

2. From the Sankrit *stūpa.* A flat or squared length of wood having roughly the outline of a reliquary tower. A *sotoba* normally stands by a grave.

3. *Gōshō,* karma of all kinds that blocks the path to enlightenment.

4. The Kasuga deity.

5. These epithets for the deity refer to the deity's identity as Shaka.

## 8.1 The Seiryōji Buddha

In the Kenpō era a former gentlewoman, now a nun, went on pilgrimage to the Shakadō in Saga.[1] She had a little something she wished to say to the Buddha. Straight off she chose the Superintendent, Hōgen Ninga,[2] to officiate, and told him how she happened to have come.

"I used to live at Bodaisen[3] near the Southern Capital," she said, "and I went regularly on pilgrimage to the Kasuga Shrine. But then for various reasons I moved to the Capital, which was so far away that I naturally could not visit Kasuga any more. This saddened me until the Daimyōjin told me, in a dream, 'I am at the Shakadō in Saga. That is close by, so you must come to see me there.' That is why I have come here specially to make my prayer."

This confirms that the Gongen's *honji* is indeed Shaka. It is a marvelous story. Ninga told it to Gedatsu-bō of Kasagi on Kenpō 6.2.15.[4]

[PICTURE: The nun's visit to the Shakadō.]

DATE. The Kenpō era (1213–19).

1. Shakadō is the popular name for the main hall of Seiryōji, a temple in the Saga area, just northeast of Kyoto. The temple was established, at his master's wish, by Seisan, a disciple of Chōnen (d. 1016), and enshrines an exceedingly famous image of Shaka brought back by Chōnen from China.

2. Unidentified.

3. A locality in the mountains about five km. southeast of Nara. It is the site of Shōryakuji, a Shingon temple founded by Kenshun in 992, and rebuilt by Shin'en (see 15.3, n. 1). Shōryakuji was attached to Daijōin.

4. For Gedatsu-bō and Kasagi, see 16.1. The date Kenpō 6 (1218) is a puzzle since Gedatsu Shōnin died in 1213. Note that the 15th day of the 2d month was the date of the Budda's nirvana, and hence of the Nehan-e (see 18.2, n. 3).

## 8.2 A Household Escape Sickness Thanks to the Merit of the Yuishiki ron

The adoptive father of Prelate Hanga[1] of Zennan'in,[2] the Lay Monk known as Ōtoneri Nyūdō,[3] was at the time a well-known warrior. One year when an epidemic was abroad and the sickness had touched every household, one of the gentleman's men dreamed that a horde of soldiers was set to break into his master's house when those in the lead peered inside, removed their helmets, bowed low, and excalimed, "The Yuishiki ron[4] is here! We must leave it in peace!" Then they all went away.

The next morning, the man went to his master's house to report the dream. "What's the Yuishiki ron?" asked his master. Hanga happened to be in the Capital at the time, staying in the house, and when he heard what had happened he made a careful search. Far back on a shelf in the guest room he discovered the ninth fascicle of the Yuishiki ron. This was where Hanga always stayed, so one of his companions must have forgotten it there.

[PICTURE: The soldiers kneeling before the gentleman's gate, while a man in the hovel next door vomits and a demon peers in from the roof; Hanga discovering the sacred text.]

DATE. Not earlier than 1183 if Hanga was prelate at the time, though he may not have been. Sōgō bunin zanketsu, rank lists for the years 1184 and 1185, does not mention him.

1. Born in 1153, Hanga was definer (ryūgi) for the Yuima-e in 1171, and lecturer (kōji) in 1183 (Sanne jōikki). "Prelate" (sōzu) was an unofficial abbreviation for either of the two sōgō ranks of shōsōzu ("minor prelate") or daisōzu ("major prelate").

2. A lesser subtemple of Kōfukuji. It does not appear in the list of forty in cited by Nagashima (1944:159), and dated to the reign of Emperor Juntoku (1210–21).

3. Unidentified. An ōtoneri was an imperial attendant.

4. The thirty verses of the Yuishiki sanjū ron ju, together with the body of commentary on them by Dharmapāla, as translated by Hsüan-tsang. The work is more formally entitled Jōyuishiki ron (Ch. Ch'eng-wei-shih-lun, Skt. Vijñapti-matratā-siddhi). It is the fundamental text of the Hossō school. Taishō 31/1, no. 1585.

## 8.3 Prelate Zōri

Prelate Zōri[1] of Kōfukuji was from Nagusa county in the province of Kii. He kept polished the jewel of conduct according to the Precepts,[2] and lifted high the lamp of devoted study. As a student of both the Exoteric and the Esoteric Teachings,[3] he could not tell which was the provisional and which was the true.[4] He therefore decided to set up an altar for each, equipped with the appropriate ritual implements and sacred texts, at either end—east and west—of the Central Pavilion.[5] He would then solicit Kasuga no Daimyōjin's presence, and have the Daimyōjin pronounce judgment.

When everything was ready, a divine person descended into the room. Bowing first before the Esoteric altar, he said, "How holy are the Esoteric Teachings!" Then bowing before the Hossō altar,[6] he said, "How profound are the Exoteric Teachings!" Each clearly received full acknowledgment.

Zōri was the first Selector for the Yuima-e.[7]

[PICTURE: A gentleman in formal dress, prostrating himself before the Esoteric altar.]

DATE. Perhaps ca. 875–85.

BACKGROUND AND RELATED MATERIALS. According to *Honchō kōsō den*, Zōri first studied Hossō at Kōfukuji, but then later, toward the end of the Jōgan era (859–77), mastered Shingon esotericism at Daianji. The court was impressed by his attainment, but insisted that if he was to practice Shingon he would have to give up Hossō. In reply, Zōri stressed the value of both, and said that he would give up one or the other only at the direction of the Three Treasures themselves. This is when he set up the Shingon and Hossō altars, as described in the *Genki*. That night a "nonordinary person" (*ijin*) came and indicated equal appreciation of both. (The account does not mention the Kasuga deity.) When Zōri reported this dream, the court approved his dual practice.

The story also appears in *Nihon kōsōden yōmonshō* 3. Zōri is said there to have studied Shingon at the urging of Shinnen, who is presented as being the one who insisted that Zōri give up Hossō and switch entirely to Shingon.

1. Zōri (836–928), a son of middle counselor Ietoki, was the teacher of Ichiwa (see 8.4). He was definer for the Yuima-e in 891, and lecturer in 903. His birthplace is

variously reported, but if the *Genki* is correct, he came from roughly the same area as Myōe Shōnin.

2. Skt. *śīla*. The Buddhist monastic rule.

3. See chapter 4, under "The origins of Kōfukuji and of its Buddhism."

4. "Provisional" *(gon)* and "true" *(jitsu)* refer to a distinction made by the Tendai patriarch Chih-i (Jap. Chigi, 538–97), regarding the two halves of the Lotus Sutra. A *jitsu* teaching is definitely superior to a *gon* teaching, since Chih-i urged one to "abolish the provisional and establish the true" (Matsunaga 1969:116). Sometimes Hossō Buddhism was accused of being *gon*, relative to the allegedly *jitsu* Tendai teachings; the Kōfukuji monk Onkaku (see 12.4) wrote an impassioned demonstration denying this.

5. The central building *(jōkai)* of the triple dormitory *(sanmen sōbō)*, the main living quarters for the scholar-monks of Kōfukuji. The complex consisted of three distinct pavilions, laid out in a U around the Kōdō and the Kondō. The east pavilion was called *chūshitsu*, and the west one *saishitsu*.

6. The esoteric altar here is *danjō*, "altar"; but the Hossō installation is actually described as a *gakusō*, a "place for study."

7. The Yuima-e is discussed in chapter 4, under "The Yuima-e." *Sanne jōikki* confirms that Zōri served as the first selector *(tandai)* in 911. The selector was the monk charged with choosing the debate topics from the *Yuima-gyō*. Later the selector came normally to be the superintendent himself, or a past superintendent.

## 8.4 Prelate Ichiwa

Prelate Ichiwa[1] of Kōfukuji, accomplished as he was both in study and in practice, displayed incomparable talent. Eventually he fled the world to live in the mountain village of Tobi.[2] There was a time before that, however, when despite his hope to be Lecturer for the Yuima-e, he unexpectedly found himself passed over in favor of a monk named Shōen.[3]

Ichiwa comforted himself with the thought that everything follows from karma accumulated in past lives, but actually he felt unendurably bitter. He decided to have nothing further to do with the Temple's debates,[4] and to take up the life of a wandering ascetic. Without breathing a word to his disciples, he simply put his personal *honzon*[5] and sutra texts in a bamboo *oi*[6] and stole out of the Triple Dormitory. First he visited the Four Sanctuaries, where he no doubt made a last, tearful sutra-offering[7]—with what feelings one can well imagine. But painful though it was for him to leave the Temple where he had lived so long, and all his familiar companions, his mind was made up. Wandering off wherever his steps might lead him, he happened to start off toward the East.

[PICTURE: Ichiwa at the shrine, saying good-by.]

At Narumigata in Owari[8] he waited for low tide, then went on to
the Atsuta Shrine,[9] where he made repeated sutra-offerings. While
he was doing so, a strange medium[10] approached him.

"You've wandered off from your temple," she said, "because you're
bitter. Of course it's only human to give in to resentment, but one's
fellow men are always a source of frustration and discontent. You
may aim for Michinoku and the strongholds of the Ebisu,[11] but if you
find even there people who grate on you, where will you go *then?*
Hurry back to your temple and achieve your ambition."

Ichiwa hung his head. "I've no idea what you're talking about," he
said. "What cause for resentment could a beggar ascetic like me
possibly have? This is absurd. What do you mean?"

The medium laughed, and spoke this divining poem:

| | |
|---|---|
| No concealment | *tsutsumedomo* |
| Shall succeed in hiding | *kakurenu mono wa* |
| what from the summer fly | *natsumushi no* |
| shines abundantly: | *mi yori amareru* |
| the heart's own fires. | *omohi narikeri* |

"Is it possible," she continued, "that you're naive enough to doubt
me? Very well, I'll tell you. You're angry, are you not, because you
were passed over as Lecturer in favor of Shōen. You see, the names
of the Lecturers are recorded on a golden tablet in the palace of
Taishaku,[12] and their order is Shōen, Ichiwa, Kisō, and Kanri.[13] I'm
sure it's been many an age since they were written there. Certainly *I*
had nothing to do with it. So cheer up and hurry back to your temple.
'The tempering of the light and the merging with the dust initiate the
link with enlightenment; the achieving the Way through all eight
phases finishes accomplishing all creatures' weal.'[14] Kami and Buddhas may differ in name, but both are equally kind to sentient beings,
just as a loving mother is to her own dear child. You may thought-
lessly have left *me,* perhaps, but I haven't left *you,* and that's why I'm
giving you this affectionate advice. Ah, Kasuga-yama's old bones are
tired!" And with these words the Deity ascended.

Ichiwa was deeply impressed, and could not refrain from shedding
tears of longing devotion as he hurried home. The next year he

became Lecturer, and sure enough, the order of the four monks turned out to be exactly as the oracle had said.

[PICTURE: Ichiwa and the medium (a woman) at Atsuta. Since the medium is the Kasuga deity, her face is hidden.]

DATE. 949, since Ichiwa was lecturer in 950.

POSSIBLE SOURCE. This telling is so close to the version in *Senjūshō* 2/1 that it must draw on *Senjūshō* or on a common source. However, in *Senjūshō* the names of the lecturers are a little garbled.

RELATED MATERIALS. (1) *Honchō kōsō den* includes a rather different telling. At Atsuta, Ichiwa sat near the shrine with the beggars. One day the medium *(kannagi)* distributed rice to this assembly but gave none to Ichiwa, explaining that Ichiwa was under the protection not of the Atsuta deity but of the deity of his own province. Nearby a fine stallion, sexually excited, was neighing and stamping so wildly that no one would go near it. When Ichiwa approached the stallion, the onlookers were amazed to see it stand still and prick its ears. The medium then gave Ichiwa much the same oracle from the Kasuga deity as in the *Genki*.

(2) A still more different version occurs in *Sanne jōikki* (DNBZ:289).

This Lecturer [Ichiwa] did not go through [the normal process] of studying and serving as Definer. He left the Temple, went to Owari province, and was appointed a county magistrate. There was in that province a manifest deity *(arahitogami)* whom people would question on matters of concern to them, and whose answers were invariably correct.

Now, a horse that Ichiwa owned suddenly vanished, and despite diligent searching, Ichiwa was unable to find it. When he tried questioning this deity, the deity replied, "If you return to your temple you will be the Lecturer for the Yuima-e." Astonished, Ichiwa asked how this could be. "The order of the Lecturers," the deity replied, "is recorded in the palace of Taishaku. The two before you are Enkū and Zen'en; the two after you are Kisō and Kanri." So Ichiwa went back to the Temple and served as Lecturer, as the deity had foretold.

"Zen'en" is wrong, but the rest of the list of lecturers is correct.

1. Ichiwa (890–970) was lecturer for the Yuima-e in 950, and rose to the rank of minor prelate *(shōsōzu)*. He was a disciple of Zōri (see 8.3) *(Honchō kōsō den, Kasuga genki ekotoba kikigaki)*, and a resident either of Tōin (Nagashima 1944:171) or of Tōbokuin *(Kasuga genki ekotoba kikigaki)*, which were, in any case, closely related. Ichiwa was the only lecturer in the history of the Yuima-e after 885 not to have served first as definer *(ryūgi)*. In fact, in 1146 the monks rejected a designated lecturer precisely because he had not been definer first (Miyai 1978;195).

2. A locality within Sakurai-shi, Nara-ken, immediately east of Sakurai and south of Mt. Miwa. Later, Ichijōin had an estate there.

3. Shōen (891–966) served as lecturer in 949, and was named minor prelate in the year of his death.

4. Debates *(rondan)* were an essential feature of monastic life and practice. Their purpose was to clarify aspects of doctrine, or to define the proper interpretation of a passage or a whole text.

5. A *honzon* ("principal object of worship") is an image, painted or sculpted, that is central on an altar, or otherwise the focal point of a rite.

6. A sort of backpack carried by foot travelers of all sorts, especially wandering ascetics.

7. *Hosse.* It was normal to read or recite a sutra text as an offering to a kami. Important shrines like Kasuga had a special little pavilion *(kyōsho)* from which this could be done.

8. The shore south of what is now Nagoya, along the western side of the very base of the Chita Peninsula.

9. A major shrine, now within the modern city of Nagoya. Atsuta enshrines the sword that is one of the imperial regalia.

10. *Hijiri (Gunsho ruijū* and Kadokawa texts); *kannagi (Kasuga go-ruki).*

11. Michinoku was the northern end of Honshu. The Ebisu were the "barbarian" people who lived there.

12. The Indian deity Indra, incorporated into Buddhism. His palace is on top of Mt. Sumeru (Jap. Shumisen).

13. Kisō (b. 890) and Kanri (895–972) were both Sanron monks of Tōdaiji. Kanri was the third head of Tōnan'in (see 12.3, n. 1).

14. *Wakō dōjin wa kechien no hajime, hassō jōdō wa rimotsu no owari na{ri}.* The expression *wakō dōjin* ("tempering the light and merging with the dust") comes ultimately from the Tao-te-ching. It was used by Chih-i, the Tendai patriarch, in the sixth fascicle of his *Mo-ho-chih-kuan* (Jap. *Makashikan).* The *Tao-te-ching* states that the wise man "tempers his light," etc. so as not to stand out among those who are not wise. Chih-i proposed that the Buddha does the same so as not to blind and confuse ordinary beings with the full radiance of enlightenment. He manifests himself in various familiar forms, and so makes the thought of enlightenment accessible to all. That is why *wakō dōjin* "initiates the link with enlightenment" *(kechien no hajime).*

*Hassō jōdō* ("the achieving the Way through all eight phases") alludes to the eight phases of the Buddha's career: (1) coming down from the Tosotsu Heaven; (2) entering his mother's womb; (3) birth; (4) leaving home, (5) subjugating Māra; (6) attaining enlightenment; (7) turning the wheel of the Law; and (8) entering nirvana. Thus the Buddha "finishes accomplishing all creatures' weal" *(rimotsu no owari).*

## 8.5 Prelate Hōzō

Prelate Hōzō[1] of Tōdaiji belonged to the Hossō school. When he was due to serve as Definer for the Yuima-e,[2] he spent his time studying so unremittingly that he never visited Kōfukuji or the Kasuga Shrine.

On the last day of the ceremony, Hōzō cut off a page and discarded it before replacing his text between its covers. The Selector asked why. Hōzō replied, "Because that was a passage which does not actually belong in the part of the text which concerns us today. That is why I removed it, and will not read it."

The Selector reproved him severely, and when he intoned the text as it was in current usage, the puzzled Hōzō gave the responses. Afterwards, Hōzō examined the current version of the text and found the passage written in it perfectly plainly. Later on, Kasuga no Daimyōjin told Hōzō in a dream that he had temporarly concealed the passage from him.

From then on, on the last day of the Yuima-e a Definer from Tōdaiji has always had the original text with him in the fold of his robe.

[PICTURE: A view of the Yuima-e assembly.]

DATE. Ca. 955. Hōzō was lecturer in 960, but oddly enough, *Sanne jōikki* does not list him as definer at all.

RELATED MATERIALS. *Kasuga Gongen genki shō* states that when Hōzō was definer, he used to go on pilgrimage to Kasuga every day. This hardly tallies with the *Genki* version.

1. Hōzō (904–68) was a Fujiwara who studied Hossō, Sanron, and Shingon at Tōdaiji. He became superintendent of Tōdaiji in 965 and reached the rank of minor prelate in 968, in the thick of a quarrel with Kōfukuji over an estate.

2. For the Yuima-e and its associated offices, see chapter 4, under "The Yuima-e."

## 8.6 An Oracle for a Monk Who Had Left the Temple

Of old a monk of Kōfukuji[1] no longer felt at home at the Temple and went to live in the East. One autumn the moon was shining down in brilliant majesty. The monk in his peaceful solitude was weeping to recall the Kasuga Sanctuaries when—whether dream or reality he could not tell—the Daimyōjin descended in august guise and said, "You have left me, but I have not left you. Whoever has lived a while at My Temple, be he of high or low degree, I love him as an only son, and my love extends as well to his future lives."

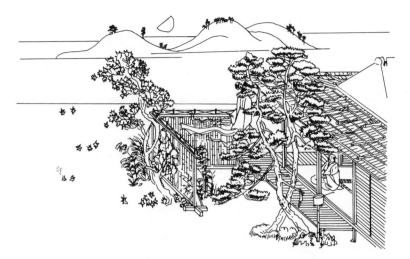

[FIGURE 8.6: In a lovely autumn setting, the monk gazes up at the deity, in the form of a noble gentleman, floating in mid-air before him.]

DATE. Ca. 1150–57.

BACKGROUND AND RELATED MATERIALS. This monk can only be Kakuei (1117?– 1157), whose story appears in *Senjūshō* 9/11. The identification is confirmed by *Kasuga genki ekotoba kikigaki*. The *Honchō kōsō den* account of Kakuei draws on *Senjūshō* to tell his tale, though its version differs in some respects from the *Senjūshō* text published in the Iwanami Bunko series. The account below will fuse the two.

Although a brilliant scholar and debater, Kakuei became deeply dissatisfied with his spiritual condition. He then prayed to the Kasuga deity, who in an oracle promised him help if he would devote himself to serious practice. So Kakuei, still in his twenties, left Nara. He ended up at Kuzu-no-matsubara in Shinobu county of Mutsu. The spot was a pine wood in a rolling landscape. He built himself a hut, begged for a living, and gave himself to a life of practice.

The year after Kakuei died, Saigyō (the ostensible narrator of *Senjūshō*) came and found his hut falling to ruin. In it were some hempen clothing, an old *oi*, some essential passages from the Lotus Sutra, and a copy of the *Yuishiki sanjū ju* (see 10.1, n. 12). The following verse, in Chinese, was attached to a pillar:

> Once I was a Hossō scholar in the Southern Capital,
>> and I sat among the dharma-assemblies of the Great House;
> now I am a beggar hermit in the East,
>> inhabiting a poor dwelling in a remote village.

(The Iwanami text has, "now I am a beggar wandering the provinces/ and I meet my end at Kuzu-no-matsubara".) Another verse read:

When the moon rises in the evening, I remember Mikasa-yama and long for Kasuga;

when the clouds disperse at dawn, I lift my gaze to the Tosotsu Heaven and think upon
the Lord of Compassion.

The Iwanami text includes a *waka* as well, and gives a final inscription in prose:
"Provisional Minor Prelate Kakuei passed away at the hour of the Monkey [ca. 4P.M.]
on Hōgen 2.2.17 [1157], in his forty-first year."

A MIRROR-SYMMETRICAL STORY. *Senjūshō* 2/2 concerns a son of Emperor Toba (not a
Fujiwara) who fled Mt. Hiei (not Kōfukuji) to reappear in Chikuzen (Kyushu, not
Mutsu) as a nameless, beggar *hijiri* living in a hut on a remote hillside. A year or two
later the villagers who had been feeding him missed him. He had disappeared, leaving
written on a post a verse similar to Kakuei's, signed and dated 1155—almost the same
year as Kakuei's.

1. Kakuei, described by *Honchō kōsō den, Kasuga genki ekotoba kikigaki,* and the
Ichijōin lineage in *Shomonzeki fu* as a son of the regent Fujiwara no Moromichi (1062–
99). If this is true, then the birthdate indicated in *Senjūshō* (1117) cannot be correct.
However, Kakuei is listed in *Shomonzeki fu* as a head of Ichijōin; and only a monk of
such birth could have been, however briefly, the head of Ichijōin. Kakuei's name does
not appear in *Sōgō bunin* or *Sanne jōikki,* as it should if he really held the rank of
provisional minor prelate. Perhaps it was expunged from the records because of his
flight, or perhaps Kakuei fled because of whatever caused him to be stricken from the
records. At any rate, his conduct was clearly a problem a century and a half later, since
the *Genki* refrained from naming him, and put his story 200 years out of place in its
chronological sequence.

## 9.1 Filial Zeal for the Lotus

In the Capital there once lived a poor woman who heard a monk
preaching at a temple in the Eastern Hills.[1] "People value their
children above all else," the monk was saying, "and when one of these
children leaves the world and receives the Precepts,[2] the Three
Treasures[3] accept him and King Enma himself is filled with joy."

This made the woman want to have her son, then in his eighth
year, enter religion. Since the Buddha's Teaching seemed to be flourishing particularly at Kōfukuji, she decided that she might as well
make him a monk *there;* and so, all excited, she set out with the boy
for the Southern Capital.

They found lodgings near the Temple's west gate.[4] "Who is the
most famous scholar at Kōfukuji?" the woman asked the proprietor.

"Prelate Kūsei at Kitain,"[5] the proprietor replied. "He is the light
of the Hossō school, and the whole Temple gathers around him in
awe. He has many disciples and is universally revered."

The woman found a way to put her son under this master. The boy turned out to be wonderfully quick and intelligent, and Kūsei, delighted to have found a capable student, treated him very kindly. The anxious mother continued to live near the west gate.

[PICTURE: Mother and son hear the preacher; they arrive in Nara; Kūsei interviews the boy.]

The boy was in his eleventh year when his mother fell seriously ill. Aware that she was dying, she called her son to her and spoke to him in tears. "The only reason why we left our home and came here to Nara," she said, "was to make sure you became a monk and a scholar. But now, before my dream is realized, I find myself near death. This is the greatest disappointment of my life, and I am afraid it may well hinder me as I go. Please tell this to your master, and let my own eyes see you as a monk. Once I have seen that sight I can go in peace." She spoke urgently, under her breath.

The boy went to Kūsei, as she had asked, and told him the whole story. The compassionate Kūsei allowed him to become a monk, and after the deed was done, the boy went straight to his mother by the west gate. She was very, very happy to see him. "Now I have nothing more to wish for in this life," she said, and breathed her last.

[PICTURE: The dying mother and her boy; he receives the tonsure.]

Since the woman was a widow and far from home, there was no one to look after her once she was gone. Being too young himself for that sort of thing, her son the novice could only sit before the body, weeping tears of farewell. Three days later his mother returned to life and told him the following story.

"After I died," she said, "I knelt before King Enma's court. Countless sinners were gathered there, and such hordes of hell-fiends that I was fainting with misery and terror. Then a noble boy, with his hair in twin loops,[6] arrived all alone. King Enma came down from his dais, inclined his jeweled crown, and displayed the deepest awe.

"I wondered who the boy could possible be. Then he spoke. 'I am Kasuga no Daimyōjin, he said. A certain small matter has brought me here. This woman is raising a monk of my Temple, and is not without merit toward me. You must pardon her. King Enma bowed, and ordered a dark minion[7] to open the Great Register. The minion read aloud, 'The present woman's son is a novice in his eleventh year, at Kitain of Kōfukuji.' 'In that case,' said King Enma, 'I have no objection to make. I shall release her immediately.' Then I came back to life. You have already pleased the Deity. Oh, it makes me so happy!" She wrung her hands and wept in an ecstasy of joy.

All who heard her story praised her to the skies. The novice amassed many splendid achievements until he became a celebrated scholar. Meanwhile, years later, the mother's life again came to a close, and she was born at last, as she had ever hoped to be, in paradise.

Seeing impermanence thus at work before him, her son's eyes were opened. In order to go on serving his mother, he withdrew from all society at the Temple and secluded himself in quiet retirement. Morning and evening he read the Lotus Sutra for his late mother's benefit, so that the people of the time called him Kishin or Jikyō.[8] He ended up on Mt. Kōya,[9] where he realized his deep yearning for Rebirth.

[PICTURE: The mother in hell, where a cloud covers the deity's face; she revives; her son chanting the Lotus in solitude.]

DATE. According to his biographies, Jōyo entered Kōfukuji in his thirteenth year, which would have been 969, and died in 1047. (The *Genki* puts his entry into Kōfukuji a little earlier.) However, he cannot then have studied with Kūsei, who lived 878–957. Perhaps he studied instead with Kūsei's disciple Shinki (930–1000).

KŪSEI AND HIS LINE. As a disciple of Shinki (10.1, n.2), if not Kūsei, the young Jōyo would have been in interesting company. Kūsei seems to have belonged to, or perhaps started, a line of esoteric adepts. The remarkable Chūsan (935–76; see *Senjūshō* 6/3, 7/4, 7/5 and *Konjaku* 28/8) was another of his students. Rin'e (10.1), a student of both Kūsei and Shinki, was a teacher of Kyōe (10.6), and according to *Konjaku* 14/43 knew the famous ascetic and visionary Nichizō (905?–985?).

1. Higashiyama, the range of hills that borders Kyoto to the east.
2. That is, makes basic religious vows.
3. The Buddha, the Teaching, and the community of the faithful.
4. A gate in the outer wall of the Kōfukuji compound. It must have been near the present Kintetsu railway station. In theory, at least, vegetable gardens were planted in its vicinity to feed the temple monks (*Kōfukuji ruki*).
5. Kūsei (878–957), a son of Fujiwara no Takamitsu, was a disciple of Enpin in Hossō studies, but also mastered Shingon. Lecturer for the Yuima-e in 932, he was promoted to minor prelate and appointed superintendent in 949 (the year Ichiwa, in 8.4, fled Kōfukuji), and remained in office until his death. Kūsei seems to have

practiced *shugendō,* for he is said to have brought a miraculous jewel back from Kongōzan in the Kazuraki mountains, and buried it in a gold box under the main altar of the main Kondō of Kōfukuji *(Kongōzan naige ryōin daidai kokon kiroku).* Moreover, *Honchō kōsō den* states that on Tentoku 1.12.9 (957), he stepped onto a rock in the garden of his residence and flew off into the sky. He founded Kitain, an important subtemple.

6. *Binzura,* the normal way for a boy of good family to wear his hair.

7. *Myōkan,* a minor official in hell.

8. *Kishin* means "prays for his parents," and *jikyō,* "upholds the Lotus Sutra." Jōyo (957–1047), who rebuilt Mt. Kōya, was known as both Kishin Shōnin and Jikyō Shōnin. Gorai Shigeru (1975:88–97) has described his career. He did not stay long at Kōfukuji but went on to study elsewhere with other masters, and was associated especially with the line of Shingon adepts from Kankakuji (Koshima-san). He is said to have gone to Mt. Kōya because of a dream command from the Kannon of Hasedera, who told him that he should go there if he wished to see his mother and father reborn in paradise. When he arrived, in 1016, he found Mt. Kōya deserted and in ruins. A great fire had destroyed the monastery in 994, and the institution had then been plundered of wealth and land. No one at all lived on the mountain from 1001 to 1016. Jōyo lit an eternal flame there (it still burns), and was largely successful in restoring the temple to life.

9. The great Shingon monastic complex on the mountain of his name in Waka-yama-ken. The temple, Kongōbuji, was founded by Kūkai in 816.

## 10.1 Prelate Rin'e

There lived in Retired Emperor Ichijō's time[1] one Prelate Rin'e,[2] a disciple of Grand Prelate Shinki,[3] the Superintendent of Yamashi-na-dera.[4] After finishing up as Lecturer for the Yuima-e, Rin'e visited the Kasuga Shrine. At the sutra-place[5] of the Wakamiya he recited silently, by heart, the whole debate over which he had just presided, as an offering of the Teaching.

While he was doing so the shrine attendants began beating drums and shaking bells,[6] disturbing his recitation. "I suppose this is only to be expected at the Shrine," thought Rin'e to himself, "but it's very irritating of them to break in this way just when I'm sincerely offering up the true excellence of the Buddha's Teaching. If I manage to become the Senior Monk of the Six Schools,[7] as I sincerely hope I shall, I'll put a stop to this sort of thing, and make sure it no longer disrupts offerings like mine." And with this thought in mind he withdrew.

[PICTURE: Rin'e at the Wakamiya.]

Through the years, Rin'e never forgot the incident. Meanwhile he reached his goal and became Superintendent. He then acted on his plan, and had the priests of the Shrine silence the drums. The Shrine became so cold and lifeless that people were afraid, but fearing Rin'e's power as well they said nothing.

Rin'e, meanwhile, began a seven-day retreat at the Shrine to pray for something very close to his heart. Day and night he tearfully implored the Deity as follows: "In this life I have gained the pinnacle of glory. May the Future Welcome not fail me; and although my past karma be yet unresolved, and normal Rebirth impossible for me, may I still, under the Gongen's protection, tread the path of liberation!"

Seven days passed without his getting any answering sign, so he stayed on another seven days to pray even more fervently than before. At dawn on the last day, he had just dozed off when he saw emerge from the Second Sanctuary a noble gentleman in formal dress, bearing a *shaku*. Rin'e assumed that the Gongen had accepted his prayer and granted his wish. Tears of gratitude and devotion sprang from his eyes, moistening the sleeves of his joy.[8]

The Gongen quietly descended two or three of the Sanctuary steps and looked at Rin'e. His angry countenance was set in a terrible scowl.

"What does this mean?" Rin'e wondered, and said fearfully, "In Your vast compassion You do not exclude from Your blessing the most uncouth mountain dweller or village woman, lazy and without faith though they may be. What then of Rin'e who, ever since he first opened the Thirty Verses,[9] until now when he is head of the entire Temple, has committed no fault at all, and who cannot imagine that his heartfelt prayer for enlightenment should fail to elicit Your divine approval! Yet now he sees You displeased, and this causes him the greatest bewilderment and dismay!" Rin'e wept as he spoke.

The Gongen did not answer directly. He only said:

The drums' sprightly beat resounds in the Palace of Enlightenment;
the Mirror of Fourfold Wisdom Perfected reflects the lightly shaken
    bells.[10]

Then he vanished.

The thunderstruck Rin'e rued his folly. Before leaving, he carefully ordered that the sound of drum and bell should never again be silenced for any reason whatsoever.

[PICTURE: The deity on the steps. His face is hidden.]

DATE. Rin'e was lecturer in 998, and superintendent 1017–25.

RELATED MATERIALS. Lady Nijō told exactly the same story in *Towazugatari*. She heard it when she visited the Kasuga Shrine in 1290. However, in her version the monk is Shinki, Rin'e's teacher. Lady Nijō remarked, "This tale strengthened my faith and filled me with awe" (Brazell 1973:203–4).

1. 986–1011.

2. Rin'e (950–1025) was a student of Kūsei and Shinki at Kitain, and a teacher of Kyōe. Lecturer in 998, he was named superintendent in 1017 and died in office. *Senjūshō* 6/3 tells how he awoke to impermanence as he watched the autumn leaves being torn from the trees by the early winter rains; while *Jikkinshō* 7 relates how his familiar spirits healed a woman by the Kizu River.

3. Shinki (930–1000), a student of Kūsei, was lecturer in 975 and became superintendent in 983. A story in *Kongōzan naige ryōin daidai kokon kiroku* tells how in 986 he visited Kongōzan and expounded the *Yuishiki ron* for the deity there; and how "the old man of Kasuga" then appeared to him. According to *Honchō kōsō den*, when Shinki recited the Heart Sutra at Nachi, the great waterfall reversed its flow. The same miracle is told of Shinki's disciple Chūsan in *Senjūshō* 6/3; Chūsan and Rin'e were together at Nachi at the time.

4. Another name for Kōfukuji.

5. *Kyōsho*, a designated spot at a shrine, from which a monk could offer his recitation of a sutra text *(hosse)* to the deity.

6. Drums and bell-rattles *(suzu)* are the main instruments of the music offered at shrines.

7. The superintendent of Kōfukuji was defined (at least by Kōfukuji) as the senior monk among all the temples of Nara, which represented the "six Nara sects."

8. This striking expression is a literal translation.

9. The thirty verses of the *Yuishiki sanjūron* (Skt. *Triṃśikā-vijñapti-karikā*) by Asanga, as translated by Hsüan-tsang (*Taishō* 31/60, no. 1586). They were the first text given a novice at Kōfukuji, even before his ordination.

10. I cannot identify this as a quotation, but the following passage occurs in *Kyōkunshō* 1: "Music plays forever in paradise, . . . and in the Inner Sanctum of the Tosotsu Heaven, the Lord of Compassion forever plays *Manshūraku* while the host of saints eternally lauds the Guide Who Is to Come." "Fourfold Wisdom Perfected" is *shichi enmyō*, the perfection of the four kinds of wisdom achieved when one attains enlightenment "without outflows" *(muro)*.

## 10.2 Prelate Eichō

When the evening session of the Yuima-e of Kōhei 1 was over, after dark, the Imperial Envoy, Middle Controller of the Left Lord Sukenaka,[1] dozed off for a moment. He dreamed that the Regent and Head of the Clan,[2] surrounded by a throng of attendants, went to the Triple Dormitory where, before a room in the west pavilion, he straightened his *shaku* and bowed thrice in homage.

Sukenaka awoke very surprised, and went to peer discreetly into the room. He saw that after having done his part at the morning session, Graduate Eichō,[3] an Auditor[4] at the ceremony, had withdrawn for a while to wait for the evening session. He was not resting, however, but was still in his ecclesiastical robes, having thrown off only his *kesa.*[5] There was a lamp by him, and before him a book. No wonder the Daimyōjin had given respectful expression to his admiration. Sukenaka was delighted, and when he got back to the Capital he reported the event to His Majesty. The following year Eichō received the imperial appointment as Lecturer.

[PICTURE: Sukenaka's dream.]

DATE. Kōhei 1 (1058). Eichō was lecturer in 1059. However, according to *Sanne jōikki,* the imperial envoy in both 1058 and 1059 was middle counselor Korefusa. Sukenaka served in 1060 and 1061.

1. Fujiwara no Sukenaka (1021–87) supervised, in 1047, the immense task of rebuilding Kōfukuji after the original temple buildings had burned down the previous year *(Zō Kōfukuji ki).* He also served as deputy governor-general of Dazaifu. His title, middle controller of the left *(sachūben),* suggests that he held the fifth rank.

2. At the time, Fujiwara no Yorimichi (990–1074), the son of Michinaga and the man who built the Byōdōin at Uji. He was regent 1017–67.

3. Eichō (1002–83, also read Yōchō) was a Tachibana. According to *Hosshinshū* 8/ 11 he started his career on Mt. Hiei, but came to Kōfukuji in hope of finding better opportunities for advancement. Lecturer in 1059, Eichō became a major prelate in 1092, and in 1094 was named superintendent of Hōryūji. At Kōfukuji he lived in Kaya-no-bō, a part of Bodaiin where Zōshun (see 10.6, n. 5) lived later on. A highly respected scholar, Eichō compiled *Tōiki dentō mokuroku. Kojidan* 3 (no. 259) tells a curious story about him, similar to one told in *Jikkinshō* 7 about Rin'e.

4. *Chōshu,* one of the forty monks (ten from Kōfukuji, two or three each from

other major temples) who formed the assembly for the rite.

5. Sometimes translated "stole." An outer vestment the details of which differed from rank to rank and from school to school.

## 10.3 (No Separate Title)

Eichō bore the title of Prelate when he lived in the main dormitory at Hōjōji[1] in the Capital, and it was there that he was visited by a nonhuman monk. "I have been down in the demon realm[2] ever since the Buddha Kuruson's[3] time," the monk said, "and I have no idea when I shall escape. You, Your Grace, are the teacher of the age. Please instruct me so that I may find my way out."

Eichō answered as best he could, and his visitor talked on about how this spot was very special, and about how there had always been a temple on it since the time of the previous Buddha.[4] Frightened, Eichō called on Kasuga no Daimyōjin. He then glimpsed behind the curtains at his side the form of a shrine servant, and heard the sleeves of the man's outer robe rustling. The sound alarmed the strange monk, who suddenly vanished. The shrine servant told Eichō to leave so dangerous a place, and so Eichō moved elsewhere.

One version has it that "Isagawa no Daimyōjin"[5] was written on the pendant tail[6] of the shrine servant's cap.

[PICTURE: Eichō and the strange monk.]

DATE. Between 1082, when Eichō was named prelate, and 1096 when he died.

A RELATED STORY. Another story (*Hosshinshū* 4/5; *Shūi ōjōden* 2/20) speaks of a demon that began its career in the time of the Buddha Kuruson. Ever since, it had been either the husband or the wife of another soul—always the same one—and had sought to hinder that soul's salvation.

1. A great temple built in 1020 by Fujiwara no Michinaga. It burned down many times, and had vanished by the Edo period.

2. *Makai,* a canonically vague, evil realm, which in the *Genki* is associated only with monks.

3. Skt. Krakuccanda. The fourth (counting from the earliest) of the Seven Buddhas of the Past.

4. Presumably Shaka.

5. The Isagawa Shrine in Nara is older than the Kasuga Shrine, being mentioned in *Nihon shoki* and *Kojiki*. *Kōfukuji ranshōki* claims that it was established in 158 B.C., when the capital was moved to Kasuga. The shrine takes its name from the Isa-gawa, a

brook that runs down from the Kasuga hills to join the Saho-gawa. Note that there is (or was) also an Isagawa Shrine at Kashima.

In the time of the *Genki,* the Isagawa Shrine was under the supervision of Kōfukuji. However, it was also claimed by the Ōmiwa Shrine, and in the Meiji period was officially designated a *sessha* of Ōmiwa. In the Muromachi period it was usually known as "Komori-sha," and is still called that today. It enshrines three deities, the names of which have varied over time. The *honji* of the Isagawa Shrine was Miroku. The Isagawa deity's association with the Nan'endō of Kōfukuji is discussed in chapter 4.

6. *Ei,* the stiff, curved "tail" on the lacquered hats still worn by shrine priests.

## 10.4 (No Separate Title)

Once Eichō caught sight of the Daimyōjin from behind. "I have long devoted myself to the Holy Teachings," Eichō said, "and have at last accumulated some merit. Who at this Temple besides myself could set eyes upon the Gongen? But even though He is now before me, I may not yet see His face. How very much I wish it were otherwise!"

"I appreciate your feelings," answered the deity, "and they please me very much. Here in my domain, however, you are not yet seeking the path of true liberation. That is why I will not face you."

At this Eichō prayed, in tears, then returned to his room at Saionji[1] where he gave himself to studying the *Kanpotsu bodaishin shū,*[2] and other such writings.

[PICTURE: Eichō before the sanctuaries. The deity of the First Sanctuary is standing at the top of his steps, turned away from Eichō.]

DATE. Perhaps between about 1060 and 1096.
RELATED MATERIALS. The story is told similarly in *Shasekishū* 1/2. *Hosshinshū* 8 tells it too, describing Eichō as having visited the Kasuga Shrine often, and as having seen the Daimyōjin repeatedly in dreams.

1. A temple located in present Amagatsuji-chō, Nara-shi, just north of Tōshōdaiji near Saidaiji station. It disappeared in the seventeenth century, but records indicate that it existed as early as 792, and that it was a Fujiwara clan temple. Having a special relationship with it, Eichō was known as "Eichō of Saionji" *(Kōfukuji ruki).* The "Makuonji" of the Kadokawa and *Gunsho ruijū* texts is an error; *Kasuga go-ruki* is correct.

2. Ch. *Ch'uan-fa-p'u-t'i-hsin-chi.* A collection in three fascicles of canonical pas-

sages on arousing the aspiration to enlightenment, complied by the T'ang monk Hui-chao in 714 (*Taishō* 35/375, no. 1862).

## 10.5 Abbot Kyōen

When the Tendai Abbot Kyōen[1] was reading through the *Yuishiki ron* early one morning at his window on Mt. Hiei, a delighted old man danced *Manzairaku*[2] on the pine in the garden. The old man was Kasuga no Daimyōjin.

[PICTURE: The old man dancing on a branch of the pine.]

DATE. Between 1039, when Kyōen became the Tendai abbot *(zasu)*, and 1047 when he died.

EARLIER, VARIANT VERSIONS. Chikazane in *Kyōkunshō* told this story as follows: "While Abbot Kyōen recited by heart the ten fascicles of the *Yuishiki ron,* from start to finish, our Daimyōjin, Kasuga Gongen, danced beneath the pine by his dwelling." An almost identical version appears in *Gōdanshō*. *Zoku kyōkunshō* (1270, by Koma no Tomokuzu) also includes the tale, stating that Kyōen dedicated his reading of the *Yuishiki ron* each evening to the Kasuga deity, and that the deity appeared on one such evening. All three versions have the deity dancing under the pine.

THE PINE TREE. This story is so famous that it was included among one or two others, at the end of *Honchō kōsō den,* to evoke the Kasuga deity. The pine in question is said to be the celebrated *yōgō no matsu* ("pine of the appearance of the god") so closely associated with Noh. It is traditionally identified with a large, old tree presently on the grounds of the Kasuga Shrine, near the First Torii. A sign before this pine names it as the *yōgō no matsu;* states that the pine's story is told in the *Genki;* and tells how Kyōen saw the deity dance at the spot before he became the Tendai abbot.

Actually, being as straight as a telephone pole, the present tree is obviously different from the twisty one in the *Genki* illustration. Moreover, the *Genki* says clearly that Kyōen was on Mt. Hiei. The earlier versions can be taken either way, and their description of Kyōen as abbot could apply to either the present or the future of the story. There certainly could have been a *yōgō no matsu* on Mt. Hiei as well, for the term seems to be a common rather than a proper noun. *Kasuga genki ekotoba kikigaki* notes one at Saionji (10.4, n. 1), and an Edo period map shows one at Kaijūsenji where Gedatsu Shōnin died.

A SIMILAR EVENT ELSEWHERE. On the night of Myōe Shōnin's first lecture on an important Kegon treatise at Jingoji, in 1195, Kasuga no Daimyōjin appeared outside his room and danced for joy (Tanabe 1983:84).

1. Kyōen (979–1047) was a son of Fujiwara no Takatada. Learned in Hossō, Shingon, and Tendai, he served as lecturer in 1020. The dramatic circumstances under

which he was appointed as the twenty-eighth Tendai abbot, in 1039, are related in *Kokonchomonjū* 1.
2. An extremely felicitous *bugaku* dance.

## 10.6 The Venerable Kyōe

There lived in the Southern Capital a monk known as the Venerable Kyōe.[1] Having been since his youth devoted to the Way, Kyōe retired to Odawara,[2] then later lived on Mt. Kōya.

Day and night for three years, he sat in perfect form, praying for Paradise and contemplating the True Refuge.[3] In the process his lower back went so bad that he could no longer stand up. Then he remembered the past and invoked Kasuga no Daimyōjin, begging the Deity to heal this affliction. As he prayed, a noble lady visited him in a dream and said, "You left me, but I have not left you. My home is in the west." Then she flew off through the sky. After that, Kyōe's back was suddenly well again, and he had no more trouble getting up and lying down. In other words, any sick person who invokes the Daimyōjin will surely have relief.

Perhaps the Daimyōjin's help reached as far even as Kyōe's next life, because at his death a purple cloud floated in the air and music resounded in the heavens, and he achieved Rebirth. In fact, on the night when Azari Ihan,[4] also of Mt. Kōya, passed away, someone dreamed that the Venerable Kyōe came singing and dancing, with greater glee than all the rest, before the host of saints.

The Fourth Sanctuary is said to be Eleven-Headed Kannon, and to appear in the form of a noble lady. Zōshun,[5] the Posthumous Grand Prelate of Bodaiin,[6] rejoiced particularly, and observed: "When of old Prince Shōtoku entered the womb, he said, 'I have vowed to save the world. My home is in the west.'[7] The Gongen now has said just the same thing."

[FIGURE 10.6: The divine lady flies off into the sky after visiting Kyōe; Kyōe comes to welcome Ihan at the head of the host of saints.]

DATE. The fourth quarter of the eleventh century.

RELATED MATERIALS. (1) Gedatsu Shōnin told the same story briefly in his *Kasuga Daimyōjin hotsuganmon*. He observed that the lady who appeared to Kyōe "was Aidono-hime-no-ōkami, a manifestation of Kanzeon." Aidono-hime is Ise, identified at Kasuga with the Fourth Sanctuary.

(2) *Kōshō Bosatsu no go-kyōkai chōmon shū* (Kamata 1971:204–5) tells the following story. Retired Emperor Shirakawa heard of Kyōe and decided to visit him on Mt. Kōya. Kyōe would not even acknowledge Shirakawa's presence. Finally, when Shirakawa asked Kyōe about Rebirth, Kyōe gave him a curt reply and declined to speak further. The text praises his refusal to be distracted. Then it notes that near the end of his life Kyōe fell ill, prayed to the Kasuga deity, and had the vision related in the *Genki*.

1. Kyōe (1001–93) was a son of Fujiwara no Noriyuki and, while at Kōfukuji, a disciple of Rin'e *(Kasuga genki ekotoba kikigaki)*. According to *Kōyasan ōjōden*, Kyōe's whole family was killed by the angry spirit of a man whom his father had tortured to death while governor of Sanuki. Kyōe became a monk so as to lay the curse to rest, but continued to suffer from it so acutely that he moved from Kōfukuji to Odawara. He moved to Mt. Kōya in his seventieth year. Gorai (1975:100) counted him as the direct founder of the *Kōya hijiri*. The account of Kyōe in *Shūi ōjōden* lacks this story, though it notes that he did suffer from an illness. An ancient note appended to the account relates the dream about Ihan and Kyōe. "The Venerable" *(shōnin)* is an affectionately respectful title for especially holy monks.

2. A *bessho* (community of Amida *nenbutsu* devotees) associated with Kōfukuji. It

was located at present *ōaza* Shimotsuya, Kumiyama-chō, Kuse-gun, Kyōto-fu, along the north bank of the Kizu River and near the old road between Kyoto and Nara. According to *Kōyasan ōjōden*, Kyōe was known as "Odawara no Gōshō-bō." There is still a Jōdo-shū temple named Gōshōji at the spot.

3. *Eshō*, the sixth of the *jūfunimon*, the ten gates to the perception of nonduality as expounded in *Hokke gengi shakusen* (Ch. *Fa-hua-hsüan-i-shih-ch'ien*) by the T'ang monk Chan-jan (Jap. Tannen).

4. *Shūi ōjōden* contains an account of Ihan (d. 1096).

5. Zōshun (1104–80) can only have heard about Kyōe's vision long afterwards. A commoner of the Kose clan, from near Unebi-yama in Yamato, he managed to serve as lecturer only in 1168. Nevertheless he was a great scholar. Zōshun was appointed deputy superintendent of Kōfukuji in 1179. In his lifetime he rose no higher than provisional minor prelate (a modest rank by that time), but was raised posthumously to grand prelate by Taira no Kiyomori. Zōshun is said to have been born in answer to a prayer addressed by his parents to Kasuga no Daimyōjin; and he himself wrote that he was called to become a monk by Gyōki Bosatsu, who appeared to him in a dream.

Zōshun lived in Kaya-no-bō of Bodaiin, where Eichō had lived before him, and was in Eichō's line. Moreover, as described in *Shōdai senzai denki*, he studied with Jippan (1086–1144), who restored the *ritsu* transmission in 1122. Zōshun then passed the transmission on to his student Kakuken, who gave it to Gedatsu Shōnin. The Shōsen and Jōon of 13.2 were his students *(Kasuga genki ekotoba kikigaki)*. Zōshun founded Sanzōin, later the residence of the Hanken consulted by Kakuen, the *Genki* compiler.

6. An important subtemple, the former residence of Genbō (d. 746). The local protector *(chinju)* of Bodaiin was Futagami Gongen, the deity of Futagami-no-take (see 19.1).

7. Prince Shōtoku (574–612) needs no introduction. He was believed to be an incarnation of Kannon, and to have sought birth in Japan (the east) in order to save beings there. According to *Shōtoku Taishi denryaku,*

A monk, golden and very beautiful, appeared to his future mother and said, "I have vowed to save the world, and I wish to lodge in your womb." "Who are you?" the lady asked. The monk replied, "I am the Bodhisattva Savior of the World. My home is in the west."

## 11.1 Hōin Egyō

Hōin Egyō of Shūnan'in[1] had plumbed the depths of the Two Wisdoms,[2] and stood as a model for the whole Temple. So fine a scholar was he that he had no need to blush before the sages of the past.

Once Egyō lay as though dead from evening until the hour of the Serpent[3] the following morning. After he revived he was asked what had happened. "I was summoned to the palace of King Enma," he replied, "and so I made my way there. King Enma ordered me to read the Lotus Sutra, so I did."

In his youth, Eygō was disappointed in a little quarrel over an estate, and secretly thought of leaving the Temple. Then the Daimyōin told him in a dream, "I had planned to have you serve Me as Deputy Superintendent. Why do I now hear that because of some trifling difficulty you wish to leave the Temple?" Egyō completely gave up the idea after that, and did in the end come to serve as Deputy Superintendent.

[PICTURE: Egyō lying asleep; Egyō reading the sutra in hell.]

DATE. Egyō's disappointment in the quarrel may date from ca. 1110–25. His visit to hell probably belongs to 1135–64.

1. Egyō (1085–1164) was a son of Fujiwara no Iemichi, and a student of Raison at Ichijōin. Lecturer in 1129, he became deputy superintendent in 1159. He founded Shūnan'in.

2. *Nimyō,* the last two of the *gomyō* ("five wisdoms"), which are languages, the arts and crafts including mathematics, medicine, logic, and Buddhist doctrine. The *nimyō* were essential fields of study at Kōfukuji.

3. Ca. 10 A.M.


## 11.2 *(No Separate Title)*

Egyō was surprised to find himself condemned by Retired Emperor Toba,[1] and exiled to Harima province. He lived for years on Shoshazan.[2] When no pardon was forthcoming he became anxious, and decided to call down the Daimyōjin in the hope of learning when he was to return to the Capital. The Daimyōjin, however, did not descend, and so Egyō brought in an adept[3] to call down the Deity for him. Shortly the Daimyōjin did appear, and announced that Egyō would return to live at his home temple after five years of exile. On hearing this oracle, Egyō could not help weeping with happiness.

Finally, after five years, Egyō returned to the Temple and served as Questioner[4] at the Yuima-e, expressing his happiness on that occasion with this self-deprecating verse:

My grass hut gathered dew day after day
while I garnered alone the pearl of the One Vehicle;

my pine gate has been shrouded in smoke these five years,
but now I am back to dim the moon of the Two Wisdoms.

All who heard him shed tears of sympathetic joy.

[PICTURE: The Yuima-e assembly.]

DATE. Egyō's exile lasted from 1129 to 1133 or 1134.

RELATED MATERIALS. *Kōfukuji ruki* (DNBZa:304) notes Egyō's "five-year exile" to
Shoshazan and gives the following account:

> During that time he went on pilgrimage to Kinpusen, and prayed at the Sanjū-
> hassho [Shrine on Kinpusen] that he should return to his home temple. Some-
> one then dreamed that Zaō [Gongen, the Kinpusen deity] visited Kasuga.[Zaō
> Gongen] said, "I am sorry for Egyō. You must consider calling him back." The
> Daimyōjin said, "I have not forgotten Egyō, and will give some thought to the
> matter immediately." Soon afterwards, Egyō was recalled.

BACKGROUND. As noted in *Kōfukuji bettō shidai,* Egyō's exile had to do with "the affair
of the buddha-image maker *(busshi)* Chōen." The affair is related in *Kōfukuji ruki,* and
a day-by-day account of it appears in *Chūyūki* for Daiji 4.11.11 to 11.29. The Kōfukuji
superintendent, Genkaku of Ichijōin, had appointed Chōen as superintendent of Kiyomizudera. However, the Kōfukuji monks *(daishu)* violently opposed his choice.
When Chōen came to visit Genkaku, the monks attacked him, stripped him of his
clothes, smashed his carriage, and wounded him in the head. The disturbance apparently occurred on Daiji 4.11.10. Retired Emperor Toba was furious. It was determined
that the ringleader was none other than Egyō, who had coveted Chōen's post himself.
Egyō and six other monks were exiled, each to a different place (Daiji 4.11.29).
Munetada, the author of *Chūyūki,* was horrified. He wrote on 11.12 that he had never
before heard of sending the imperial police *(kebiishi)* down to Nara, although of course
this was not the first time there had been trouble at Kōfukuji. "Is this the end of
Hossō?" he wondered. "It is frightful and outrageous."

1. Toba (1103–56) reigned 1007–23 and was retired emperor 1129–56. He
commissioned the building of the Kasuga east pagoda in 1140.

2. A great Tendai temple, formally named Enkyōji, near present Himeji. It was
founded in 988 by Shōkū Shōnin.

3. *Ugen no sō,* probably a yamabushi and healer.

4. *Ichimon,* or *monja.* The questioner put the questions chosen by the selector
*(tandai)* to the definer *(ryūgi).*

## 11.3 The Dream of the Eiman Era

On the 23d day of the 7th month of Eiman 2, the following notice
was posted before the First Torii[1] of Kasuga.

"The monks of the Temple were up in arms, though I do not know why, when I went on pilgrimage to the Shrine. The northernmost door[2] of the Four Sanctuaries opened, and there were sounds of human presence within. Then a cloud issued from the Sanctuary and moved off southward. By the Main Shrine stood a man as tall as the Mountain.[3] I asked who he was, and got the reply, 'He has come to greet Kasuga no Daimyōjin, who is returning to His Home Shrine.[4] Enomoto[5] is seeing the Daimyōjin off.' Towering aloft, the cloud, now south of the Main Shrine, turned toward the southeast. In it I could see a brilliantly green *sakaki.*[6] Then a voice said to one whom I took to be the Third Sanctuary,[7] 'I leave the world now to a rare youth'; and the one who had spoken started down the steps of His Sanctuary. Then the people of the Temple groaned and lamented. Some shed tears, while others cried out that they were lost; and in the dream I too, who relate these things, like all the others present, wept unconsolably.

"Though I tremble to publish such a dream, I have posted the above account because it is a divine oracle.

"A dream vision of the night of the 22d. Eiman 2.7.23."

[PICTURE: Monks and laymen gathered before the notice, which looks just like some notices posted in Nara Park today.]

DATE. Eiman 2.7.23 (1166).

RELATED MATERIALS. The fear that the deity might become displeased and leave seems to have been real. The Kasuga priest Nakatomi no Sukesada wrote in his diary for Kanki 4.7.20 (1232):

Many people have dreamed that because of the laxness of the monks of the Temple, the Daimyōjin is going to return to His homeland. As a result a council was held at the Temple, and it was decided to hold a ceremony of ten discourses spread over two days. Today was the first day.

Sukesada noted again, on Katei 2.7.28 (1236), a dream that someone had made public by posting it on a pillar of the First Torii. The dream referred to the turmoil then reigning at Kōfukuji and Kasuga (see 20.1, "Background"), and transmitted verse oracles that recommended a certain action. It is interesting that all three events (including the one in the *Genki*) should have occurred late in the 7th month.

1. This torii marked the boundary between the Kōfukuji precincts and those of the Kasuga Shrine.

2. The door of Takemikazuchi's First Sanctuary.

3. Mikasa-yama.

4. *Honsha,* the Kashima Shrine whence Takemikazuchi originally came to Kasuga.

5. "The Deity Beneath the Hackberry Tree": the local protector *(chinju)* of Kasuga. The following account draws upon Hakusen (1779), *Kasuga Daimyōjin suijaku
shōsha ki, Kōfukuji ranshōki, Shun'ya shinki,* and *Nara-ken no chimei.* Enomoto's sanctuary is in the gallery *(kairō)* of the shrine, to one's left as one enters through the south
gate. It is presently known as Kasuga no Jinja, the name under which it appears in
*Engi-shiki.* The name Enomoto no Myōjin first appears in a document dated 1084, and
was used consistently until the sanctuary was officially designated a *sessha* of the Kasuga
Shrine in 1877. Until the Muromachi period the deity was understood to be Kose-
hime or Kose no Myōjin, but thereafter came to be defined as Saruta-hiko. Enomoto's
*honji* was Tamonten or Bishamon (both forms of Vaiśravana, one of the Four Celestial
Kings); and his messenger, sometimes shown in Kasuga art, was the giant centipede
*(mukade).* His *suijaku* form was that of a thin old man in Chinese cap and dress.
Enomoto's role in the founding of the Kasuga Shrine is described in chapter 3.

6. A broadleaf, evergreen shrub or small tree sacred in Shinto, and which is the
particular vehicle of the Kasuga deity. (See chapter 3.)

7. Amenokoyane, the Fujiwara ancestor.

## 11.4 (No Separate Title)

This troubled the whole Temple. For ten days, from the 19th to
the 28th of the 8th month, a debate on the *Shingyō no yūsan*[1] was
held at the Kasuga Shrine, and the *Yuishiki ron* was expounded. The
Attesters[2] were Provisional Grand Prelate Jinpan,[3] Provisional Minor
Prelate Kyōkaku,[4] and Provisional Master of Discipline Gen'en.[5] The
Readers[6] were Lecturer Designate Renson,[7] Lecturer Designate
Kyōkō,[8] Past Lecturer Kakuken,[9] Past Lecturer Shingyō,[10] Graduate
Jōen,[11] and Graduate Zōshun. The Auditors were Chōga,[12] Saishū,[13]
Kakkō,[14] Shunkaku,[15] Kinkei, Jōshō,[16] Ehan,[17] Shōkō, and others.

On the 22d, after the debate had begun, Inkei,[18] a resident of
Bodaiin, dreamed that someone came and told him, "The Third
Sanctuary of Kasuga is back, and is at the First Torii. He has the form
of Jizō Bosatsu." Other people too had various portentous dreams.

[FIGURE 11.4: The debate; Jizō returning to Kasuga.]

DATE. Eiman 2.8.19–28 (1166).

1. The *Hannyaharamitta shingyō yūsan* (Ch. *Pan-ro-po-lo-mi-to-hsin-ching-yu-tsan*), a work in two fascicles by K'uei-chi, a discipline of Hsüan-tsang. It is a commentary on the *Heart Sutra* from the standpoint of Hossō thought (*Taishō* 33/523, no. 1710).

2. *Shōgisha,* "he who attests the meaning." The attester critiqued the definer's answer to the questioner.

3. Jinpan (1101–74) is recorded as the seventeenth son of Fujiwara no Morozane, although Morozane died in 1101. A head of Daijōin, he was lecturer in 1126. Having been allied with the wrong side in the Hōgen insurrection (1156), Jinpan had his personal estate confiscated. He was pardoned in 1162 and became superintendent of Kōfukuji in 1164.

4. Kyōkaku is mentioned as a past lecturer *(ikō)* in 1145 *(Nanto daishu nyūraku ki)* and in 1151 *(Kasuga mōde burui ki),* but is not present in more formal records.

5. Gen'en (1113–ca. 1179), a son of Takashina no Muneakira, was appointed superintendent of Hasedera in 1176, and of Kōfukuji in 1179.

6. *Tokushi,* those who read out the passages debated during the rite.

7. Renson (b. 1083) was definer in 1143, "Lecturer Designate" *(gikō)* was the title borne by a monk who had been appointed lecturer for one of the "three imperial rites of Nara," but had not yet served.

8. Kyōkō is mentioned among those who prayed at the Kasuga Shrine in 1151 for the success of Yorinaga's formal pilgrimage to Kasuga *(Kasuga mōde burui ki).* In the *Gunsho ruijū* text and in *Kasuga go-ruki* the name appears as Kyōson.

9. Kakuken (b. 1102) retired in 1195, but his death date is not recorded. The fifth son of Fujiwara no Michinori, he was an uncle and the teacher of Gedatsu Shōnin. He was lecturer in 1159 and deputy superintendent of Kōfukuji 1181–89. "Past lecturer"

*(ikō)* designated a monk who had served as lecturer for one of the "three imperial rites of Nara." The *Gunsho ruijū* text and *Kasuga go-ruki* have a different *ken* character for the name.

10. Shingyō (b. 1102) was definer in 1158 and lecturer in 1165.

11. Jōen is unknown. The *Gunsho ruijū* text and *Kasuga go-ruki* repeat the name Gen'en. A "graduate" *(tokugō)* was a monk who had served as definer for the Yuima-e, for the Hokke-e of Kōfukuji, and for the Saishō-e of Yakushiji.

12. Chōga is unknown.

13. Saishū (b. 1116) was definer in 1170.

14. Kakkō (b. 1117) was definer in 1172 and lecturer in 1181. The *Gunsho ruijū* text and *Kasuga go-ruki* have the name as Kakuson.

15. Shunkaku is mentioned in *Sanne jōikki* only as having been present at the Yuima-e of 1142.

16. Kinkei and Jōshō are unknown.

17. Ehan is mentioned in *Kōfukuji bettō shidai* as a disciple of Zōshun. *Kōfukuji ryaku nendai ki* states that Daihōshi Ehan was appointed Hokkyō on Angen 1.12.29 (1175).

18. Shōkō and Inkei are unknown.

## 12.1 Posthumous Grand Prelate Zōshun

With respect to learning, Posthumous Grand Prelate Zōshun, a Deputy Superintendent of Kōfukuji, was fully versed in the Canon; and in practice he had attained the Two Wisdoms. No one since middle antiquity[1] could compare with him. Since he was conceived after his mother dreamed that a brilliant spring sun entered her mouth, his parents, who doted on him, gave him the childhood name "Kasuga."[2] Zōshun was a precocious youth, in no way inferior to Kanro,[3] and in adulthood he remained unawed by Gankai.[4] Every day his genius grew in fame until he was truly a master in his line.

On the night of the 29th of the 5th month of Hōen 6, Zōshun dreamed that he was traveling south past the closed east gate[5] of Kōfukuji when he saw the Daimyōjin's palanquins coming in through this gate from the Torii.[6] He had his bearers let him alight, and saluted the Daimyōjin immediately. As the First Sanctuary was fully exposed, Zōshun could see him clearly, though he could not make out the expression on the divine countenance. The other three Sanctuaries were invisible inside their palanquins.

"It does not bother you at all never to visit the Shrine," the First Sanctuary remarked.

"I thought studying amounted to much the same thing," Zōshun replied.

The Deity nodded, but he still looked displeased.

"I know it's very wrong of me not to visit the Shrine," Zōshun acknowledged to himself, prostrating himself toward it.

He could tell that the First Sanctuary was Shaka, the Second Miroku, and the Fourth the *gohō,* but he woke up without learning anything about the Third.[7]

[PICTURE: Zōshun kneeling, facing the four palanquins. The First Sanctuary is about to walk through the gate.]

DATE. Hōen 6.5.29 (1140).

1. *Chūko.* The range of time designated by this term is not entirely clear. Perhaps it means the period since Zenshu (723–97) and Gomyō (750–834), two important Japanese Hossō scholars.

2. "Kasuga" is written with the characters for "spring" and "sun."

3. According to the *Shih-chi,* Kanro (Ch. Kan-lo) in his twelfth year was sent by Ch'in-shih-huang-ti as an emissary to the king of Chao. He persuaded the king to destroy five fortresses and to accept the hegemony of Ch'in. On his return to Ch'in, he was awarded an exalted court rank.

4. Yen-hui (513–482 B.C.), Confucius's best disciple. *Shasekishū* 1 describes Lao-tsu, Confucius, and Yen-hui as forms of three buddhas of the past, who appeared in order to prepare the minds of the Chinese for the Buddhist teaching.

5. Tōmon, also called the "servants' gate" since, at least in theory, temple servants lived in its vicinity.

6. The First Torii, between Kasuga and Kōfukuji.

7. Zōshun's identification of the First Sanctuary as Shaka thus precedes Gedatsu Shōnin's. Miroku for the Second Sanctuary is unusual, although not unknown elsewhere. *Gohō* for the Fourth Sanctuary, however, is otherwise unheard of. At first sight this *gohō* seems to be the Japanese name of Dharmapāla (530–61), the great Hossō patriarch. Kameda Tsutomu (1970a:374) took it that way, noting how basic both Miroku and Gohō are to the Hossō tradition. However, exactly the same characters designate the aspect of the Kasuga deity that was called down and questioned by a healer. (See chapter 5, under "The Fourth Sanctuary as *gohō.*")

## 12.2 *(No Separate Title)*

While the *Inmyō daisho*[1] was being read during a Chōkō-e[2] at the Temple, in the Hōgen era, deer came and lay down in the Yōgō Doorway,[3] completely unafraid. Apparently they wanted to hear the

Teaching. They came every day, causing wonder and a good deal of talk among those who saw them.

[PICTURE: The assembled monks, with the deer lying in the doorway.]

DATE. The Hōgen era (1156–59).

1. The common name for the *Inmyō nisshōri ron sho* (Ch. *Yin-ming-ju-cheng-li-lun-shu*), a commentary by K'uei-chi on the *Inmyō nisshōri ron*, a translation by Hsüan-tsang of the *Hetu-vidyā-nyāya-praveśa* by Saṃkarasvāmin. The commentary incorporates Hsüan-tsang's oral teachings. Widely used as a manual of Yogācāra logic, it too inspired many commentaries.

2. A "long lecture assembly," that is, a forty-day course of lectures, held irregularly at Kōfukuji and Enryakuji. The first, on the *Nehan-gyō*, was held in 846 at Kōfukuji under the patronage of Fujiwara no Yoshifusa (804–72), and lasted thirty days. In 900, Yoshiyo, Yoshifusa's brother, revived the Chōkō-e and lengthened it to forty days, so that it could deal with the entire Canon. In the years when it was held, this Chōkō-e lasted from the 24th day of the 7th month to the 4th day of the 9th month.

3. One of the entrances to the Kōdō (Lecture Hall), where the Chōkō-e was normally held.

## 12.3 Keichin's Dream

At Tōnan'in[1] of Tōdaiji there was a scholar-monk named Keichin[2] who made it his daily practice to visit the Kasuga Shrine. Keichin once dreamed that just west of the First Torii he met someone riding in a carriage. When the person opened the carriage's little window, their eyes chanced to meet. Keichin found that he was looking at Jizō Bosatsu.[3]

"This is enough of a meeting for today," said Jizō to Keichin. "I am on my way there[4] to protect Shingyō and Chinshō."[5] And he set off toward the east. Shrine servants in yellow robes, and wild deer, followed in great numbers after his carriage.

[PICTURE: Jizō's carriage and train.]

DATE. Probably 1165, the year Shingyō was lecturer for the Yuima-e.

1. A subtemple of Tōdaiji, founded by Shōbō in 875, immediately east of the temple's great south gate. Tōnan'in gave many Shingon-oriented superintendents to Tōdaiji in the Heian period, and was also the center of Sanron studies at the temple.

2. Keichin (1118–1169), a son of Fujiwara no Akikuni, was a Sanron monk and

the eighth head of Tōnan'in. His name can also be read Echin, but "Keichin" was preferred by Hiraoka Jōkai in *Tōdaiji jiten.*

3. The *honji* of the Third Sanctuary.

4. Probably the Kōdō, where the Yuima-e was about to begin.

5. Chinshō is unknown. For Shingyō, see 11.4, n. 10.

## 12.4 Onkaku

Onkaku (Hōmyō-bō)[1] of Kōfukuji was as much respected for his learning as any scholar of antiquity, but despite his constant study he still had no stipend. As a result his three robes[2] were in tatters, and his one bowl was always empty. This sometimes made him angry that the Daimyōjin was so stingy with his blessings, and sometimes inspired him to reflect that his poverty was due to his own miserable karma. Finally he gave up his studies at Kōfukuji and went wandering.

At the shrine-temple of Hachiman[3] he happened to lodge with a certain monk who bore the title of Entrant.[4] Clever as he was, Onkaku explained very nicely to this monk the deepest Hossō teachings. Since Hachiman Daibosatsu specially protects the Hossō school,[5] the other monk took refuge[6] with Onkaku, and did so well by him that Onkaku began living much more comfortably than he had in the Southern Capital.

By the time two or three years had passed, Onkaku felt so grateful for Hachiman's generosity that he was going regularly to Hachiman's shrine, to keep all-night vigil there and to make sutra-offerings.

[PICTURE: Onkaku and his patron monk.]

One night at the shrine, Onkaku dozed off and had the following dream. A very grand gentleman, accompanied by a host of attendants, arrived at the shrine. Hachiman Daibosatsu opened the doors and greeted his visitor. They talked for some time about various weighty matters of the court, until at last the visitor seemed about to go. Then he suddenly glanced at Onkaku.

"Well," he said, "I see you've got that monk in your service now. I had him with me for years. Much to my regret as the guardian of the Hossō doctrine—after all, he was an outstanding scholar—his pure karma[7] was already fully mature, which meant that he was sure eventually to be reborn into the Inner Sanctum of the Tosotsu Heaven.[8]

His being rewarded with wealth instead would only have stood in the way of this Rebirth, so I kept him on purpose from prospering. Now you're providing him with food and clothing, his reward is bound to end up being the Evil Realms.[9] It's too bad, it really is!"

Then Onkaku woke up, very sorry indeed that he had so often been foolish enough to be angry with the Deity, and realizing now more than ever the generosity of the Deity's beneficent ways. Overcome at once with joy and grief, he could not even stay to let the Entrant know what had happened, but instead went straight back to the Southern Capital. He built a hut at Yake-Kasuga,[10] near Kasuga-yama, and worked only toward liberation. In the end he passed away with right thoughts, so that music resounded in the heavens, marvelous fragrances filled his dwelling, and he achieved his wish for Rebirth.

[PICTURE:] Onkaku before Hachiman's shrine; Onkaku leaving.]

DATE. Perhaps the second quarter of the twelfth century, since Onkaku was born ca. 1102.

RELATED MATERIALS. (1) *Kokonchomonjū* no. 23 is a briefer, less interesting version of the same story. Onkaku is not named. (2) *Shasekishū* 1/7 and *Hie Sannō rishōki* 6 both include a parallel story about one Kanshun of Mt. Hiei. Sannō plays the part of Kasuga and Inari the part of Hachiman.

1. Onkaku (born ca. 1102) is the author of a tract *(Onkaku sōjō)* refuting the Tendai contention that Hossō is a "provisional teaching" *(gongyō)*. *Kasuga genki ekotoba kikigaki* and *Honchō kōsō den* agree that he was a disciple of Ryūkaku (see 14.2–4). There is no record of his having obtained a *sōgō* rank. *Honchō kōsō den* relates that at Kōfukuji he lived by the temple's great south gate. Once a deer entered his room there and circumambulated him, and the event was taken as a mark of the Kasuga deity's respect. Onkaku apparently kept very much to himself, and the other monks were rather in awe of him.

2. The Buddhist monastic rule allowed a monk to own three simple robes and one begging bowl.

3. *Hachiman no miyadera:* Iwashimizu-dera, or Gokokuji, the temple associated with the Iwashimizu Hachiman Shrine on Otoko-yama, southwest of Kyoto at the confluence of the Katsura, Uji, and Kizu rivers. It had been aligned since at least 1067 with the teaching and practice of Mt. Hiei. Hachiman, originally from Usa in Kyushu, was enshrined in 749 at Tōdaiji (Tamuke-yama Hachiman), and was established on Otoko-yama in 860 to protect the Capital. Hachiman claimed the title of Daibosatsu in 783, the first deity to do so.

A *miyadera* (or *jingūji*) was a temple associated with a shrine, in a complex centered upon the shrine. The temple's role was to serve the shrine deity by offering Buddhist rites and teachings. Kōfukuji was not a *miyadera* to Kasuga, and neither was Shion'in (see chapter 3, under "A history of the Kasuga Shrine"). Kasuga's *miyadera* was a small building in the precincts enclosed by the gallery *(kairō)* of the shrine. It is visible in some *Kasuga mandara.*

4. *Nyūji:* a modest monastic rank, beneath *azari* and above *shubun.*

5. This claim no doubt alludes particularly to Tamuke-yama Hachiman at Tōdaiji.

6. *Kie:* the act of acknowledging a monk as one's teacher.

7. *Jōgō:* action conducive to enlightenment.

8. The Tosotsu (Skt. Tuṣita) Heaven is the paradise whence buddhas are born; and the Inner Sanctum (Naiin) is where Miroku, the future Buddha, dwells. In the Hossō tradition, Seshin (Skt. Vasubandhu) received the Hossō teaching directly from Miroku in the Tosotsu Heaven. According to *Kōfukuji engi,* Kōfukuji was a living model of the Tosotsu Heaven.

9. *Akudō:* the less desirable realms of reincarnation, especially those of hell, hungry ghosts, and beasts.

10. The vicinity of Byakugōji (formerly a dependency of Kōfukuji), about 1.5 km. south of the Kasuga Shrine, below Takamado-yama. According to *Shun'ya shinki,* Amenokoyane rested there in 768, on his way to Kasuga from Hiraoka; later on, Kōbō Daishi invited the Kasuga deity to reside there, and made the spot a *shidarin* (Skt. *sītavana*), a place for the disposal of the dead. *Shun'ya shinki* also says that Yake-Kasuga was the place where Kasuga shrine servants took Buddhist vows *(tokudo).* Today, the Yake-Kasuga Jinja enshrines Amenokoyane and his consort Himegami.

## 13.1 Master of Discipline Seiga

Master of Discipline Seiga,[1] of Kanjuji,[2] was the son of Taira no Masahiro, a Lieutenant of the Left Gate Guards,[3] and of the adopted daughter of the poet Taikenmon'in no Horikawa.[4] He was conceived after his mother, who could not bear being childless, had prayed to the Gods and Buddhas. The event made his parents very happy.

When her time was near, his mother went to offer prayers at Hasedera.[5] Kasuga being on her way, she stopped the palanquin before the First Torii to pray for a safe delivery, and suddenly gave birth, right there, to a son. She left her pilgrimage unfinished in consequence, but instead of returning to the Capital, she spent thirty days in the Southern Capital making thank offerings. Only then did she go home.

[PICTURE: The lady giving birth (inside her palanquin) before the First Torii.]

In time her son grew up, and when he was in his fourteenth year she availed herself of a chance to put him under the Shōren'in Prince Abbot (the seventh son of Retired Emperor Toba).[6] Thereafter the boy was constantly upset or ill, till a healer was summoned and made to perform his rites.

While the healer was at work, an oracle came through a young girl of the household. "I am Enomoto no Myōjin," the divinity said. "Kasuga no Daimyōjin sent me. Since this boy was born in front of the Shrine's First Torii, the Daimyōjin assigned a minion to guard him, but now the boy has moved to another establishment. Being displeased, the Deity has set a curse on him."

This inspired the boy's parents to special faith. They decided not to send their son up to Mt. Hiei, but to offer him instead to the Daimyōjin. Their son's illness then vanished.

[PICTURE: The boy lying ill, with the medium delivering her oracle to the healer.]

Soon the father passed away, and the mother lived on alone. Despite her concern she got nothing done, and never managed to move to the Southern Capital. The Prelate Gahō[7] of Kanjuji, with whom she had a modest connection, asked for the boy. She told him that having given the boy to the Daimyōjin, she could not send him elsewhere without the Daimyōjin's permission.

Finally, mother and son reached the Southern Capital. At the Wakamiya, the Daimyōjin suddenly gave an oracle: "This boy was born before the First Torii, and afterwards I assigned someone to serve and watch over him at all times. Now he is here, let him sing me a song!" This was because the boy had mastered secular music and was an exceptional performer. From her palanquin, his mother begged him in tears to obey.

The boy sang two or three times the *imayō*[8] "The Five-Needled Pines on Noble Mt. Ryōzen."[9] Then the medium spoke again. "There's something in particular you're praying for," she said. "This time He surely won't put any curse on you. Go ahead with your wish." Everyone who heard her was amazed, and wept.

The boy was then put under Prelate Gahō, learned Shingon, and became a monk with the name Seiga. After being appointed Provisional Master of Discipline he fell seriously ill, but recovered instantly once he had copied out the *Yuishiki ron* and dedicated it at the Shrine, with Hōin Hanshin[10] presiding.

Later on Seiga went into retirement, taking the name Kūin (Gonen-bō), and lived, among other places, at Ninnikusen[11] and Tennōji.[12] In Kangi 2 he placed his hands in the mudrā of meditation and met his end repeating the Buddha's Name, sitting straight up, as though falling asleep.

[FIGURE 13.1: The boy singing before the Wakamiya.]

DATE. Seiga must have been born in 1165, since he was in his fourteenth year when he moved to Shōren'in, and since Kakukai was at Shōren'in only in 1178–79. Gahō died in 1190, and Seiga in Kangi 2 (1230).

1. Seiga lived ca. 1165–1230. "Master of Discipline" *(risshi)* was the lowest of the *sōjō* ranks.

2. A great Shingon temple in southeastern Yamashina (Kyoto), fairly near Uji. It was founded in 900 at the wish of Emperor Daigo's mother, having formerly been the residence of the lady's father, Fujiwara no Takafuji. Kanjuji received continuing support from the Fujiwara, and its head monk was normally the son of a high-ranking member of the clan. Its name can also be read Kajūji.

3. *Sonpi bunmyaku* notes only that he was the son of Sadahiro, a governor of Dewa, and that he held the junior fifth rank. *Chūyūki* for Daiji 4.11.12 mentions him as one of the *kebiishi* sent down to Kōfukuji to deal with the outrage committed by Egyō and his colleagues (see 11.2). A "Lieutenant of the Left Gate Guards" *(saemon no daibu)* was a third-level officer in the contingent.

4. Taikenmon'in, or Shōshi (1101–45), was the consort *(chūgū)* of Emperor Toba. In 1140 she commissioned the building of the East Round Hall (Tōendō) at Kōfukuji, which enshrined Fukūkenjaku and Jizō. Taikenmon'in no Horikawa was one of her ladies-in-waiting. Taikenmon'in no Horikawa's personal poetry collection survives, and verses by her appear in *Kin'yōshū, Shinkokinshū,* and elsewhere. No. 1858 in *Shinko-kinshū* is an oracle spoken to her by the Kasuga deity.

5. A great Shingon temple, and an important pilgrimage center, in the mountains along the valley that extends eastward from Sakurai. Its Eleven-Headed Kannon is especially revered.

6. Shōren'in, one of the "three *monzeki"* of Enryakuji, was founded by the Tendai abbot Gyōgen (a son of Fujiwara no Morozane) in 1144. Kakukai (1134–81) was the son of Emperor Toba by the daughter of the kengyō of the Iwashimizu Hachiman Shrine. He was Tendai abbot when he became the second head of Shōren'in in Jishō 2.4 (1178); he resigned in Jishō 3.11.

7. Gahō (1131–90), a son of Fujiwara no Akiyori, was the ninth abbot *(chōri)* of Kanjuji *(Kanjuji chōri shidai).*

8. *Imayō,* the popular songs of the middle and late Heian period, are here referred to collectively as "secular music" *(eikyoku,* "music of Ying") after the ancient Chinese state whose music, according to Confucius, was lascivious and inimical to social or spiritual harmony. It was normal for an artist to sing an *imayō* for a deity, or indeed, as in 16.2, for a deity to sing one himself. In *Ryōjin hishō kudenshū,* Emperor Go-Shirakawa (a passionate singer of *imayō*) related some striking instances in which he or members of his entourage sang *imayō* at shrines in response to a dream request from the deity. When he visited Itsukushima in 1174, surrounded by many ranking members of the court, the deity asked him through a medium to sing an *imayō,* exactly as the Kasuga deity does here in the *Genki.* Go-Shirakawa was flustered by the request since "the setting was much too public and, moreover, it was broad daylight" (Go-Shirakawa 1979:263). However, he had no choice but to comply.

9. This *imayō* is not in what survives of *Ryōjin hishō,* the collection made about 1179 by Retired Emperor Go-Shirakawa, but has been preserved elsewhere and is included in Kawaguchi (1965:473):

| | |
|---|---|
| The five-needled pines | *ryōzen miyama no* |
| on noble Mt. Ryōzen | *goyō matsu* |
| have, so they say, | *chikuyō nari to* |
| the Leaves of the bamboo. | *hito wa iū* |
| I myself shall see: | *ware mo miru* |
| bamboo leaves or no, | *chikuyō nari tomo* |
| pick and bring them to me! | *orimote ko* |
| With them I shall deck | *neya no kazashi ni* |
| the room where we lie. | *maro sasan* |

Ryōzen is originally Vulture Peak in India, where the Buddha preached the Lotus Sutra, but it has more than one namesake in Japan. Pine and bamboo are both associated with long life and noble constancy.

10. Hanshin (1176–1226) was the head of Tōin, a Kōfukuji subtemple. He was

lecturer for the Yuima-e in 1204 and became superintendent of Hōryūji in 1222.

11. A locality in the hills about 20 km. east of Nara, not far south of Mt. Kasagi. It is the site of Enjōji, a Shingon temple founded, according to its own tradition, in 756. Enjōji was a dependency of Ichijōin *(Kōfukuji matsuji chō)*. The temple has two protector shrines, Kasuga and Hakusan, which date from 1288 and are presently classed as national treasures.

12. Shitennōji, also known as Arahaka-dera. A temple in what is now Osaka, founded by Prince Shōtoku in 593. In medieval times it was an important pilgrimage center.

## 13.2 Prelate Shōsen

In the Angen era, Prelate Shōsen[1] of Kakuin[2] at Kōfukuji moved to the Central Pavilion in order to serve as Lecturer for the Yuima-e. Graduate Jōon,[3] meanwhile, lived as usual in the West Pavilion. He had been studying hard so as to take part in the Imperial Envoy's Debate[4] when, having lain down to sleep, he dreamed that a boy came and touched him on the shoulder. "Who are you?" Jōon asked. "The Fourth Sanctuary of Kasuga," answered the boy. "I came down to protect Shōsen, and thought I would just come by for a look at your study."

[PICTURE: The boy touching the sleeping monk's shoulder.]

DATE. 1174, the year Shōsen was lecturer for the Yuima-e.

1. Shōsen (b. 1109) was definer in 1166 and lecturer in 1174. According to *Kasuga genki ekotoba kikigaki,* he and Jōon were both disciples of Zōshun.

2. A subtemple of Kōfukuji. *Kasuga genki ekotoba kikigaki* describes it as "the present Kezōbō, and adds, "There is a rock there, where the Myōjin appeared." Of the *Genki* texts, only *Kasuga go-ruki* has Kakuin; the others have Nan'in.

3. Jōon (b. 1140) was definer in 1187 and lecturer in 1203. Like Shōsen he was a disciple of Zōshun.

4. *Chokushi bōban rongi.* A debate held at the superintendent's residence, under the patronage of the imperial envoy to the Yuima-e. Ranking scholars up to the superintendent himself took part. According to *Sanne Jōikki* for Jōhei 7, the first debate was held in 937, the year of the oracle recounted in 1.2.

## 13.3 Zōkei

At Bodaiin, a sub-temple of Kōfukuji, there lived a monk named Zōkei (Jōsen-bō).[1] Late in the summer of Bunji 5, a junior monk he lived with came down with an ague, so he went to stay for a while at a spot in the country named Wani.[2] The quiet there being so pleasant that he had no wish to leave, he decided to stay on until the thirteenth anniversary of his master's death.[3]

That fall, a fellow monk came visiting and offered Zōkei some wine. Zōkei drank only moderately, but he nonetheless became horribly drunk, and from dusk to dawn was too ill to sleep. The next day at the hour of the Sheep[4] he got just as sick as the day before, though he had drunk no wine at all. These attacks of fever came three days in a row. Then one day Graduate Kunkei[5] sent Zōkei a messenger from Nara. Zōkei started back, with due regard for the state of his health. When Kunkei told him that he would read the Canon of the Shrine[6] for him, Zōkei assented; and without even returning to Wani, he went straight to his room at Bodaiin. The fever came on him again, as usual, at the hour of the Ox.[7]

[PICTURE: Zōkei suffering from his fever, at Bodaiin.]

It returned day after day, just like an ague. By the fifth day after his arrival in Nara, Zōkei could no longer bear the agony. "I've lived in the Temple ever since my twelfth year," he reflected, "and all those years I've invoked the Daimyōjin especially, and offered Him many readings of the Sutras. So I'll worship Mikasa-yama now, even if I die in the effort."

He tried to crawl out of his room toward the east but was too weak to move more than a few feet, and had not the strength to open the door. Everything he saw looked yellow. Then he heard first thrice, then twice over the ceiling the crack of a *sakuhōshi*.[8] Next, a lovely female voice sang, to the accompaniment of a koto,[9] "Yes, turn by turn the start is done, the middle, then the end, and now, ah . . ."[10] Next the voice chanted, "Because of composure and detachment he causes his mind to eradicate all defilements and dwell in quiescence."

"That's a passage from the *Yuishiki ron!*" thought the awed Zōkei. "It must be a message from the Daimyōjin!" He wanted to write it down but had no inkstone or brush, so he waited till he heard someone coming. Finally the head monk of the pavilion passed by. Zōkei called him, and had him note down right away what the voice had said.

Still having some doubt about the matter, however, the head monk summoned the *gohō*. The Fourth Kasuga Sanctuary came down and cried, "I've won! I've won! This monk has trusted in me deeply ever since he was a boy, so I gave him a permanent living. Why did he leave the Temple without a word of farewell? That's why I tormented him for eight days. I never meant to take his life, I just wanted to give him a warning. It's Mizuya[11] I had do it. Today's divine manifestation was Mizuya's work too."

When the oracle was over, Zōkei opened his eyes and saw that things were back to their normal color. Immediately he prayed that if this really had been a reproof from the Daimyōjin, the Daimyōjin should return him by tomorrow to his ordinary state of physical and mental health. The next day he was as well as ever.

Now, the *Yuishiki ron* text normally reads, "Because of composure and detachment he eradicates all defilements . . . ," but since this does not differ markedly from what the Deity recited, the Deity's must be the proper version of the passage.[12]

[PICTURE: The medium delivering the oracle.]

DATE. Bunji 5 (1189).

1. Unknown.

2. The place where the Bodaisen-gawa flows out of the mountains into the Yamato plain, in present Wani-chō, Tenri-shi. Daijōin had an estate there, as did Tōdaiji. Wani was the name of an ancient clan with close ties to the area known, in pre-Nara times, as "Kasuga." This ancient "Kasuga" included the locality described here.

3. Apart from the rites held during the first forty-nine days after death, the dead were commemorated on the 100th day, then on the first, third, thirteenth, and thirty-ninth anniversaries.

4. Ca. 2 P.M.

5. Kunkei (b. 1127) was definer in 1183.

6. Presumably the Canon given the shrine by Shirakawa in 2.1.

7. Ca. 2 A.M.

8. A rhythm instrument used in *kagura*. Its form is simply that of a *shaku* cut lengthwise so that the two halves can be clapped smartly together.

9. The koto, a stringed instrument of the zither family, seems to have been particularly significant at Kasuga. The shrine still owns a magnificent instrument, in perfect condition, which was probably made in 884 to replace one presented to the shrine at its official founding in 768.

10. This snatch of song is actually hard to make much of.

11. The Mizuya Jinja, a Kasuga *sessha,* is said to have been founded in 943, when the Kōfukuji monk Ennyo brought to its site the deity of the Gion Tenjin-dō. Certainly it is not listed in the *Engi-shiki.* The shrine is located a few hundred meters roughly north of the Kasuga Shrine, on the Yoshiki-gawa (or Mizuya-gawa), which flows down from behind Mikasa-yama. In Bun'ei 4.4 (1267) the brook was divided above the Mizuya Jinja, and part of it was made to flow through the Four Sanctuaries complex, as it still does today (diary of Nakatomi no Sukekata).

The Mizuya deities are now Susanoo, Ōnamuchi, and Kushi-nada-hime. The Edo-period *Kōfukuji ranshōki* agrees. However, according to *Kasuga shaki* and *Kasuga Daimyōjin suijaku shōsha ki,* the deity in the twelfth century was Gozu Tennō. *Kasuga shaki* adds Inada-hime, noting that she is *nankai tennyo,* a "celestial lady of the southern ocean." Kasuga records agree that Mizuya looks like Bishamon, who happens also to be the *honji* of Enomoto. However, Mizuya's *honji* is Yakushi.

12. This translation is proposed only with the greatest hesitation. *Gunsho ruijū, Kasuga go-ruki,* and the Kadokawa text all have a slightly different passage after the quotation.

## 14.1 *The* Yuishiki ron *Escapes the Flames*

A certain scholar-monk of the Temple was suddenly inspired to leave the Southern Capital, and ended up finding himself a teacher of Tendai *shikan.*[1] Having selected some essential texts, he made them into a little bound book that he put on his shelf.

One night he dreamed that the book unaccountably caught fire. When someone beside him woke up and tried to put the fire out, a large hand, white and plump, reached down and cut the man's arm with a sword. Terrified, the man gave up. Once the fire had burned itself out, the monk saw that all the parts about *shikan* had been reduced to ashes. Only the *Yuishiki ron* was left.

As the monk remarked later on, "I hadn't wanted to change schools, but without even meaning to, I shunned one school and followed the other. I suppose this displeased the Deity. But certainly my link with the *Yuishiki ron,* which I had hardly read until then, is well worth having. I think it *will* guide me toward liberation."

[FIGURE 14.1: The monk reaching for the burning book, with the sword-wielding hand above him.]

REMARK. *Senjūshō* 1/1 speaks of "those who set before their eyes *yuishiki* and *shikan*," referring to monks at large. Apparently one did not lightly study both at once.

1. *Shikan* is a kind of meditation practiced in Tendai: *shi* (Skt. *śamatha*) refers to calming the mind, and *kan* (Skt. *vipaśyanā*) to insight into truth. Here, however, the word may simply be an abbreviation for *Maka shikan* (Ch. *Mo-ho-chih-kuan*), a great work by the Tendai founder Chih-i. Mujū Ichien referred to the *Maka shikan* this way in his *Tsuma Kagami*.

## 14.2 Grand Prelate Ryūkaku

Soon after Ryūkaku,[1] the Mitsugon'in[2] Grand Prelate, became the Superintendent of Kōfukuji, the monks rose up and drove him out. Ryūkaku was furious, and his vengeful fulminations caused a tremendous uproar.

Then someone on retreat in the gallery[3] of the Shrine dreamed that the doors of the Fourth Sanctuary opened of themselves. The Deity, in the form of a noble lady, stood by the curtain[4] in the entrance. "Ryūkaku is engaged in a contest of power with me," she said. "What shall I do?"

"How could he, a man, dare to pit himself against the Divine Majesty?" the dreamer asked.

"Yes," she answered, "but just look at what he has made me wear!" She showed him the inside of her robe. Awestruck, the dreamer obeyed, and saw written there on the reverse side of her beautiful robe, character by character, the *Daihannya-kyō*.[5] It turned out later that Ryūkaku had been offering the *Daihannya-kyō* by reading through it solemnly, in silence.

[PICTURE: Ryūkaku reading before the sanctuary.]

DATE. 1139.

CIRCUMSTANCES. Ryūkaku was a Genji, not a Fujiwara, and his appointment as superintendent was therefore unusual. This alone may have set the monks (here, *shuto*) against him. Already when Ryūkaku was appointed deputy superintendent, the *Chūyūki* diarist remarked (Chōshō 2.7.17 [1133]), "It is said that the superintendent of Kōfukuji cannot be a Genji. This monk is a Genji. Now they have their precedent." However, this motive is not mentioned in *Kokonchomonjū* no. 18 or in *Nanto daishu nyūraku ki*, both of which provide information about the affair.

According to *Nanto daishu nyūraku ki*, the incident began with the killing of a Kōfukuji practitioner (*shugakusha*) during a quarrel with Hōtōin of Kinpusenji, though Ryūkaku's fault in this connection is not described. On Hōen 5.3.9 (1139), the practitioner monks of Kōfukuji (*dōshu*) burned down Ryūkaku's residence. They started for Kyoto (led by the Kasuga deity's *sakaki*) on the 26th of the same month, but the Kasuga priest Tokimori warned Retired Emperor Toba. Toba sent troops to stop them, then dispatched an emissary to parley with them. Having gotten as far as Uji, the monks returned to Nara on the 28th.

On 11.9 of that year Ryūkaku sent a force to punish the *dōshu*, and several dozen men were killed in the ensuing fight. *Kokonchomonjū* adds various curious details to the episode. It says that Ryūkaku's army of several hundred mounted warriors surrounded Kōfukuji on three sides, but that before it could attack, the *shuto* sallied forth and defeated it in battle. Many of Ryūkaku's men were killed, and twenty were taken prisoner. It turned out that Ryūkaku must have ordered his warriors to burn down the temple, since they were discovered to be equipped for setting fires, and indeed had set fire to several houses just outside the temple. Fortunately, rain put the fires out.

Still according to *Kokonchomonjū*, a "divine fire" *(shinka)* was seen shining from Kasuga-yama during the battle, and vanished when the battle was over. In fact, someone dreamed that the Kōfukuji troops were deer. Tokimori himself dreamed he saw tens of thousands of mounted warriors approaching. They said that the "Fujiwara Lay Monk" had sent them as reinforcements for Kasuga no Daimyōjin, though Tokimori did not know who this gentleman might be.

*Nanto daishu nyūraku ki* simply says that the matter was reported to the regent (Tadamichi) and to the retired emperor, with the result that three emissaries were sent to Kōfukuji. On 12.2 the imperial police arrested fifty of Ryūkaku's warriors. Ryūkaku too made representations to Kyoto. Then on 12.10, the Kōfukuji monks and Ryūkaku's men fought once more. The palace minister Fujiwara no Sukenobu sent Fujiwara no Nobusuke, the governor of Musashi, to resolve the affair.

A decade later, on Kyūan 6.8.5 (1150), the Kōfukuji monks, several thousand strong, marched into Kyoto behind 200 Kasuga priests and shrine servants hearing the *sakaki.* Of the persons mentioned in the *Genki,* at least Gen'en (11.4), Kyōkaku (11.4), Egyō (11.1), and Tokimori were with them. They wanted a superintendent appointed, there having been none since 1148. Ryūkaku, Jinpan (11.4), and Kakkei all hoped to be named, but Ryūkaku was reappointed since both Tadamichi and the retired emperor favored him.

1. Ryūkaku (1074–1158) was a son of Minamoto (Koga) no Akifusa, and hence a Murakami Genji. Lecturer in 1106, he was named superintendent of Yakushiji in 1131, of Hokkeji in 1132, and of Kōfukuji in 1138. In 1139 he resigned, but was reappointed in 1150.

2. A Kōfukuji subtemple. Mitsugon is the name of the paradise of Dainichi.

3. The *kairō,* around the precincts of the main sanctuaries.

4. The blinds *(mi-su)* that hung before the sanctuaries with sacred mirrors *(mishō-tai)* attached to them.

5. The deity did not really dislike the *Daihannya-kyō* that much, and in *Genki* 6.3 even asked for it. A Daihannya-e was held annually on 4.15, at least in the thirteenth century, for the whole shrine (Diary of Nakatomi no Sukekata for several years between 1265 and 1280).

## 14.3 (No separate title)

One of those who lived with Ryūkaku was a practitioner monk. Every night for a hundred nights this monk went to the Shrine from near the Yakushi-dō,[1] and prayed earnestly that Ryūkaku might return to the Temple in peace. The Daimyōjin said to him in a dream, "Your master is a man who never in all his days has offered me a single sheet of paper."

The monk quickly communicated this by letter to Ryūkaku, who recognized that it was true. Ryūkaku bitterly regretted that he had done nothing but store up merit as a scholar, forgetting completely about material offerings.[2]

[PICTURE: The monk on his way through the woods to the shrine; Ryūkaku reading his letter.]

DATE. 1139.

1. The location of this building is unclear. Nakatomi no Sukekata noted in his diary for Kōan 3.3.6 (1280) that one shrine servant had wounded another with a knife just east of the Yakushi-dō; and his entry for 5.6 in the same year includes "Yakushidō" in a list of personal appellations for "villagers" (*kyōmin*) who came to a party at the Wakamiya. There is a remote possibility that Ryūkaku's colleague hid out at Kōzen (see 16.4), high in the Kasuga hills, since the temple there (if it still existed in 1139) was dedicated to Yakushi.

2. Perhaps Ryūkaku had not thought of making material offerings because he was not a Fujiwara.

## 14.4 (No separate title)

Meanwhile Ryūkaku secretly visited the Shrine by night and laid various arguments before the Deity. "No monk in all the Temple measures up to me," he said reproachfully. "It is tragic that you should reject me."

He got this divine response. "I am happy to agree, by all means, that you are a fine monk. But shall a man of sufficient stature to run the Temple show the young novices no mercy, and devote no time to giving them complete instruction?[1] No, no, I am not at all pleased."

Ryūkaku awoke from his dream. Before leaving, he vowed that if he managed to return he would immediately give a full course of instruction at length. Very soon after that he did return, and made good his vow.

[PICTURE: Ryūkaku at the shrine.]

DATE. Apparently 1139, like the two preceding items, although the "very soon after that" *(ikuhodo naku)* in the last paragraph then does not make awfully good sense.

1. The nature of the deity's complaint against Ryūkaku is unclear. The key word is *chōkō*, which means literally "long discourse." I have translated it as "complete instruction." Moreover, one wonders what this problem has to do with the monks' general rejection of Ryūkaku.

## 14.5 Tonkaku-bō

It must be roughly that long ago too that ninety ruffians[1] were expelled from Kōfukuji. The master of the worst offender of all was one Tonkaku-bō,[2] a permanent resident of Ninnikusen.[3] Lamenting what had happened to his disciple, Tonkaku-bō began coming down at the hour of the Ox[4] from his mountain temple to the Kasuga Shrine, meaning to intercede with the Daimyōjin on the fellow's behalf. After chanting the Lotus Sutra by heart inside the shrine fence, he would return at dawn to his mountain. He kept this up for one hundred nights.

On the last night, worn out with chanting the Sutra. Tonkaku-bō dozed off for a moment and dreamed that a beautiful little boy came and played about on his lap. The little boy's hair was wet. Tonkaku-bō asked him why. "Because it's so inspiring to hear you chant the Lotus Sutra," the little boy replied. "My hair is wet with tears of joy. Still, I'd have been even more impressed if you'd read the *Yuishiki ron*.[5] Anyway, you oughtn't to do your chanting so close. Stay outside the fence next time. And by the way, after careful consideration I've decided that you're not going to get what you're asking for."

[PICTURE: Tonkaku-bō before the main sanctuaries, inside the fence.]

DATE. Mid-twelfth century?

1. *Akuto* (or *akutō*), "evil bands." Bands of peasants or local warriors who caused trouble on estates *(shōen)*. Much of the community at Kōfukuji was armed and had close ties with the temple's estates, so that it is not surprising to find *akuto* directly connected with Kōfukuji.

2. Unknown.

3. A "permanent resident" *(kujūsa)* was a practitioner monk who had vowed to remain on a certain mountain (i.e., at a certain temple) for life. For Ninnikusen, see 13.1, n. 12.

4. Ca. 2 A.M.

5. The Kasuga deity was not really opposed to the Lotus Sutra. He listened to it regularly (see chapter 3, under "Rites, festivals, and offerings"). He also did not mind hinting that Mikasa-yama and Vulture Peak (where the Buddha preached the sutra) were the same place (18.1). Moreover, the Hokke-e at the Nan'endō (intimately linked to Kasuga) was one of the most important annual events at Kōfukuji.

## 14.6 A House with the Yuishiki ron Inside It Escapes a Fire

At about that time, too, there was a great fire in the Capital. Everything was a smoldering waste except for one house that did not burn, and so escaped turning to smoke. This caused quite a stir. People said it was an unheard-of wonder.

Then a neighbor related that before the fire he had had a dream. Several shrine servants in yellow robes had come and found the house burning. They had then felt over the main front beam[1] for something, and from there had extinguished the fire.

It certainly was strange that only this house had survived the flames. At the suggestion that there might be something special about the beam, the people went for a look. They found a single fascicle of the *Yuishiki ron.* Everyone who saw the event or heard the story was amazed. Obviously it was the Daimyōjin's protection of this book that had saved the house.

[PICTURE: People inspecting the scroll, while all around the house lie smoking ruins.]

DATE. Perhaps the twelfth month of 1125, when there was a great fire in Kyoto (*Shingonden* 7). However, there were many other fires as well.
RELATED MATERIALS. *Koshaki* states that once when there was a great fire in the Capital, Fujiwara no Tadamichi saw that his residence was directly in the path of the flames. Prostrating himself toward the south (the direction of Kasuga), he begged the deity to protect him. A cool breeze immediately sprang up, and the fire went out. Since Tadamichi lived 1097–1164, *this* fire could certainly be the one of 1125.

1. *Nageshi,* a horizontal beam linking the pillars of a house, under the ceiling.

## 15.1 The Tōin Graduate

When a monk known as the Tōin Graduate[1] entered the Shrine's east gallery, he found a practitioner lying there. He was so irritated when the fellow did not get up that on his way out he gave him a kick in the head. The practitioner could only lie there, helpless and hurt.

[PICTURE: The monk kicking his hapless colleage.]

The Graduate then fell ill, and when his condition became serious he summoned a medium and called down the Daimyōjin. "You did something barbarous," announced the medium, "and you are not going to get any help from *me.*"

The Graduate had forgotten the whole thing. "What are you talking about?" he asked.

"You gave a kick," said the Deity, "to a practitioner who was lying down because he was worn out from reading the *Yuishiki ron,* and whom I therefore found admirable. It was an absolutely barbarous thing to do."

Only then did the Graduate remember the incident.

[PICTURE: The monk lying sick, with the medium and the healer nearby.]

1. Unidentified. Tōin was a subtemple of Kōfukuji, originally the residence of Genbō (d. 746), and the place where Genbō deposited the 5,000 volumes of Buddhist texts that he brought back from China. *Kōfukuji ruki* notes that the presence of the *Yuishiki ron* and other Hossō texts in this collection inspired the Kasuga deity to come to Mikasa-yama in order to protect so sacred a teaching.

## 15.2  Graduate Kyōei

Kyōei, the Consultant's Graduate,[1] was worried because he was an Annual Leader of the Eight Discourses of Kasuga,[2] yet lacked what are called "host gifts."[3] The Vestal of Ise[4] then dreamed that a noble gentleman in formal dress came to her and said, "You must help the Adjunct Annual Leader."[5] When she woke up, she realized that she was to provide someone something, so she sent off a set of layered robes to one Jōkei, the Tanba Lay Monk,[6] with the message, "Who is the Adjunct Annual Leader, and what does he do? I had a dream about him, and am supposed to send him help." Jōkei sent the package straight on to Kyōei, who was very happy and grateful for what the Daimyōjin had done for him. He used the robes for host gifts.

[PICTURE: The deity standing by the sleeping lady; Kyōei receiving her gift.]

1. Unknown. Since he was called *saishō no tokugō,* his father or a close relative was probably a consultant, *saishō* being the "Chinese" term for *sangi.*

2. "Annual Leader" *(toshigashira* or *kitō)* designates one assigned the annual responsibility for a rite. The "Eight Discourses" were a series of lectures on the Lotus Sutra, held twice annually at the shrine. The practice was instituted in 947, under Fujiwara no Tadahira. In 1018, the beginning dates for it were set at 2.28 and 10.28, but by the late twelfth century the observance began on 4.9 and 9.4. The entries on it in the diary of Nakatomi no Sukesada, for example Kangi 4.4.9, are particularly detailed. A *hakkō-ya* ("pavillion for the Eight Discourses") was set up before the main Kasuga sanctuaries, and high-ranking monks took part *(Shatō go-hakkō nikki).*

3. *Torikaburimono.* The word appears as *kaburimono* in the diary of Nakatomi no Sukeshige for Bunji 2.9.6 (1186), as a synonym for *hikimono* (entry for Genryaku 2.9.6 [1185]). A *hikimono* is a gift made by the host to a guest at a banquet or celebration. In this case, Kyōei was the "host" and the Kasuga sanctuaries the "guests."

4. *Saigū,* an unmarried imperial princess who was head priestess of the Ise Shrine.

5. The annual leader presided on the first day of the rite (4.9 or 9.4), while the adjunct annual leader *(soe-toshigashira* or *soe-kitō)* presided on the second day (4.10 or 9.5). On 4.11 or 9.6, the annual leader presented gifts to all five Kasuga sanctuaries, while on 4.12 or 9.7 the adjunct annual leader did the same. These gifts could include cloth and horses as well as robes. Sukeshige's diary for Bunji 2.9.6 states clearly that each sanctuary received a robe of a different color, as well as other things. Both monks received return gifts likewise on 4.12 or 9.7.

6. Unidentified. According to *Sonpi bunmyaku,* a former governor of Echizen named Fujiwara no Tsunesuke took the religious name Jōkei at the end of his life, but Tsunesuke must have lived too late (ca. 1300) for this story.

## 15.3 The Daijōin Grand Prelate

On the 27th day of the 11th month of Gennin 1, after the demise of Senior Grand Prelate Shin'en[1] who rebuilt Bodaisen, Grand Prelate Jisson[2] of Daijōin[3] moved to Bodaisen as his successor, and conducted the mortuary rites. He was to perform a particularly solemn ceremony on the 26th of the 12th month,[4] but the night before, an attack of chronic asthma made it unlikely that he would be able to go through with it. He was extremely vexed.

Having dozed off for a moment, leaning on his armrest, he woke up and remarked to the monk Raiken[5] who was before him, "How extraordinary! I just dreamed I saw a deer right there in the garden behind you, with his head almost in the room, looking straight at me."

Raiken, who realized that this meant divine protection, wiped away tears of emotion. Jisson's asthma cleared up that minute. The next day he performed the rite as planned.

Then a monk known as Graduate Sonpen,[6] also in residence at Bodaisen, told how he had dreamed that on glancing around his room, he had seen a curtain hanging the full width between two pillars. When he drew the curtain aside, he found behind it a large deer, standing there in silence.

The two stories tallied nicely. It was wonderful how the Daimyōjin protected Jisson.

[FIGURE 15.3: The deer looking at the dozing Jisson; Sonpen drawing the curtain aside and discovering the deer.]

DATE. Gennin 1.12.25 (1224).

RELATED DREAMS. (1) Fujiwara no Munetada wrote in *Chūyūki* for Chōji 1.11.10 (1104) that he had dreamed of seeing four deer at the Kasuga Shrine, and observed that this was "an extremely good omen." (2) Fujiwara no Yorinaga wrote in *Daiki* for Kyūan 4.9 (1184), "Last night I dreamed of a deer. I think it was a fortunate sign. It shows the protection of Kasuga."

1. Shin'en (1153–1224), a son of Fujiwara no Tadamichi (1097–1164), was there-

fore a younger brother of Kujō Kanezane (1147–1207) and of the Kōfukuji superintendent Eshin (1114–71). He studied at Kōfukuji under Eshin, Jinpan, and Zōshun. At various times he was head of both Daijōin and Ichijōin. He became superintendent in 1181, and presided over the "eye-opening" of the new Great Buddha of Tōdaiji in 1185. Shin'en restored the temple at Bodaisen in 1213.

2. Jisson (1180–1236), a son of Fujiwara no Motofusa, was a nephew of Kujō Kanezane and a disciple of Shin'en. Lecturer in 1199, he was named superintendent in 1225. In 1228 he resigned, after certain monks of Kōfukuji attacked and burned Tōnomine, but the monks objected and he had to be reappointed. Jisson's principal connection was with Ichijōin. He died at Bodaisen.

3. See chapter 4, under "Fujiwara monks and the rise of the *inke.*"

4. Apparently the observance for the twenty-eight day after Shin'en's death.

5. Unknown.

6. Sonpen appears in a list of *daihōshi* who attended the Yuima-e of 1224 (Hiraoka 1958–60:1:313); according to *Kōfukuji bettō shidai,* Jisson delegated his administrative duties *(hōmu)* to Sonpen in 1229. Sonpen seems not to have been a member of the temple council *(sangō),* since he does not appear in *Kōfukuji sangō bunin.*

## 15.4  The Kii Superior

When the Naka Grand Prelate Jisson[1] was Superintendent, his Director of Repairs[2] was a monk known as the Kii Superior.[3] At the time there was famine in the land, and many people both high and low were starving to death. In secret, this Superior had a servant store a little rice up above his ceiling, just in case the Superintendent should need emergency provisions.

Now Hōsen-bō,[4] a scholar-monk of the Central Pavilion who had many children and students lodging with him, was out of food to the point where his disciples were threatened with starvation. Reflecting that the whole Temple counted particularly on the Director of Repairs, he discreetly sent him an appeal. The Kii Superior replied, "I am deeply devoted to all the monks' welfare, for I had an oracle from the Daimyōjin instructing me to give them full support. I am therefore prepared to make every possible effort. At the moment, however, I unfortunately can do nothing for you."

The disappointed Hōsen-bō now felt wholly abandoned. "To think that I always trusted him so!" he murmured, and gave himself up, with all his disciples, to despair.

Then a boy knocked on the door, opened it, and carried in some rice. "From the Kii Superior!" he announced. Hōsen-bō cheered up, roused a recumbent junior monk, and had him prepare some immediately. Everyone ate.

Early the next morning, the Superior came round. "I'm awfully sorry about my answer last night," he said, "so I came over as quickly as I could."

"No, no," Hōsen-bō protested, "you made me so happy that I should have gone to thank *you*. Your visit really does me too much honor!"

"I thought the Superintendent might need some rice to entertain an unexpected guest from the Court, you see," the Superior went on, "so I kept some back and resisted letting you have it. Then I dreamed an old monk came to me and said, '*I* know what to do with that rice you're hoarding!' He scattered it far and wide. That frightened me, I tell you! I came to apologize."

[PICTURE: The superior lying asleep, while the old monk pitches the rice bales out of their hiding place; the boy knocking on Hōsen-bō's door.]

DATE. Between 1225 and 1230.

1. See 15.3, n. 3. I cannot explain the "Naka" of his title.

2. *Shuri* (or *suri*) *no mokudai*. See chapter 4, under "the organization of Kōfukuji."

3. "Superior" is *jishu,* a title borne by certain officers of the temple council *(sangō).* This one is Keijitsu (1173–1239), who was *jishu* 1219–39 *(Kōfukuji sangō bunin).* The illustration shows him lying beside his wife, with a sword at his pillow and a sleeping warrior outside.

4. Unknown.

## 15.5 Shōzō

Hokkyō Shōzō,[1] a member of the Temple Council, was once very ill and almost certain to die.When he had the Daimyōjin brought down, and the *gohō* questioned, this oracle came through the medium: "The sick man does not interest me. However, he has not set his face toward any other shrine but mine, he has trusted in none but me, and his loyalty to me is sure. Therefore I will have pity on him. Nothing more will happen to him, and I will not cast him from my thoughts."

In the end, Shōzō had an honorable career and enjoyed a long life.

[PICTURE: Shōzō lying ill, with the medium giving the oracle to her companion monk.]

DATE. Perhaps ca. 1180, before Shōzō became a *jishu.*

1. Shōzō appears in the diary of Nakatomi no Sukeshige for Juei 3.1.1 (1184) as one of the two officials *(shoshi)* of Kōfukuji who accompanied the superintendent Shin'en to the Wakamiya on that date; and as "Echizen no [ji]shu Shōzō," who was among the monks accompanying the superintendent to the Kasuga Shrine on Genryaku 2.1.1. (1185).

## 16.1  The Venerable Gedatsu

The Venerable Gedatsu[1] of Kasagi,[2] admired by the whole Temple as a pillar of the Two Wisdoms, detested nonetheless the noise of the crowd, and finally acted on his long-standing wish to live in retirement. The waters of his faith being vigorous, the Gods shone their light upon him.

In the 9th month of Kenkyū 6, while he was ill in Uda county of Yamato province,[3] the Daimyōjin spoke to him. The Venerable Gedatsu felt that if the Daimyōjin really had possessed him he should have lost normal consciousness, whereas that had not happened; and this made him a little doubtful.

Then came a second oracle. "How suspicious you are!" exclaimed the Deity. "Surely you are not going to doubt the Gods! When Kashō,[4] Zengen,[5] and the rest were inspired by the Buddha to preach the most profound Teaching, they knew perfectly well where their knowledge came from. Since the monks of this latter age all lust after name and gain, most of them are rewarded in their next life with a fall into the demon realm. It takes two or three years, or perhaps half a dozen, to redeem lingering attachment,[6] after which one is born into the human or the celestial realms; but for *them,* so splendid a recompense is hardly to be expected. Anyway, *you* have an enduring karmic bond with me. Say you pass on with right thoughts[7]—why would I not then protect you? After all, it is thanks to me that you conceived the aspiration to enlightenment. When you read the *Shingyō no yūsan,* you know, you were consulting the *Yuga ron*[8] passages that I had abstracted for you. And your faith in relics[9] comes from the passage about the realm without outflows."[10]

Then he turned to the *taiyō* acolyte.[11] "Long ago I heard Shaka Nyorai preach on Vulture Peak," he said. "If you don't obey your master, how will you hear *my* voice?"

[FIGURE 16.1: Gedatsu seated at a reading desk, with two monks before him, gesturing as he talks.]

DATE. Kenkyū 6.9 (1195).

1. Gedatsu Shōnin (Jōkei, 1155–1213) is a major figure in early Kamakura Buddhism. This account of him is based mainly on Tanaka Hisao's biography in Kamata (1971:461–69). He was a grandson of Fujiwara (Takashina) no Michinori (Shinzei, d. 1159), a highly influential courtier close to Go-Shirakawa and Toba. Although triumphant in the Hōgen insurrection of 1156, Shinzei had to commit suicide after the Heiji insurrection of 1159–60, and the prospects of his many children were ruined. Sadanori, Gedatsu Shōnin's father, was exiled, while many of his brothers became monks. One was Kakuken (1131–1212), a superintendent of Kōfukuji, from whom Gedatsu Shōnin received the precepts in 1165. Four of Gedatsu Shōnin's brothers were likewise monks at Miidera, Tōdaiji, or Enryakuji.

At Kōfukuji, Gedatsu Shōnin lived in Ryūgejuin, which was aligned with Daijōin. He was lecturer for the Yuima-e in 1186, and played a distinguished role in many other such ceremonies. Kujō Kanezane greatly admired him, and lamented in his diary (*Gyokuyō*) Gedatsu Shōnin's decision to retire from Kōfukuji to Kasagi. (Though he seems to have made the decision in 1192, he did not actually move there until the fall of 1193.) In 1208 he moved to Kaijūsenji, a Kannon temple not far from Kasagi, where he died.

# THE MIRACLES OF THE KASUGA DEITY

Gedatsu Shōnin left many writings on such subjects as Hossō doctrine and monastic discipline. Perhaps his most famous work is *Kōfukuji sōjō* (1205), a petition on behalf of Kōfukuji to punish Hōnen. Like Myōe Shōnin, he vehemently opposed Hōnen's Amida Nenbutsu teaching, championing instead the Shaka Nenbutsu and the Miroku Nenbutsu. His Kasuga faith is discussed in chapter 5, under "The Kasuga faith of Gedatsu Shōnin." *Kojidan* 3 (no. 303) relates his miraculous conception, while *Shaseki-shū* 1/2 and *Sangoku denki* 12/27 tell how Hachiman guided him to Ise.

2. A mountain (288 m.) in extreme southwestern Kyoto-fu, some 20–25 km, northeast of Nara. Gedatsu Shōnin moved there in 1193. Kasagi rises steeply on the south bank of the Kizu-gawa, and commands a dramatic view of the valley. Kasagidera, the Shingon temple upon it, claims ultimately to have been founded in the seventh century. En no Gyōja is said to have practiced in a cave there in 686. A *shugendō* center, Kasagi was sacred especially to Miroku. The famous Miroku incised on a rock face behind the temple's main hall was almost wholly destroyed in 1331, when Hōjō troops routed the forces of Emperor Go-Daigo. Nothing is left now of what Gedatsu Shōnin built. Kasagidera, like Hasedera, was claimed as a dependency by both Tōdaiji and Kōfukuji. As far as Kōfukuji was concerned, the temple was under Daijōin.

3. A mountainous area of Nara-ken, roughly east of Sakurai.

4. Kashō (Skt. Mahākāśyapa) is one of the ten great disciples of the Buddha. In chapter 2 of the *Nehan-gyō*, the Buddha declares that Mahākāśyapa will be the great teacher of those who lived on after the Buddha's death; some Ritsu texts describe him as teaching a great assembly of arhats.

5. Zengen (Skt. Subhuti), another of the Buddha's ten great disciples, appears under that name especially in Hsüan-tsang's translation of the *Daihannya-kyō* where, in chapter 36, he explains the nonattachment of a buddha in terms that elicit the Buddha's praise.

6. *Yoshū*, apparently the remnants of worldly attachment that detain even good monks a little, before they proceed to better places.

7. *Rinjū shōnen*, the correct thoughts at the moment of death that allow one to pass on to higher spiritual realms.

8. More fully known as *Yugashiji ron* (Ch. *Yu-ch'ieh-shih-ti-lun*, Skt. *Yogācāra-bhūmi*). A fundamental Hossō treatise traditionally attributed to Miroku, and translated by Hsüan-tsang (*Taishō* 30/279, no. 1579).

9. *Shari* (Skt. *śārira*). Small, whitish, pebblelike grains traditionally supposed to be fragments of the Buddha's bones or teeth, recovered from the ashes of his cremation. They may be seen in the crystal, inner vessels of medieval reliquaries, many examples of which are associated with the Kasuga cult. The cult of relics was strong at Kōfukuji and among the aristocracy. Gedatsu Shōnin had some of the venerable relics brought from China by Ganjin (688–763), and he gave two of these to Myōe Shōnin in 18.4. Hakusen wrote in *kan* 5:

> Once, so they often say, Gedatsu Shōnin dreamed that Kasuga no Daimyōjin gave him relics. Gedatsu Shōnin woke up immediately and found thirty relic particles gleaming brightly in the sanctuary before him. Little by little he gave away to one person or another these relics that the Deity had granted him, and people generally called them "Kasuga *shari*."

10. *Murokai,* the realm of perfect enlightenment. The term appears in the *Yuishiki ron.*

11. A *taiyō* is a verse to pray for the flourishing of the Teaching, said at the conclusion of various Buddhist rites. Apparently it was this acolyte's *(shōsei)* duty to read the *taiyō* at the proper time.

## 16.2 (No separate title)

The Venerable Gedatsu built Kasuga no Daimyōjin a small shrine, so at to install him as the local protector[1] of the Hannya-dai[2] on Kasagi. On the night of the 27th of the 9th month in Kenkyū 7, he arrived at the Shrine with his companions. Since neither the Overseer nor any other ranking priest happened then to be available, Gedatsu spoke to the clansman[3] on duty.

He had the clansman cut a Sakaki branch five or six feet long from the Mountain, then carry it to the First Sanctuary and recite a *norito.*[4] Then he himself took the Sakaki and laid it outside the South Gate,[5] to the west of the entrance. Next he went before the Wakamiya.

While he was at the Worship Hall[6] a verse came unbidden to his mind:

> Yes I shall go,      *ware yukite*
> go and adore . . .    *yukite agamen*

Then he paused before adding.

> the Hannya-kyō . . .    *hannya kyō*

He was just north of the Worship Hall, having left the Wakamiya, when he suddenly felt something weighing on him. His sight dimmed and his normal awareness vanished. The weight was like two fingers pressing heavily on his head. Then the words came unbidden, as before:

> so long as Shaka's Teaching   *shaka no minori no*
> shall live on.                 *aran kagiri wa*

He turned back to worship again at the Wakamiya, then went on to the Main Shrine. There his companion Shin'e-bō[7] wrapped the Sakaki in rough matting and lifted it in his arms. The Venerable Gedatsu then felt the Deity move to the Sakaki, and the weight on his head was gone. Shin'e-bō carried his burden up Hatchō-zaka[8] at Kasagi without even pausing to rest, whereas before he had always had to stop seven or eight times on the way up.

Later on the Venerable Gedatsu dreamed that Chikahiro, Kasuga's Director of Offerings,[9] came to him and asked, "I understand the Daimyōjin is here. Where will I find Him?" Also, Shin'e-bō dreamed there were two huge deer on the mountain behind the newly built shrine. They were ten feet long and seven feet tall, and their antlers were five feet long.

Once the Venerable Gedatsu dreamed that a divine voice from the sky spoke this verse:

| | |
|---|---|
| Know me as I am! | *ware o shire* |
| The Buddha Shakamuni | *shakamuni butsu no* |
| came into this life, | *yo ni idete* |
| and lo! the bright moon | *sayakeki tsuki no* |
| now illumines the world. | *yo o terasu to wa* |

Then the same voice sang an *imayō:*

| | |
|---|---|
| From My Shrine at Kashima, | *kashima no miya yori* |
| riding a stag, | *kasegi nite* |
| I came to find | *kasuga no sato o* |
| the hamlet of Kasuga; | *tazunekoshi* |
| and now at last | *mukashi no kokoro mo* |
| a human being | *ima koso wa* |
| has seen | *hito ni hajimete* |
| what moved Me to come. | *shirarenure* |

[PICTURE: Gedatsu Shōnin and his companions at the Wakamiya; Shin'e-bō carrying his burden up Kasagi; the deer behind the shrine, with Chikahiro looking as though he is questioning two sleeping monks.]

DATE. Kenkyū 7.9.27 (1196).

RELATED MATERIALS. *Shasekishū* 1/5 notes briefly that the Kasuga deity, in the form of a child, rode from Kasuga to the Hannya-dai on top of Gedatsu Shōnin's head. The text has the two *tanka* given here, but not the *imayō.* It says that the *ware o shire* verse was spoken in the air over the Hannya-dai. Otherwise, the *ware yukite* verse occurs in *Gyokuyōshū* 20 (no. 2720), while *ware o shire* is no. 687 in *Zoku kokinwakashū.*

1. *Chinju,* the deity enshrined at a place so as to protect the family or institution occupying the spot.

2. A shrine constructed on Kasagi, by Gedatsu Shōnin, to house a complete copy of the *Daihannya-kyō* written in gold on a dark blue ground. Gedatsu Shōnin dedicated the copy on Kenkyū 6.11.19 (1195), with a prayer that it should serve to provide sutra-offerings *(hosse)* for Ise, Hachiman, Kasuga, and Kinpusen (Fujita 1976:3:98). The shrine was a six-sided hall whose central image was Shaka. *Kasagidera engi* describes it in detail.

Apparently the idea was Chinese. According to *Bukkyō deijiten* there was a Hannya-dai on Lu Shan. Judging from the context, this seems to have been a natural feature (perhaps a knoll), but a structure may have completed it. At any rate, Hui Yüan built a "Hannya-dai Temple" on Lu Shan in A.D. 403. Moreover, according to Alexander Soper (1959:89), Hui Yüan's patron, Yao Hsing, had "a Prajñā Terrace . . . raised in the Middle Palace."

3. *Ujibito,* the term for a younger son of a Kasuga priestly house, who had not yet been appointed to a formal rank.

4. A ritual prayer addressed to a deity.

5. The main gate into the precincts of the four principal sanctuaries of Kasuga.

6. This *haiden* still stands before the Wakamiya sanctuary. According to *Kasuga shaki* it was first built in 1144.

7. Unknown.

8. The steep path to the top of Kasagi.

9. *Ku no azukari:* apparently the shrine servant in charge of offerings at the Kasuga Shrine. Chikahiro is unidentified. Read Shinkō, his name could be a monk's, but the picture shows a shrine servant.

## 16.3  (No separate title)

In the fall of Shōji 1, the Venerable Gedatsu fell gravely ill in his hut on Kasagi. Then at the hour of the Bird[1] on the 22d of the 8th month, an unusual look came over him. He called his fellow monks together, and they hurried to clean up around him. Next he donned a white robe and quickly spread a length of brocade on his chapel altar, which he understood now to be the Daimyōjin's seat. Finally, when he and his companions had performed ablutions, he assumed an air of grave formality and proceeded to a general invocation. These were his words.

"Hail Shakamuni Nyorai, our Great Benefactor! Hail most profound and subtle scripture, the *Jōyuishiki ron!* Hail Gohō and the Ten Great Bosatsu,[2] Kaigen,[3] Genjō,[4] and Kōdō,[5] and all our great Founders!"

Then he held the censer high and said, "Shaka and Miroku are one in substance. Our Original Teacher, after His perfect passing, dwells in the world as Miroku. Vulture Peak and Chisoku[6] are nondual."

Next he lifted up his voice, as though singing a *rōei*,[7] in praise of the Middle School:[8] "Subtle! Most subtle! Exquisite subtlety! Profound! Most profound! Depth upon depth!" And he continued: "This Hossō Middle School of ours began when, nine hundred years and more after the Nyorai's extinction, Miroku first proclaimed it in the far place where He resides.[9] Mujaku[10] was the Bosatsu who first brought it to earth, while Seshin was the great master who put it into practice. Gohō was one of the Thousand Buddhas,[11] while Kaigen was the teacher of his age. Genjō manifested the realization of Jōtai[12] in the East, and Kōdō Daishi conveyed the full form of enlightenment in China. Now the Hossō School survives only at our Temple, among its scholars.

"How could I not call you the lamp of the Hossō teaching? How sorry I was when you left the Temple!—though I could do nothing to stop you, since it was your own karma that drove you to do so. Yet although you *do* return to your home temple, you keep coming back here again, and still insist on living here. You are wasting the gold of the True Teaching this way, and must soon sink needlessly into the ocean of suffering.

"Ever since middle antiquity[13] scholars have failed, either through indolence or through jealousy, to teach others what they themselves knew perfectly well, so that what each had to pass on has died with him. The Most Worthy Zōshun's[14] deep commitment moved him to write down the teachings of our school. If he had not done so, the school might have perished forever. Hurry now, write too, and complete what you have begun! Are you afraid your work will be worthless because it contains errors? Well, by no means everyone studies the works even of Zenshu[15] or Gomyō,[16] and no doubt even fewer will read yours. Still, your writings will be quite unlike anyone else's.

"I give you the practice of calling the Name.[17] As I have told you before, this calling should be done 10,000 times. Use the other 40,000 callings' worth of time for study—though as for your companions, you can let them practice as they please. For yourself, call our Original Master's name and chant, 'Death with right thoughts, Rebirth in the Inner Sanctum.' I often go to the Tosotsu Heaven and worship there the Lord of Compassion.[18] Even my eyes cannot encompass the sixteen yojanas[19] of His marvelous form.

"Now, I understand that you have been on pilgrimage to Amaterasu Ōmikami, our Imperial Sovereign, and talked about calling the Name. It is old karma that prompts you in this, and half of it is contrived by the demon realm. The demon realm is not a place that really encourages calling the Name. The whole thing is actually a ploy to keep you from your scholarly work. The Grand Shine protects the Buddha's Teaching even more than I do. Bonden,[20] Taishakuten, the Four Kings,[21] and the Eight Races of Protectors[22] all receive the Buddha's lofty instruction and carefully guard the True Teaching. Not that you do not know all this, but you still go wrong. I created this illness of yours. Please tell the Provisional Grand Prelate[23] all about it immediately."

In the seventh month of that year, the Venerable Gedatsu had gone to the Grand Shrine and had declared to the Deity that the precious Name of Shaka should be called 50,000 times a day. That must be what the Daimyōjin meant when He spoke of Gedatsu addressing Amaterasu Ōmikami.

[PICTURE: Gedatsu Shōnin speaking, censer in hand. Since he is the deity, his face is covered.]

DATE. Shōji 1.8.22 (1199).

1. Ca. 6 P.M.

2. Gohō (Skt. Dharmapāla, 530–61) was a great Hossō patriarch. The "Ten Bosatsu" are apparently ten Hossō founders.

3. Śilabhadhra, a disciple of Dharmapāla and eventually head monk of Nālanda. When Hsüan-tsang visited him there he was said to be 106 years old. Śilabhadra is counted as Hsüan-tsang's predecessor in the Hossō lineage.

4. Hsüan-tsang (600–64).

5. K'uei-chi (Jap. Kiki, i.e., Jion Daishi, 632–82).

6. The Tosotsu Heaven of Miroku.

7. A Chinese poem chanted in a manner popular in Heian times.

8. *Chūshū*. The Hossō school claimed particularly to represent the "middle way" taught by the Buddha.

9. Miroku was believed to have thus begun the Hossō teaching.

10. Asanga (fifth century?), who is said to have obtained the Hossō teaching directly from Miroku. He was the elder brother of Seshin (Skt. Vasubandhu), below.

11. I cannot identify these "Thousand Buddhas" unless they are simply a mistake, present in all *Genki* texts, for "Ten Buddhas." In this case they might be the same as the "Ten Great Bosatsu," above.

12. Jōtai Bosatsu (Skt. Sadāprarudita Bodhisattva) is a parotector of the *Daihan-nya-kyō.*

13. Probably the Nara and early Heian periods, when Zenshu and Gomyō flourished.

14. See 10.6, n. 5. "Most Worthy" is *daitoku,* a respectful title for an especially holy monk.

15. Zenshu (723–97), a Hossō scholar and a disciple of Genbō (d. 746), was well known at Kōfukuji for his many writings. He appears in *Nihon ryōiki* 3, nos. 35 and 39.

16. Gomyō (750–834) was a distinguished Hossō monk especially active at Gangōji. The account of him in *Shūi ōjōden* calls him the teacher of Kūkai, and states that he lived many years in the Yoshino mountains before becoming a Hossō monk.

17. The name of Shaka.

18. Jishi, another name for Miroku.

19. An immensely great unit of length.

20. The Indian god Brahma, transformed into a protector of Buddhism. Taishakuten is Indra.

21. The Shitennō, guardians of the four directions: Zōjōten (south), Kōmokuten (west), Tamonten (north), and Jikokuten (east).

22. Tenryū hachibu, the eight kinds of beings who protect Buddhism: *ten (deva), ryū (nāga), yasha (yaksha), kendatsuba (gandharva), ashura (aśura), karura (garuḍa), kinnara (kiṃnara),* and *magoraga (mahoraga).*

23. Probably Gaen (1138–1223), a son of Minamoto no Masamichi. Gaen was superintendent 1198–1207, 1208–13, 1217–18, and 1220–23.

## 16.4 Shōen

There once lived in the Southern Capital a monk named Shōen, the "Deputy's Prelate,"[1] a disciple of the Venerable Gedatsu. Although known as a scholar, he fell into the demon realm. Then he possessed a woman and said many things, among which were the following.

"Our Daimyōjin's ways are certainly wonderful. He will not have anyone who has done Him the least honor, however great a sinner that person may be, go to any other hell than the one He himself holds ready beneath the Kasuga Meadows.[2] Each morning He fills the ablution vessel of Jizō Bosatsu, and from the Third Sanctuary asperses this hell with a wand.[3] A single drop in a sinner's mouth relieves for a moment that sinner's pain, and the sinner comes a little closer to right thoughts. Then He intones for the sinners essential passages and *darani*[4] from the Mahayāna Canon. He does this every single day. Thanks to His ministrations, the sinners gradually rise and pass out of hell.

"The scholar-monks listen to the Daimyōjin discourse on *hannya*[5] at Kōzen,[6] east of Kasuga-yama, where they hold discussions and debates exactly as in the human realm. Those who were once scholars are all scholars here. It is an awesome privilege to hear the Daimyōjin preach, and to see Him with one's own eyes."

Jizō is the *honji* of the Shrine's Third Sanctuary. People say his blessings are especially wonderful. He serves the Guide whom we invoke when we call the Buddha's Name. As *honji* or as *suijaku* He is equally worthy of trust.

[PICTURE: The medium delivering Shōen's oracle.]

DATE. Ca. 1240?

RELATED MATERIALS. This story is told in much the same way in *Shasekishū* 1. It appears too in *Sangoku denki* 10/27, where the monk's name is given as Chin'en. The account of hell there is given not by Chin'en through a medium but by a magical being *(kenin)* who appears to Chin'en. The being prefaces his account with an ornate passage that recalls the first paragraph of 1.1.

A PAINTING OFTEN SAID TO SHOW SHŌEN'S REBIRTH. A famous *Kasuga mandara* owned by Nōman'in of Hasedera shows a monk being led toward a complex paradise by Jizō, who has emerged from the third Kasuga sanctuary. A group of monks at the lower right of the picture may be listening to the deity's preaching. The paradise floats over Mikasa-yama. The monk has been identified traditionally as Shōen, since no other known story combines all these elements. Susan Tyler (1987) discussed the painting in the final chapter of her work.

AN ANALOGOUS AFTERWORLD ON MT. HIEI. The afterworld placed here at Kōzen has been described by some writers as a "hell" *(jigoku)*, but this seems not to be the right word. "Purgatory" gives a better idea of its function. This is clear from *Hie Sannō rishōki* 6, which describes an analogous world maintained by Sannō in Hachiōji-dani on Mt. Hiei. A scholar-monk of the mountain meets a deceased colleague in a dream. The deceased monk relates that his sins were about to land him in "the evil realms" when "our Gongen" saved him. The monk explains.

> He does not abandon anyone, not the lowest of men, or even a bird or beast, who has lingered at His Shrine. How natural it is, then that He should summon all the shrine priests and temple officers who have been on retreat at the Shrine, and install them in Hachiōji-dani, in the depths of these mountains. There He protects them day and night, confers constant blessings upon them, and sees to it that they at last reach enlightenment.

The deity's solicitude toward his shrine priests is perhaps related to the special paradise for Ise priests discovered in a dream by Gedatsu Shōnin (see 5.1). It is curious that one should not hear of the Kasuga deity doing the same thing for Kasuga priests.

1. Shōen (1174–at least 1237) was lecturer for the Yuima-e in 1223 and presided over ceremonies at Hōryūji in 1227, 1231, and 1237 (Fukihara 1975:117). He is here called *Shōyū no sōzu,* which suggests that a close relative must have held the title of *shōyū* (an official of the junior fifth rank, lower) in one of the ministries of the civil government.

2. Kasuga-no, the slightly sloping ground below Mikasa-yama. Hakusen (1779, vol. 5) discussed the location of the hell beneath it, noting that "the thickly wooded ravine south of the Enomoto shrine and the Chakutō-den has always been popularly called Jigoku-dani (Hell Valley)."

3. This ablution vessel is *shasuiki.* Laurence Berthier (1981:82) described as follows the bowl and wand used for the Omizutori rite at Tōdaiji: "Le plus important d'entre eux [ritual implements used in the rite] est l'aspersoir à eau lustrale, *shasuiki,* qui est composé d'un bol et d'un bâton; on emploie pour la Réunion un instrument d'un type très archaique, un grand récipient de métal où repose un bâton de bois."

4. A *darani* is typically a formula or short passage from a sutra, often said to carry, in a mystical sense, the meaning of the whole sutra.

5. Skt. *prajñā,* "wisdom." The deity probably discussed the *prajñā-pāramitā* philosophy expressed in the *Daihannya-kyō* and related texts.

6. A roughly flat-topped prominence near the southern end of the Kasuga hills, in an area that has been of exceptional religious significance since early times. The spot overlooks the valley of the Noto-gawa, which flows down through southern Nara. Many rock-carved buddhas are to be found nearby, and so is another Jigoku-dani (see n. 2, above), the name of which suggests that at one time the bodies of the dead were disposed of there. The Hagai of the *Man'yōshū* has been identified with Kasuga-yama, and Hakusen (1779, vol. 5) insisted that it is Kōzen. *Konjaku* 19/19, without naming Kōzen, speaks of a Tōdaiji monk who went to gather flowers in the Kasuga hills (he was therefore a practitioner from the Hokkedō, engaged in the practice called *tōgyō*), who met there a dead monk being tormented by hell-fiends. *Konjaku* 20/4 and *Nihon kiryaku* for Kōhō 4.3.28 (967) make it clear that there were once Buddhist ascetics living at Kōzen. The Tōdaiji map of 756 notes a "Kōzen-dō" at the spot, and a full-scale temple dedicated to Yakushi was first erected there in 762. However, only broken tiles are left there now, and the temple may have been gone already by the Kamakura period.

In Kamakura and Muromachi times, Kōzen was important because of its role in rainmaking. The dragon of Kōzen appears in *Kojidan* 5 and in *Kōfukuji ruki.* Near Kōzen is the Naruikazuchi jinja (listed in the *Engi-shiki*), which in medieval times was known as Ryūō-sha ("Dragon King Shrine"). Prayers for rain have been addressed to Naruikazuchi Jinja, now a *massha* of Kasuga, even in the twentieth century.

## 17.1 The Venerable Myōe

For the Venerable Myōe of Toganoo,[1] the wind of the Ten Profound Dependent Originations[2] had swept away the dust of the
passions, and the moon of the Sixfold Harmony[3] shone brightly in
the window of his contemplation. He was therefore rich in virtue for
the nation, and a refuge for all sentient beings.

Having encountered trouble on Takao,[4] the Venerable Myōe had
gone for a time to Shirakami,[5] a locality in the province of Kii. While
there, he vowed to cross the ocean without delay.

Then on the 19th of the 1st month of Kennin 2, a lady of the
Tachibana clan began abstaining from water and gruel, and of course
from solid food as well. She did so for eight days. The household was
afraid some disorder was making her starve herself,[6] but her face
never lost its color and she seemed if anything more plump than ever.
Every day she bathed, read the Sutras, and invoked the Name.[7]
Puzzled, people asked her what her conduct meant. "I've no special
purpose in mind," she answered. "It's just that my heart is full of the
perfection of the Three Treasures, and quite untouched by the things
of this world."

At the hour of the Horse[8] on the 26th she hung a new mat over
the main beam,[9] then mounted the beam and spoke as follows.

"I am Kasuga no Daimyōjin. Good monk,[10] I am very sorry that
you should be planning to go to China, and so have come to dissuade
you from doing so. You are wiser than anyone else, you see. Do
please visit me sometimes. I live in the Southern Capital."

The Venerable Myōe received this utterance with awe, and said he
would give up his journey.

Then she came down from the beam. Though pregnant, she went
up and came down with the greatest of ease, like a moth fluttering its
wings.

[PICTURE: The lady fasting; the lady sitting on the beam, speaking to Myōe,
his companions, and some members of the household.]

# THE MIRACLES OF THE KASUGA DEITY

DATE. 1203 (Kennin 3.1.19). The Kennin 2 of the text is an error, as proven not only by all earlier source materials but also by 18.1.

THE LIFE OF THE VENERABLE MYŌE. The material presented in 17.1–18.4 deserves separate study, and can be introduced only briefly here. Since the circumstances surrounding these oracles really cover Myōe's whole life up to 1206 when he was granted Kōzanji, it seems best to provide a summary biography. This one is based on Tanabe (1983:53–143). Note that nothing quite explains why Myōe was so close to the Kasuga deity.

Myōe Shōnin (Kōben, 1173–1232) was one of the most distinguished monks of his time, and a champion of both Shingon and Kegon Buddhism. Born into the Yuasa family in the Arita district of Kii, Myōe was the maternal grandson of Yuasa no Muneshige, who supported Taira no Kiyomori in the Heiji insurrection (1159–60). Myōe's father, a Taira warrior, died in battle in 1180, and his mother died soon after. Having a clear vocation, the young Myōe was sent in 1181 to Jingoji near Kyoto, where his uncle Jōgaku was a disciple of the celebrated Mongaku Shōnin.

Myōe studied at Jingoji from 1181 to 1195, and was ordained in 1188 at Tōdaiji. In 1195 he went back to Kii and built a hut at Shirakami, near the sea. There he dreamed of going on pilgrimage to India, and studied accounts of Hsüan-tsang's pilgrimage. In 1198 he returned to Jingoji where Mongaku asked him to teach, and where he had his first recorded vision of the Kasuga deity (see 10.5). That same year, Go-Toba formally censured Mongaku, who was intimately associated with Minamoto no Yoritomo. To avoid trouble, Myōe left again for Kii. This time he settled at Ikadachi, some way inland, where his uncle Yuasa no Munemitsu built him the facilities he needed. Early in 1199 he returned to Jingoji. Then Yoritomo died, and Go-Toba immediately exiled Mongaku. Myōe went back to Kii and settled at Itono, not far from Ikadachi.

All this time, Myōe was doing his best to help and instruct the laymen around him. He wrote expositions of doctrine for them, and he became a healer. Early in 1201, his rites and prayers healed the wife of his uncle Munemitsu, who was then pregnant. A few months later, after she had given birth, his ministrations miraculously saved her life. This woman, Myōe's aunt by marriage, was the medium described in the *Genki*. At the time of the *Genki* oracles she was in her twenty-ninth year.

Alas, Munemitsu too was linked to Yoritomo, and he was now dismissed as the steward of the estate that included Itono. Myōe had to move again to a locality called Hoshio, where Munemitsu continued to serve as steward. Such troubles seem to have decided Myōe to act at last on his longing for the land of the Buddha's birth, and he began to plan his journey. This was when the *Genki* oracles occurred, at Hoshio. It was at Hoshio too that the monk-artist Shunga painted likenesses of the Kasuga and Sumiyoshi deities, according to the instructions received by Myōe in the oracle of 18.2.

In 1204, on the anniversary of the oracle of 17.2, Myōe held a gathering, then spent the night reciting Fa-tsang's *Wu-chiao-chiang* (Jap. *Gokyōshō*). When Munemitsu's wife asked Myōe to pray for those present, Myōe thought the Kasuga deity might be speaking through her again. She said no, but added that the deity would surely support her request.

# THE MIRACLES OF THE KASUGA DEITY

Shortly Myōe started for Kyoto at the invitation of Mongaku, who was back from exile, but a dream he attributed to the Kasuga deity prompted him to return to Kii the next day. Sure enough, Mongaku was soon exiled again. However, Munemitsu was now dismissed entirely from his position in Kii, and summoned with his family to the Kanto. Myōe moved to a small mountain temple nearby, then (still in 1204) visited Kyoto. By the fall of 1204 he was back in Kii, called there by the illness and death of another uncle to whom he was devoted.

The homeless Myōe, who could not forget his abiding grief at having missed the assemblies of the living Buddha, now decided again to go to India. But after a few days of preparation, in 1205, he became desperately ill. Suspecting that his illness was a warning from the Kasuga deity, he questioned the deity, together with Shaka and the "spiritual friends" of the *Ganda-vyūha,* by a simple form of divination. The answers being unanimously negative, he gave up his journey once more.

In 1205 and 1206, Myōe made several journeys back and forth to Kyoto. Then in late 1206, Go-Toba granted him land and the old temple at Toganoo, which was then a dependency of Jingoji. Myōe renamed the temple Kōzanji, and installed the Kasuga deity there as the temple's local protector. In 1207, Go-Toba appointed Myōe concurrently head teacher of Sonshōin at Tōdaiji, in order to support the Kegon teachings. However, Myōe continued to spend a good deal of time in Kii as well.

During all these years, Myōe had been writing on Kegon and Shingon. When Hōnen's *Senchakushū* appeared in 1212, just after Hōnen's death, Myōe swiftly replied with his biting *Zaijarin.* Thus Myōe and Gedatsu Shōnin together became the most eloquent defenders of the old Buddhism. Myōe went on writing during the rest of his life, which he passed at Kōzanji, near the Kamo shrines, and in his home district in Kii. He also wrote a good deal of poetry. Though sought after by some of the greatest nobles in Kyoto, he often refused their invitations. Toward the end of his life he seems to have achieved a measure of peace, and a feeling that he had done what needed to be done.

Devotion to the Buddha was essential in Myōe's complex, intense spiritual life, filled as it was with visions, dreams, and ecstatic moments. He seems to have striven above all to bridge the gulf of time and space between himself and Shaka. In 17.1–18.4, the Kasuga deity demonstrates to him that this gulf is illusory—a thought taken up again particularly in 20.2.

SOURCES AND RELATED MATERIALS. (See the discussion following 18.4.)

1. A spot in the hills just northwest of Kyoto, and the site of Kōzanji. At this time he had not yet been granted Kōzanji.

2. *Jūgen engi:* the ten aspects of *jiji muge* ("unobstructed *dharmadhātu"*) in Kegon thought, that is, the ten ways in which things interpenetrate freely and without obstruction.

3. *Rokusō en'yū:* the six aspects of the harmonious interpenetration of all things according to Kegon thought.

4. A hill near Toganoo, and the site of Jingoji where Myōe was trained.

5. A locality in Arita-gun, Wakayama-ken, near the coast and just northwest of the town of Yuasa. It is also known as Suhara-yama.

6. They feared she was suffering from *fushoku no yamai* ("no-eating disease"). Perhaps the lady was prone to this disorder, since she seems often to have been ill.

7. The name of Shaka.

8. Ca. 12 noon.

9. The *kamoi* beam of her room. This beam runs below the ceiling, providing the upper groove for the sliding partitions between rooms.

10. This is rather an overtranslation of *go-bō*, a word that was little more than a second-person pronoun used when addressing a monk. However, in this passage and in 17.2, the lady (or the deity) needs a term with which to address Myōe in the vocative case.

## 17.2 *(No separate title)*

On the 19th of the same month, at the hour of the Bird,[1] the lady began fasting, etc., as before. She stayed in her room, from which a marvelous fragrance spread to fill the whole garden. When the Venerable Myōe, with many companions, went to the room and slid open the doors, he found her lying down with the covers over her face. She lifted her head when she saw him and smiled.

"What is this scent?" he asked.

"I don't know," she answered, "but when I noticed how fragrant I was, I got ready to receive you. I want to be high, so I'll go up to the ceiling. Please close the doors."

Myōe did so, and she immediately rose to the ceiling. When he opened the doors again one of the ceiling planks had been removed, and the unearthly fragrance was stronger than ever. Myōe and the others all gathered below her and prostrated themselves, saying, "Namu Kasuga no Daimyōjin."

The lady then began speaking in a soft, sweet voice. "It is rude of me to sit so high up," she said, "but as persons like me are used to being elevated, I have raised up the one through whom I am addressing you. I am here because our last meeting seems to have left you in some doubt.

"You *must* stop prostrating yourselves to me," she interjected, but the Venerable Myōe and the others nonetheless went on doing so. She insisted they were being unmannerly.

"There is not one of the Gods, good monk," she then continued, "who does not protect you. Sumiyoshi no Daimyōjin[2] and I attend you particularly. And I, especially, am always with you in the center

of your body,[3] so that even if you were across the sea we would not
be parted, and I would not personally mind. But when I remember
all the people who can be inspired by you to faith, as long as you are
in Japan, my happiness at the thought turns to grief that you should
mean to undertake so long a pilgrimage. I love all those who have
faith in the Buddha's Teaching, and among them I think particularly
fondly of three: yourself, Gedatsu-bō, and another in the Capital.[4]
But I am not as devoted to the other two as I am to you."

[FIGURE 17.2: The lady sitting on the ceiling, addressing those gathered
below her through the hole left by the missing plank.]

Then she descended from the ceiling as silently as a swan's feather
falling. The fragrance as she spoke had grown still more pronounced.
Though not musk or any such scent, it was very rich, and quite unlike
any fragrance of the human world. Transported with delight, those
present licked her hands and feet, which were as sweet as sweetvine.[5]
One woman's mouth had been hurting for days, but when she licked
her the pain was gone.[6] Despite everyone pressing in to lick her, the
lady kept her loving expression and seemed not to mind. She never

moved. In color she was as bright as crystal,[7] and every detail of her was beyond the ordinary. Her wide-open, unblinking eyes showed much less pupil than white. Everyone was weeping.

"Never before have I shown my true form this way and come down into human presence," she said, "and I never will again. I have done so now, good monk, because I have such supreme regard for you. That you should have your heart set on the mountains and forests of distant lands is wonderful as far as your own practice is concerned, but it makes those whom you would otherwise touch lose a chance to establish their link with enlightenment, and that is what distresses me."[8] She continued a while in this vein.

"I have stayed a long time," she said at last. "I meant to go earlier, but I was so happy to be with you that I could not bring myself to do so." She pressed her palms together and saluted the Venerable Myōe. Myōe protested, but she insisted on renewing her gesture of homage. "As for Gedatsu-bō," she then went on, "consider that both of you are the same age.[9] It is extraordinary how deeply one feels for him!" She repeated this four or five times. "However," she continued, "I cannot accept his living in seclusion. Do tell him so."

"In your ardor to adore Lord Shaka where He actually lived, you are unique in all the world. This gives me particular pleasure. I love you more than ordinary people love an only son. In fact, I feel just as Zenzai's spiritual friend did when Zenzai[10] conceived the aspiration to enlightenment. Now I will leave you. You *must* come to Kasuga-yama. You may not actually see me then, but I will be there and will come to greet you. Yes, you need have no doubt about that! Ah, it's so late! I must be going!"

She drew the Venerable Myōe's hands to her, while the unearthly scent grew still more intense. Those present were sobbing so pathetically that she spoke again.

"Do not weep!" she said. "Ours is a latter age, when none give themselves heart and soul to practicing the Buddha's Way. Since everyone loves what is not the Teaching, the True Teaching cannot prevail. Please, please do not let your time slip wastefully by, but study the sacred writings until you grasp their deep meaning! Good monk, your wisdom is of the highest, but your learning is still immature. If you will stop allowing your energy to be scattered hither and yon into this worthy task and that, and set your eyes only on the sacred Teachings, then you will come to known what the Buddha meant. Be willing to take on many students, a hundred or a thousand of them, even if all they have in mind to gain from their study is fortune and fame. And you, groan and weep that hearts cannot well be other than base in this latter, evil age!" The tears streaming down her cheeks showed plainly her grief and pain. In her, the unspeakably moved company beheld inconceivable compassion.

Lifting her head again, she addressed them one last time. "Now I *am* going," she said. "I will leave you my fragrance a while, to remind you all of me and to give you comfort. You, good monk, come quickly to Kasuga-yama!"

As before, the Deity prepared to leave. Then she said, "If you undertake to gather each month[11] on this same night, to talk and to study, then I will come down and join your assembly,[12] no matter where it may be."

[PICTURE: The monks and laymen gathered around the lady. One woman is licking her.]

DATE. 1203 (Kennin 3.2.29). The "19th" indicated in the text is an error.

1. Ca. 6 P.M.

2. The deity of the Sumiyoshi Shrine, now enveloped by modern Osaka: a patron especially of poetry and of seafaring. At Kasuga, Sumiyoshi is present in the Iwamoto-sha that appears on the earliest extant list of Kasuga *massha* (1133). However, according to *Kōfukuji ranshōki*, Sumiyoshi was brought to Kasuga in 1155. Myōe later enshrined Sumiyoshi and Kasuga together at Kōzanji.

3. Literally, "in your *hara.*"

4. The source materials described following 18.4 mention only *two* persons so favored: Myōe and Gedatsu. Regarding "another in the Capital," Kujō Michiie (1193–1252) wrote in his *Mine-dono go-gan* (ST:198): "When Kōben [ = Myōe] Shōnin of Toganoo received the divine oracles, [my grandfather, Kujō Kanezane] suggested to me that *I* might be one of the three blessed by the Deity." Certainly, this unnamed person is likely to be a present (in 1203) or future senior Fujiwara in Kyoto—perhaps Kanezane himself, or the then head of the clan, Kujō Yoshitsune.

5. *Amakazura* or *amachazuru*, a common vine in Japan. The leaves and stems were boiled to make a sweet liquid called *misen.*

6. The sex of this person is ambiguous in the text, but the picture shows a woman.

7. *Kasuga Daimyōjin go-takusen ki* (DNBZ:260a) has:
Her color was as bright as crystal. She was completely transparent, and [watching her] was like watching the lines in a crystal. Every detail of her movement and gestures was characteristic of a greater being *(daijin)*. When she looked around, she turned not her head but her whole body. . . . When she spoke, the

fragrance of her breath was particularly intense, and one felt as though one was being sprinkled with something *(mono no furikakaru kokochi su)*.

8. The pronoun *warera,* which is more likely to be plural than singular, suggests that the deity may be speaking for Sumiyoshi as well.

9. Gedatsu Shōnin was eighteen years older than Myōe. The deity wishes Myōe to forget any feeling that Gedatsu is senior to him.

10. Zenzai (Skt. Sudhana) is the pilgrim on the great journey described in the *Nyūhokkai-bon* (Skt. *Gaṇḍa-vyūha*) section of the *Kegon-gyō* (Skt. *Avataṃsaka-sūtra*). In his travels he consults fifty-three spiritual friends (Skt. *Kalyāṇamitra*) and finally achieves enlightenment. Myōe was deeply interested in this story. In fact, the medium and her family had recently given him the money to commission a painting of Zenzai's pilgrimage (Tanabe 1983:91).

11. *Kasuga Daimyōjin go-takusen ki* has "each year."

12. *Mondō kō,* or "dialogue lecture." *Kanbun gyōjō* (p. 113) uses this term for the ceremony that Myōe conducted exactly a year later to commemorate this moment. Apparently Myōe asked questions of the gathering, and developed his teaching according to the answers he received.

## 18.1 (No separate title)

In the 2d month of Kennin 3, the Venerable Myōe left his province on the 5th day to make the pilgrimage to Kasuga. On the 7th he ended his journey at Sonshōin[1] of Tōdaiji. When he reached the Middle Gate[2] of Tōdaiji, more than thirty deer went down on their knees all together, and bowed their heads before him. Once again that unearthly fragrance floated on the air.

On the 11th of the same month, he was before the Kasuga Sanctuaries when he dozed off a little and dreamed that he went to Vulture Peak and served our Great Teacher Shaka. This happened half a dozen times. While he was on his way back to Kii, people dreamed night after night that they saw the Daimyōjin's minions by his side, while others caught hints of the unearthly fragrance coming from Myōe himself.

[PICTURE: The deer bowing to Myōe. Two companions are with him.]

DATE. 1203 (Kennin 3.2.5 and after).

1. A powerful subtemple, founded by the Tōdaiji superintendent Kōchi in 990. It emphasized Kegon studies, in contrast to Tōnan'in. Myōe knew it well, having often stayed there and borrowed books from its library.

2. Naka no mikado, the gate into the immediate precincts of the Daibutsu-den.

## 18.2 (No separate title)

Later, Myōe decided to go back to Kasuga to pray for help as to how the Daimyōjin should be painted. On the 22d, as he was preparing to leave the next day, the Daimyōjin descended into the woman as before.

"Since you are so interested in how I am to be shown in painting," she said, "I have come to tell you." She gave him detailed instructions.[1] "You know," she went on, "the deer kneeling before you at the Middle Gate of Tōdaiji were a sign that I had arrived three days ahead of you, and had come out to greet you. And at Imadegawa[2]— I had gone to hear the Nehan-e[3] on the night of the 15th of this month, and I was about three feet up, just to the left of the officiant's dais and a little toward the altar. You read the passage in the Nirvana Sutra that says, 'The light of the Nyorai, having gone forth, returned. This was not without reason. It meant that in the ten directions his actions had dissolved. This was the mark of his final extinction.'[4] Then you expounded the text. I was so overcome with awe that I dropped to the floor and listened from there."

The Deity spent several hours relating all sorts of similar secrets. Finally Myōe begged for a verse as a parting gift.

"What memory could be better than our meeting itself?" the Deity answered. "Besides, my parting gift to you will be my picture. But since you wish it:

| | |
|---|---|
| Very swift and mighty | *chihayaburu* |
| our Lord: at His shrine fence, | *kimi ga igaki ni* |
| come, gather in a ring, | *madoi sen* |
| and know that for parting gift | *katami ni megumi* |
| the circle will have blessings. | *taruru to o shire* |

[PICTURE: Myōe talking to the medium.]

DATE. 1203 (Kennin 3.2.22).

1. Myōe could not establish the observance he had in mind until he had a proper *honzon*. The deity's instructions included the portrait of Sumiyoshi. The monk-artist

Shunga painted both deities at Myōe's request, and the portraits were dedicated on Kennin 3.4.19.

2. Imadegawa was a brook that ran north-south through the present Shōkokuji grounds, and down into the present imperial palace grounds at least as far as Ichijō, giving its name to that area *(Kyōto-shi no chimei)*. Hōjōji, founded by Fujiwara no Michinaga in 1023, was in that neighborhood.

3. An important ceremony held annually on the 15th day of the 2d month to commemorate the Buddha's passing. Myōe had gone to Kyoto and presided at this Nehan-e before returning to Kii.

4. From the first chapter of the Nirvana Sutra *(Taishō* 12/611a).

## 18.3 *(No separate title)*

On the 23d he left his province, arriving in the Southern Capital on the 25th. At the hour of the Dog[1] he went to the Shrine. On retiring to sleep after this visit, he dreamed that he went to Vulture Peak and served our Great Teacher Shaka. When he dozed off a moment before the Sanctuaries, it seemed to him that he held in either hand a brightly polished steel hammer.

[PICTURE: Myōe dozing before the sanctuaries.]

DATE. 1203 (Kennin 3.2.25–6).

1. Ca. 8 P.M.

## 18.4 *(No separate title)*

On the 27th, he went to Kasagidera to meet the Venerable Gedatsu. "There's an extraordinary scent in the air," Gedatsu-bō observed. "The Daimyōjin must have come with you. He must be here now. Let me offer the Teaching before we talk." He closed his eyes and made an offering.[1]

Afterwards they spent several hours together. "It's been such a pleasure to talk to you today," said Gedatsu-bō, "that I want to give you some precious relics."[2]

On the 28th, as Myōe was about to leave Kasagi, Gedatsu-bō wrapped up in paper the relics that he had promised the evening before, and presented the package to Myōe. Myōe-bō did not presume to inspect it, but put it straight into his sutra-purse.[3] He returned to Tōdaiji without even knowing how many grains there were.

[PICTURE: Gedatsu giving Myōe the relics.]

Going directly to the Shrine, he closed his eyes before the Sanctuaries and offered the Teaching. As he hovered between sleep and waking, it came to him that the two steel hammers of the other day were two relic grains. Then he woke up and at last opened his gift. He found two relic grains. Astonished, he wrapped them as before, put them back in his purse, and hung the purse at his left side.

He then prayed, "Surely You summoned me this time just so that I should be given these relics. From now on, I will trust in them as in the tokens of Lord Shaka himself, and as the very body of the Daimyōjin. May the Gongen in His body come to inhabit these relics!" As he prayed intently, with closed eyes, there came to him a vision of the Daimyōjin standing near him to the left. This must have been a sign that the Daimyōjin had entered in His body into the relics that Myōe had hung at his left side.

[FIGURE 18.4: Myōe examining the relics.]

DATE. 1203 (Kennin 3.2.27–8).

1. That is, he recited a sutra passage as an offering to the deity.

2. According to *Kasuga Daimyōjin go-takusen ki,* these relics came originally from Ganjin and had been given to Gedatsu Shōnin by Kujō Kanezane.

3. *Kyō-bukuro,* a bag for carrying sacred texts, worn slung around the neck.

JINSON'S COMMENT. The Kōfukuji superintendent Jinson noted in his diary (*Daijōin*

# THE MIRACLES OF THE KASUGA DEITY

*jisha zōjiki* for Chōroku 2.11 [1458]) that he had read an account of these events. His comment was, "Absolutely amazing!" *(shushō shushō)*.

SOURCE MATERIALS. There are three possible, known sources for 17.1–18.4. (1) *Sō Jōben ganmon,* dated Genkyū 2.12 (1205), a copy of which has been preserved at Kōzanji. The relevant passage was cited in full by Itō (1983:426), who referred to the copy as *Sō Jōben (Kōben) ganmon sha.* (2) *Kōzanji Myōe Shōnin gyōjō (kanbun gyōjō), kan* 2:112–13. This *kanbun* translation of the earlier *kana gyōjō* passage (now lost) by Myōe's disciple Kikai (1178–1250) is dated 1255. (3) *Kasuga Daimyōjin go-takusen ki,* also known as *Myōe Shōnin jingon denki,* written by Kikai in 1232 or 1233. (A later copy, dated Eikyō 6 [1435] is entitled *Kōben ki.*)

Myōe wrote *Sō Jōben ganmon* less than three years after the events in question. Though brief compared to the *Genki* or to *Kasuga Daimyōjin go-takusen ki,* this document fully confirms both in outline. It also contains several touches that appear in the *Genki.* For example, Myōe has the deity say, roughly as in *Genki* 17.2, "I have never before manifested such a wonder as this, nor will I ever do so again." Myōe also wrote:

> Furthermore, during my pilgrimage to the Shrine (some say I was traveling [between Yuasa and Nara], while others speak of my being at the Shrine itself), there occurred countless wonders. That is to say, an ineffable fragrance filled the air, a group of deer went down on bended knee [before me] outside the gate, and so forth. . . . I also witnessed all sorts of other marvels, both in dream and in waking consciousness.

This passage touches particularly on the content of 18.1, but also suggests 18.3 and 18.4. Regarding *Kōzanji Myōe Shōnin gyōjō* and *Kasuga Daimyōjin go-takusen ki,* the former is relatively short, while the latter is more detailed than the *Genki* version. The *Genki* account seems to be related to both since it includes characteristic vocabulary from the first and many details present only in the second. However, it departs from both in certain respects. In short, by the time the *Genki* was made, there seem to have been variant traditions on the subject. *Mine-dono go-gan* suggests that the events of 17.1–18.4 were known at court, and no doubt at Kōfukuji as well, outside the written accounts of them by Myōe and Kikai. Moreover, *Kokonchomonjū, Shasekishū,* and *Kingyoku yōshū* (discussed below under "Related Materials") apparently represent a variant written tradition.

The *Gyōjō* version states plainly the writer's fear of offending the Kasuga deity by revealing too much. The following discrepancies between *Gyōjō* and *Go-takusen ki* are worth noting. (1) Concerning the material of 17.1, *Gyōjō* says nothing about the medium sitting up on the beam. (2) *Gyōjō* but not *Go-takusen ki* notes how people licked the medium and found she tasted sweet. (3) Concerning the material of 18.1, *Gyōjō* states that the dozing Myōe "saw the Shrine suddenly turn into Vulture Peak," a much clearer expression than in *Go-takusen ki* or the *Genki.*

THE ACCOUNT IN KASUGA DAIMYŌJIN GO-TAKUSEN KI. One striking difference between *Go-takusen ki* and *Genki* 17.1–2 is that, in the older account, the deity speaks of himself several times as "this old man," and that he describes himself as Myōe's "adoptive father" *(yōiku no chichi).* This conveys a sharp distinction between the deity and the medium, one that is easy to forget in the *Genki.* The *Go-takusen ki* version suggests that the presence is principally that of the First Sanctuary. Here is a summary of the *Go-takusen ki* account.

*The first oracle (17.1).* Myōe did not immediately promise to give up his journey. Instead, once the oracle was over and the deity gone, he prayed before a mandala of the fifty-three "spiritual friends" for an unequivocal sign that the oracle had been either genuine or false. Meanwhile his companion monks were chanting the *Kegon-gyō*. As Myōe began his prayer, a light appeared on the altar.

*The second oracle (17.2).* Some seventy or eighty people witnessed the second oracle. *Go-takusen ki* begins by describing the medium. It lacks the scene in which people press forward to lick her, nor does the medium in this version rise again to the ceiling, as she did for the first oracle.

In *Go-takusen ki,* the deity starts by insisting at length that Myōe must study more. This passage in the *Genki* comes near the end of 17.2. "You must not take time out," the deity says, "just because you are a healer *(genza)*. I will do the healing for you. If sick people come to you, send them to Kasuga-yama." Then the deity tells Myōe that he has no time to waste because he is unlikely to live past forty.

To comply with the deity's wishes, Myōe must live in the Capital. The deity reproaches him for living in seclusion, and then, as in the *Genki,* asks him to pass that message on to Gedatsu Shōnin as well.

India comes up only once in all this, since the deity has dismissed the idea of a pilgrimage from the start. But the deity assures Myōe that he will achieve rebirth in the Tosotsu Heaven *(tosotsu ōjō),* and that all those who follow him will "see the Buddha and hearken to the Teaching."

At this point, *Go-takusen ki* has a long passage to which 17.2 alludes only in its final paragraph. Myōe questions the deity about perpetuating the cult for which this visitation is to be the founding event. He says he wants to paint a likeness of the deity so that he can worship it after the deity is gone; and that he wants to hang this painting as a *honzon* for the meetings at which he will formally teach. The deity is both pleased and shocked at the suggestion. He assures Myōe that "such as I" only serve the buddhas of past, present, and future, and that he could not possibly be a *honzon.* The *honzon* must be Miroku.

When Myōe asks whether he may then hang Kasuga and Sumiyoshi on either side of Miroku, the deity readily assents. One gathers here, as in the *Genki,* that Sumiyoshi is in partnership with Kasuga regarding Myōe and the future cult. Later on in *Go-takusen ki,* it appears that Sumiyoshi has been present all along during this visitation, though mute.

Next Myōe says he intends to enshrine Kasuga in his own dwelling, and he implores the deity to "divide yourself and reside there." The deity earnestly promises to do so. Myōe then asks if the *Yuishiki sanjū ju* and the *Yuishiki ron* are what the deity would like for scripture-offerings. The deity replies that these would be a bit much for people who, unlike the present company, have little knowledge of Buddhism; and he recommends instead the *Jūjū yuishiki.* The deity clearly has in mind popular gatherings under his patronage.

Myōe's last question is about the annual commemoration of this night. "Each year," he says, "we [or I] will celebrate this night of your descent. We will hold a meeting *(kōen)* and make scripture-offerings. Please come down to be with us as you have done this evening." The deity, apparently speaking also for Sumiyoshi, promises to do so.

The deity now says he must be going. He (that is, she) embraces Myōe and holds him a moment "with his face against hers." Tears stream from her eyes as she admonishes Myōe a last time to do as he has been bidden. Myōe cries out in grief and, sobbing, implores the deity to stay a while longer. Everyone else is of course weeping too, and it is now that the deity urges them to weep not for his departure but for the decline of the Teaching.

The deity leaves, but is drawn back again "from near the window" by the intense emotion of the gathering. (Myōe himself has almost fainted.) "Here I am! Here I am!" he calls as he returns. "You must come to Kasuga-yama," he then tells Myōe. "I will be waiting for you, and we will finish our conversation then." But Myōe now has a speech to make. He describes at length his longing to visit India where the Buddha himself preached, and his intense disappointment at not having been able to hear this preaching in person. But having rehearsed all this, Myōe assures the deity that his "old, old sorrow" *(mukashi no urami)* is gone now, and he goes on to evoke his present joy.

The deity caresses Myōe's head affectionately, repeats the invitation to come to Kasuga-yama, and once more leaves. Myōe rises to go, but the deity comes back briefly, a final time, to make it clear that he is not inviting Myōe to reside in Nara. Myōe is only to *visit* Nara sometimes, for his place is in Kyoto.

The deity's last words are, "Sumiyoshi no Ōkami is soaring away too."

*The deer bow to Myōe (18.1)* The *Genki* text smooths out the choppy little *Go-takusen ki* entries. It also omits a dream that Myōe had the night before leaving Kii again for Nara. Myōe dreamed that he went to the Kasuga Shrine and found a feast prepared there, but left again without eating.

*The parting poem (18.2).* Among the material corresponding to 18.2, *Go-takusen ki* lists the present locations and owners of four paintings of Kasuga and two of Sumiyoshi; these include the originals made by Shunga in Kii. Otherwise, the two versions remain close to one another. However, the *Genki* omits an exchange that follows the deity's explanation of why the deer had gone down on bended knee. Myōe says, "At the time I didn't understand what was gong on, so I didn't dismount. That was very rude of me, and I apologize." "Well," replies the deity, "they say a beloved child can do no wrong. It never occurred to me to reproach you. Besides, there was no harm anyway, since I was already higher than you!"

*The steel hammers and the relics (18.4).* In what the *Genki* includes, there is no significant divergence from *Go-takusen ki*. However, *Go-takusen ki* goes on to say that after the deity had "entered in his body" into Myōe's relics, Myōe dreamed again of a feast spread for him at the shrine. This time he ate, for he realized that the food was the relics now fully inhabited by the deity. *Go-takusen ki* also notes Gedatsu Shōnin's words: "These relics are those of Sairyūji. They are the same as the ones at Tōshōdaiji, which Abbot Ganjin brought from China. I had them from Tsukinowa no Zenjō Denka [Kujō Kanezane]."

*Other material omitted by the* Genki. Otherwise, *Go-takusen ki* notes that at about the time of 18.4, a Tōdaiji monk named Shōsen dreamed that he saw seven or eight "treasure boats" moored by "the bridge at Rokudō" (see 6.3). These flew through the sky toward the Hongū Shrine at the top of Mikasa-yama. Shōsen was told in the dream that Myōe was riding in the lead boat, and that the others were carrying those who had entrusted themselves to Myōe's guidance. Thus those who had taken refuge with Myōe passed over the six realms *(rokudō)* and achieved direct rebirth in paradise. There follows a discussion of the discovery that the Kasuga deity had a special affinity with *saru* days.

*Go-takusen ki* further describes how Myōe took the monk-artist Shunga with him down to Kii on Kennin 3.4.9, and how he held the "eye-opening" for the likenesses of Kasuga and Sumiyoshi on Kennin 3.4.19. That night someone dreamed that Myōe's voice, as he preached at the ceremony, resounded from heaven to heaven and filled the cosmos.

*A story about these paintings.* These paintings seem to have inspired an amusing story, recorded in *Kōfukuji ranshōki* (p. 326a). There apparently arose a legend that Myōe, in the presence of the Kasuga and Sumiyoshi deities, noticed that while Kasuga was young and plump, Sumiyoshi was old and thin. Myōe is supposed to have asked Sumiyoshi why he looked so poorly. Sumiyoshi replied, "Kasuga has the Teaching offered him every morning, so age hasn't touched him. But since Sumiyoshi gets no such offerings, his form is an old man's." That started the custom of reading the *Daihannya-kyō* monthly at Kasuga for the benefit of Sumiyoshi. Actually, Kasuga and Sumiyoshi do appear, as described, in a painting still owned by Kōzanji: Sumiyoshi is a thin, white-haired old man, while Kasuga is a healthy-looking, black-haired gentleman (Kyōto Kokuritsu Hakubutsukan 1981:pl. 74).

RELATED MATERIALS. (1) *Kokonchomonjū* no. 64 contains narrative that corresponds to 17.2 but differs from the source versions. The differences are intriguing, since *Kokonchomonjū* is dated 1254, a year earlier than *Kōzanji Myōe Shōnin gyōjō*. The deer have already bowed before Myōe; the medium not only rises to the ceiling but sits there for three days; an extraordinarily fragrant white foam issues from her mouth; and there is no mention of people licking the medium. The passage has been translated in full by Robert Morrell (1982).

(2) *Shasekishū* 1/5 briefly mentions the Kasuga deity's oracles to dissuade Myōe from going to India, and notes that the deity once called Myōe and Gedatsu his "Tarō" and his "Jirō." It notes the deer bowing before Myōe, and specifies that Myōe and Gedatsu were together at the time.

(3) *Kingyoku yōshū* (an unpublished work of which undated, probably Muromachi-period manuscripts are owned by the Shōkōkan Library and the National Diet Library) contains a passage entitled "Kasuga Daimyōjin no on-koto." The passage is quoted in full by Itō (1983: 426–27). It deals with the content of 17.2 and 18.1, making no separate mention of the oracle of 17.1. Like *Shasekishū*, *Kingyoku yōshū* specifies that Myōe and Gedatsu Shōnin were together when the deer went down on bended knee (18.1), and it too tells how the Daimyōjin referred to the two monks as his Tarō and Jirō. Like *Kokonchomonjū*, it places the episode with the deer *before* the great oracle corresponding to 17.2. According to *Kingyoku yōshū*, this was the first time the Daimyōjin had heard of Myōe's plan, and he was horrified. Once the deer had knelt to him, he manifested himself to Myōe on the spot, in human form, and admonished him right away. Myōe then returned to Yuasa, where the great oracle took place. *Kingyoku*

*yōshū's* description of this oracle is unlike that in the documents discussed above as possible sources for the *Genki,* and unlike *Kokonchomonjū* as well. Moreover, *Sō Jōben ganmon* in particular proves that *Kingyoku yōshū* and *Kokonchomonjū* have the order of events wrong. In this respect, and despite the fairly early date of *Kokonchomonjū,* they apparently represent a variant and somewhat garbled tradition. Interestingly, *Kingyoku yōshū* has the Daimyōjin name his *honji* as Jizō. This idea, thoroughly uncharacteristic of Myōe, Gedatsu, or the *Genki,* is much easier to associate with the Muromachi period. (See chapter 6, under "Jizō.")

(4) *Shingonden* 7 has a summary account that follows the order of events in the *Genki.* This passage too has been translated by Robert Morrell (1982).

THE NOH PLAY KASUGA RYŪJIN. (This play, a radically different version of how the deity stopped Myōe from going to India, is discussed in chapter 7.)

## 19.1 The Sacred Mirrors in the Shōan Era

Not long ago the scholar-monks of Kōfukuji rose up in anger,[1] and prayed that the bandits of Yamato province should be rearrested and exiled. Meanwhile on the 25th of the 10th month of Shōan 3, at the hour of the Rat,[2] the bandits broke into the Shrine. They stole both mirrors from each of the Four Sanctuaries and the six from the Wakamiya: fourteen in all.[3] Then they barricaded themselves at a place in the same province known as Takao-no-wakeno.[4]

On the 28th the monks[5] led troops to capture them, and a great battle ensued. One among the motley crew, Ikejiri Nayakuōzaemon-no-Jō Iemasa,[6] was killed in the fight, and the three sacred mirrors he was carrying were retaken.

[PICTURE: The well-armed bandits stealing the mirrors; the fight at Takao-no-wakeno.]

On the 8th of the 11th month of that year, the sky being beautifully clear, a chapel at Tokiwa,[7] a place in the same province, suddenly emitted a miraculous light resembling a rainbow. Peering into the chapel, the amazed passersby and villagers saw three sacred mirrors hanging in white cloth bags before the altar, with a scribbled message beside them. These were the mirrors stolen by Masayasu no Kanja of Ryōfukuji.[8] The steward of the Hirata estate[9] was informed, and hastily mobilized local people to move the mirrors to Konshōji.[10] Meanwhile black clouds rose over Futagami-no-take[11] and a fierce hail fell, while clouds of the five colors hung over Kasuga-yama. Everyone who witnessed the event, whether monk or layman, was moved to tears.

[FIGURE 19.1: The rainbow light at Tokiwa; the procession carrying the mirrors back to Kasuga, attached to a *sakaki* branch.]

On the 30th of the same month, at the hour of the Tiger,[12] the Kasuga shrine servant Yasukage[13] received a dream oracle. At daybreak he made straight for Takao-yama[14] and saw from afar, before he had even set foot on the mountain, a miraculous light. Awed, he sought out the spot, and the next day, at the hour of the Horse,[15] dug up a sacred mirror that he moved immediately to Konshōji. Then he transported all seven mirrors back to the Shrine, in a manner commensurate with their dignity.

[PICTURE: Rainbow light over Takao-yama; a large procession of shrine servants returning the mirrors to Kasuga.]

On the 13th of the 12th month, the shrine servant Morimoto[16] set out for Takao-no-wakeno to look for the remaining sacred mirrors. After he arrived, the mountain gave forth a deep rumbling sound. Caught between fear and amazement, Morimoto questioned the resident monks. They told him that the mountain had often rumbled since the bandits had invaded the Shrine. Pursuing his search with renewed faith, he discovered five flower-shaped sacred mirrors[17] inside the body of the main Buddha in the lower hall. On the 15th of the month he returned these to the Shrine.

[PICTURE: The discovery of the flower-shaped mirrors.]

On the 23d, two sacred mirrors were found on the peak above Fuse-zan,[18] also in Yamato. These were the ones stolen by the *hōshi* Enshun.[19] They were returned to the Shrine on the 25th. When Enshun tried to put the five flower-shaped mirrors where they did not belong, sweat ran from them like water and they glowed. Enshun had stayed behind alone, at great personal risk, to report this wonder, and swore in a pledge that he addressed to the scholar-monks that his account was accurate.

It is extraordinary that the fourteen sacred mirrors should have returned to the Shrine safe and sound within three months.

[PICTURE: Shrine servants looking for the mirrors on Fuse-zan.]

DATE. 1301 (Shōan 3).
BACKGROUND. As outrageous as this incident seems, it is worth knowing that in Einin 3.11 (1295), the Kasuga mirrors were stolen by none other than the *shuto* of Daijōin, in order to gain the advantage in a quarrel with Ichijōin (Nagashima 1963:22).

In the present case, the *akutō* ("bandits") were based on the vast Hirata estate, in the area of Taimadera on the west side of the Yamato plain. They were headed by the Oka and Manzai families (Nagashima 1944:105). The fort at Takao-no-wakeno was at a spot controlled by the Manzai, who in theory managed the estate for Ichijōin.

According to *Kōfukuji ryaku nendaiki*, the *sakaki* of Kasuga had been moved to the Kondō of Kōfukuji on Shōan 3.4.5, because of fear of the "local bandits" *(tōgoku akutō)*. The diary of Nakatomi no Sukeharu, summarized by Nagashima (1963:22), confirms that according to rumor the bandits were going to invade Nara. Kōfukuji therefore strengthened its defenses and requested help from court and bakufu troops. On 9.20, "retainers from seven provinces and warriors resident in the Capital" proceeded to Yamato. Of twenty bandits summoned to appear, five failed to respond and instead barricaded themselves in a stronghold on Futagami-no-take. They fled when the troops attacked, and the troops destroyed their fort before returning to Kyoto. Meanwhile the *sakaki* returned to the shrine on 9.30.

On 10.25 the bandits struck. *(Kōfukuji ryaku nendaiki* mentions ten mirrors stolen from the Wakamiya rather than six.) Everyone at Kasuga and Kōfukuji, from the scholar-monks to the nearby populace, pursued them to their lair, which was the same as before, and fought with them for several hours. On 10.28 the sanctuaries were purified. Then on 12.2 and 12.14 the mirrors were returned to the shrine from the several places where they had been discovered. That year the *Onmatsuri* was delayed until 12.17.

AN ANALOGOUS WONDER ON MT. HIEI. *Zoku Hie Sannō rishōki* tells how a set of paintings, just as sacred as the Kasuga mirrors, were equally miraculously recovered unharmed in the aftermath of a fire. The incident happened in 1290.

1. *Hōki*, the normal term used when the angered monks contemplated or undertook action.

2. Ca. midnight.

3. The mirrors would have been easy to take because they hung on the outside of the blinds at the front of the sanctuaries.

4. According to *Kasuga genki ekotoba kikigaki*, a spot on the Hirata estate, "in the Manzai area." In other words, probably Manzai-yama, just south of Futagami-no-take, where at least in later times the Manzai had a fort *(Nara-ken no chimei)*.

5. *Shuto*. The enforcement of Kōfukuji's police power was their responsibility.

6. Ikejiri is a locality just east of Konshōji on the former Hirata Estate. Iemasa is unknown.

7. Probably a spot close to Ryōfukuji, but the name no longer exists at this location.

8. Ryōfukuji is still a locality in Kashiba-chō of Kitakatsuragi-gun, about five km. north of Taimadera. Masayasu is unknown.

9. An Ichijōin estate, and the largest single estate in Yamato, situated in present Shinjō-chō and Taima-chō of Kitakatsuragi-gun. A steward *(jitō)* was an estate manager appointed by Kamakura; his chief duties were to collect taxes and exercise police powers. There had probably been a steward on the Hirata estate since 1236. In 1307 he would become an issue in another conflict between Kōfukuji and Kamakura, one that got Saionji Kinhira into trouble with Kōfukuji.

10. A small temple at a spot known as Ichiba in present Shinjō-chō. It retains only a vestigial existence today.

11. The twin-peaked mountain (540 m.) over Taimadera, in Taima-chō.

12. Ca. 4 A.M.

13. Unknown.

14. Apparently the location of Takaodera, a temple below Futagami-no-take. It was a dependency of Kōfukuji.

15. Ca. 12 noon.

16. Identified as Fujii no Morimoto in the *Shintō taikei* text of the *Genki*.

17. The picture shows mirrors with five deeply notched "petals."

18. Chionji, a temple in Shinjō-chō and once a dependency of Kōfukuji. It is just below Iwahashi-yama (659 m.). Chionji is now nearly abandoned.

19. Unknown.

## 20.1 The Spirit Fires of the Kagen Era

In Kagen 2, there were among the monks of Kōfukuji some who had driven out a Yamato steward. This made the Kanto very angry. Many monks[1] and shrine servants were arrested and a steward was reappointed to the province. Horrified, the whole Temple went into hiding.

Meanwhile, early in the 7th month, long before the season for the leaves to turn, the trees on Kasuga-yama suddenly lost their green. Soon the branches were bare and the trees were dying. Now, a divine oracle of Jingo-Keiun 2 states, "Know this well! It is for the glory of the Fujiwara clan and for the protection of the Hossō School that I manifest myself upon Mikasa-yama. Whenever in future generations there shall be any deviation from the established rites, or any disobedience toward the imperial Will, the trees shall instantly die, and I shall leave the Mountain and return to My Celestial Palace." Therefore everyone groaned in the belief that the portals to the Divine Presence were now closed, and that the Deity had returned to the Citadel of Original Enlightenment.[2]

This news reached the ears of the Kanto, which, greatly astonished, removed the steward.

On the evening of the 28th of the 9th month, before word of the Kanto's action ever reached the Southern Capital, a rumor that the Daimyōjin was returning caused a great stir. People hurried to see. In all four directions the clouds glowed as with the lingering light of a conflagration, while a cooling breeze blew softly and a fine rain fell. Far and near, dazzling fires, as many and as bright as stars, were dancing through the air and into the Sanctuaries. On the Shrine grounds there appeared lights formed in two lines, like the ranks of torches lit when the Deity returns to His Seat;[3] and the flames in the lanterns before the Sanctuaries went out all at once, although no one had extinguished them. It has always been the custom to put out the lanterns both when the Daimyōjin goes out and when He returns. *Kagura* commissioned by the Head of the Clan[4] was being performed at the time, so that many excited musicians, guards, and servants witnessed the spectacle.

[FIGURE 20.1: The fires dancing over the Kasuga hills and meadows into the shrine.]

DATE. Kagen 2 (1304).

BACKGROUND. This quarrel with Kamakura was one incident in a protracted conflict that began in 1235 with a dispute between Kōfukuji and Iwashimizu over water rights in neighboring estates. The affair is discussed by Uwayokote Masatake (1975:58–59), and in greater detail by Kuroda Yoshio (1975:79–140). It became so violent that the court asked Kamakura to intervene. When Kōfukuji vigorously defied the bakufu's authority, the bakufu appointed a constable *(shugo)* to the province—which in recognition of Kōfukuji's power it had never done before—and installed stewards on the Kōfukuji estates. In 1236 Kōfukuji capitulated, and the constable and stewards were removed. However, stewards were reappointed almost immediately to those estates that had been a base for the leaders of the Kōfukuji resistance. Presumably the Ikoma estate, the one involved in the present incident, was among these.

The tension established in 1235–36 was never really resolved, and continued to break out in one way or another. Another flare-up occurred in 1281–82. After the quarrel in 1304, another broke out in 1307 over the steward on the Hirata estate.

IMMEDIATE CIRCUMSTANCES. *Kōfukuji ryaku nendaiki* records that on Kagen 2.5.28, the *shuto* of Kōfukuji decided to expel the steward from the Ikoma estate. Kamakura responded by sending troops, then exiling the instigators of the affair and reappointing the steward. On 7.5 of that year Kōfukuji looked deserted, its population having gone into hiding, and by the middle of the 7th month one-third of the trees on Kasuga-yama were dead. Then on the night of 8.7, in the midst of fierce wind and rain, five shining objects (perhaps one for each Kasuga sanctuary) flew off from Kasuga-yama toward the northeast. They were "as bright as suns."

On 9.23, *kagura* commissioned by the regent began at the shrine. On the 26th, two envoys from Rokuhara (the Kyoto office of the bakufu) announced that in response to the pleas of Kōfukuji, those who had been exiled as a result of this affair would be allowed to return. Finally on the 29th (the *Genki* has the 28th) there occurred the prodigy of the spirit fires.

THE DYING TREES. The oracle mentioned here, recorded in *Koshaki* although worded somewhat differently there, is discussed in chapter 3. The deity's threat was taken seriously. On Katei 2.7.16 (1236), in the midst of chaos caused by the conflict just described, Nakatomi no Sukesada noted in his diary that many trees on Mikasa-yama had died. Then in Shōhei 2 (1352), according to *Kōfukuji rayaku nendaiki,* "more than 6,000 trees died." This too was in the midst of chaos: the war between Daijōin and Ichijōin described in *Saisai yōki nukigaki.* The author of this chronicle noted the report about 6,000 trees having died, and took the trouble to check it personally. He was astonished to find it true. The monks were so alarmed by this and other signs that they spent days chanting the *Yuishiki ron* and the *Yuishiki sanjū ju* for the deity. *Saisai yōki nukigaki* also mentions *kagura* that was intended, as in 1304, to persuade the deity to come back.

THE SPIRIT FIRES. The return of the deity to his shrine in the form of spirit fires is mentioned nowhere else. However, the *Kōfukuji rayaku nendaiki* mention of the deity's departure, in the form of five lights, has a counterpart. *Saisai yōki nukigaki* notes that on the night of Shōhei 7.4.27 there was a terrible storm, after which spirit fires were seen flying off Kasuga-yama. Mentions of the mountain simply shining are more common. The earliest example is in *Hyakurenshō,* under the date Kanji 7.8.26 (1093), where the Hongū shrine on the top of Mikasa-yama is said to have emitted light, while the mountain rumbled.

1. *Shuto.*

2. *Hongaku no shiro.* The expression stresses that the deity's true nature is enlightenment, as discussed in chapter 5. "Portals of the Divine Presence" is *suijaku no toboso:* access to enlightenment as the deity manifests it in our world.

3. The deity returned to his seat this way after every *shinboku dōza* expedition.

4. The head of the clan was then Nijō Kanemoto (1268–at least 1308). This sort of *kagura* was offered in time of crisis. According to *Kasuga genki ekotoba kikigaki,* the first instance was in 1235. This one was the second. Similar *kagura* was offered again starting on Engyō 2.11.8 (1309), then on Shōhei 7.6.26, and half a dozen times thereafter until the Ōei period (1394–1428).

## *20.2 (Conclusion)*

Ours is a divine realm, and each of our three thousand or more shrines and ancestral tombs has its own history and confers its own blessings; yet wonders like these have never been seen or heard of before. It is indeed after a frost that one recognizes the enduring pine, and in time of general peril that the loyal minister appears. No doubt that is why the Deity has vouchsafed wondrous signs to sentient beings without faith; for this is the latter age, when men's hearts are doubting and devious.

What do these wonders mean for us? Lord Shaka has already lived, while the Three Assemblies of the Lord of Compassion lie far ahead in time.[1] Lord Shaka therefore had pity on those who are born into the interval between the past and future Buddhas, and who consequently must be deprived of blessing in this life and the next. Although He vanished into the smoke of the Crane Grove,[2] He still tempers the brilliance of the moon over Vulture Peak, mingles with the dust of an age rife with polluted views, and saves those who "from darkness enter a dark way."[3] To reflect upon the depth of His compassion is to shed unceasing tears. For He surely does not bestow the advantages of office in this present life simply for the sake of momentary profit and fame. Since "the tempering of the light and the merging with the dust initiate the link with enlightenment,"[4] once this link is established, He "finishes accomplishing all creatures' weal" by achieving the Way through the eight stages of His career, and so brings them to illumination. In other words, the manifestations of His wisdom-in-action[5] correspond exactly to the capacity of beings of the various kinds.

How glad a thought! We ordinary beings who turn upon the wheel of transmigration have encountered the transforming guidance of the Buddha's manifestation! Since purity in accordance with the mind[6] is itself the Pure Land, our own Kami are the Buddhas. How could the Shrine not be the Pure Land? Jōruri and Vulture Peak[7] are present within the shrine fence. Why seek Fudaraku and Shōryōzan[8] beyond the clouds? Surely that is why the Venerable Myōe revered the Mountain as Vulture Peak, and why He told Lord Toshimori that it is the path to enlightenment.[9] Those whose sins are heavy, and whose karma binds them, fall into a hell where (since awakening does not distinguish between pure and impure) the Daimyōjin manifests himself as the active emanation of His *honji*, the Body of Law;[10] so that the sinner is at last drawn toward liberation. It is quite true, as Prelate Shōen said through the medium,[11] that the guidance He gives each kind of being, according to that being's own needs and mind, passes all understanding. Hence even those who turn among the six realms and the four modes of birth[12] are touched without exception, once their link with Him is established, by the August Deity's saving influence. Consider, after all, that the Esoteric teachings place Hell, Hungry Ghosts, and Beasts side by side in the mandala with the host of the blessed.[13]

1. According to the *Miroku geshō-kyō* (Skt. *Maitreya-vyākaraṇa)*, Miroku will preach to three assemblies when he at last appears in the world as the successor to Shaka.

2. The Sala Grove where Shaka died and was cremated.

3. A line from the famous poem by Izumi Shikibu (late tenth–early eleventh century):

| | |
|---|---|
| From darkness I come | *Kuraki yori* |
| and a dark way | *kuraki michi no zo* |
| now is mine to go: | *irinubeki* |
| illumine me from afar, | *haruka ni terase* |
| moon at the mountains' rim! | *yama no ha no tsuki* |

The image is from chapter 7 of the Lotus Sutra.

4. See 8.4, n. 16 for a discussion of this passage.

5. *Jōjichi* (Skt. *kṛtyānuṣṭhāna-jñāna)*, the fourth element of "fourfold wisdom perfected" (10.1, n. 11).

6. *Zuishin jōsho*, an expression that appears to mean that the mind cognizes purity in accordance with its own capacity or attainment, so that an awakened mind will see no difference between the world as it is and the Pure Land.

7. Jōruri is the paradise of Yakushi (Skt. Bhaiṣajyaguru), the most common *honji* of the Secondary Sanctuary. It lies toward the east. Vulture Peak is the paradise of Shaka, identified with the First Sanctuary.

8. Fudaraku (Skt. Potalaka) is the paradise of Kannon, the *honji* of the First Sanctuary understood as Fukūkenjaku, and in any case of the Fourth. Shōryōzan is another name of Wu- t'ai-shan (Jap. Godaisan), a mountain in China believed to be the paradise of Monju (Skt. Mañjuśrī), the *honji* of the Wakamiya.

9. See, respectively, 18.3 and 5.1.

10. The Kasuga deity as a manifestation of the *hosshin* (Skt. *dharmakāya*) is discussed in chapter 5.

11. See 16.4. However, this statement is not actually reported in the *Genki*.

12. The four modes of birth are birth alive and fully formed; birth from an egg; birth from moisture; and metamorphic birth. Together they represent all forms of life.

13. The outermost region of the Taizōkai mandala, which shows a complex array of holy beings, is considered to represent the three worlds *(sangai)* and the six realms *(rokudō)*.

# Bibliography

Unless indicated otherwise, all Japanese books are published in Tokyo.

## ABBREVIATIONS

DNBZ    Bussho Kankōkai, ed. 1915. *Dainihon bukkyō zensho*. Bussho Kan-kōkai. 151 vols.

DNBZa    Zaidan Hōjin Suzuki Gakujutsu Zaidan, ed. 1972. *Dainihon bukkyō zensho*. Kōdansha. 100 vols.

GR    Hanawa Hokiichi, comp. 1938–39. *Gunsho ruijū*, ed. Sakamoto Kōtarō et al. Zoku Gunsho Ruijū Kanseikai. 24 vols.

KGG    *Kasuga Gongen genki e.* Kadokawa Shoten. (Nihon emakimono zen-shū, vol. 15.) Rev. ed. 1978. (Shinshū Nihon emakimono zenshū, vol. 16.)

KSK    Takeuchi Rizō, ed. 1979. *Kasuga-sha kiroku.* Kyoto: Rinsen Shoten. (Zōho zoku shiryō taisei, vols. 47–49.) 3 vols.

KT    Kuroita Katsumi, ed. 1929–66. *Shintei zōho kokushi taikei.* Yoshi-kawa Kōbunkan. 66 vols.

NARA    *Nara,* vol. 11. 1929. Nara: Tōdaiji Ryūshōin.

NDK    *Nihon daizōkyō.* 1914–21. Nihon Daizōkyō Hensankai. 51 vols.

NKBT    Takagi Ichinosuke et al., eds. 1957–68. *Nihon koten bungaku taikei.* Iwanami Shoten. 102 vols.

NST    *Nihon shisō taikei.* 1970–. Iwanami Shoten. 67 vols.

ST    Nagashima Fukutarō, ed. 1985. *Kasuga.* Shintō Taikei Hensankai. (Shintō taikei, jinja-hen, vol. 13.)

ZGR    Hanawa Hokiichi and Hanawa Tadatomi, eds. 1923–30. *Zoku gun-sho ruijū*. Zoku Gunsho Ruijū Kanseikai. 71 vols.

ZZGR    *Zoku zoku gunsho ruijū.* 1906–9. Kokusho Kankōkai. 22 vols.

Arnesen, Peter J. 1982. "Suō Province in the Age of Kamakura." In Jeffrey P. Mass, ed., *Court and Bakufu in Japan: Essays in Kamakura History.* New Haven and London: Yale University Press.

Aston, William G., tr. 1972. *Nihongi.* Rutland, Vermont and Tokyo: Charles E. Tuttle.

Bender, Ross. 1980. "The Political Meaning of the Hachiman Cult in Ancient and Early Medieval Japan." Doctoral thesis submitted to Columbia University.

Berthier, Laurence. 1981. *Syncrétisme au Japon. Omizutori: Le Rituel de l'eau de jouvence.* Paris: École Pratique des Hautes Études, Ve section: Centre d'études sur les religions et traditions populaires du Japon. (Cahiers d'études et de documents sur les religions du Japon, vol. 3.)

Brazell, Karen, tr. 1973. *The Confessions of Lady Nijō.* Stanford, California: Stanford University Press.

Brown, Delmer M., and Ishida Ichirō. 1979. *The Future and the Past: A Translation and Study of the* Gukanshō, *an Interpretative History of Japan Written in 1219.* Berkeley, Los Angeles, and London: University of California Press.

Chidori Suketada. 1978. "Takatsukasa Mototada fushi no idai na keishin no kōseki." In *Emaki (Shinshū Nihon emakimono zenshū, geppō* no. 16, January). (Insert in KGG.)

*Chūyūki* (Diary of Fujiwara no Munetada). 1932–33. Naigai Shoseki. (Shiryō taisei.) 5 vols.

*Daijōin jisha zōjiki.* 1931–37. Ed. Tsuji Zennosuke. Sankyō Shoin. 12 vols.

*Daiki* (Diary of Fujiwara no Yorinaga). 1929. Naigai Shoseki. (Zōho zoku shiryō taisei, vol. 23.)

Darling, Leonard Bruce, Jr. 1983. "The Transformation of Pure Land Thought and the Development of Shinto Shrine Mandala Paintings: Kasuga and Kumano." Doctoral thesis presented to the University of Michigan, Ann Arbor.

*Denreki* (Diary of Fujiwara no Tadazane). 1968. Iwanami Shoten. (Dainihon kokiroku.) 5 vols.

De Visser, M. W. 1935. *Ancient Buddhism in Japan: Sutras and Their Ceremonies in Use in the Seventh and Eighth Centuries and Their History in Later Times.* Leiden: E. J. Brill. 2 vols.

*Eishōki* (Diary of Fujiwara no Tametaka). 1940. Naigai Shoseki. (Shiryō taisei, vol. 38.)

Faure, Bernard. 1987. "The Daruma-shū, Dōgen and Sōtō Zen." In *Monumenta Nipponica,* vol. 42, no. 1 (Spring).

Fujita Tsuneyo, ed. 1976. *Kankō bijutsu shiryō (jiin-hen).* Chūō Kōron Bijutsu Shuppan. 3 vols.

Fujiwara no Shunzei. *Shunzei no kyō bunji rokunen gosha hyakushu.* In GR, vol. 11.

Fukihara Shōshin. 1975. *Nihon chūsei yuishiki bukkyō shi.* Daitō Shuppansha.

*Fukuchiin-ke monjo.* 1979. Ed. Hanazono Daigaku Fukuchiin-ke Monjo Kenkyūkai. Kyoto: Hanazono Daigaku.

Fukunaga Shizuo. 1975. *Kamigami no shisha—Kasuga no shika.* Tōkyō Shinbun Shuppankyoku.

Fukuyama Toshio. 1961. "Kasuga Taisha, Kōfukuji sōsetsu." In *Kasuga Taisha, Kōfukuji*, ed. Kinki Nihon Tetsudō Sōritsu Gojūshūnen Kinen Shuppan Henshūjo. Ōsaka: Kinki Nihon Tetsudō K.K. (Kinki Nihon sōsho, vol. 6.)

*Fusō ryakki*. In KT, vol. 12.

*Fuyuhira kō ki* (Diary of Takatsukasa no Fuyuhira). 1969. Zoku Gunsho Ruijū Kansei Kai. (Shiryō sanshū.) 2 vols.

*Gaun nikken roku*. 1961. Ed. Tōkyō Daigaku Shiryō Hensanjo. Iwanami Shoten. (Dai Nihon kokiroku.)

Geddes, Ward, tr. 1984. *Kara monogatari: Tales of China*. Tempe, Arizona: Arizona State University. (Center for Asian Studies, Occasional Paper no. 16.)

Gedatsu Shōnin (Jōkei). *Kasuga Daimyōjin hotsuganmon*. In NDK, Hossō-shū shōsho, vol. 2.

———*Kasuga kōshiki (Betsugan kōshiki)*. In Hiraoka Jōkai 1958–60, vol. 3, pp. 216–19.

*Genkō shakusho* (Kokan Shiren). In KT, vol. 31.

*Gōdanshō*. In GR, vol. 27.

*Go-Nijō Moromichi ki* (Diary of Fujiwara no Moromichi). 1956–58. Ed. Tōkyō Daigaku Shiryō Hensanjo. Iwanami Shoten. (Dainihon kokiroku.) 3 vols.

Gorai Shigeru. 1975. *Kōya hijiri*. Kadokawa Shoten. (Kadokawa sensho, no. 79.)

———1977. "Yama no Yakushi, umi no Yakushi." In *Dainhōrin* (July).

———1978a. "Taidan: engi emaki no haikei," with Minamoto Hōshū. In *Emaki (Shinshū Nihon emakimono zenshū, geppō* no. 16, January). (Insert in KGG.)

———1978b. "*Kasuga Gongen genki e* no musō to takusen" ("Emaki to min-zoku," no. 10). In *Emaki (Shinshū Nihon emakimono zenshū, geppō* no. 16, January). (Insert in KGG.)

———1982. "Jisha engi no sekai." In *Kokubungaku kaishaku to kanshō*, vol. 47, no. 3 (March 1982).

Go-Shirakawa (Emperor). 1979. Ryōjin hishō kuden. In *Ryōjin hishō*, ed. Enoki Katsurō. Shinchōsha. (Shinchō Nihon koten shūsei.)

*Goshūi ōjōden*. 1974. In *Ōjōden, hokke genki*, ed. Inoue Mitsusada and Osone Shōsuke. Iwanami Shoten. (NST, vol 7.)

Grapard, Allan G. 1982. "Flying Mountains and Walkers of Emptiness: Toward a Definition of Sacred Space in Japanese Religions." In *History of Religions*, vol. 20, no. 3 (February 1982).

———1984. "Japan's Ignored Cultural Revolution: The Separation of Shinto and Buddhist Deities *(shimbutsu bunri)* and a Case Study, Tōnomine." In *History of Religions*, vol. 23, no. 3 (February 1984).

Hagiwara Tatsuo. 1975. "Jingi shisō no tenkai to jisha engi." In Sakurai Tokutarō (1975).

Hakusen. 1779. *Kasuga-yama no ki*. Nara: Jakushō Shōja. 5 *kan*.

Hardacre, Helen. 1986. "Creating State Shintō: The Great Promulgation

Campaign and the New Religions." In *The Journal of Japanese Studies*, vol. 12, no. 1 (Winter 1986).

*Hasedera engibun.* In DNBZ, vol. 118.

Herbert, Jean. 1967. *Shintō at the Fountainhead of Japan.* London: George Allen & Unwin.

*Hie Sannō rishōki.* In ZGR, vol. 2b.

Hiraoka Jōkai. 1958–60. *Tōdaiji Sōshō Shōnin no kenkyū narabini shiryō.* Nihon Gakujutsu Shinkōkai. 3 vols.

———1981. *Nihon jiin shi no kenkyū.* Yoshikawa Kōbunkan.

*Honchō kōsōden* (Mangan Shiban). In DNBZ, vols. 111, 112.

Hori Ichirō. 1974. *Folk Religion in Japan: Continuity and Change.* Chicago and London: The University of Chicago Press.

Hurst, G. Cameron III. 1976. *Insei: Abdicated Sovereigns in the Politics of Late Heian Japan.* New York and London: Columbia University Press.

*Hyakurenshō.* In KT, vol 14.

*Ima monogatari.* In GR, vol. 27.

Inokuma Kaneshige. 1963. "Murō no ryūketsu." In *Murōji*, ed. Kinki Nihon Tetsudō Sōritsu Gojū Shūnen Kinen Shuppan Henshūjo. Osaka: Kinki Nihon Tetsudō K.K.

*Ishiyamadera engi.* In ZGR, vol. 28b.

Itō Masayoshi, ed. 1983. *Yōkyoku shū,* vol. 1. Shinchōsha. (Shinchō Nihon koten shūsei.)

Jien. 1979. *The Future and the Past (Gukanshō).* (See Brown, Delmer M.)

*Jikkinshō.* 1942. Ed. Nagazumi Yasuaki. Iwanami Shoten. (Iwanami Bunko, vol. 30-120-1.)

*Jikkinshō.* In KT, vol. 18.

*Jizō Bosatsu reigenki.* In ZGR, vol. 25b.

Kageyama Haruki. 1961. "Kasuga mandara to *Kasuga Gongen genki.*" In *Kasuga Taisha, Kōfukuji*, ed. Kinki Nihon Tetsudō Sōritsu Gojūshūnen Kinen Shuppan Henshūjo. Ōsaka: Kinki Nihon Tetsudō K.K. (Kinki Nihon sōsho, vol. 6.)

———1962. *Shintō bijutsu no kenkyū.* Kyoto: Shintōshi Gakkai.

———1965. *Shintō no bijutsu.* Hanawa Shobō. (Hanawa sensho 48.)

———1973. *The Arts of Shinto.* Tr. Christine Guth. New York and Tokyo: Weatherhill and Shibundō. (Arts of Japan, vol. 4.)

Kamata Shigeo and Tanaka Hisao, eds. 1971. *Kamakura kyū bukkyō.* Iwanami Shoten. (Nihon shisō taikei, vol. 15.)

Kameda Tsutomu. 1970a. "Hase Nōman'in no Kasuga jōdo mandara." In Kameda Tsutomu, *Nihon bukkyō shi josetsu.* Gakugei Shorin.

———1970b. "Kujō Kanezane no Kasuga-sha to Nan'endō e no shinkō." In Kameda Tsutomu, *Nihon bukkyō shi josetsu.* Gakugei Shorin.

Kamei Katsuichirō. 1975. *Chūsei no shōji to shūkyō kan (Nihonjin no seishin-shi,* vol. 3). Kōdansha. (Kōdansha bunko.)

Kamo no Chōmei. 1976. *Hosshinshū.* In *Hōjōki, Hosshinshū*, ed. Miki Sumito. Shinchōsha. (Shinchō Nihon koten shūsei.)

*Kanjuji chōri shidai.* In ZGR, vol. 4b.

*Kanmon gyoki.* In ZGR, *hoi,* vol. 2b.

*Kasagidera engi.* In DNBZ, vol. 118.

Kasanoin Chikatada. 1987. *Kasuga no kami wa shika ni notte.* Shimizu Kō-bundō.

*Kasuga Daimyōjin go-takusen ki.* In ZGR, vol. 2a; DNBZ, vol. 123.

*Kasuga Daimyōjin suijaku shōsha ki.* In GR, vol. 2.

*Kasuga genki ekotoba kikigaki.* In Kondō Kihaku (1953).

*Kasuga Gongen genki.*
  (1) Text and paintings
    *Kasuga Gongen reigenki.* 1929. Yūzankaku. 2 vols. (Nihon emakimono zenshū, vols. 3–4.)
    *Kasuga Gongen genki e.* In KGG.
    *Kasuga Gongen genki e.* 1982. Chūō Kōronsha. (Zoku Nihon emaki taisei, vols. 14–15.)
  (2) Text only
    *Kasuga Gongen reigenki e mokuroku.* In GR, vol. 2.
    *Kasuga genki kotobagaki.* 1940. Yōmei Bunko.
    *Kasuga Gongen genki (Kasuga-bon).* 1983. Nara: Kasuga Taisha.
    *Kasuga genki e kotobagaki.* In ST.

*Kasuga go-ruki.* In DNBZ, vol. 124.

*Kasuga mōde burui ki.* In ZGR, vol. 2b.

*Kasuga ryūjin.* In Sanari Kentarō, ed. 1930. *Yōkyoku taikan,* vol. 1. Meiji Shoin.

*Kasuga shaki.* In GR, vol. 2.

Kasuga Shamusho, ed. 1981. *Kasuga no mori no mukashibanashi.* Nara: Kasuga Taisha.

*Kasuga-sha sanjikkō saisho go-ganmon.* In GR, vol. 24.

Katagiri Yōichi, ed. 1972. *Heian waka utamakura chimei sakuin.* Kyoto: Daigakudō Shoten.

Katō Bunnō, Tamura Yoshirō, and Miyasaka Kōjirō, trs.; with revisions by W. E. Soothill et al. 1975. *The Threefold Lotus Sutra.* New York and Tokyo: Weatherhill/Kosei.

Kawaguchi Hisao and Shida Nobuyoshi, eds. 1965. *Wakan rōei shū, Ryōjin hishō.* (NKBT, vol. 73.)

Kawamura Tomoyuki. 1980. "Kasuga jōdo to Kasuga mandara." In *Bijutsu shi kenkyū,* no. 17.

——1981. "Kasuga mandara no seiritsu to girei." In *Bijutsu shi* 110 (vol. 33, no. 2, March).

Keene, Donald, tr. 1967. *Essays in Idleness.* New York: Columbia University Press.

Kidō Saizō. 1987. *Nijō Yoshimoto no kenkyū.* Ōfūsha.

Kinki Nihon Tetsudō Sōritsu Gojū Shūnen Kinen Henshūjo, ed. 1961. *Kasuga Taisha, Kōfukuji.* Osaka: Kinki Nihon Tetsudō K.K.

*Kinpusen kengyō shidai.* In GR 5.

*Kōben ki.* In *Kōzanji shiryō sōsho,* vol. 1. 1971. Tōkyō Daigaku Shuppankai.
*Kōfukuji bettō shidai.* In DNBZ, vol. 124; ZZGR, vol. 2.
*Kōfukuji engi.* In DNBZ, vol. 119; DNBZa, vol. 84.
*Kōfukuji matsujichō.* In DNBZ, vol. 119; DNBZa, vol. 84.
*Kōfukuji ranshōki.* In DNBZ, vol. 119; DNBZa, vol. 84; ZZGR, vol. 11.
*Kōfukuji ruki.* In DNBZ, vol. 119; DNBZa, vol. 84.
*Kōfukuji ryaku nendaiki.* In ZGR, vol. 29b.
*Kōfukuji sangō bunin.* In ZGR, vol. 4b.
*Kōfukuji shinboku dōza chōjō.* In ZZGR, vol. 16.
*Kōfukuji sōjō.* In Kamata (1971).
*Kojidan* (Minamoto no Akikane). 1981. Ed. Kobayashi Yasuharu. Gendai Shichōsha. (Koten bunko, vols. 60, 62.) 2 vols.
*Kokonchomonjū* (Tachibana no Narisue). 1966. Eds. Nagasumi Yasuaki and Shimada Isao. Iwanami Shoten. (NKBT, vol. 84.)
*Koma-shi keifu.* In ZGR, vol. 7b.
Kondō Kihaku. 1952. "Saionji Kinhira shosha no *Fukūkenjaku shinju-kyō.*" in *Kokka,* no. 725.
——1953. "Kasuga genki ekotoba kikigaki ni tsuite." In *Kokka,* no. 739.
——1957. "Emaki ni kansuru shiryō oboegaki: *Nōe Hōshi den* to *Kasuga Gongen genki.*" In *Bijutsu shi,* vol. 7, no. 1 (July).
——1958. "*Kasuga Gongen genki* no seiritsu." In *Nihon rekishi,* no. 126.
——1959. "Zoku Kasuga shinkō no kodaiteki igi." In *Shintō shigaku,* no. 20 (May).
*Kongōzan naige ryōin daidai kokon kiroku.* In NDK, Shugendō shōsho, vol. 3.
*Konjaku monogatarishū.* 1961–63. Ed. Yamada Yoshio et al. Iwanami Shoten. (NKBT, vols. 22–26.) 5 vols.
Koresawa Kyōzō. 1963. "Kasuga Daimyōjin no shin'i." In KGG.
*Koshaki.* In ST.
*Kōshō Bosatsu no go-kyōkai chōmon shū.* In Kamata (1971).
*Kōyasan ōjōden.* In ZGR, vol. 8a.
*Kōzanji Myōe Shōnin gyōjō (Kanbun gyōjō).* In *Kōzanji shiryō sōsho,* vol. 1. 1971. Tōkyō Daigaku Shuppankai.
*Kugyō bunin.* In KT. 5 vols.
Kujō Kanezane. *Gyokuyō.* Ed. Kokusho Kankō Kai. Kokusho Kankō Kai, 1898–1907 (3 vols.).
Kuroda Toshio. 1975. *Nihon chūsei no kokka to shūkyō.* Iwanami Shoten.
——1980. *Jisha seiryoku.* Iwanami Shoten. (Iwanami shinsho, no. 117.)
*Kyōkunshō* (Koma no Chikazane). In ZGR, vol. 19a. Also in *Kodai chūsei geijutsu ron,* ed. Hayashiya Tatsusaburō. 1973. Iwanami Shoten. (NST, vol. 23)
*Kyōto-fu no chimei.* 1981. Heibonsha. (Nihon rekishi chimei taikei, vol. 26.)
Kyōto Kokuritsu Hakubutsukan. 1981. *Kōzanji-ten.* Kyoto: Asahi Shimbunsha.
*Kyōto-shi no chimei.* 1979. Heibonsha. (Nihon rekishi chimei taikei, vol. 27.)

Mass, Jeffrey P., ed. 1982. *Court and Bakufu in Japan: Essays in Kamakura History.* New Haven and London: Yale University Press.

Matsunaga, Alicia. 1969. *The Buddhist Philosophy of Assimilation.* Tokyo: Sophia University Press, in cooperation with Rutland, Vermont and Tokyo: Charles E. Tuttle. (Monumenta Nipponica Monographs.)

McCullough, Helen Craig, tr. 1980. *Ōkagami: The Great Mirror.* Princeton, N.J. and Tokyo: Princeton University Press and University of Tokyo Press.

McCullough, William H., and Helen Craig McCullough, trs. 1980. *A Tale of Flowering Fortunes.* Stanford, California: Stanford University Press. 2 vols.

*Meigetsuki* (Fujiwara no Teika). 1911. Kokusho Kankōkai. 3 vols.

Meisezahl, R. O. 1962. "The Amoghapāśahṛdaya-dhāraṇī: The Early Sanskrit Manuscript of the Reiunji, Critically Edited and Translated." In *Monumenta Nipponica,* vol. 17, nos. 1–4.

Miya Tsugio, ed. 1983. *Kasuga Gongen genki e.* Shibundō. (Nihon no bijutsu, no. 203.)

Miyai Yoshio. 1978. *Ritsuryō kizoku Fujiwara-shi no ujigami ujidera shinkō to sobyō saishi.* Seikō Shobō. (Jingi shinkō no tenkai to Nihon jōdokyō no kiso, vol. 2.)

———1979. *Chihō shomin kara mita jōdai no shinbutsu shūgō to jōdokyō.* Seikō Shobō. (Jingi shinkō no tenkai to Nihon jōdokyō no kiso, vol. 3.)

Mochizuki Shinkō. 1931–36. *Bukkyō daijiten.* Bukkyō Daijiten Hakkōsho. 7 vols.

Moore, Jean. 1982. "A Study of the Thirteenth Century Buddhist Tale Collection 'Senjūshō.' " Doctoral thesis presented to Columbia University.

Mori Atsushi. 1965. "Chikei kara kansatsu shita Kasuga-yama no bunka." In *Nara Kokuritsu Bunkazai Kenkyūjo nenpō.* Nara: Kokuritsu Bunkazai Kenkyūjo.

Mōri Hisashi. 1947. *Shin'yakushiji kō.* Kyoto: Kawara Shobō.

Mori Ikuo. 1987. "Kasuga no saishi iseki." In *Kasuga Myōjin,* ed. Ueda Masaaki. Chikuma Shobō.

Morrell, Robert E. 1982. "Passage to India Denied: Zeami's *Kasuga Ryūjin.*" In *Monumenta Nipponica,* vol. 37, no. 1 (March).

———1983. "Jōkei and the Kōfukuji Pettion." In *Japanese Journal of Religious Studies,* vol. 10, no. 1 (March).

Mujū Ichien. 1966. *Shasekishū.* Ed. Watanabe Tsunaya. Iwanami Shoten. (NKBT, vol. 85.)

*Myōe Shōnin jingon denki.* In *Kōzanji shiryō sōsho,* vol. 1. 1971. Tōkyō Daigaku Shuppankai.

Nagashima Fukutarō. 1944. *Nara bunka no denryū.* Chūō Kōronsha.

———1955. "Kaisetsu." In *Kasuga-sha kiroku,* vol. 1. Ed. Mizuyagawa Tadamaro. Nara, Kasuga Taisha Shamusho. Repr. as KSK, vol. 1.

———1959. "Kōfukuji no rekishi." In *Bukkyō geijutsu,* no. 40.

———1963. *"Kasuga Gongen genki e* no seiritsu to sono jidai." In KGG.

———1977. *"Genjō Sanzō e* no seisaku kankyō—kotobagaki shosha nendai no suitei o chūshin ni shite." In Minamoto Toyomune, ed., *Genjō sanzō e.* Kadokawa Shoten. (Shinshū Nihon emakimono zenshū, vol. 15.)

———1987. "Kasuga Taisha no rekishi." In *Kasuga Myōjin,* ed. Ueda Masaaki. Chikuma Shobō.

Nakamura Yoshio. 1984. "Emaki to setsuwa." In *Kokubungaku kaishaku to kanshō,* vol. 49, no. 11 (September).

Nakano Genzō. 1975. "Shaji engi e ron." In *Jisha engi e,* ed. Nara Kokuritsu Hakubutsukan. Nara: Nara Kokuritsu Hakubutsukan.

Nakatomi no Sukefusa. *Diary (Kyūki shōshutsu).* In KSK, vol. 1.

Nakatomi no Sukeharu. *Diary.* In KSK, vol. 3.

Nakatomi no Sukekata. *Diary.* In KSK, vols. 1–3.

Nakatomi no Sukesada. *Diary.* In KSK, vol. 1.

Nakatomi no Sukeshige. *Diary.* In KSK, vol. 1.

*Nanto daishu nyūraku ki.* In ZGR, vol. 29a.

Nara-ken Kyōikukai, ed. 1914. *Yamato shiryō.* Kōdōkan. 2 vols.

*Nara-ken no chimei.* 1981. Heibonsha. (Nihon rekishi chimei taikei, vol. 30.)

Nara Kokuritsu Hakubutsukan, ed. 1964. *Suijaku bijutsu.* Kadokawa Shoten.

———1982. *Kasuga seitō tōtō seki no hakkutsu.* Nara: Nara Kokuritsu Hakubutsukan.

Nara Rokudaiji Taikan Kankōkai, ed. 1968, 1970. *Kōfukuji.* Iwanami Shoten. (Nara rokudaiji taikan.) 2 vols.

Nara-shi Henshū Shingikai, ed. 1985. *Nara-shi shi (shaji-hen).* Yoshikawa Kōbunkan.

*Nihon kōsōden yōmonshō.* In KT, vol. 31.

Nijō Yoshimoto. *Sakakiba no nikki.* In GR, vol. 2.

Nishida, Nagao. 1978. "Kasuga Taisha no seiritsu: bunken shiryō o chūshin ni shite." In *Nihon shintō shi kenkyū,* vol. 9 ( *jinja-hen,* vol. 1). Kōdansha.

Noma Seiroku. 1963. *"Kasuga Gongen genki e* no gaikan." In KGG.

*Ōhigashi-ke shikan keifu.* In *Kasuga Jinja monjo,* vol. 3. Comp. by Kasuga Jinja Shamusho. Nara: Kasuga Jinja Shamusho. 1928–42. 3 vols.

Ōhigashi Nobuatsu. 1929. "Kasuga shashi ni tsuite." In NARA.

———1972. *Shinshū Kasuga-sha shashi bunin ki.* Nara: Kasuga Miyamoto Kai. (Private printing.)

Ōhigashi Nobukazu. 1980. "Kasuga sanjō no shōjin gun." *Kasuga* (periodical issued by the Kasuga Shrine).

———1983a. "Edo-jō ni hakobareta *Kasuga genki—Kuwana-bon* no seiritsu no ikisatsu." In Miya (1983).

———1983b. *"Kasuga-bon Kasuga Gongen genki* no seiritsu." In *Kasuga Gongen genki (Kasuga-bon).* Nara: Kasuga Taisha.

———.1985. "Kasuga no shake no saijin denshō ni tsuite." In ST *(geppō).*

Okudaira Hideo. 1973. *Narrative Picture Scrolls.* Tr. Elizabeth ten Grotenhuis. New York and Tokyo: Weatherhill/Shibundo. (Arts of Japan, vol. 5.)

*Ōmine tōzan honji Kōfukuji tōkondō sendatsu kiroku.* In NDK, Shugendō shōsho, vol. 3.

Ōya Tokujō. 1929. "Kasuga no shinroku ni taisuru chūsei kizoku no shinkō." In NARA.

Pigeot, Jacqueline. 1982. *Michiyuki-bun: Poétique de l'itinéraire dans la littérature du Japon ancien.* Paris: Maisonneuve et Larose.

Piggott, Joan R. 1982. "Hierarchy and Economics in Early Medieval Tōdaiji." In Mass (1982).

Reizei Tamekane. *Tamekane-kyō shika hyakushu: Kasuga-sha hōraku.* In GR, vol. 11.

Rosenfield, John M., et al., eds. 1973. *The Courtly Tradition in Japanese Art and Literature: Selections from the Hofer and Hyde Collections.* Cambridge, Mass.: Fogg Art Museum, Harvard University.

Rotermund, Hartmut O. 1972. "La Conception des kami japonais à l'époque de Kamakura: Notes sur le premier chapitre du 'Sasekishū.' " In *Revue de l'Histoire des Religions* (July).

Saeki Ryōken. 1929. "Kasuga gyōkō gokō rei kō." In NARA.

*Saisai yōki nukigaki.* In DNBZ, vol. 124.

Sakaida Shirō and Wada Katsushi. 1976. *Zōho kaitei nihon setsuwa bungaku sakuin* (shukusatsu-ban). Seibundō.

Sakamoto Tarō et al., eds. 1967. *Nihon shoki.* Iwanami Shoten. (NKBT, vols. 67, 68.) 2 vols.

Sakurai Tokutarō. 1975. "Engi no ruikei to tenkai." In *Jisha engi,* ed. Sakurai Tokutarō. Iwanami Shoten, (NST, vol. 20.)

*Sanekata no Ason shū* (Fujiwara no Sanekata). In GR, vol. 14.

*Sangoku denki.* In DNBZ, vol. 128.

*Sanne jōikki.* In DNBZ, vol 123.

*Senjūshō.* 1970. Ed. Nishio Kōichi. Iwanami Shoten. (Iwanami bunko, vol. 30-024-1.)

*Shadan dōei kiu hyakushu.* In GR, vol. 11.

*Shatō go-hakkō nikki.* In ZGR, vol. 2a.

Shikinaisha Kenkyūkai, ed. 1982. *Shikinaisha chōsa hōkoku: Kyō, Kinai.* Ise-shi: Kōgakkan Daigaku. (Shikinaisha chōsa hōkoku, vol. 2.)

*Shingonden.* In DNBZ, vol. 106.

*Shinpen kokka taikan.* 1984. Kadokawa Shoten. 10 vols.

*Shintōshū.* 1967. Ed. Kondō Kihaku. Kadokawa Shoten.

*Shōdai senzai denki.* In ZZGR, vol. 11.

*Shomonzeki fu.* In GR, vol. 5.

*Shōtoku Taishi denryaku.* In *Shōtoku Taishi zenshū,* vol. 3. 1942. Ryūgin Sha.

*Shozan engi.* In *Jisha engi,* ed. Sakurai Tokutarō. Iwanami Shoten. (NST, vol. 20.)

*Shūi ōjōden.* 1974. In *Ōjōden, Hokke genki,* eds. Inoue Mitsusada and Osone Shōsuke. Iwanami Shoten. (NST, vol. 7.)

*Shun'ya shinki.* In ST.

*Sōgō bunin.* In DNBZ, vol. 123.

*Sōgō bunin zanketsu.* In DNBZ, vol. 111.

*Sonpi bunmyaku.* In KT. 5 vols.

Soper, Alexander Coburn. 1959. *Literary Evidence for Early Buddhist Art in China.* Ascona, Switzerland: Artibus Asiae Publishers.

Suzuki Ryōichi. 1983. *Daijōin jisha zōjiki: aru monbatsu sōryo no botsuraku no kiroku.* Soshiete. (Nikki, kiroku ni yoru nihon rekishi sōsho, kodai/chūsei-hen, vol. 18.)

Suzuki Shōei. 1975. "Shugendō tōzan-ha no kyōdan soshiki to nyūbu." In *Yoshino, Kumano shinkō no kenkyū,* ed. Gorai Shigeru. Meicho Shuppan. (Sangaku shūkyō shi kenkyū sōsho, vol. 4.)

*Taiheiki.* 1960–62. Eds. Gotō Tanji and Okami Masao. Iwanami Shoten. (NKBT, vols. 34–36.) 3 vols.

*Taishō shinshū daizōkyō.* 1924–34. Eds. Takakusu Junjirō and Watanabe Kaigyoku. Taishō Issaikyō Kankōkai. 104 vols.

Takagi Ichinosuke, Ozawa Masao, et al. 1959–60. *Heike monogatari.* Iwanami Shoten. (NKBT, vols. 32, 33.) 2 vols.

Takagi Yutaka. 1985. *"Kasuga Gongen genki e to Senjūshō."* In ST *(geppō).*

Takahashi Teiichi. 1959. *"Kasuga Gongen genki ekotoba no teihon ni tsuite."* In *Kokugo bungei* (November). Repr. in *Taskahashi Teiichi kokubungaku ronshū.* Kyoto: Shibunkaku. 1982.

Takeuchi Rizō, ed. 1963–68. *Heian ibun.* Tokyōdō. 13 vols.

Tamamuro Fumio. 1977. *Shinbutsu bunri.* Kyōikusha. (Rekishi shinsho 113.)

*Tamon'in nikki.* 1965. Ed. Tsuji Zennoksuke. Kadokawa Shoten. 10 vols.

Tamura Enchō. 1959. *Nihon bukkyō shisō shi kenkyū (Jōdokyō hen).* Kyoto: Heirakuji Shoten.

Tamura Yoshinaga. 1929. "Kasuga jinja no shinroku ni tsuite." In NARA.

Tanabe, George Joji. 1983. "Myōe Shōnin (1173–1232): Tradition and Reform in Early Kamakura Buddhism." Doctoral thesis submitted to Columbia University.

Tanabe, Willa Jane. 1984. "The Lotus Lectures: *Hokke hakkō* in the Heian Period." In *Monumenta Nipponica,* vol. 39, no. 4 (Winter).

Tashima Kazuo. 1986. *"Hie Sannō rishōki* no kenkyū." In *Kokubungaku Kenkyū shiryōkan hō,* no. 26 (March).

*Tatsuichi-ke keifu.* In *Kasuga Jinja monjo,* vol. 3. Comp. by Kasuga Jinja Shamusho. Nara: Kasuga Jinja Shamusho. 1928–42. 3 vols.

*Tatsuta no Daimyōjin no on-koto.* In ZGR, vol. 2b.

*Tendai zasu ki.* In ZGR, vol. 4b.

*Tōdaiji Hachiman genki.* In ZGR, vol. 3a.

*Tōgyō mikki.* Ms. in Tōdaiji library.

Tomimura Takafumi. 1976. "Gedatsu Shōnin to Kannon shinkō." In *Risshō shigaku,* no. 40.

*Toshiyori kuden shū* (Minamoto no Toshiyori). In ZZGR, vol. 15.

*Tōshōdaiji ge.* In DNBZ, vol. 105.

Tsuji Zennosuke. 1944. *Nihon bukkyō shi (jōsei hen).* Iwanami Shoten.

Tyler, Royall. 1982. "A Critique of Absolute Phenomenalism." In *Japanese Journal of Religious Studies,* vol. 9, no. 4 (December).

———1987. "Buddhism in Noh." in *Japanese Journal of Religious Studies,* vol. 14, no. 1 (Spring).

Tyler, Susan. 1987. "The Art of the Cult of Kasuga." Doctoral thesis submitted to the University of Oslo.

Ueda Kōen. 1980. "Kōfukuji no Yuima e no seiritsu to tenkai." In *Nanto bukkyō,* no. 45 (December).

———1985. *Nihon jōdai ni okeru yuishiki no kenkyū.* Nagata Bunshōdō.

Ueda Masaaki. 1987. "Kasuga no genzō." In *Kasuga Myōjin,* ed. Ueda Masaaki. Chikuma Shobō.

*Uji shūi monogatari.* 1973. Ed. Kobayashi Chishō. Shōgakkan. (Nihon koten zenshū, vol. 28)

Uwayokote Masataka. 1975. "Kamakura Bakufu to kuge seiken." In *Iwanami kōza: Nihon rekishi,* vol. 5. Iwanami Shoten.

Wada Eishō. 1917. *"Kasuga Gongen genki* ni tsuite." In *Kokka,* no. 328.

*Wakayama-ken no chimei.* 1983. Heibonsha. (Nihon rekishi chimei taikei, vol. 31.)

Waseda Daigaku Tsubouchi Hakase Kinen Engeki Hakubutsukan, ed. 1960–62. *Engeki hyakka jiten.* Heibonsha. 6 vols.

Watanabe Sumio. 1960. "Yamato no akutō." In *Nihon rekishi,* vol. 139 (January).

*Yamato monogatari.* 1957. Ed. Sakakura Atsuyoshi et al. Iwanami Shoten. (NKBT, vol. 9.)

Yoshida Kenkō. 1957. *Tsurezuregusa.* Ed. Nishio Minoru. Iwanami Shoten. (NKBT, vol. 30.)

Yoshihara Hiroto. 1986. "Chūseiteki' jisha engi no keisei." In *Kokubungaku kaishaku to kanshō,* vol. 56, no. 6 (June).

Yūgon Hōin. 1917. *Buzan gyokusekishū.* Ed. Ajiro Chimyō and Yoshida Shinryō. Nara-ken: Hasedera Jimusho.

*Yuima e e-hajime no ki.* In DNBZ, vol. 123.

*Zō Kōfukuji ki.* In DNBZ, vol. 123.

*Zoku Hie Sannō rishōki.* In ZGR, vol. 2b.

*Zoku kojidan.* In GR, vol. 27.

*Zoku kyōkunshō.* In *Nihon koten zenshū,* vol. 6. 1924. Nihon Koten Zenshū Kankō Kai.

# Index

Page numbers for Part I are separated by • from those for Part II. In entries for Part II, **boldface** shows that the item is also glossed in a note.

# INDEX

# INDEX